TRANSFORMING VIRTUAL WORLD LEARNING

CUTTING-EDGE TECHNOLOGIES IN HIGHER EDUCATION

Series Editor: Charles Wankel

Recent Volumes:

Volume 1: Educating Educators with Social Media – Edited by Charles Wankel

Volume 2: Higher Education Administration with Social Media: Including Applications in Student Affairs, Enrollment Management, Alumni Relations, and Career Centers – Edited by Laura A. Wankel and Charles Wankel

Volume 3: Teaching Arts and Science with the New Social Media – Edited by Charles Wankel

CUTTING-EDGE TECHNOLOGIES IN HIGHER EDUCATION
VOLUME 4

TRANSFORMING VIRTUAL WORLD LEARNING

EDITED BY

RANDY HINRICHS
2b3d LLC, Sammamish, WA

CHARLES WANKEL
St. John's University, New York, USA

United Kingdom – North America – Japan
India – Malaysia – China

Emerald Group Publishing Limited
Howard House, Wagon Lane, Bingley BD16 1WA, UK

First edition 2011

British Library Cataloguing in Publication Data
A catalogue record for this book is available from the British Library

ISBN: 978-1-78052-052-0
ISSN: 2044-9968 (Series)

CONTENTS

PART II: TRANSFORMING VIRTUAL WORLD DESIGN

PART III: TRANSFORMING VIRTUAL WORLD DEVELOPMENT

PART IV: TRANSFORMING VIRTUAL WORLD DEPLOYMENT

LIST OF CONTRIBUTORS

Youngkyun Baek	Boise State University, Boise, ID,USA
Simon Bignell	University of Derby, Derby, UK
Samantha J. Blevins	Virginia Tech, Blacksburg, VA, USA
Irena Bojanova	University of Maryland University College, Adelphi, MD, USA
Aimee M. Brenner	Virginia Tech, Blacksburg, VA, USA
Melissa L. Burgess	Texas Virtual Learning Center, Huntsville, TX, USA
Candido Cabo	New York College of Technology of The City University of New York, Brooklyn, NY, USA
Dona Cady	Middlesex Community College, Bedford, MA, USA
Donguk Cheong	Korea National University of Education, Chungbuk, South Korea
Sue Gregory	University of New England, Armidale, Australia
J. M. Grenier	Middlesex Community College, Bedford, MA, USA
Béatrice S. Hasler	Interdisciplinary Center Herzliya, Israel
Randy Hinrichs	University of Washington, Seattle, WA, USA
Phil Ice	American Public University System, Charles Town, WV, USA

Owen Kelly	Aalto University, Helsinki, Finland
Hoe Kyeung Kim	Cleveland State University, Cleveland, OH, USA
Reneta D. Lansiquot	New York College of Technology of The City University of New York, Brooklyn, NY, USA
Matthew Olson	Middlesex Community College, Bedford, MA, USA
Les Pang	University of Maryland University College, Adelphi, MD, USA
Vanessa Parson	University of Sunderland, Sunderland, UK
Lesley Scopes	Drury University, Springfield, MO, USA
Peter Shea	Middlesex Community College, Bedford, MA, USA
Jennifer L. V. Sparrow	Virginia Tech, Blacksburg, VA, USA
Jenny S. Wakefield	University of Texas at Dallas, Richardson, TX, USA
Scott J. Warren	University of North Texas, Denton, TX, USA
John Woollard	University of Southampton, Southampton, UK

ACKNOWLEDGEMENTS

Randy acknowledges the astute expertise of the 2b3d team who provided exemplary guidance and transformative vision to the science and art of building virtual worlds; this especially includes Kathryn, Janice, Colin, and Claire. Also, great gratitude to Charles Wankel, best-selling author and erudite colleague. Charles acknowledges the professional editorial acumen of his research associates Kyle Miller and Neil Washington, who notably improved the format and content of the bibliographic citations, and Chris Hart and Jessica Davis' world-class publishing know-how at Emerald.

INTRODUCTION: THINKING IN 3D

Transforming virtual world learning requires a new of way of thinking, thinking with depth, thinking in 3D. It means using avatars and interacting with objects in virtual places. The virtual world citizen, the avatar, practically "lives in" the virtual environment as a surviving organism, and as a consequence, must learn the environment. The more interaction between virtual objects and their relationships, the more adaptation to the virtual environment. The more experience gained in the virtual world, the more expertise is required to participate. Virtual worlds are indeed worlds. They are more than 3D game playing communities. They are in fact quite common to everyday users. Learning the principles and techniques for building 3D virtual worlds should not be new for anyone, as you are likely already an expert. As educators, we are already quite familiar with the 3D environment. We participate in it every day. It is our physical world. What is exciting for education today is that we are building the physical world inside the virtual world, and bringing the virtual world outside to the physical world. This book is designed to help integrate the physical world with the virtual world for learning in a practical way, using your experience and the experience of others.

Thinking in 3D is transformational for learning. Three-dimensional building starts with geometry and advances to near theatrical production, in which journeys, dramatic tension, and character are all utilized. The mathematics translates into space with vectors, volume within a space, or more simply a cube as a representation of a 3D concept of space or volume. Think of the difference between a square and a cube, or a circle and a sphere. How would you present material and interactions in a 3D cube? You can think of it more as a stage or the set of a movie when you have three dimensions and live participants. The theatrical production immerses the learner in a narrative, setting up a learning situation that deals with conflicts or problem solving, and engages with the other actors in the virtual world as resources. In building this way, you think more in terms of actions, activities, identifying a problem and its components, and interacting with objects until you reap a reward and secure recognition. This is the stuff from which motivation and learning outcomes are born in virtual worlds.

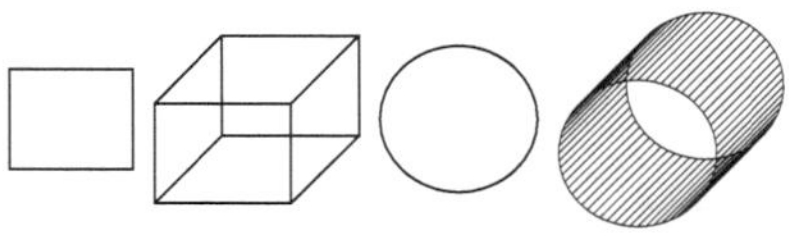

Much like our physical world, virtual world places are designed for exploration. The learner walks into the environment, picks things up, and turns them around. They encounter obstacles and develop strategies to get around them. They perform actions in front of others and feel the constraints of time. An example would be, the learner is dropped into an emergency room. They must scrub up and put on scrubs and get into place immediately. They must assess the environment as quickly as they can as patients are lying on stretches with real problems. The learner, an active agent in the environment, rushes to make critical decisions while a patient is bleeding. There is an urgency to gather information from every device and person around them. Such nail-biting activity is different from reading a case study in a book while sitting in a chair. So, our objective as thinkers in 3D is to explore how to bring visuals back into a 3D space that enhances a user's experience. We must quickly go beyond the presentation screen, the note card, and the graphic on the wall. We must head to the stage, the molecule, and the consequence of interaction.

Indeed, 3D space seems more complex and complicated compared to a linear textual model. We often fall back on 2D media techniques because we are familiar with them. You don't see text much in nature, so you cannot rely on it necessarily in critical learning situations. You see organic shapes and a delicate balance of objects and people interacting with each other. And, you are one of them. As instructors, if we imagine how we place the learner in the middle of a natural, unfolding story, in which their behavior determines the next outcome, we create a learning environment in 3D.

We are well equipped to imagine what we have to build. We understand terrain, objects, sounds, actions, interactions, and ever-changing variations that leverage our visual, audio, and sensory abilities. We understand the physics of falling and solid objects. We know water and chemistry and electricity. And, we know about human emotion, collaboration, and getting things done. We also know about the power of the Internet and access to the worldwide store of information. As we explore virtual worlds learning solutions, we envision what would be in the scene like a set director in a movie, and then we provide deep access to it all through Internet connections, communication technology, and immersion.

In fact, much like our physical world interactions, many tiny things are processing in the environment in the virtual world to attain the "immersion" or the "feel" that we are "there." When we act in and upon the virtual world, interacting with the objects and the people, unexpected things happen and we have to react. Our minds are convinced that what we are seeing is no different from what we see in our natural environment, and our flight or fight instincts come rushing forward causing us to make a decision. In building virtual worlds for education, we are constantly faced with how we insert enough meaningful activity into the environment to make the experience valuable and meaningful to our learner? The starting point begins with understanding the differences between the 2D and the 3D world engagement.

In software design, the 2D diagram describes the inflows and the outflows. We receive a learning object and think about how our student will read something, then write something about it. That is good. We sometimes show pictures, graphs, and videos and ask to discuss what we have seen. These reflections are quite useful. The exercise is linear in nature usually, sequential, rule dominant, and results often in understanding, knowing, and appreciating. In 3D design, we ask people to interact with objects in real-time within context, making the solution all more meaningful. We visit one or many locations to analyze the information and interactions between things, and we manage all the analysis of the objects in our head as we figure out a strategy for solving a problem. We encourage interacting with things by clicking on them, or manipulating them. We use video, audio, and visual elements to push the learner toward decision making, and seize their attention by limiting their field of vision and making one procedure happen before successfully moving on. And we make objects move into place as the learner responds to the stimulus.

To build on our virtual medical experience example, our user encounters a body lying on an emergency stretcher. The patient is hooked up to equipment and vital signs are pulsating on a graphic. The user can change the oxygen flow or the liquid intake and change the settings, and must do so as the patient is in extreme stress. In fact, the patient is bleeding and requires the medical technician to apply pressure to stop the bleeding. The vital signs are not changing and a bit of panic seeps in. The emergency room is filled with noise and shouting, the patient is yelling out and suddenly another patient comes in on a stretcher, and the technician, you, have to immediately turn and face that situation. You are immersed in a virtual world.

In planning for 3D learning, we encourage creating scenarios that accomplish tasks much like in the physical world. We ask you to imagine seeing yourself doing something. If you want to improve communication within a department store, we ask you to follow a store manager through his daily grind and watch how he is experiencing pain points in his communication, experience his abilities and failings. Imagine what the cashiers are saying to the frowning or even angry customers? Picture a liquid aisle spill in aisle fifteen as you assist a wandering customer. Because there is so much going on, you experience what the store manager needs to communicate to get the spilled cleaned up, you understand how many different people he must manage in conversation, and you understand how fast decisions must be made to avoid the consequences. If the learner experiences such detail in a virtual store, practicing the various scenarios over and over again, and getting points for doing it right, do they learn it better? This is on-the-job training.

When you are constructing shapes in the environment, think of them as containers of expression. Some of the objects are there to create comfort and familiarity, while other objects are there for you to process and experience. If you are in a fast-food restaurant, for example, and you want the trainee to wash his hands before preparing food, make sure the sink has a running faucet with sound, and that it has handles that turn on hot and cold water, and a soap dispenser that reminds the employees they are disinfecting their hands. There are affordances for assessments, such as a sink sending out messages to the participant to reinforce desired behavior. In this way, you reinforce standards, and/or provide reminders on correct behavior if the object was not engaged properly. Since you can collect avatar actions, capturing a metric like the average length of time that a person washes their hands is useful feedback to your program. In doing so, you may predict behaviors in your users and plan the experience and outcome. These are considerations that help to transform thinking about virtual worlds and the training environment. If actions are repeated often enough in a virtual world simulation, it could possibly become a predictable behavior. The more you fire the neurons, the more likely you are to wire the behavior.

Thinking in 3D can supercharge the results. In development, this requires a good plan, iterative analysis on usability and outcomes, and an ever-evolving plan to improve. Build it and ask others to interact with it. Once engaged, use interactive experiences to move the learner to their next activity. If they stall, try something else and make them repeat it just as you would in the physical environment. Either you motivate and captivate the learner and they seek to continue, or they leave. Either you engage the learner and immerse them in your plan, or they flounder. Making mistakes and recovering from the mistake and trying again was made for virtual worlds. During the development process, you experience this quite a lot, which helps to relate to the learner experience as well. So develop a 3D mindset that promotes rapid prototyping. Start with an experienced plan. You can always learn something new about how users interact and can change easily, usually. The key is usability analysis, and in the virtual environment, the opportunities to get user feedback is accelerated. Feedback in a virtual world comes from the environment itself and how people are reacting to it. So when you hit on the right combination of energy, activity, and environment as the authors testify in this book, you know it and so do the students!

Our objective in this book is to provide you with stories. Each author has considerable experience planning, designing, developing, and deploying learning in a virtual world. They understand the transformations they made from building classroom experiences in educational institutions, to building web-based instruction during the e-learning era. When they slipped over into thinking in 3D, they learned how to transform builders by enabling them to be collaborators, co-participants, mentors, and players along with their students. They learned to build communities in which learners belonged to their environment and built up experience over time, learning from the environment as well as from each other, and succeeding over time. They also learned about dynamic, rapid prototyping during their development phase, realizing creativity happens as organically as homesteading. They realized that you must reach out to the entire world and leverage all of the wonderful assets that are available as 3D objects, and avatar components that can be used to develop your persona to your liking. They learned that performance is the focus of the learning experience, and that formal processes work too, but cannot restrict you from thinking in 3D. The purpose of education is to change. The research here and the stories indicate that the faculty are changing, the students are changing, the learning environments are changing, and the Internet is augmenting the educator's toolkit. Virtual worlds technology is moving to the head of the class.

The book is divided into four part: Transforming Virtual World Planning, Transforming Virtual World Design, Transforming Virtual World Development and Transforming Virtual World Deployment. The planning chapters recommend bringing the faculty into the center of the process, and showing them the affordances of virtual worlds. Once they become subscribed to the notion, they work with their stakeholders by bringing them directly into a virtual world to do the planning. The virtual world design chapters encourage the planners to build people-centered communities in virtual worlds, where engagement and immersion are the goals. The objective is to create a place where learners stay in world engaged in solving problems together. The development chapters underscore that virtual world development is dynamic, relies on a distributed workforce for building, and should leverage commercial virtual worlds in order to accelerate time to deployment and access to social networks and assets. The compelling recommendation is to think outside of the classroom metaphor from the start. And finally, when deploying your virtual world, consider international and intercultural perspectives. If you are using the full scale Internet and open access to learning, accommodate for how people are going to interact together. Similarly, rely on narrative in your virtual world and plan for diverse learning outcomes.

TRANSFORMING VIRTUAL WORLD PLANNING

The part covers the planning process from the perspective of the instructor. Our global set of authors span Europe, Asia, and the Americas. The principle concept is that the science of learning, the cybergogy, that has emerged in technologies like virtual worlds requires faculty to think in terms of learning archetypes. As faculty plan for activities and ways to manage attention in activity-based learning environments, they will think in terms of building around avatars, engaged in finding things, and responding to critical incidences. In doing so, teaching and learning grows around visual stimulation, engagement, collaborative motivation, personal interest, context in the subject matter, and "contemporarity" of the learning environment. The process for teaching in virtual worlds mirrors other emerging technology. Educators need to lead by example, using the technology themselves to build their expertise. They must garner support from their stakeholders and create and engage in professional development courses that focus on virtual worlds so they can prepare and be prepared for delivering in the environment.

The planning part includes the following chapters: *A Cybergogy of Learning Archetypes and Learning Domains: Practical Pedagogy for 3D Immersive Virtual Worlds* by Lesley Scopes, Visiting Fellow, from the School of Education, University of Southampton, UK; *Initial Teacher Training in a Virtual World* by John Woollard also from the School of Education in University of Southampton; *Faculty Development for and in Virtual Worlds* by Jennifer L.V. Sparrow, Samantha J. Blevins, and Aimee M. Brenner, from the Virginia Polytechnic Institute and State University and *Pre-Service Teachers' Teaching Practice in Second Life®* by Donguk Cheong, Korea National University of Education, Adjunct Professor, Youngkyun Baek, Boise State University, Professor and Hoe Kyeung Kim, Cleveland State University, Associate Professor.

A common theme in this part recommends the faculty build their virtual world applications with the learner in the center of the activities. Planning is a comprehensive activity; it requires all the stakeholders to contribute their requirements to the planners. The planning part shifts its focus from the student onto the drivers of the plan: the faculty. It looks at teacher training and how it affects all of the elements of virtual world learning in a seamless process of engagement and interaction. The authors in the planning part report on individuals who host, provide, and support the learning environment. The overarching message of this part reminds builders to construct safe and productive places that allow the student to explore their environment and to make decisions. It emphasizes connecting everyone in the virtual world and immersing the user in activities that result in discovery. It also positions the faculty as a responsible player engaged as an equal, and guiding as a mentor.

Scopes provides us with a practical way of planning for virtual world development. She expands on a model called cybergogy, whose intention is to provide content in a way that takes advantage of the distinct features of virtual worlds. There are two categories of virtual worlds: game-centric and social-centric according to Scopes. The former is story and narrative oriented and relies on reward systems. The latter is social in nature, open ended, without stated goals, and can be used for content that is oriented around communications, affiliations, and relationships. Among these domains, faculty are encouraged to plan using learning archetypes and domains. The archetypes include role play, peregrination, simulated actions, meshed experiences with assessment, and evaluation integrated into the activities. She frames the archetypes around four learning domains: cognitive, dextrous, social, and emotional. These domains combine to create full experiences for learners that can be crafted to result in predictive outcomes from learners. Scopes breaks down her framework in practical applications to understand how they work. She looks at classes in the history of Christianity, astronomy, social psychology, and Arab-Israeli conflict studies. Her chapter is targeted to show the framework and how it can be used to plan for virtual world learning.

Woollard references cybergogy and speaks directly about faculty preparation in its use. He discusses the social rules that are required for conducting virtual world based learning. He explains that knowing what the social rules are for interacting is critical for instructors, as the stakes are high, especially in the use of avatars, explicit content, and live environments, where self-management is vital. He explains what kind of intervention is required with regard to cyber-safety. He reminds faculty to communicate effectively in the virtual world by preparing note cards, scripted material, and sending notifications both in-world and in e-mail to guide training. He cautions that it is the faculty's responsibility to secure the mental and physical well-being of classroom avatars in the virtual world. He provides ample dialogue from his teacher training program to demonstrate how users interacted with others in the learning environment to reinforce his teachings here. He identifies a framework for thinking about e-safety: looking at content as a recipient, contact as a participant, and conduct as an actor. He frames this interaction model around four domains: commercial, aggressive, sexual, and values, so the appropriate material and behaviors are considered during the planning phase. He rounds out his discussion by explaining the essential elements of acceptable use policy to ensure faculty understand the netiquette, legal requirements, and consequences of their actions. Woollard's contribution to the dialogue around e-safety is a key planning element.

Sparrow, Blevins, and Brenner, stress the importance of focusing on faculty development as well, providing easy-to-implement virtual world instructions that they have used. Their objective is to participate in the faculty planning process, using proven methods for teaching in world. Before embarking on the design and development process, they recommend examining good learning practices and understanding how to get and maintain attention in the virtual world. Maintaining avatar attention when engaging in a new activity requires good communication among groups, as well as between the faculty member and each individual. These three authors from Virginia Polytechnic Institute and State University present the mechanical issues such as how to address issues of access, how to meet technology requirements, and how to prepare for student orientation. They advise how to make sure you set expectations on student behavior in world as well as communicating how assessment will work in the virtual world. They discuss both single workshops and conducting entire conferences as models that work.

Cheong, Baek, and Kim have formally engaged in a long-term pre-service teachers' teaching practice in Korea. Their pre-service teacher educators not only provide the tools for planning, but also prepare students to practice their teaching in a virtual world, so they can bring their experience to life. It is one thing to read about a framework and see how others teach in a virtual world, it is quite a different experience to do it yourself. This chapter shows that many kinds of objects supporting teaching and learning should be designed and created in advance for successful teaching practices in virtual worlds. Procedural learning is vital, and these authors show pre-service teachers' teaching practices that work such as how to close the distance and increase the amount of communication. In physical classrooms, conversation is limited by formal turn taking and interruption civilities. In a virtual world, conversation flows more freely. Individuals chat in local or group chat, providing insight both to the other students in terms of what they are thinking, as well as to the faculty and mentors who are dynamically presenting. Cheong, Baek, and Kim take us through eight weeks of training among 160 college students who were completing a practicum at Korea National University of Education using a cognitive apprenticeship model. Like these authors, there is guidance on transforming learning in virtual worlds from all of the various authors located in the lesson plans that accompany these chapters.

These chapters in the planning part remind us of the need for faculty to work through communication issues, Internet policy issues, attention management, student preparation, and Q&A support. They advise us that the virtual world classroom is a unit, and that it enables real-time connections and seamless corrections. As a rich environment for interaction and engagement, make sure you plan for access to URLs, definitions from expert sources, and expertise during regular class time to enhance the flow of the class. We are reminded here that people are at the core of virtual world learning, be they faculty who have to manage the experience, students who engage as active participants, or outside mentors. Virtual worlds can provide pre-service teachers and experienced instructors with a creative and relevant classroom experience. Faculty can engage in cognitive apprenticeships, demonstrating how virtual spaces can be used to create a continuous experience of participation and observation to all their stakeholders before, during, and after the length of the course.

TRANSFORMING VIRTUAL WORLD DESIGN

The part is dedicated to designing virtual worlds as a dynamic process that includes much more than just the builders. It also requires the participants. Design in virtual worlds centers first around building the learning community first, and then the shared activities that make the community meaningful. Design in virtual world learning requires users to show up in the virtual world to begin the process of building. The traditional instructional designer or the teacher oftentimes falls back on traditional activities – writing, reading, lecturing, discussions, or brainstorming. These are all great. However, virtual worlds are a stage and the students are actors. The more narrative you build, the more engagement occurs. The more character development is required, the more the students invest in their participation. And, of course the more rewards and recognition, the more sense of a community is built. From the moment the first person lands in the environment, the story must unfold, the problem must present itself, and the tasks must begin as though the user were on an adventure. What is this place and how do I shape it to express myself and interact with others to communicate and learn? How do I set it up so that people feel a sense of belonging, ownership, and knowing where to go and what to do? This happens as much to the faculty member as it does to any of the students and mentors who share the space.

Present in the stage of design are the following: *A Practical Model and Assignments for Using Virtual Worlds in Higher Education* by Dona Cady, Matthew Olson, Peter Shea, and J. M Grenier from Middlesex Community College, in Bedford, MA; *Instructional Design Frameworks for Second Life Virtual Learning* by Scott J. Warren and Jenny S. Wakefield from the University of North Texas; and *Using the Community of Inquiry (CoI) Model and Bloom's Revised Taxonomy to Support 21st Century, Virtual Teaching and Learning in Multiuser Virtual Environments* by Melissa L. Burgess from the Texas Virtual Learning Center and Phil Ice from the American Public University System.

Cady, Olson, Shea, and Grenier provide the rationale and background for designing in virtual worlds, as they come together as a community of practice. They discuss practical concerns for instruction in commercial virtual worlds including committing to providing a strong online presence. By integrating virtual worlds into instruction, the Virtual Education Research Group (VERG) at Middlesex Community College in Massachusetts provides students with collaborative experiences through a sustained community of practice and experimentation with a variety of virtual world commercial platforms. Why not leverage what is already there as a start is sound advice. Their experience has students entering various virtual worlds. As a consequence, some general principles and specific learning activities have emerged for instructors integrating virtual worlds into the classroom. The basic concepts of connecting technical and administrative support, choosing worlds with thematic connections to the discipline, creating scheduled opportunities for play, and providing a strong online presence are vital to their design. Such principles have been used to bring social virtual worlds into the classroom and classrooms into the virtual world. Through the work at VERG, virtual worlds are used in a wider context in a variety of instructional disciplines, ranging from humanities to psychology to business.

Several case studies illustrating unique and effective practices are provided. The story revolves around leveraging commercial virtual worlds to enhance the learning experience and getting to the rapid design process quickly. The VERG group believes in experimentation and learning by doing.

Burgess and Ice offer a traditional framework for a modern technology, using the community of inquiry (CoI) model and Bloom's revised taxonomy to support 21st century online teaching and learning in multiuser virtual environments. Inquiry-based learning creates student participation. Bloom's taxonomy for learning, a well-known format for instructional design, is modernized by these authors' dive into communities that come alive with people and 3D content. The authors argue that online learning in higher education has delivered e-learning instruction primarily through learning management systems (LMS) such as BlackBoard, Moodle, and others. They recognize that budgetary constraints and mushrooming enrollments have required designers to look at delivery of online learning via multiple open source (free) formats. In investigating open environments, the emerging technologies of multiuser virtual environments, or MUVEs, were identified as an option. Keeping in mind the authors are looking for CoIs and shopping for models that engage as Bloom recommended, they found interactive and socially rich learning experience for learners in virtual worlds and adopted them, while adapting their models of learning to match the affordances of virtual worlds. In their chapter, Burgess and Ice propose a dually fused pedagogical framework that, when used together, have the potential to provide both asynchronous and synchronous online learning activities that elicit critical thinking skills and that also align with skills to compete in today's global society. Their learning models advance our thinking about converting physical spaces and experiences in virtual worlds to help transform the way we learn.

Warren and Wakefield have also provided a process for designing virtual worlds based off of their work at the University of North Texas. They have a five-step formula for designing virtual worlds. They offer:

- Build community – Develop activities to sustain virtual community beyond classroom tasks so that learning can take place after the course is long over.
- Allow experimentation – Permit learners to freely experiment with the new technologies in and out of the virtual world.
- Support creative play – Know that learners will go off-task and will want to creatively use these experiences and their real-world lives to give context to what they learn.

- Be there for your learners – Provide extensive support in the form of direct and indirect instruction and address technical issues quickly.
- Give learners time to think – For many, virtual worlds are brand new. Provide meaningful opportunities for learners to reflect on their individual experiences and learn from them.

They provide examples of how to utilize their framework. They discuss designing their student Second Life (SL) success program and their SL design course highlighting the communication features that enhanced learning: local text-based chat, private channel instant message (IM), group text chat, and voice calls. They used rapid prototyping to produce in-depth knowledge on building, avatar management, scripting, and avatar animations to meet diverse student needs. They designed four principles to inform other designers: Principle One: Create opportunities for sustaining virtual community beyond a task, Principle Two: Provide social communication opportunities to participants, Principle Three: Promote and advertise new community to leverage excitement, Principle Four: Leverage participant experience with new technology to experiment.

The transforming design chapters demonstrate the culture of interaction, where people and experts come together with similar interests to learn from each other, grow with each other, and take feedback in safe and conducive places. Such experiences allow teams to form skills to be shaped from collective practices, supporting team members with caring explanations of what worked and what did not. In worlds that work, it seems that students assist each other more through participation than critique. Value and trust are used more as the currency of learning transactions in the virtual world. And after years of experience, these authors show how their communities are designed around individual's experience, and the collective experiences that come with entering into the virtual world at any time of the day and engaging with others looking for interactions. Happenstance in a virtual world is actually a design element. These chapters support the notion of designing the community first, and then the spontaneous activities to support the community. Realizing this is an iterative process that requires using the technologies of community and the tools of design is important to note. Advancing the theories of instructional development that have supported learning so elegantly is a stalwart activity, but the needs of the technology simply call for it. The technology has become network oriented and has connected large groups of people from around the world. These authors have delivered those progressions.

TRANSFORMING VIRTUAL WORLD DEVELOPMENT

Transforming development in virtual worlds looks at three examples of dynamic development, in which the community is doing the development. Development is different in the virtual world because it utilizes people from anywhere in the world. Since logging into the virtual world is universal, it allows people to participate from anywhere in the world where they have an Internet connection and credentials. Inviting people to build and test in the virtual world is key to accelerating development. Not every virtual world allows for building. Many virtual worlds allow users to come into the world and experience the content, rather than create it. These virtual worlds are valid examples of using 2D content often in which lectures occur, breakout groups form to discuss lectures, and presentations are provided as the key construct in the environment. The more common virtual worlds that have been used for learning seem to allow for user-generated content creation and highlight the social networking aspects of learning. So, in this part, we look at those virtual worlds where content creation is the norm, where universality is the value, and cocreation is the objective. We do this because the nature of learning is doing. It is not just about being there, it is about doing there. This is a phrase that has defined every virtual world that seems to make a difference in learning. The question for the virtual world developer is how often can you get your whole class to visit a genetics laboratory, fly into the center of a hurricane, or meet other people worldwide to engage in problem solving and return to a sandbox and build something that helps to solve a real-world problem?

Our authors that have transformed the nature of development in virtual world learning include: *Marinetta Ombro: A Culture Not a Classroom* by Owen Kelly from Arcada University of Applied Sciences in Finland; *Enhancing Graduate Courses through Educational Virtual Tours* by Irena Bojanova and Les Pang from the University of Maryland University College; and *Using Problem-Based Learning within 3D Virtual Worlds* by Vanessa Parson, University of Sunderland and Simon Bignell, University of Derby, both located in the United Kingdom.

Kelly describes the development of Marinetta Ombro, an eight-year project intended to find innovative ways of using a synthetic culture for learning purposes. He tells us that Arcada is a small university of applied sciences in Helsinki, Finland and its ethos is vocationally directed, therefore the idea of building in a virtual world fits their social constructivist model. They decided to supplement their online media students with a virtual world environment to create a laboratory where students could test out their ideas.

But instead of building a classroom, they decided to build a culture. They wanted it to be unpredictable and multipurpose to accommodate for several users in different departments across Arcada. But, they didn't enter the world first and start creating, instead they engaged in a deep research and design process. Once they had created the culture of Marinetta Ombro, they began building content on the islands. They built on concept design and branding, research methods for health care, entrepreneurship, foundations of Photoshop, tourism and media, and cross media production. Kelly explains to us the lessons learned from developing the virtual world in this way. He identifies three key learnings: (a) we need to look not just how virtuality might be used for learning, but how learning might be changed through exposure to virtuality; (b) we need to understand more about the nature of the relationship between what is modeled in virtuality and what is perceived in the real world; and (c) we need to examine the extent to which skills are gained merely through prolonged experience in a virtual environment, and the extent to which these skills are themselves transferable to the physical world. Distinguishing between virtual spaces, virtual worlds, and virtual reality by creating a place for residents to evolve is at the center of Kelly's experiment in Marinetta Ombro. Kelly believes that virtual worlds should be viewed more as living labs or Petri dishes than as classrooms.

Bojanova and Pang use virtual tours as their technique for developing engagement in virtual world experiences. Tours can be both synchronous and asynchronous. The authors believe educational virtual tours offer many advantages over traditional field trips in terms of cost, logistics, and safety. So, they provide clear guidelines on how to effectively conduct educational virtual tours and discussion on key lessons learned. It is not always so easy to herd cats, when moving people from location to location, especially when you can't see all of them. The buddy system is a good solution, as well as preplanning where you are going and making sure that there is a map with meeting locations on it. Bojanova and Pang treat the environment seriously as they observe and record. Their chapter shares results of a survey conducted on virtual tour participants that provide a revealing insight on this new approach. Educational field trips to virtual worlds were proven to raise the students' level of engagement, promote critical thinking, and meet pedagogical objectives. Virtual tours in SL that offer a rich palette of choices for military, enterprises, education, science, and entertainment help to demonstrate the variety and diversity in incorporating tours into the learning platform. As the virtual world arena expands and as interoper-ability between virtual worlds becomes more within our reach, moving across virtual worlds, experiencing their various interfaces, and returning back to a home base will be ways to expand this technique that Bojanova and Pang recommend. The open access to their content and their tours through the university island provide a community experience that adds the practical touch to this book that helps anyone developing in virtual worlds and inspired our adding lesson plans to each chapter.

Developing in virtual worlds is different from developing for the classroom. In virtual worlds, you want to make sure to focus on the learner and the experience and avoid recreating the classroom itself. Using the classroom metaphor may help to orient people to show up and sit down, know where the teacher is going to stand, and know when to be silent when something is about to begin. But, if all we wanted people to do was to listen, then the metaphor works, and it indeed does have a place in virtual world development. But ignoring other users, or regarding them as distractions, prevents educators from harnessing the power of their activities to fuel learning experiences. So, the idea is not to create more interesting learning places, like volcanoes, or sitting in trees or under the ocean, but to use virtual worlds as virtual spaces not only defined by their gorgeous geometry but also by the depth of communication and sociality and the recognition that comes with success. Learning becomes more organic in this environment, allowing users to adapt to the environment, rather than just to do the exercises in it. The concept of "virtual worlds" is not as simple as it may appear when developing because the default is to go back to what you know.

Parson and Bignell, suggest that using problem-based learning (PBL) in virtual worlds leads to a deeper approach to learning, emphasizing team skills, and students developing problem-solving skills. These authors claim that virtual worlds facilitate learning in an active way, enabling students to use planned scenarios and case studies. PBL sets the user up to think in terms of creating solutions to real problems. What you can do to enhance learning by using PBL is to provide physical world experiences within a safe and controlled environment free from the consequences associated with typical problems. They recommend avatar-driven scenarios, information-driven scenarios, group formation, and scavenger hunts to find information to solve the problem at hand. To exemplify the development model, they present a case study in which learners examining a virtual world house identifying the social interactions and symptoms of people with clinical conditions such as depression, schizophrenia, and anorexia nervosa. They discuss the role of the teacher in virtual world education describing how teachers have to juggle their roles as directors and facilitators in both synchronous and asynchronous support environments for PBL-based students. They discuss the components of a virtual classroom: access, materials, group formation, communication, and texting. They also explain how to prepare the students for the virtual world by providing instruction on avatars and user accounts, the user-interface, use of space, impact and management of "lag." The more practice and performance, the more learning and changing takes place. The more contact with others, the more reinforcement takes place. The more PBL, the more engagement and immersion takes place.

TRANSFORMING VIRTUAL WORLD DEPLOYMENT

Deployment is engaging the community over time and making improvements to sustain the interaction. When deploying virtual worlds, it is useful to recognize some of the long-term effects. Deployment has a lot to do with socialization, so many current, successful builders incorporate metrics onto their islands so they can observe social patterns of avatars. Some techniques include using polls and feedback kiosks placed throughout the virtual world environment to capture student impressions. More robust methods conduct usability studies to investigate ethnographies, heuristics, common uses, and failing patterns. In this part, we will examine three components of deployment that likely need to be measured for determining social impact. They include intercultural collaborative learning, narrative continuity, and the observation of the diversity of learning outcomes. When deploying virtual worlds there are many human factors that need to be regarded. The research in this area is just beginning. The attention to recognizing some of the components is important for building sustainable learning environments.

The contributors to this part include: *Intercultural Collaborative Learning in Virtual Worlds* by Béatrice S. Hasler from the Sammy Ofer School of Communications, Interdisciplinary Center Herzliya, Israel; *Alice's Adventures in Programming Narratives*, by Reneta D. Lansiquot and Candido Cabo from the New York City College of Technology of The City University of New York; and *Teaching Higher Education Students with Diverse Learning Outcomes in the Virtual World of Second Life* by Sue Gregory from the University of New England, Armidale, NSW, Australia.

Hasler embraces intercultural collaborative learning. Her data suggests that language has become less of a barrier in virtual worlds than might have been expected. She explains the concepts of intercultural literacy and intercultural collaborative learning, and looks at the core elements of virtual worlds from a cross-cultural perspective. She provides a case study of a global lecture series that used a collaborative virtual environment (virtual world CVE) as a platform for intercultural student collaboration. Hasler's evaluation results show that real-world cultural conventions are transferred into the virtual world, which are reflected in the deployment of avatars. She was able to capture the perceived usefulness of virtual world CVE for intercultural collaboration and provides what the participating students have learned from working in an intercultural virtual team. Her work identifies the cultural differences between individualist and collective thinking and how that can affect the usefulness of the virtual world experience. She discusses "identity tourism" and its consequences on human interaction. She provides useful information on the role of nonverbal communication in virtual worlds and the implications of visual metaphors. These are all issues of concern that extend beyond the initial design and development, and reinforce the need for virtual worlds to be dynamic and observant of the differences among us as much as the similarities between us.

Lansiquot and Cabo take us into the narrative through a virtual world programming class that provides us some reflection on the importance of narrative in education. They compare teaching Visual Basic and an Immersive Learning Programming environment known as Alice in a computer science class. The students that used the virtual world programming environment which leveraged narrative storytelling, seemed to improve their performance in general problem-solving abilities while programming in Visual Basic alone did not. Increasingly significant is that the narrative component also increased participation and retention. Examining this aspect of narrative in a computer science programming class is significant as programming classes tend to be quite difficult for users as a content area and even more difficult to teach in a relevant way. Seeing narrative at work in such a course provides insight into what the impact could be on many other subject matter areas. The authors support that the narrative is vital to improved learning outcomes. In thinking through virtual world deployment, taking the human story into account is vital.

Gregory finalizes the transformation process by reminding us that teaching with a diverse set of learning outcomes is imperative for completing the picture. How can an educator teach students in a virtual world when the students have diverse learning outcomes? This is a question that crosses all designers and developers of virtual worlds. Gregory becomes the actor avatar and takes us into the narrative of the Jass Easterman, a well-established teacher avatar, who engages her students to liaise together as pre-service instructors. Jass, aka Gregory, explains the outcomes are diverse. Some of her community are academic, some are social, some are political, and the in-world play is fascinating. Some of the outcomes result in new communication strategies, and working with others from around the world who have different expectations and different technical mannerisms. Her innovative tutorial model serves students through virtual tours, visiting other educational institutions, attending guest lectures together, undertaking role play activities and learning the basic building and scripting skills of virtual worlds, all from their own homes. Jass is the virtual world. She has come to live in it, accept it as a norm, and adapts to it effortlessly. The future of learning is upon us now, she reminds all of us, and invites us to meet many in-world residents who are ready to take anyone by the hand and transform virtual world learning and practice together. When you meet Jass or any of our author avatars, you instantly have mentors, guides, and community organizers who can help transform learning in virtual worlds with you.

This book argues that setting up learning in a virtual world requires a transformative approach. First, you must look at the entire group of stakeholders who will be affected by the new learning community and you must include them in the planning process. These stakeholders include the enablers: funders, visionaries, administrators, and faculty. They also include the builders: learners, designers, developers, testers, implementers. They also include the facilitators: the helpers, evaluators, visitors, guests, mentors, and finally they include the chroniclers: the people who write about and market virtual world learning environments both inside and outside the organization. Second, design requires building communities in which the stakeholders spend significant time in the environment adapting to the environment and practicing in the fluidity of the environment. Third, virtual world development is real time and iterative and uses the principles of rapid prototyping and dynamic production with an international work force. And finally, virtual world deployment encourages you to grow your world internationally, build around narrative, and acculturate to diverse learning outcomes. If users adhere to these principles, their execution and stakeholder adoption might be complete. When a community is born and grows organically, it hosts learning, evolves user-generated content for reuse, celebrates experience, and provides a launch pad for continued belonging – the Petri dish for lifelong learning.

The advice given in this book comes from real-world implementers of virtual worlds. It is meant to transform your thinking about creating and using innovative virtual world applications. The perspective and practical applications orientations come from those virtual world users who are actively learning, teaching, or supporting those who do. Each chapter provides sound advice, personal experience, a framework, and a lesson plan. The objective is to address the stakeholders, enable activity-based learning, and assess through performance. In short, the collective wisdom here suggests building a virtual biodome for learning. It is our hope that this book inspires current educational institutions and business, both large and small, to build creative virtual worlds that are persistent, scalable, and can be used to create communities of education, where the choice is viable and complete for everyone in the learning value chain: K-12, community college, university and industrial strength educational solutions to educate the work force, and of course lifelong learning. Who knows when you will be tapped as a mentor in a virtual world?

Randy Hinrichs
Editor

PART I
TRANSFORMING VIRTUAL WORLD PLANNING

A CYBERGOGY OF LEARNING ARCHETYPES AND LEARNING DOMAINS: PRACTICAL PEDAGOGY FOR 3D IMMERSIVE VIRTUAL WORLDS

Lesley Scopes

ABSTRACT

Our university demonstrates a strong investment in online education and as part of continuing development delivers some existing online programs in a 3D virtual world. Faculty members need a plan to engage, so they were guided in the adoption of our cybergogy of learning archetypes and learning domains to draw together various aspects of learning. Together we weave threads from orthodox theories with a doctrine of educational technologies that encompasses social-centric 3D interactive virtual environments. This chapter documents the growth of the model from theory into practice to provide a framework for instructors to plan their virtual courses. Five Second Life®-enhanced courses were developed, scheduled and marketed to enrolled students to test the framework. The teaching and learning strategies adopted are reported and outcomes are presented.

Keywords: Virtual worlds; cybergogy; learning archetypes; learning domains

Transforming Virtual World Learning
Cutting-edge Technologies in Higher Education, Volume 4, 3–28

ISSN: 2044-9968/doi:10.1108/S2044-9968(2011)0000004005

> Pedagogy is a complex affair, and there are many ways of writing its history– states Gabriel Compayré in the 1899 publication *The history of pedagogy*.

It is true that pedagogy has had millennia to develop philosophically and in terms of processes. Compayré refers to 'the beautiful spectacle of humanity in a state of ceaseless growth'. The recent emergence of 3D immersive virtual worlds (3DiVW) provides a computer-mediated digital environment for people to develop pedagogical practices and to continue humanity's perpetual growth. At centre stage is the student and faculty as avatars, described by Kapp & O'Driscoll (2010, p. 57) as a person's virtual character. The backdrop is the digital environment in which an avatar is immersed, described by Meadows (2008, p23) as 'The avatar is the character (protagonist), the system is their story environment and the events that happen to the avatar are all steps along a narrative chosen by the driver of the avatar'.

3DiVWs provide a milieu within which educational content can be delivered to widely dispersed cohorts of learners. Owing to the distinct features that comprise virtual worlds, however, many aspects of pedagogy need to evolve. We have implemented a model of Cybergogy, honed to embrace the affordances of the 3D environment as a powerful learning medium. This theory addresses the sensibilities of the digital learner and presents educational content in a way which takes advantage of the distinct features in 3DiVWs which are mostly absent in traditional e-learning scenarios.

The Model of Cybergogy of Learning Archetypes and Learning Domains is presented here as a structure for teachers using virtual worlds to conduct virtual world teaching (v-Teaching), enabling them to demonstrate stringent planning and execution of imaginative, reflective practices that are felicitous for 3D virtual worlds.

This chapter describes the further developed model of cybergogy that is born out of the product of a masters (MSc) dissertation (Scopes 2009) under the hospice of The University of Southampton, School of Education, UK, which set out to combat with earlier notions (circa 2004) that emerging 3DiVWs, such as Second Life® (SL), provide not much more than a frivolous setting for a parody of meaningful educational pursuits. The notions are easy to qualify when the emergence of 3DiVWs is put into context along with the look and feel of the interface with some perceptions being shaped by media reactions, many of which were initially particularly negative (Greenfield, 2008; McDougall, 2010; Sigman, 2009). The context in terms of time of initial emergence places the arrival of 3DiVWs approximately 10 years after the rising popularity of computer and video games that were evolving from their 2D ‘platform jumping’ roots (Super Mario, Prince of Persia) to 3D games for the PlayStation and Nintendo game consoles. Along a parallel thread, the Internet had provided an opportunity for communities to be formed in cyberspace with text-based Multi-User Dungeon (MUD) chat rooms as the vehicle. 3DiVWs are seen by some, as a marriage of these two paradigms, a graphical chat room and a 3D real-time gaming environment epitomised by game-centric virtual worlds such as World of Warcraft which provides a story narrative, a quest and reward-driven world where affiliations and collaborations can be formed. Given the common association, it is of little surprise that social-centric 3DiVWs such as Second Life® (SL) can flounder in terms of comfortable contextualisation wherein there is no story narrative provided, no obvious way to ‘win’ and no pre-defined purpose. It is difficult to point to a niche in which such an environment fits within the existing strata of educational technologies and no prior indication as to whether these new social-centric 3D environments should be taken seriously as a valid educational tool (Table 1).

In fact, SL provides something toward emancipation for educators. People and places are transitory. SL – software that epitomises the capability of a virtual world that is user created, the content is generated by the users, referred to as residents, of the virtual world for purposes ranging from the altruistic to the promotional, engendering environments from the mundane to the phantasmagorical. This, like some of the other user created virtual worlds is capable of supporting almost any category of activity chosen by the user. But the success of the world of experiences is largely dependent upon the quality of design standards that underpin the activity and environmental conditions. Many ventures in 3DiVWs do not transition well using real-life strategies. In terms of commerce, this 3D trend has not been especially productive for many. Daniel Voyager (2011) provides a list of approximately 15 real-life ‘big’ companies who remain active currently (March 2011) in SL. Voyager blogs that ‘Many real life organizations and businesses have left SL in recent years with their own reasons for doing so’. Evidence suggests that a virtual presence representing real-life commercial

Table 1. 3DiVW Centricities.

Two Categories of 3D Immersive Virtual Worlds (3DiVW)	
Game-centric	Social-centric
Story narrative (quests)	Open ended
Reward system	No way to ‘win’

operations is often unpopulated, attracting disappointingly little interest or return on investment. This can also be said for many educational institutions. Is there an operational force that could turn around the utility of this environment for education? The implication is that, of the 50,000 plus regular denizens, many do not necessarily inhabit a 3DiVW to experience a direct replication of real life, but perhaps rather, to participate in a contradistinctive experience, a foot in both worlds, producing a blending of realities whereby one feeds into the other and definitive boundaries become blurred. Whilst not discussed in detail here, the term 'v-Terial' is meant to describe the subjective and un-quantifiable point in an individual's perception where the *virtual* blends with the *material* in a form of synergy.

In terms of educational affordances, effectiveness is subject to careful re-engineering of pedagogy to align content, delivery and receptivity toward taking strategic advantage of the aspects of 3DiVWs which splice them away from traditional methods of online education. Hence, the emergence of Cybergogy of Learning Archetypes and Learning Domains, set somewhat apart from the Wang and Kang (2006) model of cybergogy for Web 2.0 applications, this is cybergogy for 3DiVW. The purpose of cybergogy is to install a valid pedagogical approach for educationists by bringing together threads from orthodox theory, weaving them into a doctrine of educational technologies that encompass social-centric 3Di virtual environments. This model caters to the 3DiVW optimisation of the affordances for the transfer of real-life knowledge and skills in a v-learning context. Techniques can supplement learning experiences in face-to-face seated classes or in the ability to facilitate real-time training experiences amongst globally distributed teams of individuals. This model allows educators to demonstrate that their v-teaching practices are as stringently planned, documented and executed as their standard pedagogical practices.

The theoretical model is explicated by accounts of the practical application of cybergogy by Drury University (Springfield, MO) online education faculty members following structured formal teaching along with extended informal developmental support.

THE RATIONALE

The model of cybergogy is situated within a social constructivist epistemology deriving philosophically from the Vygotskian socio-cultural approach of knowledge internalisation supported by social processes leading to the development of higher cognitive functions. Social constructivism is pertinent with regard to the qualities and affordances typically present within a social-centric 3DiVW, the provision of multiple channels for communication both synchronous and asynchronous, opportunities for collaboration, co-creation and networking, purposeful affiliations with groups and communities of practice, not underestimating the value in serendipitous encounters that may provide an opportunity for informal learning and the formation of meaningful social and working relationships in genuine human collaborations. Communications, affiliations and relationships forged between people within the 3DiVW are not necessarily confined just to the virtual environment, but often branch out into other social networking sites such as LinkedIn, Twitter, and Facebook, even further, allegiances formed in the virtual worlds can sometimes extend into the physical world, whereby people meet up face to face, often travelling internationally for occasional social or business purposes. Conversely, new residents may be drawn into the virtual world as a result of connections, affiliations and associations emanating from social media influences.

LEARNING ARCHETYPES AND LEARNING DOMAINS

The model of cybergogy is composed of two interacting components: learning archetypes and learning domains (Fig. 1).

Learning archetypes are categories of learning activities that capitalise on the affordances of the 3D environment, crafted to elicit learning outcomes that engage four learning domains. Originating from concepts expressed by Karl Kapp and Tony O'Driscoll's (2007) e-Learning Guild essay 'Escaping Flatlands', learning archetypes are the fundamental building blocks of educational activities whose locus is the plasticity of possibilities afforded by 3DiVWs. Activities can often be virtually constructed that are not possible in other mediums or indeed in physical life. The model of cybergogy harnesses five overarching categories of archetypes named and defined in Table 1. More recently, Karl Kapp & Tony O'Driscoll have reviewed their library of archetypes as published in their book 'Learning in 3D' (2010, pp. 91–118) and have included detailed descriptions that have been presented in prior publications (Scopes 2009, pp. 33–43); however, the concept remains unchanged. Learning archetypes are indigenous to the design process in providing a conceptual framework to support learning activities, serving as

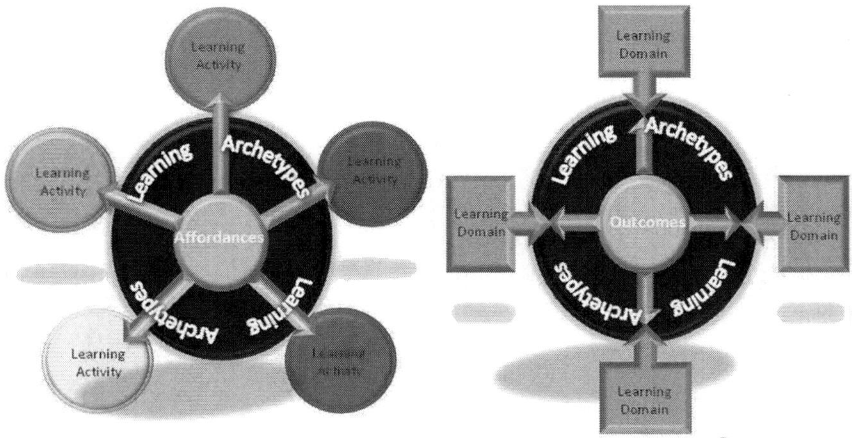

© Scopes 2009

Fig. 1. Two Interacting Components – Learning Archetypes and Learning Domains.

a vehicle towards attaining a condition of immersion whilst undertaking tasks designed to provide learning opportunities. They are a tool for the designer and an activity for the learner. Newer archetypes as they develop can be absorbed under the umbrella of this model of cybergogy adding instructional techniques for further enrichment of the currently defined archetypes (Table 2).

Each classification of learning archetypes is further broken down into frames and sub-frames that serve to both contextualise and hone the activity, but more so to design them in a way to accommodate the deeper dynamics of specific learning domains (outlined later). For example, the role-play archetype can be broken down into frames and sub-frames as seen in Table 3.

The second intrinsic component of the model of cybergogy is four learning domains: cognitive, dextrous, social and emotional. These represent strands drawn from the physical world and an understanding of pedagogy, assimilated to form a new blended taxonomy designed to draw forth all of a person's available sensibilities into the virtual environment. Currently, two domains not accommodated by this model are haptic and sensory. This restriction is subject to logistic issues and common availability of technical equipment and facilities needed to provide a full virtual reality experience. The lack of haptic and sensory domains serves to partially demonstrate the divergence of 3D virtual worlds from virtual reality, discussed by Castronova (2007) as

Table 2. Classifications and Definitions of Learning Archetypes.

Classification of Learning Archetypes	Definition
Role play	To assume a role in an alternative form (living or inanimate) with the objective of undertaking aspects of action, interaction or portrayal of emotions
Peregrination	Travel to locations or the very action of journeying to a destination provides the circumstances under which learning can take place
Simulation	The implementation of an environment designed to represent real or virtual conditions for the purposes of imitation, enactment, exploration, rehearsal and evaluation
Meshed	Creation of opportunities to not simply network but to combine and interconnect individuals and groups in various ways for desired purposes and outcomes
Assessment and Evaluation	Execution of appropriate methods of assessment, evaluation and feedback as part of the learning process

Table 3. The Role-Play Archetype Showing Frames and Sub-Frames.

Archetype	Frame	Sub-Frame
Role play	Free form (*Not organised or planned in a conventional way*)	Individual (*A single role played by individual learners*)
	Structured (*Organised according to a plan*)	
		Multiple (*Groups or Teams of Roleplayers*)
	Dramatised (*A presentation of a vivid expression of informed performance*)	
		Synergetic (*In synergetic combination with another Learning Archetype such as Simulation*)
	Morphic (*To assume a role in an alternative form, living or inanimate*)	

'practical virtual reality', having 'emerged unannounced from the dark imagineering labs of the video gaming industry' and as such is distinguishable from the scientific virtual reality of the 1990s. Castronova reflects that the lack of access to these domains has not impoverished the appeal of or engrossment and immersion in television, radio, movies or of books!

Catering to the four learning domains pivots upon planned learning outcomes fostered by the subsequent selection of learning archetypes, sometimes necessarily in synergetic combination. They can be crafted to elicit required responses from the learning domains. By catering to all four domains, a teacher can create compelling, holistic experiences that can transport the learner into an immersed condition of learning.

BLENDED TAXONOMY OF ESTABLISHED PARADIGMS

Established, validated theoretical paradigms were selected to support the four learning domains and their relationship to desired learning outcomes at the appropriate level of implementation in Table 4. The cognitive learning domain is addressed from the perspective of Bloom's Taxonomy, adapted

Table 4. Blended Taxonomy of Learning Domains Showing Associated Learning Outcomes.

Level of Implementation	Learning Outcomes in the Cognitive Domain	Learning Outcomes in the Emotional Domain	Learning Outcomes in the Dextrous Domain	Learning Outcomes in the Social Domain
6 (high)	Creating	Influencing	Authoritative	Channelling
5	Evaluating	Self Regulating	Naturalising	Networking
4	Analysing	Understanding others	Articulating	Affiliating
3	Applying	Understanding Self	Developing precision	Communicating
2	Understanding	Using Emotion	Manipulating	Contextualising
1 (low)	Remembering	Perceiving Emotion	Imitating	Personalising

by Anderson and Krathwohl (2001) with an additional adaptation to accommodate Web 2.0 applications considered (Churches 2008). At the fundamental level of implementation, learning outcomes should reflect the learner's ability to archive and recall information. Higher levels of implementation require that learning outcomes demonstrate abilities of hypothesis construction/destruction and abstract conjecture.

The emotional domain is extracted from models of emotional intelligence (Goleman 1998; Salovey & Mayer 1994). Aspects included are techniques for tapping into 'whole brain learning', accelerated learning techniques, self-motivation, change adaption and the re-evaluation and adjustment of restrictive patterns of thought, feeling and behaviour that may interfere with efficiency and can increase stress. Within a 3DiVW, the perception of an emotional constituent in a simple situation such as a fear of falling from a height or a moment of aesthetic appreciation contributes to a deepened level of immersion and learning. Kapp and O'Driscoll (2010, p. 63) report that experiences in the 3DiVW can cause real physical reactions from participants such as increased heart rate, laughter and perspiration. In a similar vein, emotional experiences encountered in a virtual world translate to real emotions and as such provide the teacher with an almost tangible portal to the person represented by the avatar. Having said that, emotional manipulation should be handled with caution owing to the somewhat impoverished feedback mechanisms normally interpreted such as body language and facial expression. Learning outcomes in the emotional domain range from a low level of requiring a learner to internally acknowledge their own emotional reaction, to, at the higher levels, becoming capable of influencing the emotional experiences of others. The emotional domain can be further stimulated by impromptu events encountered in the 3DiVW, for example, in social situations, managing interpersonal interactions, experiencing a range of personalities, cultures and opinions, effects of conversations held, affects of the actions of others, observations of behaviours and the critical evaluation of new experiences. All of these are aspects of a rounded social constructivist paradigm.

The dextrous domain was initially inspired by Bloom's incomplete psychomotor domain re-engineered to accommodate requirements that provide dexterity at the interface with the virtual world and also within it; however, within this model of cybergogy, dexterity extends further than manual manipulation of virtual objects using a keyboard and mouse; it includes an authoritative command of the functionality of the virtual world viewer. (There are several viewer versions which offer different affordances along with different viewers for 3DiVWs other than SL.) Dexterity is not simply limited to 'physical agility' but also includes on the spot problem solving (not necessarily just of a technical nature), and it can include certain types of conflict resolution, diplomacy, correct management of environmental conditions to protect events, property and content from malicious or inadvertent disruption and the identification of compromises and solutions especially to ensure the safety and welfare of learners whilst in the virtual world.

The social domain has been adapted from Wang and Kang (2006) whose model of cybergogy was intended for the inclusion of Web 2.0 applications into classroom activities and has been extended to accommodate the affordances of 3DiVW in terms of the establishment of a sense of personal presence and the awareness of the presence of others. In communication, contextualisation of interpersonal interactions includes the ability to accurately interpret meaning within a somewhat impoverished text-based communication system that can sometimes be influenced by cultural diversity and language complications and, equally, to be able to convey accurate meaning using the same medium. Seemingly trivial incidents such as taking too long to type, combined with typing too much, can have a negative impact on the flow of textual conversations, delivering conflicting messages to all of the learning domains to a greater or lesser extent. Whilst voice over Internet protocol (VOIP referred to as 'voicing' or 'voice') is available, text-based communication in local chat (synchronous) and instant message (IM) (both synchronous and asynchronous) is by far the most widely used, especially between users who are not closely associated. Further levels of implementation in the social domain are intended to propel the learner towards forming useful affiliations with individuals and groups, networking between these and channeling reasonable amounts of filtered information, connections and inventory to selected recipients for their genuine benefit.

This tool of cybergogy provides a detailed breakdown of individual learning outcomes, offering indicators of 3Di-specific objectives in conjunction with real-life transfer of demonstrable learning within each domain at all levels of implementation. For example, instructional developers would be prompted to build in an opportunity for learners in the emotional domain at level 2 (using emotion):

- As a motivational factor
- For creative thinking
- To portray a topic vividly
- To convey a notion, message or information with passion or with neutrality
- To invest a facet of self into an event, action or interaction.

Table 5. Sculpting the Archetypes.

Level of Implementation	Learning Outcomes in the Cognitive Domain	Learning Outcomes in the Emotional Domain	Learning Outcomes in the Dextrous Domain	Learning Outcomes in the Social Domain
6 (high)	Creating	**Influencing**	Authoritative	Channelling
5	Evaluating	Self Regulating	Naturalising	**Networking**
4	Analysing	Understanding others	Articulating	Affiliating
3	Applying	Understanding Self	**Developing precision**	Communicating
2	**Understanding**	Using Emotion	Manipulating	Contextualising
1 (low)	Remembering	Perceiving Emotion	Imitating	Personalising

Further, with reference to Table 4, each of the domains at any particular level should ideally be engaged with each other. For example, to make emotional experience plausible, aspects from the cognitive, dextrous and social learning domains are important as facilitators in the emotional engagement. As in the hypothetical example shown in Table 5, a learning archetype such as the meshed archetype, implementing small group work could be sculpted at the design stage to be primarily focused at eliciting a level 6 learning outcome in the emotional domain (influencing the emotional responses of others), but the cognitive domain at level 2 (understanding), the dextrous domain at level 3 (developing precision) and the social domain at level 5 (networking) would all have a part to play in supporting the achievement of the primary learning outcome and should be included in considerations at the design stage to ensure the potential affordances are integrated.

PRACTICAL APPLICATION OF THE MODEL OF CYBERGOGY

Drury University (MO, USA) has a strong investment in online education and with the backing of senior management procured a SL island in 2008 for the purpose of delivering part of their existing online programs in 3DiVW.

After a period of time taken up in developing the island facilities, willing faculty members were solicited, developed and guided in the adoption of the model of cybergogy, and SL-enhanced courses were scheduled, marketed and student enrolments were accepted. The first wave of faculty members to transition their materials and strategies were Online Education Director Skyhook Inglewood and Assistant Director Semaj Susanowa, and instructors Fenix Muhindra, HG Vayandar, Grendel Minotaur, Orion Haystack. Five courses were provided initially: Introduction to SL (as a precursor to studentship) Social Psychology, Arab Israeli Conflict Studies, History of Christianity and Astronomy.

IMAGINATION AND CONJECTURE

In the position of faculty developer, this author suggested to the cohort that 'all learning experiences start in the imagination of the designer' in this case, the instructors themselves, who were experienced online facilitators and used 2D web-based VLE platforms; however, transitioning courseware design from 2D to 3DiVWs was to present new challenges. The primary consideration in terms of designing courseware for a virtual world is to ensure that the selected learning activity is the wisest choice in providing the desired learning outcomes. The 'efficacy analysis matrix' (EAM) was devised and introduced as a pragmatic measure to assist the faculty in discerningly evaluating the overall effectiveness of delivering content using SL. Application of the EAM for each learning instance under consideration entails individuals to conjecture the score on a scale which provides a preliminary opportunity for them to subjectively and critically analyse the environment in conjunction with their own skills and other practical constraints for potential implementation of *specific* learning activities in terms of three key aspects:

- Conjectured effectiveness for learners (is the use of SL gratuitous)
- Feasibility of implementation and management (is the activity sustainable in the environment)
- Viability of content quantity and quality (can the learning activity produce the desired learning outcomes in a timely, economic, effective manner).

The objective was to encourage faculty members to re-examine their syllabus under the lens of 3DiVWs and to exploit opportunities which could enhance their teaching by providing a learning experience with a greater level of immersion than by other means available and to identify incidents where straightforward delivery via a learning management system (LMS) such as blackboard or even a practical activity in a classroom would be more effective, therefore minimising counter arguments that SL is being used frivolously or without substantiation.

INTRODUCTION TO SECOND LIFE FOR LEARNERS (INSTRUCTORS: SKYHOOK INGLEWOOD, SEMAJ SUSANOWA)

Learners enrolling into the variety of SL-enhanced courses were invited to participate in the introductory sessions. The purpose was to personalise their avatar and contextualise themselves and their part in the learning environment and to make the acquaintance of peers and tutors from all available disciplines using the communication channels available: local chat, IM and voice.

A peregrination archetype (travel to locations) was included, learners were escorted to another SL location to acquire free clothing and accessories to further personalise their avatar and they focused initially upon fine tuning the user interface in terms of acquiring headsets, adjusting volume levels and learning commands and functions within the interface and adjusting their physical computer systems to accommodate SL. As the learners progressed in dexterous skills, training based around a dexterity course enabled learners to practise opening doors, navigating a narrow path, sitting on chairs and the manual manipulation of virtual objects such as books and bicycles. Further dextrous activities included flying through aerial hoops at varying heights and angles, navigating spiral staircases and walking a roller coaster inspired narrow aerial track through ascent and descent. Learners were introduced to the 'time tunnel' which is a cave-type construction that is too narrow to accommodate an avatar and therefore can only be traversed using camera controls. By learning to zoom, pan and manoeuvre the camera along the tunnel, and around a series of bends, learners eventually find a clock which reflects the SL time which they report back to instructors. An assessment archetype based primarily in the dextrous domain concludes the sessions. For this, learners were required to create a structure which is intended to be their individual personal space on the island for the duration of their academic course. Initially, learning takes place by imitation, a level one learning outcome in the dextrous domain. The learners imitate the instructor (level 1), manipulate building objects (level 2) and develop precision (level 3) in the dextrous domain along with personalisation of their structure engaging level 1 in the social domain. Prizes for outstanding achievement are available, one awarded by a guest judge and one voted for by peers.

The instructors made exemplary use of the EAM which helped focus their efforts upon the creation of new topic-specific materials for virtual world skill acquisition. The meshed archetype appealing primarily (but not exclusively) to the social domain was used predominantly to enable learning in the dextrous domain occur. Learners were coached in elementary mastery of their avatars and social etiquette along with the virtual world user interface. In a few cases, learners needed to upgrade some of their equipment (headsets, mice etc.) to meet the standards required for functioning effectively in SL in preparation for confident uptake of their enrolled courses. In formal lesson construction and execution, these instructors carefully matched resources and activities to the model of cybergogy, adapting them to include the maximum number of learning domains possible, they also reviewed and re-aligned their e-teaching good practice procedures by applying the supportive systems and procedures inherent in the model of cybergogy such as the EAM and documented lesson planning.

HISTORY OF CHRISTIANITY (INSTRUCTOR: GRENDEL MINOTAUR)

The primary setting for this class was a raffia style circular platform elevated a few metres above the island land level. Around the edge were large pictures symbolically representing the diversity of peoples and cultures around the world. Learners in this class experienced an opportunity within the role-play archetype to dress their avatars in robes and historical attire comma and the peregrination archetype was used to travel to SL locations which represent religious ideologies other than Christianity. These excursions were intended to spark group discussions. Old Testament Biblical events were represented by 3D objects and, after reading an issued text, learners were required to manoeuver the objects into an accurate timeline, an activity that addressed Cognitive and Dextrous Learning Domains. Much of the course content was delivered via a meshed archetype, in small group forums which cater predominantly to the cognitive, emotional and social domains. Learners were supported in contributing to evaluation of materials, perceiving, understanding and influencing emotions and were encouraged to communicate their ideas and opinions to peers and the instructor.

This course used a blended learning approach fairly strongly. Most of the background reading was done in the physical world from specified texts and the university's LMS was used as a group forum medium. The instructor used SL to hold twice-weekly office hours, making himself available to the learners for enquiries and discussions using 'voice' often on a one-to-one basis. The students benefited from a sense of 'co-presence' of the instructor and their peers, receiving guidance and support in real time which sets the experience apart from most distance learning situations previously encountered by the learners. The students were also able to leave text-based note cards in a drop box at the classroom to be collected and dealt with by the instructor asynchronously. Some assessment material was submitted using the same method. The instructor applied the model of cybergogy to a lesser extent than anticipated but settled into a comfortable adoption of the technology to service the more social, interpersonal aspects of distance learning that are normally not catered for. A video of an interview conducted by this author with a student of this course (not made for the later purposes of this chapter but for the development of Drury University's online presence) is available at http://www.blip.tv/file/4063427.

ASTRONOMY (INSTRUCTOR: ORION HAYSTACK)

Astronomy classes take place in and around the observatory on Drury's online education island. There is a viewing platform with one major telescope, surrounded by several individual telescopes for each student's use (Fig. 2).

The telescopes provide an opportunity to implement the simulation archetype. Whilst gazing into the telescope lens, the learner is presented with

Fig. 2. Virtual World Stargazing.

multiple choices of categories of authentic images of galaxies, comets, planets, moons and so forth. Each category contains further multiple choices of images to view. The images are not web-based; they are embedded into the telescope's functionality and are contained within SL; they subsequently address the cognitive domain primarily, and the social domain to a lesser extent as students share their experiences with peers because they are not solitary observers. It is hoped that the emotional domain may be accessed at the level of 'perceiving' (level 1), depending on the personality of the user and perhaps their passion for the subject; images accompanied by the expertise of the instructor may induce a 'WOW' experience! A further activity employs the role-play archetype in conjunction with a meshed archetype to address the cognitive and social learning domains primarily; learners assume the role of detectives and work together to solve scientific mysteries of the cosmos using clues given by the instructor.

A simulation archetype addressing the cognitive and dextrous domains is employed as students are required to manipulate 3D models of planets into the correct order around the sun. Formative assessment takes place in stages with the grading of assignments submitted via the university's LMS, but summative assessment of learning takes place in SL using a meshed archetype, a presentation to peers, instructors and guests on a course-related item of the student's choice.

After a slightly unsure start, the instructor enthusiastically adopted the model of cybergogy to support his teaching. As opposed to using a peregrination archetype to visit other SL destinations, the instructor was, during the faculty developmental sessions, guided to enrich his own environment, for example, installation of the individual telescopes. He also included streaming video into SL. It could be argued that video could more easily be made available on the LMS; however, after an EAM analysis, it was decided that by presenting it in SL, learners were able to watch together and interject with questions and comments in a meshed archetype addressing cognitive and social learning domains. This instructor now speaks with confidence to other educators about teaching in virtual worlds.

SOCIAL PSYCHOLOGY (INSTRUCTOR: FENIX MUHINDRA)

The instructor created a novel underwater environment to take advantage of one of the affordances of the 3DiVW, which enables a shift from the re-creation of a real-life classroom scenario. As a part of the course students were required to experiment with the psychological effects of gender role reversal within the role-play archetype. Learners re-gendered their avatars in terms of physical appearance, and sought to play out a stereotypical trans-gendered role in terms of persona outside of the safety of the Drury Island in a peregrination archetype combined with the social domain, travelling to locations where other avatars might interact with them with a focus on observing what interpersonal differences occur that may be attributable to gender perception. Learners reported back their experiences, and (addressing the emotional domain) extracts from the feelings and impressions generated by the experiment are reported here:

> I found that talking like a guy was hard to do because I kept wanting to elaborate on what I was talking about or in my comments back to other people in SL. I really could feel the control of one side of my brain trying to control the other. I wonder if people with personality disorders feel like that.
>
> The difference that I noticed in SL was that guys kept trying to give me clothes; they did not feel that I was pimped out enough. I also noticed that guys just do not talk that much to each other on a one on one with men that they do not know. On the occasion that they did talk they were just interested in how to make gestures and noises. I really had to work on trying to come up with topics to talk about to strangers and then also having to keep in mind that it had to be one that a guy would like. So what I decided to do was to travel to a few sand boxes and see if I could find some conversation there. Not really much of an improvement but at least I did not have to pull their teeth out. I found a couple of new guys and was able to share some of my knowledge about building. Now my knowledge is not great but staying in character I was able to help them out a little.
>
> When I would talk to woman they would ask if I knew how to do technical things, like building and scripting but were not willing to just stop and chat. This I found to be a big change because when my avatar was female I found that woman were willing to just chat for awhile about our mistakes in SL and be more forthcoming about places they had visited and their adventures there.
>
> I now realize that I like being a girl a lot more than what I thought.

During the gender experiment, learners were also required to extend the role play into physical life for a period of 24 hours. Learner's reflections indicate that it was more awkward than and not as effective as the virtual trans-gendering experience:

> After I put on the outfit, I already felt more like, well not really male, but more lesbian-ish. It was easy to walk like a male since the shoes were too big. It felt weird trying to be someone I wasn't though, but I was with my family most of the day so it just made them laugh.

> It [the role-play experiment] went down since I was clearly a woman dressed like a male. I think a lot of people thought I was a lesbian and most of the people in this area don't accept gay/lesbian.

Of all faculty members transitioning courseware into SL, this instructor had already experienced SL for approximately 1 year. Fenix had developed dextrous abilities over the time and was extremely capable of producing materials and locating resources already in existence in-world (within SL). She was aware of the scope of the environment and readily adopted the structure made available by this model of cybergogy and used its various mechanisms, especially the peregrination archetype to scaffold learning experiences that were imaginative. Fenix strove to collect evidence by means of the assessment archetype conducted in-world which often involved students reporting on their experiences in the emotional domain.

ARAB-ISRAELI CONFLICT STUDIES (INSTRUCTOR: HG VAYANDAR)

These classes followed a general format in which the instructor felt to be most effective for the subject matter. Beginning most teaching sessions with a meshed archetype, an informal lecture appealing to the social domain, contextualising and communicating (level 1 and 2) and understanding in the cognitive domain (level 2), which sets the scene for the peregrination archetype that follows, travel to locations that provide the opportunity for learning to occur in the cognitive, emotional and dextrous domains. Examples of Peregrination destinations pertinent to the subject matter are SL Israel, Palestine Holocaust Memorial Museum, Camp Darfur, Islam Online or the Hajj where Guided Tours take place lead by the instructor.

The Darfur camp in SL sets out to illustrate how an unregulated government can cause suffering and misery to its people who struggle with starvation and disease due to the lack of essential resources and it brings awareness to the learners that this sort of thing is still occurring (http://slurl.com/secondlife/Better%20World/176/245/21).

The Palestinian Holocaust Museum tells the stories of the Palestinian people who are being victimised by a Zionist government. The experience brings to life that these are real people caught up in the war and they have no decision-making power. Learners are able to investigate deaths of Palestinian children by the Jewish military and to blog about particular cases.

HG Vayandar comments: 'The students really feel the loss when they read the horrific stories of Palestinians losing their lives to Israeli attacks'. This example demonstrates the impact on learning that can be made possible by directly addressing the emotional learning domain using a peregrination archetype at the content design stage (http://slurl.com/secondlife/IslamOnline%20dot%20Net2/32/212/24).

The SL Israeli site allows students to visit the Western Wall, the Church of the Holy Sepulchre, Dome of the Rock and Tel Aviv. Students can participate in praying when it comes to the Western Wall or the Dome of the Rock. These are representations of real places where other Jews and Arabs come to worship virtually. Drury students experience and even participate in it while becoming aware of real-world Jewish custom which is closely observed in the virtual world (http://slurl.com/secondlife/Israel/168/45/22).

Islamonline.net Virtual Hajj is a contemporary Middle Eastern 3D environment in SL where students can experience a different culture and meet people from other countries. HG Vayandar comments: 'There is a tendency to think of the Middle East as a non-developed region, on the contrary, during the course students come to realise it is highly developed and this SL destination allows students to embrace modernity in the Middle East using a Peregrination Archetype designed to address emotional and social learning domains' (http://slurl.com/secondlife/IslamOnline%20-dot%20Net/14/22/2).

HG Vayandar comments 'Our conversations are limitless. Learners seem to break out of their normal roles and dismiss the social norms and protocols that we are used to in a traditional classroom. Students who would not normally communicate in class are now dominating the virtual classroom'.

This course benefited greatly from the use of the peregrination archetype focused on learning in the cognitive, emotional and social domains. Activities conducted in the 3DiVW were enriched by the broad array of virtual content established in SL by residents passionate to represent their customs, cultures and beliefs for the benefit of raising awareness for educational purposes. The instructor carefully orchestrated group discussions to filter out any personal biases or prejudices that a learner may have and instead promote open-mindedness and appreciation of diverse political standpoints.

It is hoped that the examples of teaching and learning in virtual worlds described in this chapter provide evidence of the values and affordances of this model of cybergogy. They illustrate differing emphasis on the four learning domains but, importantly, show the inter-connectivity between them and how successful teaching can be established.

CONCLUSIONS

Activities in the form of learning archetypes form a thematic structure for active, experiential learning in the virtual world. As with physical world learning in a classroom scenario, a learner pursuing an active part in learning automatically invests personal energy (on more levels than simply the physical) into the event, therefore gains more of a return for their efforts than in a passive learning situation. 'When immersed in a 3D environment, a person is cognitively encoding the sounds, sights and spatial relationships of the environment and is behaviourally engaged' (Kapp & O'Driscoll, 2010, p. 63). Carefully selected, sculpted learning archetypes enable participants to be aware of the purpose, direction and desired outcomes of the learning activities, minimising floundering and time wasting in favour of productivity. Kapp and O'Driscoll (2010, p. 63) observe 'The person becomes emotionally involved and behaves and acts as he or she would in the actual situation'.

The nature of virtual worlds supports the creation and habitation of 3D digital spaces. Once a level of immersion is attained, perception of the 3D world evolves to feel as a real destination as any other geographical location, a persistent place to visit, travel around, establish a presence, set up a home base, create things and/or buy virtual items created by other residents, enjoy live music and drama performances, experience various art forms and forge meaningful relationships. On the other hand, it must be acknowledged that there may be some risks associated with deep levels of immersion such as the effects of shifting priorities, e-security and exposure to offensive comments and content in some rare instances. It is important to note that while a SL account which generates the initial avatar is free, a deep level of immersion trades upon personal investment and can require monetary expenditure as well as diligence.

As noted by Kapp and O'Driscoll (2010, p. 25) Bill Gates, referring to the information revolution, suggested that people overestimate the short-term implications and underestimate the long-term impact of disruptive technologies. 3D virtual worlds are disruptive in terms of their potential scope of influence on educational strategies, the provision of avenues into brand new educational opportunities that have not been possible before. These are some of the long-term impacts that are dependent on innovations that are happening now. Whilst virtual worlds may appear to be somewhat game-like or fictional, and there can be a tendency to trivialise exercises and activities purposed for teaching and training, but there is a growing body of evidence of people's commitment to the promotion of good quality academic intentions and endeavours occurring in virtual places. There is a growing network of international contributors, collaborating through blogs, wiki's and lists such as SLRL (Second Life Researchers List), SimTeach, Educause and SLED (Second Life Educators List) to spread innovation and best practice. There are certificate programs such as that offered by the University of Washington which teaches about virtual worlds over the course of an entire year.

There is a growing library of publications as people's virtual world research forms the basis of papers, journals and books. As well as virtual conferences lasting over days, such as the annual Virtual Worlds Best Practises in Education (VWBPE), there are also annual conferences organised in the real world such as the Second Life Community Conference (SLCC). Avatars emerge from the screen into physicality to engage face to face as a real community to drive the virtual environment forward into the mainstream landscape and to celebrate and showcase achievements. No one expects this to be a rapid process nor one without hurdles because the technology *is* disruptive; however, the journey has begun and appears to be gaining momentum based on the quality of contributed intellect, community spirit and the movers and shakers investing themselves in it.

> I am my avatar, my avatar is me. I am beholden by any promises my avatar makes on my behalf and my avatar will honour any contract I make.
>
> Light Sequent aka
>
> Lesley Scopes MSc, BSc Hons, PGCE, FIfL

REFERENCES

Anderson, L. W., & Krathwohl, D. (Eds). (2001). *A taxonomy for learning, teaching and assessing: A revision of Bloom's taxonomy of educational objectives*. New York, NY: Longman.

Castronova, E. (2007). *Exodus to the virtual world*. New York, NY: Palgrave Macmillan.

Churches, A. (2008). Edorigami, Bloom's taxonomy and digital approaches. Educational Origami [Online]. Available at: http://edorigami.wikispaces.com/Bloom%27s+and+ICT+tools. Retrieved on 11/09/10.

Compayré, G. (1899). *The history of pedagogy* (W.H. Payne, Trans). Boston: D.C. Heath & Co.

Goleman, D. (1998). *Working with emotional intelligence*. New York, NY: Bantam Dell.

Greenfield, S. (2008). *ID: The quest for identity in the 21st century*. London: Sceptre.

Kapp, K. M., & O'Driscoll, T. (2007). Escaping flatlands: The emergence of 3 D synchronous learning. Guild Research 360 Report on Synchronous Learning Systems, 111–153.

Kapp, K. M., & O'Driscoll, T. (2010). San Francisco, CA.

McDougall, B. (2010). Kids lost to a virtual world. *The Daily Telegraph*, June 7. Retrieved from http://www.heraldsun.com.au/news/kids-lost-to-a-virtual-world/story-e6frf7jo-1225876496588.

Meadows, M. (2008). *I avatar: The culture and consequences of having a second life*. Berkeley, CA: New Riders.

Salovey, P., & Mayer, J. (1994). Emotional intelligence. *Imagination, Cognition and Personality*, *9*, 185–211.

Scopes, L.J.M. (2009). *Learning archetypes as tools of cybergogy for a 3D educational landscape: A structure for eTeaching in second life*. Masters thesis, University of Southampton, School of Education. Available at http://eprints.soton.ac.uk/66169//

Sigman, A. (2009). *The spoilt generation*. London: Piakus.

Voyager, D. (2011, March 24). Active RL companies that have a presence in SL 2011. Daniel Voyager's Blog [Web log post]. Available at http://danielvoyagerblog.wordpress.com/2011/03/24/active-rl-companies-that-have-a-presence-in-sl-2011/.

Wang, M. J., & Kang, J. (2006). Cybergogy of engaged learning through information and communication technology: A framework for creating learner engagement. In: M. S. Khint & D. Hung (Eds.), *Engaged learning with emerging technologies* (pp. 225–253). New York, NY: Springer.

COURSE PLAN: CYBERGOGY OF LEARNING ARCHETYPES & LEARNING DOMAINS: IMPLEMENTATION OF VIRTUAL WORLD TEACHING STRATEGIES FOR EDUCATORS

Course Title: **Cybergogy of Learning Archetypes & Learning Domains: Implementation of Virtual World Teaching Strategies for educators**	**Session Title:** Conceptual Clarification	**Session Number:** 1 of 6	**Instructor:** Light Sequent
		Duration: 100 m	**Number of attendees:** 6
Session Aims: To deliver a broad initial overview of (a) Social Constructivist approaches (b) Five Categories of Learning Archetypes (c) Four Learning Domains (d) A justification as to how 3DiVWs benefit from different teaching strategies (cybergogy) from established online teaching methods (pedagogy).			
Session Objectives: Learners will acquire familiarisation with the components making up the Model of Cybergogy in preparation for more detailed explication of the essence which follows in subsequent sessions. Learners will achieve minimum Level 1 Learning Outcomes across all 4 Learning Domains: Archive and Recall information (Cognitive), Perceiving Personal Emotion (Emotional), Imitating (Dextrous) and Personalising (Social). The session will be videoed and posted online for asynchronous review.			

The group of learners have been profiled using an online questionnaire prior to commencement. Areas for special attention have been highlighted on an individual basis.

Time Allocated	Topic	SL Activity/Learning Archetype/Additional Resources	Learning Domains Addressed	Learners RL Activity	Assessment Archetype
Introduce 20 m	Social Constructivism (SC), an explanation of theoretical underpinning and its pertinence in social-centric virtual worlds.	Learners should access email; start writing a message to record RL responses (ref: RL Activity column). Meshed: Group Forum; Synchronous Presentation using VoIP and text chat. In world Poster Display, web links posted in local chat: http://en.wikipedia.org/wiki/Social_constructivism http://tip.psychology.org/vygotsky.html	Cognitive Lv1&2 Social Lv1&2	• Write 4 short statements describing how SC can be incorporated into personal teaching style	Formative Q&A to check for remembering and understanding (Cognitive) and Personalising and Contextualising (Social)
Develop 30m	Learning Archetypes (LA), introduction to the 5 types, definitions are provided for Role play,	Meshed: Group Forum; Synchronous Presentation using VoIP and text chat.	Cognitive Lv1&2	• Record the 5 Archetypes & write how any 2 could be used in personal teaching style.	Formative Q&A to check for remembering and understanding (Cognitive) and Personalising and Contextualising (Social)

	Peregrination, Simulation, Meshed and Assessment.	In world Poster Displays and animated 3D Learning Archetypes model.	Social Lv1&2		
30 m	Four Learning Domains (LD), and the Blended Taxonomy. Instructions on design principles in providing learning activities to engage learning domains at required levels of implementation.	Meshed: Group Forum; Synchronous Presentation using VoIP and text chat. Animated 3D Learning Domains model joins Learning Archetypes model. Interactive Blended Taxonomy Display dispenses Notecards containing information regarding eliciting planned learning outcomes	Cognitive Lv1&2 Social Lv3 Dextrous Lv2	• Choose 3 LDs and describe how 1 LA could be crafted to elicit 3xLD responses	Based in the Emotional Domain, Learners are questioned regarding their feelings about and perception of the model as presented and its conjectured potential for each subject teacher + providing coaching for RL email Activity
Conclude 20 m	Summarise session. Introduce flavour of next session 'Matching Learning Activities to	Instructor to • Issue Lesson Plan template via email.	Social Lv1–5	• Send above RL responses to Instructor's email within 12 hours for feedback	**Assignment 1** (due week 2): Learners will construct a lesson plan that is consistent with the model of Cybergogy in

	Learning Outcomes' and applying the EAM.	• Issue Assignment 1 criteria and guidelines via email. • Offer 1-2-1 support opportunities			preparation for Summative Assessment of a micro-teach presentation in week 6 which is intended for learners to showcase skills
	Close session 1 and move into informal/social learning and social networking.	Learners are at liberty to leave as desired	Emotional Lv1&2		

INITIAL TEACHER TRAINING IN A VIRTUAL WORLD

John Woollard

ABSTRACT

This chapter reports on the innovative and developing use of a virtual world environment to support the training and professional development of pre-service teachers of information and communications technology (ICT), information technology (IT) and computing. The findings show that the online experience promotes confidence and competence in virtual world activity. It also stimulates thinking about the potential of alternative methods for teaching and learning in schools. The case study participants were 16 trainee teachers aged between 21 and 55 years old, with varying backgrounds including those with careers in the computing industry, those straight from university and those having spent considerable time in schools as unqualified teachers. In Second Life they experienced a number of environments and discussed the potential of virtual worlds. The tutors believe that Second Life can offer a valuable environment to promote engagement by pre-service teachers in innovative and imaginative methods of teaching and for them to better understand the affordances of virtual worlds.

Keywords: Teacher training; pre-service teachers; virtual world; e-safety; emotional engagement

Transforming Virtual World Learning
Cutting-edge Technologies in Higher Education, Volume 4, 29–46

ISSN: 2044-9968/doi:10.1108/S2044-9968(2011)0000004006

INTRODUCTION

'It feels a bit strange walking around an environment where you don't actually know the social rules, and the social rules are definitely an area that needs to be defined in an online virtual environment when considering the mental and physical well-being of pupils'. These words are from a trainee teacher making her third visit to the 'staff room' at the University of Southampton Island in Second Life. It reflects the three important aspects of teaching and learning in a virtual world:

'it feels a bit strange' – a virtual world is immersive; the sights and sounds coming through the computer engender emotion and engagement in ways similar to those of the real world; it is those feelings that can impact upon in-world behaviours.
'know the social rules' – learners, whether they are school pupils or professionals, need information, advice and guidance regarding the mores, procedures and ethics of in-world behaviours.
'considering the mental and physical well-being' – we have a duty of care to our learners to ensure that they are protected from harm, resilient to threats and informed of risks.

The traditional approach to teacher training in the United Kingdom is a programme of university-based activity inducting, briefing and informing trainees of their roles and responsibilities in the classroom and providing a safe place to explore issues of policy, behaviour management and curriculum development. This university experience is integrated with in-school placements of observation, support and teaching in real classrooms with real pupils. The pervasive and rapidly changing use of technology means that would-be ICT teachers need an increasing in-depth and wide-ranging exposure to the resources available. At this time, the virtual world is the point of challenge and opportunity. The challenge is to change our way of working and the means by which we enable trainees to develop their life-long skills for teaching and the opportunities are those of alternative and better ways of presenting the curriculum.

An important element of the developing learning environments that use online profiles, avatars, virtual worlds and social networking are the issues of e-safety. Ensuring learners are working in safe ways, are resilient to inappropriate experiences and confident in dealing with unwelcome contact.

FEATURES OF THE VIRTUAL WORLD EXPERIENCE

Features of the experience include: the physical location of the activity is the trainee's choice, elements of the activities are new to every participant, trainees have to adopt an avatar to represent them, activities develop skills relating to dexterity and peregrination. There are challenges for teaching and learning in particular virtual world environments but these activities provide experiences that enhance trainee teachers' skills, knowledge and understanding of the 3D immersive (3Di) experiences and technology-enhanced learning in general. Comments made by trainees following their first visit to Second Life include emotions of surprise, wonder and professional pleasure.

> It has a really WOW factor, with opportunities for gathering information that exceeds real life.
>
> The most striking exhibit I found to be the "hiding place", which oozed of claustrophobic dread. The authentic photo was poignant. (Holocaust Museum, 2010, in-world)
>
> 'I really enjoyed that environment (Studio 33, 2010, in-world). Some of the pieces were lovely. In the art environment I was pleased to learn how to jump and move forward so that I could scale a wall. I was surprised when I found I could fly and walk through windows.

Another trainee also reflects on the potential for use in areas of emotional intelligence. 'The social and aesthetic quality of such a task would lend it to being an emotional experience. All of these learning threads should allow for improved learning and recall due to the multi-faceted ways of encoding the learnt information through the rich experience'.

This emotional engagement is associated with cognitive engagement (ACOTT, 2008; Cobb & Mayer, 2000; Gardner, 1993; Goleman, 1995; Patrick, Ryan, & Kaplan, 2007). If a learner is surprised, shocked or inspired they are more likely to remember the topic and context. A very early consideration of the impact of audio-visual resources on learning is that of Edgar Dale who proposed a hierarchy of engagement in the learning process from the least engaging, reading about something, to the most engaging, actually carrying out the task by doing the real thing. His ideas present a realistic challenge to teachers and designers of technology-enabled learning experiences and can be used as a touchstone regarding pedagogic value (see Fig. 1).

When software-driven tasks are designed to present information in a predetermined, pre-structured and didactic way, they lead to efficient

reading

hearing words

looking at pictures

watching a moving image

looking at an exhibit of the artefact

watching a demonstration of the activity

seeing the activity being carried out on location

seeing and discussing the activity with other learners

preparing and giving a spoken presentation about the activity

preparing and then carrying out a dramatic representation of the activity

preparing, rehearsing and then simulating the real experience of the activity

doing the real thing

Fig. 1. Hierarchy of Engagement. *Source*: Based on Dale (1969) and Woollard (2011).

knowledge transfer (Maris, 2005; Pettijohn, 2004; Skinner, 1968). When those tasks enable learners' achievements to be presented and assessed then they lead to effective learning through feedback (Black & Wiliam, 1998). When those tasks are drill and practice, they heighten response and accuracy and lead to more skilled learners (Ebbinghaus, 1885). When the tasks enable collaboration and communication, they lead to socially constructed learning that is both engaged (Patrick et al., 2007; Walker, 2008) but safe (Byron, 2008, 2010). When the learner reflects that the experience is strange, different, novel, new or even perverse or wrong, then they are engaging emotionally with the activity. It is that emotional engagement that can drive or diminish the cognitive engagement – the preparedness to learn, the motivation to learn and the context for learning.

SOCIAL RULES IN VIRTUAL WORLDS

All teachers have a responsibility to provide a safe environment for learning. They have a duty of care. In the United Kingdom this is reflected in the requirement placed upon trainee teachers to 'establish a purposeful and safe learning environment conducive to learning' (TDA, 2008, p. 10). For it to be a safe environment the learners need to know how to behave; they need to know the social rules.

Many adult users of virtual worlds do so with confidence and competence gained through experience. Some adults gain that confidence and competence quickly whilst for others it takes time and they learn through 'trial and error'. There is a need to understand what makes some adults more able to deal with a new learning environment more quickly than other adults. This is called varyingly: e-literacy (digital knowledge, internet safety and security, netiquette), computeracy (computer literacy, using rather than programming a computer) or ICT capability (choosing the right application for the task in hand and being able to apply current skills, knowledge and understanding to new or more complex situations). It is a necessary element of all training programmes to ensure that the basic skills are established and enhanced. Consequently, it is necessary to set the prerequisites in terms of skills and knowledge for working in virtual world learning environments and ensure the learners are prepared.

However, when working with young people and children we must not take risks. We cannot be satisfied that they can learn through 'trial and error' as those errors may have profound emotional and physical outcomes. Teachers are expected to 'establish a clear framework for classroom discipline to manage learners' behaviour constructively and promote their self-control and independence' (TDA, 2008, p. 10). A keyword in that requirement is 'independence'. Rules, guidance and advice cannot be created for every situation. Importantly, the teacher cannot be there for the learner in their future lives. The education process must equip the learner for the current and future experience. An interesting approach is to adopt Edward de Bono's Thinking Hats strategy (1985) to support the learners.

The six coloured hats relate to six different ways of thinking, six different ways of considering a situation. As the teacher introduces learning in a virtual world, at different times the learners' attentions are drawn to those ways of the thinking. The White Hat focuses on facts and information. The tutors, trainers or teachers are responsible for ensuring that the learners know what experiences they are going to have, know how to carry out the tasks and are aware of the way they will be assessed or judged. The Red Hat is most important in immersive environments – it relates to feelings and emotions. The learners are encouraged to use intuition, feelings and hunches and to try and not be afraid; the teacher should ensure they have the knowledge to back track (Control Z, browser back/forward buttons, breadcrumbs and history) or escape from situations (Control H, landmarks). Teachers should caution learners on e-safety rules and staying safe strategies to avoid problems; but they should also be developing pupil resilience to help the learners deal with inappropriate material and actions (Byron, 2008). The Yellow Hat promotes positive behaviours by identifying values and benefits and why something might work. The teacher needs to make learners aware of functionality and affordances – what the systems can do and what the systems enable us to do. The Green Hat is all about creativity and imaginative application of their skills and knowledge. Finally, the Blue Hat sees the big picture. The learners are using virtual world learning environments as a natural part of their learning strategies and opportunities. They are becoming the competent, confident, effective, efficient, imaginative, resilient and sensitive e-learners.

Knowledge of the social rules and modes of engagement is also important for the teacher. The teacher's behaviour in a conventional classroom impacts upon the learning. Inappropriate, gauche, unusual, weird or unexpected behaviours impact negatively on learning. In the virtual world learning environment, the same applies. In studies of the use of chat rooms to support learning (Richards, 2003, 2009), a post-analysis of the context generated a set of rules relating to teacher online interventions when used in a traditional classroom. These have been adapted to the situation where learners are all in the same room but exploring and learning through a virtual world learning environment at their computers (see Table 1).

Table 1. Teacher Guidance – Using Virtual Worlds in a Computer Room.

Intervene through the virtual world wherever possible (unless there is a health or safety or school discipline issue)
Never intervene physically (in the real world).
Provide timed and timely instructions through the virtual world that are:

- copy and pasted from a pre-written file (IM) or
- read from the script (local chat) or
- issued through note cards (in-world) or
- sent by e-mail;

When appropriate, sending positive statements (rewards, compliments, acknowledgements)
When appropriate, sending suggestions/ideas (modelling answers)
Encourage non-participants by (in the first instance) asking them closed questions and
Guide off-task participants by (in the first instance) asking them closed questions.

This guidance for the teacher operating in the virtual world is intended to ensure on-task behaviour, engaged learners, attainment and progress.

Another aspect of real-world teacher behaviour that affects learning is the teacher's attire – the way they dress and appear. Bryant and Curtner-Smith (2010) cite many examples of research drawn from a range of educational settings indicating that attire, physical appearance and perceived competence influence pupils' 'perceptions of teachers' ability to teach. Other research indicates that in secondary school settings, 'pupils learned less from obese teachers than seemingly fit ones and [the pupils] perceived them to be less competent' (Bryant & Curtner-Smith, 2010, p. 312). These comments about real-world teaching may have bearing upon in-world appearance and behaviour. The refined nature of the avatar and the dexterity by which the teacher or trainer operates within the virtual world could impact upon learner attitude and learner confidence in the teaching process. However, this is a conformity issue, and whilst schools and pupils tend to be conservative in outlook, that to a degree virtual worlds are about breaking away from conformity. We have witnessed some effective and engaging sessions conducted by furries, successful trainers, teachers and developers adopting non-human forms and successful students acting in bizarre ways.

MENTAL AND PHYSICAL WELL-BEING IN VIRTUAL WORLDS

Teachers should not make the learning environment stressful or frustrating. One trainee reported, 'The major issue was finding the Staffroom and as a result, the other problem with exploring environments – it is easy to waste time!' Another said, 'The positive aspects of the day were using new software such as Second Life, which has been extremely time consuming, but has shown me that working collaboratively, I was able to grasp the basics and get on with the product. I can see that introducing a new piece of software in a classroom would need to be done in stages, with guideline and help rather than making it a self-taught class. So pupils, like me, would get frustrated with the seemingly unhelpful screen in front of them'. Hart and Staveland (1988) defined frustration as the participant's experience of feeling insecure, stressed, discouraged and annoyed versus feeling secure, gratified, content and relaxed whilst engaged in a task. That frustration with software interfaces is common and is subject to legislation and regulation. The Health and Safety Executive identify that software 'not suitable for the task or the person using it, causing frustration and distress' (HSE, 2003, p. 3). Workers should not be exposed to risks and hazards of strain or tension. In a similar way, learners should not be exposed to frustrations and distractions. Amsel (1992) identified the issues caused by frustration in the learning process. More recently, they are discussed by Hove and Corcoran (2008) who concluded that there were higher levels of frustration in learners using virtual learning environment than those being taught through traditional lectures or lectures supplemented with slide shows. The learners' 'greater frustration (i.e., insecurity, stress, discouragement)' was explained by the absence of direction and guidance provided by an instructor. 'Historically, the role of the teacher has been to explicitly and implicitly direct students, controlling the amount of information and presenting it in way that is manageable and relevant' Corcoran (2008, p. 123). Virtual worlds offer a natural opportunity for the teacher to be present in the learning environment and be in a position to offer the information, advice and guidance associated with traditional and effective teaching. The value of support and just-in-time intervention to ensure learners feel confident in the virtual world is important.

'For some reason I could not teleport and after much help from Light Sequent and John, I still could not follow the others. I recall a moment when Light Sequent said to me "Don't worry I wouldn't leave you alone", which made me giggle. How silly I thought, "it's only Second Life". Eventually Light Sequent did have to leave me alone due to her commitments to the group, and I can honestly say for a spilt second I actually did feel abandoned. Then after 10 minutes of waiting for teleportation I felt a little lonely. Feeling these emotions made me realize the full potential of building and maintaining relationships in Second Life. I felt the same frustration and disappointment about not being able to join the rest of the trainees as I would have if I had been locked out of or stopped from entering a room during a training session at University'. Lonely is a feeling that is not associated with well-being.

'This emotional response is an expression of "immersion" with the environment. Personally, I view this as an extremely healthy experience, especially at such an early stage of adoption … this example serves to demonstrate how easy it is to both project and perceive a personal presence in the virtual world … this is a powerful tool for teachers indeed' (Woollard & Scopes, 2010, p. 4), but when working online we have to be cautious exploring emotional issues. Mark Meadows noted that children online are less risk-averse in their dealings with others. 'Over 75 percent of Internet users feel safer speaking their mind when they use an avatar' (Meadows, 2008, p. 36). They feel safer and speak more readily with those that they do not know in the physical sense but only know in the virtual world. 'The lack of contextual clues frees up social inhibition but also loosens commitment and trust' (Shortis, 2001, p. 97). They more readily confide secrets and more readily expose themselves in both a physical way (Jenny's Story, 2005) and in a verbal way.

Mark Meadows describes the avatar as a tool for regulating intimacy because intimacy and interaction with others is more easily controlled. In real life it can be difficult to remove oneself physically from uncomfortable positions but in the virtual world 'isolation' or 'home' is always just a mouse click or key press away. But, as Mark Meadows explains, 'in a world where information is more important than physical proximity, we are not as safe as we might assume … I have seen some extreme tragedies unfold because of the assumption of the mask … because we can immerse ourselves more and more into these environments we let our guards down' (Meadows, 2008, p. 36).

The Byron review in the United Kingdom identified an important element of education with regard to e-safety as developing children's endurance and resolution in the face of inappropriate and potentially damaging materials and contacts that the internet presents. The report of the review states, 'we must also build children's resilience to the material to which they may be exposed so that they have the confidence and skills to navigate these new media waters more safely' (Byron, 2008, p. 8).

Using the terms presented by Freud, the learners' motivations arise from the Id and the Ego and are modified by social mores. Freud's 'cap of hearing' is the key. We have to ensure that the learner has the opportunity to 'hear' clear and actionable information about their online lives. The 'hear' includes seeing appropriate behaviour by peers and models, experiencing appropriate scenarios, being rewarded for behaving appropriately as well as being given appropriate information, advice and guidance. Teachers, tutors and trainers working in the virtual world need strategies in place to support their responsibilities, their duty of care, towards their pupils, students and trainees. The following analysis of e-safety provides such a framework of support.

The three 'Cs' of content, contact and conduct that Tanya Byron proposes help guide the provision of information, advice and guidance to learners (see Table 2).

The content of the internet can be the source of concern by parents and guardians of children, teachers of students and the tutors and trainers of older learners. No one is immune from this threat. Even the most professional and academically aware can be 'conned' by the apparent authority of internet presence and therefore the truth, validity, reliability or reasonableness of content. The Byron report identifies four areas of content that are important when dealing with younger learners: commercial, aggressive, sexual and values. The learner needs to understand and be resilient to advertising, spam,

Table 2. Content, Contact and Conduct Aspects of e-Safety (Byron, 2008, p. 16).

	Commercial	Aggressive	Sexual	Values
Content (child as recipient)	Adverts Spam Sponsorship Personal info	Violent/hateful content	Pornographic or unwelcome sexual content	Bias Racist Misleading information or advice
Contact (child as participant)	Tracking Harvesting personal info	Being bullied, harassed or stalked	Meeting strangers Being groomed	Self-harm Unwelcome persuasions
Conduct (child as actor)	Illegal downloading Hacking Gambling Financial scams Terrorism	Bullying or harassing another	Creating and uploading inappropriate material	Providing misleading info/advice

sponsorships and demands for personal information. Within the virtual world he or she needs to be aware of ownership and the nature of the owner in terms of their authoritative, commercial or personal motivations. Entering an environment controlled by the New York City Police Department and seeing information about anniversary arrangements for 9–11 is likely to be of a different nature from that owned by a non-sectarian group. Learners can be harmed by misinformation.

The learner needs to be resilient to violent and hateful content and know how to deal with it. On teleporting to a recommended location, the images being presented on the screen may have content that could be emotionally upsetting. We need to ensure that learners have strategies for dealing with it. In the United Kingdom there is a Zip It, Block It, Flag It campaign (DCSF, 2010). There is the concept of provisionality (DfEE, 1998) with regard to internet content. As teachers, tutors and learners we cannot rely on the fact that seeing a structure, environment or information point today means that it will be the same, or even present, tomorrow. The learner cannot be protected by continually policing the environments to which they are exposed. Therefore, the learner needs to be resilient to pornographic and unwelcome sexual content, and the learner needs to be able to identify bias, racism, misleading information and advice.

The second 'C' is contact – the direct communication by a third party with the learner whilst they are online. Virtual worlds have a significant element of social interaction. Some online facilities, such as Facebook and Internet Messenger, are totally dominated by social interaction. Some online facilities, such as Google Maps, Wikipedia and e-learning systems, are dominated by the content and the structure/order of that content. Virtual world learning environments have a balance between the content (the environment, the structures and the information presented) and the contact (the social interaction and social networking facilities). It is possible to have a perfectly good learning experience in a virtual word without necessarily engaging in social banter. Equally, the learning experience in a virtual world may be dominated by the socially constructed understanding of a new area of experience, concept or body of knowledge. Therefore, the contact 'C' is an important consideration of e-safety in the virtual world.

The e-safety threat is the learner unwillingly or unwittingly participating in inappropriate activity. The learner needs to be aware that there may be those tracking and harvesting personal information and the importance of the need to protect their personal information. The learner needs to be resilient to being bullied, harassed or stalked and know what action to take in such situations. Importantly, the teacher, tutor or trainer must have procedures in place so that it is clear what the learner should do if they feel any threat or uncertainty about the identity or intentions of avatars they meet. The learner needs to understand the implications of meeting strangers and being groomed and he/she needs to be resilient to unwelcome persuasions.

The final 'C' is conduct – that is, the willing actions and activities of the learner whilst working in the virtual world. It is where the learner is initiating the inappropriate action. Learners must be given clear guidance with regard to their illegal downloading, hacking, gambling, griefing, financial scams and terrorism and understand the consequences of such actions. Learners must also be given clear guidance with regard to bullying or harassing behaviour of their avatar towards another and understand the consequences of such actions. Learners must be given clear guidance with regard to creating and uploading material that might cause offence or contain misleading information or advice. An important aspect of conduct on the internet relates to sexually explicit material and sexually motivated activities. This e-safety issue arises from the combined effect of:

- Younger users of the internet feeling freer and more able to express themselves in a sexual way because of the appearance of anonymity,

caused by the mask of the avatar, including experimenting with gender, being explicit about their personal sexuality and wishing to shock others.
- The actions of paedophiles, bullies and stalkers who are freed by anonymity and false identity and an 'exhaustive potential to contact potential victims' (Powell, 2007, p. 113) to groom, victimize and solicit on the internet.

In Freud's world, it is the sex drive or libido that modifies or drives behaviour. Because he articulated that repressing sexual drive leads to problems in later life, Freud has been criticized for allowing some people to excuse their behaviours and the behaviours of others rather than taking direct responsibility for their actions. The duty of teachers is to provide e-safety information and e-safety guidance. This is both an ethical and moral issue. There needs to be a clear and firm message about acceptable behaviour, reasonable behaviour and an explicit code of conduct. The 'acceptable use policy' (AUP) is a means by which the online behaviour of both pupils and teachers can be regulated. The AUP, along with classroom-based codes of conduct, are mean by which the social mores can impact upon the learners' decision making (see Table 3).

The 'Zip it, Block it, Flag it' campaign (DCSF, 2010) raised public awareness especially amongst parents. 'Zip it' refers to the pupil keeping personal information private and thinking about what they say or do online. 'Block it' requires pupils to block people who send nasty messages and encourages them not to open unknown links and attachments. 'Flag it' is the guidance to pupils that they should flag up with someone they trust if anything upsets them or if someone asks to meet them offline. However, there still remains the issue of many mainstream providers of resources and

Table 3. Essential Elements of Acceptable use Policies (Woollard, 2011, p. 70).

- Philosophical motivation/corporate message about the underlying values
- Rationale for network and internet access
- Advice and instruction for appropriate patterns of use (netiquette)
- Advice and instruction for expected patterns of use
- Declaration of the importance of self-regulation and personal responsibility
- Statements regarding legal requirements (including computer misuse, protection of personal data, copyright and obscene materials) and
- Description of consequences of violating the policy including punishments and appeal procedures.

social networking not facilitating fast report mechanisms that would make children feel more secure. Child Exploitation & Online Protection Centre (CEOP) is the UK's law enforcement agency and encourages the use of its report mechanism and provides online support for young people and teachers (CEOP, 2010).

Another issue is that of parents condoning children's use of adult social networking sites such as Facebook (under the age of 13 years) and Second Life (under the age of 18 years). The virtual world specifically provided for teenagers was Teen Grid but Linden Labs closed the facility in 2011 (Metaversally Speaking, 2010). It had previously catered for 13–17-year olds and to move registered users to the main grid at age 16. Some adult Second Life residents are voicing concerns that under 18s should be flagged up in their profile to protect the interests of those who do not wish to inadvertently associate with children. However, there is the counter argument that to do so might highlight the identity of teens for the purposes of grooming and other abuses. e-Safety has to be a key consideration of any online educational activity. The impact of that consideration should not be to stop activities but to make those activities as safe as possible without unnecessarily affecting the pedagogic value.

SUMMARY

'It feels a bit strange walking around an environment where you don't actually know the social rules, and the social rules are definitely an area that needs to be defined in an online virtual environment when considering the mental and physical well being of pupils'.

The words of a newbie trainee teacher echoed great pertinence with regard to the actions we need to take to ensure learning in virtual worlds is to be a rewarding, effective, efficient and, importantly, safe experience. We conclude:

- Not knowing the social rules and mores makes the learner vulnerable. They can become victims of the social predators, the commercial exploiters and the purveyors of inappropriate or untruthful material.
- The popularity of online gaming, the demonstrable value of interactive programmes for teaching and training and the growing potential for teachers to design and build their own 3Di environments, makes an imperative that teacher training includes experience of virtual worlds such as Second Life in their teaching.

- An online day where trainees work on their computers, in their work or home environment, offers many opportunities for them to be independent and personalize their own learning and start to vision education of the future where their learners see them as avatars and they see their pupils as avatars.
- As noted by Kristen Moore and Ehren Pflugfelder, there is a need for pedagogical and technological scaffolding in preparation for taking students into online environments if those places are to function as 'fun and creative spaces' (2010).
- The significant challenges are of a technical nature but the structure and resourcing for the online day must be considered so that individuals do not feel isolated or unsupported.

In our work in teacher training we have seen trainees growing in confidence in their use of virtual worlds. Subsequent visits have elicited an increase in positive impressions as the students began to feel less estranged in the virtual environment. The follow-up online days are structured to give the students a choice of peregrination activities consisting of matched pairs of in-world locations that present contrasting experiences. Trainees are asked to consider the locations in terms of the impact on each of the four learning domains of cybergogy: cognitive, emotional, dextrous and social (Scopes, 2011).

Teaching and learning in virtual worlds provides trainers with the opportunity to meet another UK government requirement that teachers should 'identify opportunities for learners to learn in out of school contexts' (TDA, 2008, p. 10) – in-world is out-of-school. Teaching and learning in virtual worlds has affordances of stimulation, engagement, motivation, interest, context and contemporarity. Teaching and learning in virtual worlds has the challenges of understanding a new pedagogy called cybergogy, building environments that stimulate, structure and facilitate learning and protection of our learners from inappropriate content and contact and ensuring they conduct themselves appropriately.

REFERENCES

ACOTT. (2008). Apple classrooms of tomorrow – Today learning in the 21st century online. Retrieved from http://ali.apple.com/acot2/global/files/ACOT2_Background.pdf

Amsel, A. (1992). *Frustration theory: An analysis of dispositional learning and memory*. New York, NY: Cambridge University Press.

Black, P. J., & Wiliam, D. (1998). Inside the black box. Retrieved from http://weaeducation.typepad.co.uk/files/blackbox-1.pdf

de Bono, E. (1985). *Six thinking hats*. Toronto: Key Porter.

Bryant, L. G., & Curtner-Smith, M. (2010). Effect of a physical education teacher's disability on high school pupils' learning and perceptions of teacher competence. *Physical Education & Sport Pedagogy*, *14*(3), 311–322.

Byron, T. (2008). *Safer children in a digital world: The report of the Byron review* (Retrieved from http://www.dcsf.gov.uk/byronreview.). London: DCSF.

Byron, T. (2010). Do we have safer children in a digital world? A review of progress since the 2008 Bryon review. Retrieved from http://www.dcsf.gov.uk/byronreview

CEOP. (2010). *Child Exploitation and Online Protection Centre* (Retrieved from http://www.ceop.police.uk/report-abuse.). London: Child Exploitation and Online Protection Centre.

Cobb, C. D., & Mayer, J. D. (2000). Emotional intelligence: What the research says. *Educational Leadership*, *58*(3), 14–18.

Dale, E. (1969). *Audio-visual methods in teaching* (3rd ed.). London: Holt, Rinehart and Winston.

DCSF. (2010). *Internet safety code* (Retrieved from http://www.dcsf.gov.uk/ukccis/userfiles/file/Internet%20Safety%20Code%20FINAL%20FINAL.pdf.). London: Department for Children, Schools and Families.

DfEE. (1998). *Teaching: High status, high standards* (Annex B DfEE circular 4–98. Retrieved from http://www.dfes.gov.uk/publications/guidanceonthelaw/4_98/annexb.htm.). London: DfEE.

Ebbinghaus, H. (1885). *Memory: A contribution to experimental psychology* (Retrieved from http://psy.ed.asu.edu/~classics/Ebbinghaus/memorypref.htm.). New York, NY: Dover Publications.

Gardner, H. (1993). *Multiple intelligence: The theory in practice*. New York, NY: HarperCollins.

Goleman, D. (1995). *Emotional intelligence*. New York, NY: Bantam.

Hart, S. G., & Staveland, L. E. (1988). Development of a multi-dimensional workload rating scale: Results of empirical and theoretical research. In: P. A. Hancock & N. Meshkati (Eds), *Human mental workload* (pp. 139–183). Amsterdam: Elsevier.

Holocaust Museum. (2010). US Holocaust Memorial Museum, US Holocaust Museum in-world. Retrieved from http://maps.secondlife.com/secondlife/US%20Holocaust%20Museum1/1/35/27.

Hove, C. M., & Corcoran, K. J. (2008). Educational technologies: Impact on learning and frustration. *Teaching of Psychology*, *35*(2), 121–125.

HSE. (2003). *Understanding ergonomics at work*. Caerphilly, UK: HSE Information Services.

Jenny's Story. (2005). *Jenny's story an internet safety resource* (Retrieved from http://www.childnet-int.org/jenny.). London: Childnet International.

Maris, J.-M. B. (2005). Validation of the learning machine. *Informing Science and IT education joint conference*, Flagstaff, Arizona. Retrieved from http://www.informingscience.org/proceedings/InSITE2005/P01f90Mari.pdf

Meadows, M. S. (2008). *I, avatar: The culture and consequences of having a second life*. Berkley, CA: New Riders.

Metaversally Speaking. (2010). *Second life teen grid to close online*. Retrieved from http://blog.pradprathivi.com/2010/08/15/second-life-teen-grid-to-close

Moore, K., & Pflugfelder, E. H. (2010). On being bored and lost (in virtuality). *Learning, Media and Technology*, *35*(2), 249–253.

Patrick, H., Ryan, A. M., & Kaplan, A. (2007). Early adolescents' perceptions of the classroom social environment, motivational beliefs, and engagement. *Journal of Educational Psychology*, *99*(1), 83–98.

Pettijohn, T. F. (2004). *"Programmed learning", Psychology: A connecText* (4th ed.). McGraw-Hill.

Powell, A. (2007). *Pedophiles, child abuse and the internet*. Oxford, UK: Radcliffe.

Richards, C. (2003). Chatrooms in the classroom. *InteracTive*, *47*, 23–25.

Richards, C. (2009). *How useful are bounded online chat rooms as a source of pastoral support in a sixth-form college*? Doctoral thesis, University of Southampton, School of Education. Retrieved from http://eprints.soton.ac.uk/66451

Scopes, L. (2011). A cybergogy of learning archetypes and learning domains: Practical pedagogy for 3D immersive virtual worlds. In: R. Hinrichs & C. Wankel (Eds.), *Transforming virtual world learning*. Cutting-edge Technologies in Higher Education (Vol. 4). Bingley, UK: Emerald.

Shortis, T. (2001). *The language of ICT*. London: Routledge.

Skinner, B. F. (1968). *The technology of teaching*. New York, NY: Appleton-Century-Crofts.

Studio 33. (2010). *Studio 33 Welcome Center, Rockcliffe Gardens* [in-world]. Retrieved from http://slurl.com/secondlife/Rockcliffe%20Gardens/87/97/22

TDA. (2008). *Professional standards for qualified teacher status and requirements for initial teacher training* (Retrieved from http://www.tda.gov.uk/qts.). London: The Training and Development Agency for Schools.

Walker, L. (2008). *Learner engagement: A review of learner voice initiatives across the UK's education sectors*. Bristol, UK: Futurelab.

Woollard, J. (2011). *Psychology for the classroom: E-learning*. Oxford, UK: Routledge.

Woollard, J., & Scopes, L. (2010). *Review of the second encounter with second life online*. Retrieved from http://www.pgce.soton.ac.uk/IT/Research/SecondLife/SLevalreport2.pdf.

LESSON PLAN: ONLINE ENGAGEMENT AND VIRTUAL WORLD LEARNING

Course Title: Teacher Training	**Session Title:** Online engagement and virtual world learning	**Session: 1 of 3** Duration: 5 hours 09.30–16.00 GMT	**Instructors:** Light Sequent Stradd Ling

Session aims:

The primary aim of the session is to ensure that trainees are fully comfortable working in online environments. The day provides the time and collegiate support to explore online environments, develop new skills and understanding, build professional relationships, reflect upon potential affordances for education and identify areas for further development.

A prerequisite is that the trainee is physically located with a computer that has access to the internet and is using a web browser that supports Java and Adobe Flash. (University public workstations can support the activities of this session.) The computer will also need software that supports online communication such as Second Life, Microsoft Messenger and Skype software. Hardware required includes headphones/speakers, microphone and webcam. Online accounts that may prove useful include: Messenger, Bebo, Google, Skype, Second Life, Hotmail etc. It will also be necessary to have a PGCE IT EPS/Wiki account.

***Make sure that you have read and understood this information before the day.

Session Objectives:

During the day the trainee is expected to carry out as many activities as possible:

- make one-to-one contact with each and every other member of the group;
- participate in a chat session with several others;
- navigate around a multi-user environment (such as Second Life);
- in Second Life and on Skype, meet their tutors and make contact with other trainees;
- navigate around geographic information systems (GIS) systems such as Google Earth, Streetmap, Google Map, Locrating, Geocache; global positioning systems (GPS);
- use internet search engines to discover new information and develop personal search strategies;
- collaborate with 2 or more others to develop a single online document;
- during the day (and certainly before 4.00 pm) make a brief report of the activities undertaken;
- write an evaluation of this teacher training activity; and
- submit both by email to PGCEwork@soton.ac.uk and ccL.Scopes@soton.ac.uk

Outcomes

Using this 'writing frame' to record your activities and reflections.

During the online activities day I undertook ... [Write no more than 300 words outlining the activities undertaken using the 'objectives' above to guide the order and content.]

Then write ...

The positive aspects of the day were ... [Identify at least 3 activities that you have undertaken and the contribution that you feel they have made to your training as a ICT teacher.]

The activities that did not have a significant value were ... [Identify activities that you have undertaken where you feel the contribution they have made to your training is limited; give your reasons.]

Make specific reference to your Second Life experience and reflect upon affordances and challenges.

If there were activities that you did not do because there was not enough time during the day, please identify them.

The activities that were challenging because of software/hardware issues were ... [Identify activities that were limited in value because of outside factors.

Try to identify how the day could have been more efficient and effective through better planning and resourcing.]

My suggestions for next time are ...

Important note

Being a reflective practitioner is valued highly in the process of becoming an effective ICT teacher. Your comments will be treated confidentially by your tutors and mentors. They may be used to inform the feedback given to you. Occasionally, your comments, observations and statements will be used to inform our practice and the practice of colleagues elsewhere. In those cases the information will be fully anonymized.

FACULTY DEVELOPMENT FOR AND IN VIRTUAL WORLDS

Jennifer L. V. Sparrow, Samantha J. Blevins and Aimee M. Brenner

ABSTRACT

This chapter provides information on using virtual worlds for faculty and teacher professional development. The information presented in this chapter has been discovered through an examination of relevant literature with regard to utilizing virtual worlds in higher education. Among topics explored, the authors discuss the following: information regarding theoretical frameworks of teaching and learning, including social constructivism, experiential learning, and problem-based learning; the process for teaching instructors how to use virtual worlds across a variety of curricula; modeling of good practices in teaching and learning in a simulated environment; and the process of teaching faculty how to teach with virtual worlds. In addition, issues of access, technology needs, student training, expectations, and assessment within virtual worlds are discussed. Examples of faculty development including single workshops and entire conferences are shown with specific focus on successes and challenges of conducting these activities within a virtual worlds. In presenting these examples, it is hoped that individuals in higher education will gain a better perspective of utilizing virtual worlds in their practice.

Keywords: Virtual worlds; faculty development; Second Life®

Transforming Virtual World Learning
Cutting-edge Technologies in Higher Education, Volume 4, 47–65

ISSN: 2044-9968/doi:10.1108/S2044-9968(2011)0000004007

INTRODUCTION

While much of the theory of teaching and learning was defined and tested prior to the implementation of today's technologies, the underlying presumptions can be applied to the tools available to faculty in higher education. Good teaching encourages contact between faculty and students, interaction and cooperation between students, is active, provides timely and constructive feedback, emphasizes time on task with high expectations, and provides learning opportunities for diverse learning styles (Chickering & Gamson, 1987). As Web-based tools become more pervasive, teaching and learning theory and what is known about how students learn, of any age, it is critical to examine the technology tools within the framework of sound pedagogy (Churches, 2008). Technologies need to be matched to both the learning outcomes and the readiness of both the student and the instructor. The "wow factor" or the excitement over the technology tools alone should not be the sole deciding factor on which tools should be utilized. The learning outcomes, and application of learning theory, should drive the choice of technology tools. The use of virtual worlds can address not only Chickering and Gamson's (1987) principles of good practice but also Vygotsky's social constructivism theory, experiential learning, and problem-based learning. Virtual worlds allow for active learning opportunities that allow students interactions with faculty and other students, real-world scenarios, and the opportunity to engage in problem solving in a cooperative and collaborative environment.

SOCIAL CONSTRUCTIVISM

Vygotsky's (1997) theory on social constructivism of learning is based on the following: learning is a social and collaborative activity and students need to be engaged in learning activities that fall within their zone of proximal development (ZPD). Application of Vygotsky's theory in virtual worlds springs from a social perspective, a collaborative perspective, and through the creation of a range of activities that address various learning levels. The interactive nature of virtual worlds allows for a social component to learning that can include text, audio, and avatar-based interactions. Today's learner comes equipped with the knowledge and skills to utilize technology to interact with others on both a social and academic basis (Prensky, 2001).

Collaborative learning can occur in both predetermined learning modules within virtual worlds or through dynamic interactions that evolve as avatars move throughout a virtual worlds. Virtual worlds simulation modules have been established that reproduce emergency management scenarios, problem-solving modules, and more. These modules can include planned interactions with experts that can provide learners with access to additional knowledge. Additionally, these modules may just present problems that allow for learners to interact with a wider group of peers, allowing for more diverse perspectives and problem solutions.

Vygotsky's ZPD postulated that there is a range of skills and knowledge where learning occurs best. The ZPD includes both where a student can work independently on material and where they are challenged to understand new concepts. By working within the ZPD, with material neither too simplified nor too difficult, a learner can construct an understanding of new concepts in relation to current knowledge and understanding. Virtual worlds offer instructors the opportunity to provide a range of interactions, problems, and scenarios that can be adapted to address a range of ZPDs, allowing for learners to work within a particular range, or move freely between ranges as learning occurs.

EXPERIENTIAL LEARNING

Experiential learning theory is based on the idea that experiences of a student directly influence the student's knowledge and understanding of a topic. Dewey (1913) outlined experiential learning as allowing the learner to have a safe place to explore, experience, and test new topics. Kolb (1984) built on Dewey's emphasis on experiences in the learning process and developed a cycle of learning. These four cycles – concrete experience, reflective observations, abstract conceptualization, and active experimentation – are required stages in the learning process.

A virtual worlds such as Second Life® or Open Sim can allow for experiential learning in situations where a safe place to explore a topic, location, or problem. This could include allowing students to "virtually" explore the inner workings of a volcano, younger students can study art and architecture through a "virtual" Rome, or emergency management planners can attend a "simulated" natural disaster. These types of experiential learning modules allow for a safe exploration in terms of both physical and learning safety. Learning safety is the opportunity to try solutions without the repercussions possible in a real-world setting. Participation in a virtual worlds addressed Kolb's (1984) learning cycle by providing concrete experiences and active experimentation without the costs associated with a real-world travel experience. While a virtual worlds cannot replace the sights, sounds and smells of walking down the streets of Rome, it can provide an opportunity for a wider audience to experience the "virtual" Rome.

PROBLEM-BASED LEARNING

Problem-based learning theory furthers experiential learning theory into an opportunity for learners to identify a problem, suggest possible solutions, test solutions, and monitor outcomes. Problem-based learning allows students to utilize Bloom's (1956) higher order skills including the ability to think critically, evaluate solutions, effectively communicate alternative solutions, and analyze options. Problem-based learning also encourages students to work cooperatively in teams to think about and analyze real-world problems; to find, evaluate, and use resources; and to negotiate among team members and to others (Duch, Allen, & Groh, 2001).

Problem-based learning within a virtual worlds can be enhanced in several ways. First, the ability to bring together diverse groups of learners regardless of physical location can be seen as a benefit over a traditional classroom setting. Experts can be included in the virtual worlds. Learners have an opportunity to interact with an expert. Experts may include other students or individuals identified outside of the classroom that would otherwise not have been able to participate in the problem-solving exercise. Instructors would need to establish the problem that can be solved within the confines of the virtual worlds or with tools that can be utilized and accessed in their first life. Again, this virtual worlds provides a safe place to test multiple approaches to the problem. Final reports on the problem may include not only the justification for a chosen answer but also the reasons for not choosing other solutions. Framing the problem, providing support as needed, and introducing tools to solve the problem can be done either in a face-to-face classroom setting or in the virtual worlds.

VIRTUAL WORLDS FOR TEACHER PROFESSIONAL DEVELOPMENT PROCESS FOR TEACHING INSTRUCTORS

In order to leverage the learning experiences that virtual worlds have to offer, educators need to be aware and well versed in this virtual learning environment before employing it within their classroom. This adoption of new technology can be overwhelming to educators without proper guidance and support, and teaching within a virtual worlds is not without challenges. However, professional development courses that focus on virtual worlds or occur in virtual worlds can assist with this transition.

Learning to teach through a new technology, such as virtual worlds, offers educators the opportunity to revisit and revise their pedagogical practices instead of replicating their traditional teaching methods. Virtual worlds provide new modes of communication, collaboration, and technology that can prompt educators to discover new applications of pedagogy (Dreher, Reiners, Dreher, & Dreher, 2009). For example, Sanchez (2009b) identified digital storytelling, role-playing, and community engagement as pedagogical applications for virtual worlds that offer the freedom of creativity, active participation, and reflection to students. In particular, virtual worlds can bring faculty together to collaborate on projects and best practices for common goals, as well as provide previously created content that can be leveraged in the classroom (Waters, 2009).

Training educators to successfully implement new technology can be a challenging task. Effective faculty development programs are the key to successful implementation and execution of technology (McIsaac & Craft, 2003). Although assistance from institutional training and support is not always available, training can help faculty develop their instructional methodology and practice within virtual worlds (O'Conner & Sakshaug, 2009). According to Dembo (2008), immersion within virtual worlds is the goal of faculty training. Understanding a virtual worlds is impossible without having experience in that world; immersion within virtual worlds helps the educator understand what the learner will experience (Waters, 2009).

To begin, educators need to learn basic skills in virtual worlds, such as altering their avatar's appearance and learning to navigate between islands, just as their students would do. Once educators have learned the ropes, conducting professional workshops in the virtual environment can help them execute these basic skills. Finally, having educators present what they have learned to other educators within virtual worlds will demonstrate their mastery of the virtual environment (Dembo, 2008).

After learning their way around virtual worlds, educators can then begin to think about how they should prepare to teach their own course in virtual worlds. Careful consideration should be made to designing a course in virtual worlds (O'Conner, 2010). Replicating traditional or lecture-based classroom experiences within virtual worlds fails to both inspire students and take advantage of the rich environment that virtual worlds have to offer. Having clear objectives for virtual worlds in mind and beginning in virtual worlds with simple objectives can ensure success (Baker, Wentz, & Woods, 2009). In addition, educators should strive to create learner-centered sites or activities that actively engage students within the virtual worlds classroom (Thompson & Garetty, 2009). Students can also be involved in the design and assessment of learning activities within virtual worlds, investing them in their own learning experience (Baker et al., 2009).

Research suggests that virtual worlds have a high learning curve (O'Conner, 2010; O'Conner & Sakshaug, 2009; Sanchez, 2009a). This learning curve can be contributed to several factors, including: difficulty with using the interface, technical issues, expectations of virtual worlds, and time spent in-world (Sanchez, 2009a). Without the help of an educator or guide who is familiar with virtual worlds, students will possibly become part of the 90% of individuals who sign up for virtual worlds, but fail to maintain an active presence within the virtual environment (Sanchez, 2009a). Research also shows that students, who receive support during their beginning exploration of virtual worlds, despite their proficiency at the beginning, can reach high achievement by the end of a course (O'Conner & Sakshaug, 2009). Strategies that educators can employ to assist students with the steep learning curve associated with virtual worlds include allowing students to discover the interface and navigation of virtual worlds through play, placing emphasis on the social aspects of virtual worlds by using in-world group activities and projects, and providing only a small amount of guidance while encouraging creativity on in-world assignments (Sanchez, 2009b).

EDUCATIONAL EXAMPLES IN VIRTUAL WORLDS FOR TEACHER PROFESSIONAL DEVELOPMENT

Virtual worlds contain many spaces that educators can take advantage of in terms of networking, professional development, and free resources. Among these spaces, three Second Life islands stand out from the rest: Discovery Educator Network (DEN), Community of Academic Virtual Educators (CAVE), and the Teacher Networking Center (TNC). These three islands are described with more detail in the following paragraphs.

The DEN is an island where visitors can become oriented in virtual worlds. This island sponsors a group of DEN guides, or volunteers, who assist new teachers as they begin to use virtual worlds. Specifically, new users can learn to navigate within virtual worlds, alter their avatars, and learn how to interact with other users in formal and informal settings. These sessions can be done with groups or one-on-one (Waters, 2009).

The CAVE island is maintained by a partnership between Boise State University's Department of Educational Technology; the Association for Educational Communications and Technology (AECT); the International Association for K-12 Online Learning (iNACOL); Applied Research in Virtual Environments for Learning (ARVEL SIG), a division of the American Educational Research Administration (AERA); and the Information and Communications Technology (ICT) Library. This island offers valuable resources to educators, including free teaching and meeting spaces, opportunities to participate in virtual professional development activities, and scavenger hunts or virtual worlds-games that allow users to explore all CAVE island has to offer.

The TNC island in virtual worlds is designed to bring educators together from across the globe. This island is another resource available for educators to learn about different educational tools available in virtual worlds, as well as the opportunity to meet others from around the world who are implementing virtual worlds in their classrooms. These are just three examples of the islands that afford many educational opportunities for educators in virtual worlds. Many other exciting islands are waiting to be explored and applied as learning experiences for students in the classroom.

VIRTUAL WORLDS AS A TEACHING TOOL

Practical Applications of Virtual Worlds in Teaching and Learning

The uses for virtual worlds and their application to teaching and learning have been varied and implemented across many academic fields. Because virtual worlds are still relatively new to higher education, there exists a need for more empirical research as more institutions adopt the use of virtual worlds in courses and programs. This section highlights recent examples of virtual worlds being integrated into multiple higher education courses as a way to expose learners to emerging technologies and to take advantage of the affordances that relate to specific fields. The academic fields that are highlighted include educational leadership, teacher education, hospitality and tourism, accounting, nursing, music, and digital photography. This range of subject matter demonstrates the versatility of virtual worlds and demonstrates that it offers many authentic opportunities across many different disciplines.

Zijdemans-Boudreau, Headley, and Ashford (2009) introduced a course about communities in virtual worlds for educational leadership doctoral students during the summer of 2008; students learned how to be productive residents, investigated being part of a community, and explored the educational opportunities. Although students struggled with the learning curve presented, once they overcame this challenge, they found overall that they could experience interactions with others similar to those in the physical world; additionally, they also felt that virtual worlds definitely presented potential uses for education (Zijdemans-Boudreau et al., 2009). Penfold (2008) participated in a project involving the School of Hotel and Tourism Management at The Hong Kong Polytechnic University in 2007 where a virtual campus was created to offer real-world simulations in hospitality and tourism; teachers found that the experience provided more interactivity, variety, and enjoyment of the learning process and 57% of the students surveyed in the four pilot classes rated it to be "interesting" or "very interesting."

Hornik and Thornburg (2010) pioneered a study that situated accounting students into a virtual worlds classroom entitled "Really Engaging Accounting" and allowed students to interact with a 3D accounting equation model; the study demonstrated that virtual environments can engage students and thus promote better performance. In spring 2010, Jinyuan, Dan, and Pauline (2010) worked with a total of 50 subjects from an undergraduate course in nursing from a private college on a pre-eclampsia simulation in virtual worlds, as this type of experience is usually difficult for instructors to provide authentically for students; instructors and students found the immersive environment provides a powerful tool for role-playing and interactive engagement in a social context. In the spring of 2007, the SUNY Oneonta virtual worlds Music Project commenced when students from a large music class volunteered to take part in a project that involved organizing three concerts at the Pantheon virtual music hall; not only did the students demonstrate a high level of engagement, but the experience prepared them for future professional opportunities (Greenberg, Nepkie, & Pence, 2009).

Nie, Roush, and Wheeler (2010) reported on a pilot study involving six students studying digital photography as undergraduates and participated in a group project involving virtual worlds in October of 2008 at the London South Bank University; the students created virtual cubes with images obtained from in-world libraries. The findings demonstrated that students were engaged in the active learning project that incorporated collaboration from others. Another recent study involving teacher education students took place during a three-week January term course and involved students, after training in a computer lab, designing a school uniform for their avatar, debating the use of uniforms in schools, and then collaboratively designing a playground; following these tasks, students perceived virtual worlds as an instructional tool to add to their teacher toolbox and also recognized the potential it holds for interactive and engaged learning, as long as sufficient training has been provided for participants (Storey & Wolf, 2010). These are just a few recent studies illustrating possible uses of virtual worlds in education. The common theme found at the close of each study is that virtual worlds affords teachers and students the opportunity to take part in a learning process that is interactive, collaborative, and engaging and that may not be possible in real life.

VIRTUAL WORLDS ACCESS: FIRST LIFE REALITIES

Unfortunately, virtual worlds also possess a number of barriers in which educators need to be aware before they implement any aspect of virtual worlds in a professional manner (Warburton, 2009). The barriers include technology needs and access, student training, student expectations, and assessment within virtual worlds. By understanding each of these barriers, educators can plan accordingly and design professional development or instruction systematically. Barriers can then become part of the expectations of implementing virtual worlds and become a teachable moment for faculty and students.

TECHNOLOGY NEEDS AND ACCESS

The technology requirements are significant. Antonacci and Modaress (2008) noted that the most recent releases of the Windows and Mac OS X operating systems supported virtual worlds software, including a high-speed Internet connection and high-functioning video/graphics cards in order for virtual worlds to run smoothly on a computer. Jinyuan et al. (2010) proposed that although virtual worlds still function adequately utilizing a wireless connection, hard-wired Internet connection is much more expedient, remembering that some virtual worlds are not supported by wireless technologies. Educators need to consider what access to technology their learners might have and what alternatives are available to those who don't have access. Alternatives to utilizing their own computers should be reasonable for student access. Few students may have to travel to a physical location to participate in virtual worlds activities and should be included in course planning.

In addition to individual student computer considerations, educators also need to recognize the technical infrastructure of their institution; many higher education campuses may not be able to support an virtual worlds project that is large-scale simply because of these high-end technology requirements (Penfold, 2008). Warburton (2009) contended that when these technology requirements have not been fully met, aspects of the end-user experience can be disrupted and lead to one of the more adverse effects found within virtual worlds, "lag," which involves the downloading of environmental objects and avatars to appear in-world in a disjointed manner. Another frustration with the technology is intrusion of abundant system updates and patches. Requirements for client viewer updates on a regular basis can result in unexpected computer downtime, which takes time away from instruction (Warburton, 2009). Shedding light on these technology issues is meant to empower instructors to plan the time required to evaluate the technology and communicate to their stakeholders and procure the necessary support (Penfold, 2008).

STUDENT TRAINING

To be functional and creative, there is a pronounced learning curve. Learning simple skills to operate one's avatar edit its appearance, communicate, and travel from one destination to another (Zijdemans-Bourdreau et al., 2009) is one set of skills to plan for. Additionally, as your students aim to utilize the power of the environment, they must also engage in such advanced activities as building and scripting (Antonacci & Modaress, 2008). The steep learning curve is attributed to the abundance of features. Learners have to develop these competencies to participate in the various learning worlds and advance their skills to move around more gracefully, teleport to other islands seamlessly, and communicate with others (Zijdemans-Bourdreau et al., 2009) in meaningful ways. It is essential that teachers set aside time for learning and training in virtual worlds as well, as it directly affects the experiences of their students (Penfold, 2008).

Zijdemans-Bourdreau et al. (2009) suggested conducting basic training sessions as a prerequisite to the actual course by providing regular socials to aid individuals new to virtual worlds, or "newbies," with some of the basic skills. Strengthening the student's comfort level, instructors take students tours to popular educational islands, allowing them to participate in authentic learning tasks related to the course content, and having them keep reflection journals of their activities in virtual worlds as a way for them to share and make meaning of their experiences in-world. Completing the basics before the course begins saves the educator time. Specific training agendas and time allowed to integrate the basics and some advanced skills may differ depending upon the content of the course and the objectives.

STUDENT EXPECTATIONS

As with any course, program, or project in education, the objectives, activities, and assessments should be clearly laid out and explained by the teacher. This is also true of any activity, task, or assignment that takes place in virtual worlds. Oftentimes, the activities may be discovery based, in which the outcome is not a win or a loss. Students may perceive virtual worlds as games, but they are not. In educational settings, the environment is used more to examine how one interacts with others and the environment. This is accomplished by planning various types of tasks that are managed. Discovery does not have a real set of goals or prescribed outcomes. Sullivan (2009) suggested that because of this characteristic of virtual worlds, students who are left on their own to wander around and investigate with no real direction from the instructor may become bored and even frustrated. Students can become distracted because of the plethora of opportunities and possibilities that are available to them; this in effect can be a curse and a blessing to educators (Greenberg et al., 2009).

When this became an issue, it is beneficial to students to create more structured virtual worlds assignments six weeks into the semester (Sullivan, 2009); although the direction aided students in their engagement with virtual worlds, changing the syllabus midcourse afforded a new set of problems. In order to avoid such an issue, Greenberg et al. (2009) stated that faculty involved with a virtual worlds project, which included students from a large music class, aided their students' progression into the virtual space by providing a very decisive collection of expectations that governed their inaugural activities in the virtual space; as students gained more confidence operating in virtual worlds, the faculty were able to provide more independence to the students in accomplishing goals set forth by the course. The important principle to take away from the experiences of these faculty is to understand that in order to provide students with appropriate expectations, they need clearly structured activities within virtual worlds initially while they are just learning the fundamentals and from there, educators can provide more general goals for activities. Students, however, should be allowed to determine the process of accomplishing those goals within virtual worlds.

ASSESSMENT WITHIN VIRTUAL WORLDS

Assessment within virtual worlds, as with any project or assignment, depends upon the nature of the project, the content and, of course, the expected outcome. In reviewing the literature, assessment can take on many familiar forms dependent upon the various factors. Zijdemans-Boudreau et al. (2009) requested students to post observations detailing their interactions in-world, as well as class meetings that took place within virtual worlds to a class wiki. Storey and Wolf (2010) utilized pre- and postcourse surveys to measure student perceptions, experiences, game knowledge, and skills, as well as technology and virtual worlds. Qualitative formats relied on daily blog entries, stored on course learning management system, capturing daily activities, and reflections providing evidence that the activity's objective(s) had been accomplished. Nie et al. (2010) collected assessment data by conducting individual and focus group interviews; during which the researchers were able to capture students' perceptions regarding engagement with assigned virtual worlds activities, group work, as well as barriers in utilizing virtual worlds. They also recorded chat logs, with student permission, from each virtual worlds session in which students participated. The majority of assessment data relating to student activities within virtual worlds is qualitative in nature and employs a varied methodological approach. Because virtual worlds are still a relatively new technology, it is important for educators to analyze students' thought processes relating to the activities that they are being asked to execute in virtual worlds. This is best accomplished through the utilization of assessment tools that allow for reflective thinking. This provides a medium in which educators can determine whether learning objectives have been met and allows for remediating course structure.

CONCLUSION

Several theoretical frameworks of teaching and learning, including social constructivism, experiential learning, and problem-based learning, support the implementation of virtual worlds into the classroom or faculty development activity. When selecting a technology or virtual worlds to implement, time must be taken to ensure that the learning outcomes and readiness of the instructor and learners match the capabilities of that technology. These two factors are crucial in deciding the choice of technology or tools implemented.

The process for teaching instructors how to use virtual worlds is the same as any other implementation of new technology. Educators need to be aware and immersed in the technology before employing it in their classroom, thus ensuring that they have an understanding of the technology from a student perspective. In addition, faculty must feel supported and guided in their efforts, in order to ensure they will feel comfortable using the technology in their own classrooms. Offering professional development courses that focus on virtual worlds can assist with their transition to a virtual worlds.

Virtual worlds have been successfully implemented in a variety of curricula, and faculty can learn from these successes and good practices. A multitude of examples were previously discussed, from using virtual worlds as a simulation environment to conducting entire workshops or conferences within the virtual worlds. In addition, the challenges of implementing virtual worlds were discussed in detail, as well as the assessment of students who participate in virtual worlds. However, even given these challenges, it is easy to see that virtual worlds can breathe new life into a course or curriculum.

REFERENCES

Antonacci, D. M., & Modaress, N. (2008). Envisioning the educational possibilities of user created virtual worlds. *AACE Journal*, *16*(2), 115–126.

Baker, S. C., Wentz, R. K., & Woods, M. M. (2009). Using virtual worlds in education: Virtual worlds as an educational tool. *Teaching of Psychology*, *36*, 59–64.

Bloom, B. S. (1956). *Taxonomy of educational objectives, handbook I: The cognitive domain.* New York, NY: David McKay.

Chickering, A. W., & Gamson, Z. F. (1987). Seven principles for good practice in undergraduate education. *AAHE Bulletin*, 3–7.

Churches, A. (2008). Bloom's taxonomy blooms digitally. *Tech and Learning*. Available at http://www.techlearning.com/article/8670

Dembo, S. (2008). Virtual worlds for educators: Second Life creates a new dimension for K12 learning and collaboration. *District Administration*, October, pp. 49–52.

Dewey, J. (1913). *Interest and effort in education.* Boston, MA: Riverside Press.

Dreher, C., Reiners, T., Dreher, N., & Dreher, H. (2009). Virtual worlds as a context suited for information systems education: Discussion of pedagogical experience and curriculum design with reference to virtual worlds. *Journal of Information Systems Education*, *20*(2), 211–224.

Duch, B. J., Groh, S. E., & Allen, D. E. (2001). *The power of problem-based learning: A practical "how to" for teaching undergraduate courses in any discipline*. Sterling, VA: Stylus Publishing, Inc.

Greenberg, J., Nepkie, J., & Pence, H. (2009). The SUNY Oneonta virtual worlds Music Project. *Journal of Educational Technology Systems*, *37*(3), 251–258.

Hornik, S., & Thornburg, S. (2010). Really engaging accounting: Virtual worlds as a learning platform. *Issues in Accounting Education*, *25*(3), 361.

Jinyuan, T., Dan, L., & Pauline, W. (2010). A case study on applying virtual worlds to supplement classroom teaching in a health care curriculum. *Journal of Interactive Instruction Development*, *21*(4), 3–8.

Kolb, D. A. (1984). *Experiential learning: Experience as the source of learning development*. Englewood Cliffs, NJ: Prentice Hall.

McIsaac, M. S., & Craft, E. H. (2003). Faculty development: Using distance education effectively in the classroom. *Computers in the Schools*, *20*(3), 41–49.

Nie, M., Roush, P., & Wheeler, M. (2010). Virtual worlds for digital photography: An exploratory study. *Contemporary Educational Technology*, *1*(3), 267–280.

O'Conner, E. (2010). Instructional and design elements that support effective use of virtual worlds: What graduate student work reveals about virtual worlds. *Journal of Educational Technology Systems*, *38*(2), 213–234.

O'Conner, E., & Sakshaug, L. (2009). Preparing for virtual worlds: Two teacher educators reflect on their initial foray into virtual teaching and learning. *Journal of Educational Technology Systems*, *37*(3), 259–271.

Penfold, P. (2008). Learning through the world of virtual worlds: A hospitality and tourism experience. *Journal of Teaching in Travel & Tourism*, *8*(2/3), 139–160.

Prensky, M. (2001). Digital natives, digital immigrants part II: Do they really differently? *On the Horizon*, *9*(6), 1–9.

Sanchez, J. (2009a). Barriers to student learning in virtual worlds. *Library Technology Reports*, pp. 29–34.

Sanchez, J. (2009b). Pedagogical applications of virtual worlds. *Library Technology Reports*, pp. 21–28.

Storey, V., & Wolf, A. (2010). Utilizing the platform of virtual worlds to teach future educators. *International Journal of Technology in Teaching & Learning*, *6*(1), 58–70.

Sullivan, F. (2009). Risk and responsibility: A self-study of teaching with virtual worlds. *Journal of Interactive Learning Research*, *20*(3), 337–357.

Thompson, A. D., & Garetty, C. (2009). Virtual worlds: A tool for teacher educators. *Journal of Computing in Teacher Education*, *25*(4), 118–123.

Vygotsky, L. S. (1997). *Educational psychology*. St. Lucie Press.

Warburton, S. (2009). Virtual worlds in higher education: Assessing the potential for and the barriers to deploying virtual worlds in learning and teaching. *British Journal of Educational Technology*, *40*(3), 414–426.

Waters, J. (2009). A 'virtual worlds' for educators. *THE Journal*, *36*(1), 29–34.

Zijdemans-Boudreau, A., Headley, S., & Ashford, R. (2009). Do educators need a virtual worlds? Exploring possibilities for technology-based distance learning in higher education. In: I. Gibson, R. Weber, K. McFerrin, R. Carlsen & D. A. Willis (Eds.), *Proceedings of society for information technology & teacher education international conference 2009* (pp. 1617–1622). Charleston, SC: Society for Information Technology & Teacher Education.

LESSON PLAN: STARTING YOUR *SECOND LIFE*

Jennifer L.V. Sparrow, Samantha J. Blevins & Aimee M. Brenner

Lesson Title: Starting Your Second Life

Task(s) to be taught: Sign into Second Life® (SL), editing avatar appearance, movement and navigation, interface, and search functionalities

Time Required: 30–45 minutes

UNIT GOAL(S)

After completion of the unit, learners will be able to login to SL, edit the appearance of their avatar, and navigate to a variety of educational islands.

UNIT OBJECTIVES

1. The learner will be able to download, install, and create an avatar in SL.
2. The learner will be able to describe SL and identify two educational applications of the software.
3. The learner will be able to sign on to SL.
4. The learner will be able to identify the major components of the SL interface.
5. The learner will be able to demonstrate editing their SL avatar.
6. The learner will be able to execute basic movements with their SL avatar.
7. The learner will be able to utilize the SL search engine to teleport to islands of interest.

INSTRUCTIONAL OBJECTIVES

Performance Objectives

1. Given a computer and a step-by-step handout, the learner will be able to download, install, and create an avatar in SL without instructor aid with 100% accuracy.

Enabling Objectives: Learner will be previously familiar with the Internet and their computer.

2. Following a video about SL, the learner will be able to describe SL and identify two educational applications of the software with 80% accuracy. **Enabling Objectives: Learners will be able to identify previous or potential educational uses of SL.**
3. Given a computer with SL software, the learner will be able to sign on to SL with 80% accuracy.
   Enabling Objectives: Learner will know location of needed button/function. Learner will know their login name and password.
4. Given the SL interface, the learner will be able to identify the major components of the SL screen and each component's function with 80% accuracy.
   Enabling Objectives: Learner will know location of needed button/function.
5. Given access to a SL avatar, the learner will be able to demonstrate editing their avatar with 100% accuracy.
   Enabling Objectives: Learner will know location of needed button/function.
6. Given access to a SL avatar, the learner will be able to execute basic movements with their SL avatar with 100% accuracy.
   Enabling Objectives: Learner will know location of needed button/function.
7. Given access to a SL avatar, the learner will be able to utilize the SL search engine to teleport to islands of interest with 100% accuracy.
   Enabling Objectives: Learner will know location of needed button/function.

RESOURCES NEEDED FOR THE SESSION

'How to Get Started in Second Life' Web site

Equipment and Supplies Needed

PowerPoint, Internet access, Pen/Pencil, Computer, Projector, SmartBoard/Overhead screen

Media Attributes to be Utilized

- Audio
- Video

LESSON CONTENT, METHODOLOGY, AND RESOURCES

Content Outline	Methods, Resources, Tips
Introduction: Download, install, and create an avatar in SL Web site (http://www.uncp.edu/home/acurtis/NewMedia/SecondLife/HowGetStarted SecondLife.html) to learners before class.	Learners install SL on their computer, following the instructions on the Web site. Those learners should then bring their laptop to class.
I. Describe SL and identify two educational applications of the software. Show YouTube video about SL. (http://www.youtube.com/watch?v=CaLKFeJLnqI&feature=related)	Ask learners: 1. What educational applications have you used SL for? 2. What educational practices do you see SL has potential for?
II. Sign on to SL Ask learners to pair off into groups of two or three, making sure that each group has a computer to use. Ask learners to open the SL software and sign on.	Learners will pair off into groups, each using one computer. Learners will sign on to SL.
III. Identify the major components of the SL interface Using screenshots, the instructor will guide learners in the SL interface, demonstrating each function.	Learners should follow along with the instructor, exploring each part of the interface.

IV. Demonstrate editing their SL avatar The instructor will guide learners in editing the following attributes of their SL avatar: • Shape • Skin • Hair • Eyes	Learners should follow along with the instructor, exploring each section of their avatar available to edit.
V. Execute basic movements with SL avatar The instructor will guide learners in executing the following movements of their SL avatar: • Walking • Flying • Running	Learners should follow along with the instructor, executing each movement as shown.
VI. Utilize the SL search engine to teleport to islands of interest The instructor will guide learners in using the search box listed to find other islands of interest to visit. Instructor will direct learners to search for "Sistine Chapel" and "NOAA."	Learners will follow along with the instructor.
Summary Learners should now be prepared to navigate SL and interact with other users. Learners should also have the knowledge needed to edit the appearance of their SL avatar.	

Evaluation Instructor will have each group search for one island of educational significance, teleport there, and then explore. Each group will then be asked to share one interesting aspect of the island.	Ask learners to search for one island of educational significance, teleport there, and then explore. Learner will then share one interesting aspect of the island with the rest of the class.

REFERENCES

http://www.uncp.edu/home/acurtis/NewMedia/SecondLife/HowGetStartedSecondLife.html
http://www.youtube.com/watch?v=CaLKFeJLnqI&feature=related

PRE-SERVICE TEACHERS' TEACHING PRACTICE IN SECOND LIFE®

Donguk Cheong, Youngkyun Baek and Hoe Kyeung Kim

ABSTRACT

This chapter describes pre-service teachers' teaching practices of didactic methods based on cognitive apprenticeship. The purpose of this chapter is to demonstrate potential of Second Life® as a space for teaching practices of pre-service teachers. The participants were 160 college students who were completing a practicum at Korea National University of Education. These students enrolled in four sections of teaching methods and educational technology, which was one of the requirements for their teaching certificate. The students were placed in groups of three to five students according to their majors. In Second Life, they practiced their teaching and participated in the evaluation of other groups' teaching. They discussed Second Life's potential, such as a space for expanding their teaching experiences and explored possibilities for using it as an environment for teaching practices. The authors believe that readers will find that Second Life can offer a valuable environment to promote pre-teachers' understanding of teaching techniques.

Keywords: Teaching practice; pre-service teacher education; Second Life; virtual worlds

Transforming Virtual World Learning
Cutting-edge Technologies in Higher Education, Volume 4, 67–84

ISSN: 2044-9968/doi:10.1108/S2044-9968(2011)0000004008

POTENTIALS OF SECOND LIFE FOR PRACTICE TEACHING

The teaching skill of pre-service teachers can be improved through practice in real settings and reflection on theory-based learning. Teacher education based on authentic experience and solid theoretical frameworks lead us to an interest in "theory and practice" and "learning by doing." A practicum is one way for pre-service teachers to have an opportunity to practice teaching. Park (2007) stated that experiences such as observation of teaching, teaching performance, and receiving feedback from a cooperating teacher or peers positively influenced pre-service teachers' teaching efficacy.

There are some issues regarding a practicum in spite of its benefits. First, it is not always easy or possible for pre-service teachers to have sufficient teaching experiences or teaching practice prior to a real classroom teaching. Some cooperating teachers don't want pre-service teachers to teach their students for extended periods of time. The second issue is that teaching real students could expose students to trials and errors of pre-service teachers. In a physical classroom, any undesirable behavior or mistake made by pre-service teachers cannot simply be undone. This makes it difficult for teacher candidates to have the opportunity to practice their teaching in real situations.

Second Life, however, can be a good alternative for training pre-service teachers in these pedagogical skills. Second Life is a virtual environment in which the users are represented by avatars. Individuals can interact with one another through a variety of text or voice-based communication tools in virtual spaces that are constructed to simulate traditional classrooms. Through this technology, pre-service teachers in Second Life can experience a virtual teaching environment, practice teaching skills, and participate in problem-solving processes.

In addition, Second Life allows pre-service teachers to switch roles with their peers, role-playing a student or a teacher, in ways that are more immersive and engaging than traditional classrooms allow. These immersive role-play sessions provide an opportunity for peer teachers to evaluate the lesson from both the student and the teacher perspectives. Peer pre-service teachers can evaluate their own lessons by comparing their lesson plans with others, they can explore possibilities to enhance their teaching skills, and then modify their teaching. Although the role-playing is not a "real" teaching experience, it can be a viable alternative to help pre-service teachers acquire and improve teaching skills, as it facilitates their understanding of students' perspectives.

Second Life provides several affordances that give pre-service teachers the opportunity to have specific experiences, and it also provides them with an opportunity to reflect on the process and the results, as well as to obtain feedback from their peers and supervisors on their teaching. A well-designed teaching practice in Second Life, therefore, is expected to remove any potential negative effects on real students and to create a new kind of teaching environment combining learning theories with an abstracted model of a traditional classroom.

COURSE DESIGN FOR THE PRACTICE

Two of the authors were instructors of teaching methods and educational technology, which was a required course for a teaching certificate at Korea National University of Education. It was a two-credit course that lasted 15 weeks. During eight weeks, the participating pre-service teachers practiced their teaching skills in Second Life for two hours per week. The topics addressed in this course included theories of teaching and learning, instructional media, new instructional media, educational technology, instructional design and practice, and virtual reality for education. A short version of the course syllabus is as follows.

Course Description and Purposes

This course is designed to provide K-12 pre-service teachers with the knowledge and skills on the theoretical foundations of educational technology and their application in design practice and further in teaching practice. It is important to note that the emphasis of this course is more on how to design a lesson based on the learning theories and how to practice teaching skills using computer technologies than on how to operate computer hardware and software. A broad range of current theories of teaching and learning, instructional media, educational technology, instructional design and practice, and virtual reality for education will be explored. The course provides hands-on experiences in designing and developing a lesson and teaching materials using current theories and research. In addition, students will experience teaching practice in the course as a pre-practicum prior to their student teaching experience in the field.

This course will use Second Life, a web-based online virtual reality space, to provide students with the experience of teaching practice and to reflect upon their teaching. Students are required to have regular access to Second Life to improve the effectiveness of their practices. Students who register for the course will receive the detailed instruction on how to get started as well as get access to Second Life from the instructors when the class begins. Students are expected to actively participate in class activities and create a warm and professional learning community.

Instructional Mode

This course will be taught primarily through:

- Lectures on the theories of teaching and learning, new instructional media, educational technology, instructional design and practice, and virtual reality for education accompanied by class discussions.
- Small group discussions and activities, which will assist in developing a lesson plan, improving teaching skills and reflecting upon the teaching practice using Second Life.
- Off-line discussions, which will expand to issues discussed among students in the reflection on their practice.

Course Requirements

Attendance and Participation: Attendance, promptness, and participation are expected. Students are expected to participate in class and peer group activities. Students are expected to read assigned readings prior to class and come prepared to share ideas, experiences, and opinions.

Teaching Practice Project in Second Life: The course project allows you to apply knowledge and skills covered in class. The project requires you to design a lesson collaboratively with group members, developing presentation material for the lesson, and practicing the lesson in Second Life, respectively. To do this your group will: (1) select a lesson topic, (2) design a lesson, (3) develop presentation material for the lesson in Second Life, (4) practice the lesson in Second Life, respectively, (5) discuss the lesson with your group members, (6) modify the lesson plan and re-practice a modified lesson in Second Life, and (7) record a video clip of the practice in Second Life. Two outcomes of your project should be handed in for grading: (1) two lesson plans (original and modified ones) and (2) a video clip recording the final practice.

Open Book Exams (Online and Off-line): Students are required to take and pass two exams. The first exam will cover approximately the first half of the course and the second will cover the second half. Both exams will be administered in class.

PROCEDURES OF THE PRACTICE IN SECOND LIFE

One hundred sisty students from four sections of the methods and instructional technology course participated in this practice. There were 34 groups, with three to five students in each group. Teaching practices in Second Life were done group by group in sequence. The next section describes their preparation for teaching, their teaching procedures, and the evaluation process of their teaching in Second Life on a weekly basis. The descriptions are focused around activities of the instructors and pre-service teachers along with problem-solving processes that occurred during teaching.

First Week: Becoming a Member of Second Life

Instructors Activities: The instructors introduced Second Life to the class for the first-class hour. The instructors explained how to join Second Life, how to use basic functions, and how to search places. The instructors introduced education-related places in Second Life and encouraged participants to join. The instructors asked them to reflect on how to use Second Life for teaching and learning. The instructors discussed briefly the participants' future teaching practices in Second Life.

Pre-service Teachers Activities: With instructors guidance, each participant joined Second Life, learned the basic functions, and were given time to think about its educational usage.

Problems and Solutions: The first challenge that participants experienced began with computer hardware. Some students could not use their computers for Second Life due to graphics card incompatibility with Second Life or due to memory shortage. They had to use other classmates' computers. The second problem was that some students could not log into Second Life because they did not receive invitation emails from Second Life. The emails were sent to all participants in order to activate their accounts. Due to the failure of mail delivery, not everybody successfully activated individual accounts. One participant found the email in their spam box and informed other students of this and told them to search their spam box to find their email invitation.

Second Week: Adding Friends, Joining a Group, and Becoming Familiar with Basic Functions

Instructors Activities: The second week was spent in a computer room where each participant could access computers and the Internet. The first hour was assigned to lecture topics about the course, teaching methods, and instructional technology by the instructors and the second-class hour was spent on how to join Second Life and how to use the basic functions. During this time, the participants practiced how to use communication tools, such as local chatting, instant messaging, voice chatting, gesturing, land marking, and teleporting. Before the pre-service teachers performed these on their own, the instructors demonstrated these activities.

Pre-service Teachers Activities: All participants were able to add their instructors and classmates to their list. They created and joined their groups without difficulties. They learned the basic functions and used them to communicate with their classmates in Second Life.

Problems and Solutions: There were no difficulties for the pre-service teachers to learn the basic functions about how to navigate and search in Second Life. However, setting computer hardware for voice chatting was a minor problem. Instructors were able to help them solve the problem by telephone, email, and instant messaging in Second Life. Most of the technical problems they had were solved with support from the instructors and classmates.

Third Week: Listening to the First Demonstrative Teaching

Instructors Activities: The third week's lecture was performed in a computer room. Each participant occupied one computer to listen to the lecture. The instructors converted PowerPoint slides into images and uploaded them to their inventories in Second Life for the demonstrative lecture. For this lecture, the instructors created a virtual classroom with a screen, a projector, chairs, and desks in Second Life. These facilities made it possible for pre-service teachers to listen to the instructor's lecture while they were watching the texts on the screen. The instructors sent the information about landmarks to all participants via group notice so that they could teleport to the assigned classroom easily. The instructors' demonstrative teaching was performed in a didactic mode as shown in Fig. 1.

Pre-service Teachers Activities: Through instructors' demonstrative teaching, the participants learned about topics related to teaching methods and instructional technology. Simultaneously, they observed the instructors' usage of presentation and communication tools in Second Life.

Problems and Solutions: The participants in the first section of the course experienced some difficulties in setting at the beginning. The computers they used in the computer room were new to them and they were not the same ones they used previously. The instructors had to spend almost half of the class hour fixing a voice setting. Due to the technical problem, only 30 minutes remained for teaching in Second Life. However, the participants in other sessions were able to spend more than one hour because the computers were fixed and adjusted for voice chatting. For the participants in the last session, the instructors were able to spend one and a half hour teaching in Second Life. The video clips recorded in the last session of the class were forwarded to the participants in the first and the second sessions. At last, all the pre-service teachers in the first and second

Fig. 1. Screen Shot of the Demonstrative Teaching.

session in the course knew what the other pre-service teachers were learning during the class time.

Fourth Week: Taking the Second Demonstrative Teaching/Forming Groups, Designing Instruction, and Developing Teaching Materials

Instructors Activities: In this session, instructors and participants logged into Second Life from remote computers. For the first time, the instructors taught the class outside of the classroom. The instructors recorded the four sessions of their classroom teachings and e-mailed the video clips to participants who needed more practice in Second Life. After the second demonstrative teaching in Second Life, the instructors grouped the participants based on their majors and gave each group a homework assignment to design a didactic lesson. As part of the homework assignment, instructors asked each group to create PowerPoint slides as an instructional tool.

Pre-service Teachers Activities: The participants logged into Second Life for the class at various places such as in their dormitory, home, or in a computer room. During the class time, they observed the instructors' use of presentation tools, communication methods, and gestures. They also communicated with their instructors using local chatting and voice chatting tools. The instructors taught how to record lectures and how to save video clips of teaching in Second Life. These skills can be very useful for pre-service teachers when they teach their own class later. All the participants did their homework assignments in groups and designed lesson plans using Second Life. Lesson plans were required to include presentation, communication, and interaction features of Second Life. The instructors encouraged participants to include other features and to incorporate various teaching methods and techniques such as didactic, discussion, storytelling, or experiential learning into their lesson plans if they wanted. Some group members chose a special site, such as historic sites or cultural sites, as a teaching setting to promote experiential learning. Each group combined a classroom instruction with links to special sites for experiential learning. As required by the instructors, each group created PowerPoint slides based on its lesson plan.

Problems and Solutions: Most participants had no difficulty logging in and attending a class. However, a few participants had problems due to some technical problems caused by computer malfunctions. If they missed any part of the class, they reviewed recorded video clips to catch up with other classmates. Most groups tried to incorporate video clips into their lesson plans. Since the incorporation of video clips required an advanced skill, the instructors encouraged them not to include video clips in their lessons. Many groups tried to find places for implementing experiential learning. Some groups were able to find the site they were looking for and included it in their lessons while the other groups were not so lucky. Using the teleporting feature, participants could move in and out of the site they landmarked quickly.

Fifth Week: Learning How to Use Tools for Teaching Practices

Instructors Activities: In the fifth week, the first hour was allocated to teaching general topics about teaching methods and instructional technology, and the second hour was used for each group's teaching practice in Second Life. The instructors created and delivered necessary virtual objects for teaching, such as desks, chairs, and presentation facilities to each group's leader. The leaders distributed these objects to their group members. The instructors explained how to use objects, local chat, instant messages, voice chat, and gestures for teaching with examples. In addition, the instructors demonstrated to the participants how to set the desks, chairs, and displays according to their instructional methods and their teaching topics.

Pre-service Teachers Activities: The members of each group placed desks, chairs, and displays provided by the instructors. These virtual objects were arranged in a circle, semicircle, or in a line according to the instructional methods that they adopted. Each group members' PowerPoint slides were transformed into images and saved into Second Life inventories. Each group practiced various operational skills and techniques needed for their group teaching. These practices included voice chatting, speech gestures, synchronizing gestures with voice, local chatting and instant messaging, and presentation tools.

Problems and Solutions: After viewing the instructors' demonstrative teaching, each group member created a virtual classroom in Second Life by arranging desks, chairs, and displays. Some of the participants had difficulties in rotating and moving objects. With several trials and help from peers and instructors, they became familiar with manipulating objects in Second Life. Another problem raised with regards to communication was that there was no soundproof facility in Second Life. This problem became an obstacle when multiple users were talking at the same time. In other words, voices of each group spread out to the vicinity and affected other groups teaching and communicating. Each group had to keep the distance of 30 meters between groups in order to avoid any distracting voices. The instructors arranged a larger space to reduce this problem.

Sixth Week: Individual Teaching Practices and Recording

Instructors Activities: Two hours of class time in the sixth week were devoted entirely to each group's teaching practice. The instructors and each group logged into Second Life using remote computers. Each group member took turns teaching the other members for 20–30 minutes. Teaching in groups was recorded in a digital format and delivered to the instructors. The instructors observed every teaching practice as shown in Fig. 2. During the group teaching, the instructors facilitated each group's teaching and their use of Second Life in solving their technical problems through instant messages, local chatting, voice chatting, and telephone communication. In a few instances, the instructors intervened in participants teaching and solved problems from a remote computer.

Fig. 2. Screen Shot of Observing Teaching Practices.

Pre-service Teachers Activities: Each group member conducted his or her teaching practice as shown in Fig. 3. Each member took the role of the teacher by instructing the group's lesson plan to their group members. When one member of a group took over a teaching role, other members participated in a teaching demonstration as students. In groups, all members took turns in teaching. During the teaching practices, PowerPoint slides converted into images were used as an instructional tool. Thus, all participants played multiple roles, that is, a student, a peer evaluator, and a teacher. Each participant received feedback on his or her teaching from the group members. Although each group shared the same topic and the same lesson plan, each group member employed different languages, interactions, and communication methods in teaching practices. Each time the same lesson was taught by different members, the group members learning about the subject matter was reinforced and their understanding of the topic was enhanced. In most instances, the last teacher in each group became the most skillful, in terms of the operation of functions in Second Life. Each

Fig. 3. Screen Shot of a Didactic Teaching.

teaching practice was recorded into a video clip and shared by all the group members so that each member could compare his or her own teaching with the teaching of other members of the group. It seemed that two classroom hours was too short to accommodate all participants' teaching practices. As a result, extra hours after class were used to complete the practice teaching.

Problems and Solutions: The first problem that emerged during teaching practices was related to the participants' low level of computer literacy. Even though instructors explained the basic functions of Second Life and basic computer operation skills, each participant showed various degrees of skill in capturing movies and recording his or her teaching segment. It is believed that this discrepancy occurred mainly due to individual participant's computer literacy skills. The individual difference in computer literacy affected other members' teaching as well because teaching required all participants' involvement. This problem was overcome with the help of the peers and instructors. In the future, instructors need to help students in advance to improve their skills using Second Life. In addition, instructors were suggested to make a group heterogeneous in terms of members' computer literacy so that the students with a higher level of computer literacy could help the students with a lower level.

Seventh Week: Each Group's Teaching and Recording

Instructors Activities: The instructors and participants logged into Second Life from their own personal computers. Just like in the sixth week, two hours of class time in the seventh week were spent practicing teaching in Second Life. As in the sixth week, the instructors observed each group's teaching practices. The instructors continued to support participants' teaching whenever they asked for help. In week seven, none of the groups reported technical problems nor asked for help. The instructors asked each group to submit one recorded video clip as a showcase of outstanding teaching.

Pre-service Teachers Activities: Each group member revised and modified their lesson plans that they taught the previous week, after reflecting on their experiences. One member from each group performed group teaching. Each group recorded the teaching segment and submitted it to the instructors.

Problems and Solutions: There were no problems reported to instructors. It seemed that all participants had become accustomed to teaching in Second Life.

Eighth Week: Presentation and Reflections

Instructors Activities: Two hours of teaching time in the eighth week was spent watching the videos of each group's teaching performance. After watching the videos in a regular classroom, the instructors asked each group to explain the teaching performance in the video. The instructors asked the class to evaluate the other groups teaching performance and to compare it with their own teaching. The instructors mediated the class discussion about each group's teaching. The participants were encouraged to share their comments and feedback with their classmates. The instructors also provided their overall comments and feedback on teaching performance in the videos. When the teaching practice was over, instructors asked 59 participants to respond to a questionnaire with four items, rating the helpfulness of the role switching in their teaching practice in Second Life, based on a five-point Likert scale. The questions in the questionnaire were as follows: "Was my feedback as a teacher helpful for the peer's teaching practice?" "Was the peers' feedback as a teacher helpful for my teaching practice?" "Was participation as a student in the peer's teaching practice helpful to me?" and "Was participation as a student in my teaching practice helpful to the peer?"

Pre-service Teachers Activities: Each group watched other groups teaching in the videos. After watching the videos, they discussed their opinions about and comments on the videos in groups and compared other groups teaching with their own teaching. One member from each group presented the group's overall comments to the class after the group discussion. Group members in the corresponding video had a chance to respond to other groups' comments and feedback. In this process, all group members had an opportunity to reflect on their lesson plan and teaching practices. When the teaching practice was done, 59 participants rated the helpfulness of the role switching in their teaching practice in Second Life (see Table 1).

Problems and Solutions: There were no problems reported in this process.

Table 1. Helpfulness of Role Switching in Teaching Practice in Second Life (Cheong, Yun, & Collins, 2009).

Helpfulness of Role Switching	*N*	Mean	SD
My feedback as a teacher was helpful for peer's teaching practice	59	3.81	0.656
Peers' feedback as a teacher was helpful for my teaching practice	59	3.80	0.664
Participation as a student in the peer's teaching practice was helpful to me	59	3.61	0.616
Participation as a student in my teaching practice was helpful to the peer	59	3.58	0.593

COGNITIVE APPRENTICE METHOD FOR TEACHING PRACTICE IN SECOND LIFE

The cognitive apprenticeship model was introduced by Collins, Brown, and Newman (1989). They tried to integrate an apprenticeship model into classroom teaching. According to this model, students learn through modeling, scaffolding, and coaching. In addition, they are given opportunities for articulating, reflecting, and exploring what they learn.

Modeling helps build a conceptual model needed to acquire the target skills by observing an experts performance. For instance, the instructors performed teaching in Second Life to pre-service teachers as modeling. The pre-service teachers observed their instructors' teaching, especially the techniques and skills needed for teaching in Second Life. These experiences helped them build a conceptual model necessary for their own teaching.

Coaching provides students with hints, reminders, and an advanced model to improve their performance. Thus, the goal of a coach is to raise students' performance to the level of the expert. The expert's coaching was provided during each group's teaching. For instance, the instructors observed each group's teaching and provided each group member with feedback, suggestions, and technical help to improve the teaching practice of the member. Also, the peers played a coaching role once they completed their teaching in Second Life. Their experience of teaching in Second Life allowed them to share their skills and techniques with the inexperienced participants.

Scaffolding supports students in advancing to the next level. Once students reach the advanced level, they become less dependent learners. In the beginning stage, the instructors provided various instructional techniques, such as motivation, questioning, communication, and speech skills. These supports are gradually reduced in terms of frequency and amount. As described earlier, no support was needed from the instructors as the week progressed.

While modeling, coaching, and scaffolding refer to instructional techniques, articulation, reflection, and exploration are practiced by the learners. Articulation is student clarification of their knowledge, reasoning, and problem-solving processes. Experts can ask questions from the students: what are the performed skills they used? Or why did they adopt the particular skills that they did? Reflection is to review the performances and problem-solving procedures by students themselves and to compare their teaching with the experts' performance. Exploration is a means to search the way to apply acquired knowledge and skills to new situations. During the course, participants had to explain the lessons they designed and their teaching practices to other group members after watching the video clips. Each group explained why they selected the topic in particular, what the learning objectives were, and why they selected the activities that they did. They also discussed evaluation methods and the results. They had to articulate the processes they went through and the rationale for each step they took during their teaching experience in Second Life. Their reflections helped them explore more ideas in order to improve their teaching skills.

FOR FUTURE USE

The above description of teaching practices suggests that Second Life has a great potential as a virtual educational environment, especially for educating teacher candidates. Apparently, there are prerequisites for successful implementation of teaching practices in Second Life based on our own experiences.

First, computers with a high-quality graphics card and large capacity of memory are required for Second Life activities. These requirements are mandatory to carry out any teaching practices in Second Life. Second, pre-service teachers ICT (Information, Communication, and Technology) literacy should be advanced enough to set computers up for using Second Life. In using Second Life, more than basic computer technology skills are required. Third, pre-service teachers are expected to utilize basic functions of Second Life. If not, creative and variable teaching practices cannot be guaranteed. Fourth, many kinds of objects supporting teaching and learning should be designed and created in advance for teaching practices in Second Life. By doing so, pre-service teachers can spend their teaching time on teaching itself, not on building objects for their classroom.

The authors have a strong belief that Second Life can provide pre-service teachers with a creative and relevant classroom experience prior to their actual teaching. The described teaching practice will facilitate pre-service teachers in developing their own teaching skills and establishment.

REFERENCES

Cheong, D. U., Yun, S. C., & Collins, C. (2009). Is Second Life effective for pre-service teachers' teaching practice? In: I. Gibson, R. Weber, K. McFerrin, R. Carlsen & D. A. Willis (Eds), *Proceedings of society for information technology and teacher education international conference 2009* (pp. 1418–1421). Chesapeake, VA: AACE.

Collins, A., Brown, J. S., & Newman, S. E. (1989). Cognitive apprenticeship: Teaching the crafts of reading, writing and mathematics. In: L. B. Resnick (Ed.), *Knowing, learning and instruction: Essays in honor of Robert Glaser* (pp. 453–494). Hillsdale, NJ: Lawrence Erlbaum Associates.

Park, S. H. (2007). Impact of student teaching on prospective teachers' personal teaching efficacy and outcome expectancy. *The Journal of Korean Teacher Education*, *24*(1), 271–297.

LESSON PLAN: TEACHING METHODS AND TECHNOLOGY

Week	Lecture topics	Practices in Second Life
1	Orientation on the course (1 hr) Theories of teaching & learning (1 hr)	
2	Theories of teaching & learning (2 hr)	
3	Instructional media (2 hrs)	
4	New instructional media (2 hr)	
5	Educational technology (2 hr)	
6	Educational technology (1 hr)	First week practice (1 hr): Becoming a member of Second Life, using basic functions, and searching educational places
7	Instructional design and practice (1 hr) Open book online exams after class (1 hr)	Second week practice (1 hr): Adding friends and joining a group, using communication tools and land marking, and teleporting
8	Instructional design and practice (1 hr)	Third week practice (1 hr): Taking the first demonstrative teaching
9	Instructional design and practice (1 hr)	Fourth week practice (1 hr): Taking the second demonstrative teaching Forming a group, designing instruction, and developing teaching materials

10	Virtual reality for education (1 hr)	Fifth week practice (1 hr): Learning how to use tools for teaching practices
11		Sixth week practice: Individual teaching practices and recording (2 hr)
12		Seventh week practice: Each group's teaching and recording (2 hr)
13		Presentation and reflection on the practices (2 hr)
14	Virtual reality for education (2 hr)	
15	Open book off-line exams (1 hr)	

PART II
TRANSFORMING VIRTUAL WORLD DESIGN

A PRACTICAL MODEL AND ASSIGNMENTS FOR USING VIRTUAL WORLDS IN HIGHER EDUCATION

Dona Cady, Matthew Olson, Peter Shea and J. M. Grenier

ABSTRACT

Since the prevalence of virtual worlds in society has grown exponentially in recent years and virtual worlds have demonstrated an incredible power to engage participants in ways in which traditional education has not, virtual worlds provide us an excellent opportunity to create engaging, collaborative, and academically challenging learning situations. Also, given the new media literacy of many of younger students, we in higher education are in many ways meeting them where they already are ... or should be. By integrating virtual worlds into instruction, the Virtual Education Research Group (VERG) at Middlesex Community College in Massachusetts provides students with these collaborative experiences. Through a sustained community of practice and experimentation with a variety of virtual world platforms including ActiveWorlds, World of Warcraft, Warhammer, City of Heroes Architect, Forbidden City, and Second Life, some general principles and specific learning activities

Transforming Virtual World Learning
Cutting-edge Technologies in Higher Education, Volume 4, 87–112

ISSN: 2044-9968/doi:10.1108/S2044-9968(2011)0000004009

emerge for instructors integrating virtual worlds into the classroom. The basic concepts of connecting with technical and administrative support, choosing a world with thematic connections to your subject, creating scheduled opportunities to play and learn together, and committing to providing a strong online presence have been expanded upon to create a flexible model that can be applied across disciplines. Through the work of VERG at Middlesex Community College, virtual worlds are now used in a variety of instructional disciplines, ranging from humanities to psychology to business. Several case studies illustrating unique and effective practices are provided.

Keywords: Virtual worlds; second life; community of practice; constructivism; collaborative learning; instructional design; instructional technology; community colleges

PART I: RATIONALE AND BACKGROUND

Of the many technologies that have emerged in the last 20 years to revolutionize how people interact, few have acquired such a devoted following as *virtual worlds*, also known as immersive learning environments (Aldrich, 2009) or multiuser virtual environments (Vincenti & Braman, 2011). The grandiose name, virtual worlds, indicates the scope of this technology, suggesting god-like powers to create new worlds. Virtual worlds have been of particular interest to educators who understand the impact of learning spaces and who have longed for a platform that enables them to create environments which promote active learning and appeal to a variety of learning styles (Aldrich, 2009; Cady, Kalivas, Margulis, & Olson, 2006; Gee, 2003).

With the introduction of virtual worlds, educators recognized potential learning opportunities, but, were unsure of how to design instruction within this unique platform. While virtual worlds may offer the possibility for unique learning experiences, it takes knowledge, time, effort, and support to design such environments. Accustomed as we are to prefabricated instructional resources such as publisher websites and PowerPoints, virtual worlds are … a whole different world.

Much of the current online resources and discussion of virtual worlds falls into two categories: advocacy, praising the potential of virtual worlds but offering few concrete examples of instructional successes, and technical, offering explanations on how to move, communicate, and interact in specific social and gaming environments. Our chapter seeks to transcend these two approaches. By sharing our analysis of our virtual world experiences, we offer a model for schools and organizations thinking about using virtual worlds as a learning platform. We hope others will consider our model, thus, avoiding at least the pitfalls *we* encountered.

PART II: EARLY EXPLORATIONS WITH VIRTUAL WORLDS

In 2003, early work with virtual worlds at Middlesex was done using a platform called ActiveWorlds, a visual landscape allowing participants to create aspects of the environment as well as interact with other people who are three-dimensional (3D) representations called avatars. As today, ActiveWorlds participants interacted with each other and the virtual world through the eyes of their avatars. Within this closed, private world, avatars could walk, run, fly, and make gestures to enrich the integrated text chat (ActiveWorlds and Education, 2011).

Psychology professor and VERG member Dona Margulis was impressed with the ability of his virtual world to engage his students beyond the classroom, finding that students were more likely to take part in lengthy conversations (45 minutes or more) in ActiveWorlds than in his office or after his face-to-face classes. Professor Margulis noted, "… the increased amount of lengthy interaction seems to indicate that students are more engaged in their learning or more connected to their instructor." Conversely, that level of interaction might have been greater because the instructor himself was highly energized by this novel and interactive environment. Still another factor possibly influencing engagement was that students actually *built* this world themselves, creating their own environment and meeting spaces, and one of the outcomes of this investment was increased discussion and conversation (Cady et al., 2006).

And while Dona Cady, professor of humanities, successfully created from an ActiveWorlds template a readymade theatrical gallery for students to conduct collaborative research on literature and drama, fellow VERG member and history professor David Kalivas was somewhat frustrated in his attempt to access and import prims necessary for a virtual world that was historically accurate because of the lack of available suitable materials, though he continued for several years to use his world as a place to interact with students (Fig. 1).

Fig. 1. Dona Cady's Globe World in ActiveWorlds.

Through individual experimentation and comparing notes on successes and failures, Middlesex professors supported each other's work in these early days believing that virtual worlds would become valuable and standard tools to encourage and engage diverse learning styles and preferences of today's students. In order to use virtual worlds to their fullest potential, however, there must be ongoing experimentation in how virtual worlds support the learning process. For example, Burgess and Caverly (2009) suggest that social interaction in virtual worlds supports a community of inquiry among students, particularly important for engaging developmental learners. Moreover, because these time-consuming efforts are not always initially successful or well-received by students, they are best undertaken in a supportive community of practice (Lave & Wenger, 1991) in which faculty can share emerging insights while encouraging each other to continue pushing the boundaries of the learning environment. For these reasons, we established the Virtual Education Research Group (VERG).

The WoW Factor

The VERG continued to explore ActiveWorlds until 2007 when use expanded to a commercial online gaming world to support a fantasy and science fiction literature class. The project was largely met with success as the commercial gaming world interaction served to engage learners and support course content. This section details those experiences and concludes with a set of concrete guidelines emerging from this experience for those attempting to use commercial worlds in support of instruction as well as a set of crucial pragmatic and technical concerns.

O Brave New World that Has Such People in It

This project had the goal of extending the learning environment into the wildly popular World of Warcraft (WoW) online game. WoW, a massive multiplayer online role-playing game or MMORPG, is a virtual worldwide community of over 13 million people, all interacting online in a virtual fantasy world, all playing a game in which they set aside their true identities and take on the roles of fantastic creatures and mythical heroes. At first glance the game is pure escapism, and the idea that we could leverage its popularity to engage learners and reinforce important themes in literature was a challenge. Still, the possibilities of igniting a spark in a previously disengaged learner and extending instruction beyond the classroom and Blackboard LMS into the rapidly growing virtual universe were too enticing to resist.

One of the reasons we suspected possible success using the commercial gaming environment of WoW is that by its very nature WoW is thematically linked to the literature genre of fantasy sci-fi, the course topic. The course itself, structured by the overarching theme of the archetypal hero's journey, provided opportunity for each student in a mutually supportive environment to experience trials that lead to individual growth and self-awareness. We expected students' direct experiences in WoW to parallel the experiences of characters in the fantasy and sci-fi literature covered by the course. Our belief was that each student would personally experience the hero's journey, thus promoting deeper understandings of course topics.

Of course, we were not blindly optimistic. We entered into this experiment understanding that commercial gaming worlds can be inhospitable environments, containing other players who are sometimes annoying or aggressive and quests that require killing for advancement within the game. Still, we reasoned, the central theme behind many sci-fi and fantasy literature is about adversity and conflict, and these characteristics, while not desirable in an educational environment (although sometimes unintentionally present!), are at least consistent thematically with the course topics, *Beowulf*, the *Kalevala*, *Lord of the Rings*, and *Good Omens* come to mind to name only a few. Moreover, the ill-defined nature of the difficulties encountered in the virtual world made it a perfect platform to practice problem solving, reinforcing course goals that included collaboration on quests and taking leadership roles within the collaborative process (deWintera & Vie, 2008).

Besides the thematic and academic considerations, there were many technical and administrative concerns as well. The need for collaboration and support from various others at the college was considerable and crucial to our success. We were aware that virtual world gaming might prove addictive for students of certain personality types. While the evidence is by no means clear that online gaming is more addictive than any other hobby or recreational pastime, the novelty of this endeavor and the visibility of this issue in the popular media encouraged us to create a close connection with our colleagues in the Student Affairs division, apprising them of our project, our intentions, and assuring them that we would refer any students who experienced too close a connection to the game at the expense of their studies or this admittedly more mundane reality. Our next stop was the academic technology area where an educational technologist created an avatar within our game to provide in-world support. We received assistance from the library creating a specific area with technology sufficiently robust to run our game. And, working with the bookstore, we ordered time-based game cards that students could even purchase using financial aid. Finally, our level-70 instructors unselfishly donated a horde of gold to start our class guild! With administrative details in check, we moved on to the design of instruction.

Taking into consideration the uncontrolled and unpredictable nature of WoW, we realized specific details and structure of assignments were particularly important. For this reason, we created a multipart activity based on two components: the stages of the archetypal hero's journey (described by Joseph Campbell as the Monomyth (Campbell, 2008), a widely repeated pattern of experiences seen in numerous stories from *Gilgamesh* to *Star Wars*) and the basic elements of fiction. Specifically, the WoW assignment required students to analyze the background mythology of WoW, develop a character, join a guild, complete quests, and perhaps most importantly to create a narrative "travelogue" of their experiences in the form of an ongoing fantasy story – their avatar's own heroic journey.

Stories within the sci-fi and fantasy genres are distinguished by their creation of a complicated, multifaceted world often with its own mythos serving as not only a backdrop but also as a context for understanding plot and characters. The same is true for WoW, and consequently, we required students to watch the WoW *cinematic*, the video presentation describing the history and development of that virtual world, and to read the many pages of lore posted on the web. Students then compared the lore of the WoW, and its impact on the shape of the world with the lore of other works of literature addressed in the course.

In the WoW assignment, students were asked to create a character, for good or evil, which included selection of a gender, race, class, individual appearance, and name. Individual choice around the creation of their character was related to the notion of character development in literature. By making choices in the creation of their own character, students were provided a new lens to analyze the protagonists in the associated works of literature. In addition, we asked students to redo this assignment choosing an opposite gendered character.

An important component of the archetypal hero's journey is the establishment of a group of fellows to support and challenge the hero along his way. This experience was recapitulated through establishment of a guild consisting of students and instructors. The guild was a means of giving students mutual support and heightening interaction within the commercial world. The guild was established with a charter designed to encourage students to think about and exemplify characteristics associated with the archetypal hero. Students were expected to embody the traits of nobility, selflessness, and chivalry as well as required to complete 10 quests as part of the learning activity.

Student Comments: Truth and Consequences

Working in the commercial world, students connected socially with each other. As one student observed, "I enjoyed the camaraderie. It gave us a chance to relate on an outside level." Moreover, they enjoyed the opportunity to take on different characteristics and play roles. Said one, "In class we were discussing how everybody likes to play a different role. They [students] like the fantasy world better than the real world because you don't have to be yourself."

We were gratified to find that the majority of students felt that the virtual world work helped them to understand the literature in the course. One student commented, "It really helped me understand a lot more, like, get into the characters' minds ... and it helped me understand the stories a lot better." The imagination fueled by this role-play stimulated the in-class discussions. As another student stated, "You could use your imagination to jump off to discussions in class."

Still, there was a small minority that did not connect the virtual world work. One student noted, "... it was different; it was fun, but as far as the class, I don't know how much if it pertained..." While this opinion was in the minority, it underscored for us the importance of drawing connections between the virtual world activity and the course content.

MY CLIPBOARD, PLEASE: GUIDELINES FOR USING COMMERCIAL GAMING WORLDS IN INSTRUCTION

From several semesters using a variety of commercial worlds including WoW, Lord of the Rings, and others, we developed the following guidelines for using commercial worlds for instruction:

Space, the Final Frontier (or Maybe It's the Prime Directive!)

There was a need to have updated technology that would run the software and places for students to work together in groups for social support. Even though students logged in virtually, they felt the strongest sense of community when online together. Given the schedules of students, it makes sense for colleges to provide a place for students to work together and connect socially online analogous to Oldenburg's notion of, "…'the great good place, those hangouts that 'get you through the day''' (Putnam, 2000, p. 102). And, while the course was offered as a hybrid, this did not serve us well. We felt that working online would compensate for missing class time: it did not. Students wanted more structure and more class time to incorporate the online game play. It was there they felt the greatest sense of community.

What Happens When It's Not Fun Anymore?

When escapism becomes part of what you *have* to do, it is not fun anymore. When it becomes a requirement for students and faculty, some of the intrinsic attraction (i.e., fun) dissipates, disappears, and dissolves. We initially chose to experiment with WoW because students were there already, but by turning it into a classroom, we squelched some intrinsic desire to be there. The very nature of role-play involves the denial of mundane reality for the escapism of the virtual world. This may make commercial worlds intrinsically challenging to instructional intentions. Furthermore, if students are to put themselves out there, the separation of private and public selves remains a concern, a concern we address in our *Model for Virtual Worlds* at the end of this chapter.

Stop the World! I Want to Get Off!

In undertaking this project, we made a concerted effort to link students to information on the web regarding online gaming and Internet addiction as well as to connect with our counseling office at our college. In fact, one of our members almost withdrew from the project due to these issues, but happily in our case as no students experienced a problem, our concerns proved groundless.

Order from Chaos

One reason our project had success was the heroic nature of the commercial virtual worlds dovetailed neatly with the instructional themes of the course. For the use of a virtual world to be instructionally effective, the details of any specific assignment must be consistent with, emphasize, and provide opportunities to assess the student learning outcomes.

The Devil's in the Details

There were many small details that were crucial to the success of this effort. Getting video cards purchased and installed, purchasing time-based game cards so students didn't need to provide credit card information, approval of financial aid vouchers to pay for game cards, earning the necessary "gold" to establish the guild, and creating "in-game" technical support in the form of an instructional technologist who created a character to help students were all small crucial factors in making this work.

Beware Volunteer Work

Because all the instructors were committed to this project, they were willing to donate their time, lacking an established structure to provide workload credit. This informal collaboration, while initially exciting for the participants, was just that, an informal collaboration. Because it was not formal, the investment of time on the part of the faculty members not receiving workload credit became a heavy concern toward the end of the semester. It is our advice to institutions seeking to implement this form of learning to adequately support professors willing to take such risks.

Through this project we advanced our understanding of the potential of virtual worlds for instruction. Our next steps were to develop a learning community course using a new virtual world, City of Heroes (CoH) Architect Edition as it fit more thematically with the new course themes. The workload structure provided by a learning community allowed for increased collaboration and mutual support and CoH provided a unique opportunity for students to author their own adventures. Still, there was a pull from a large and growing virtual world that we had not yet used. By 2009, the gravity of Second Life (SL) was drawing us in.

Here on Middlesex Isle

With a mini-grant, we established the Middlesex Second Life Island during the summer of 2010. We decided to license a simulated private location, or "Island," consisting of 65 km^2 as a flexible learning and social networking space to be used by faculty, staff, and students. We elected to license a full Island partially due to the constraints of college purchasing processes (e.g., only full islands can be paid on an invoice) and consideration of privacy needs as full Islands allow for more restrictive access.

Researching In-World: Our Starter Home

Our first step was to explore various options for virtual learning spaces. We had to determine an appropriate look and feel including a necessary feature set using best practices as a guideline (Collins & Jennings, 2007). We wanted to create a space that was positive, welcoming, and user-friendly with useful tools for instruction. Unlike our previous efforts, our explorations of SL quickly led us to many helpful groups of like-minded educators.

Immediately, we joined several professional groups in SL, consisting of teachers and instructional designers from around the real world, to identify best practices and challenges. Open and communicative, these groups such as Community Colleges in Second Life (CCSL) were willing to share research, learning tools, and even instructional spaces with other educational and not-for-profit groups. Members often initiated chats in order to answer questions and provide suggestions to help facilitate in-world learning with a futuristic focus on the nature of learning and societal change.

Our next step was to investigate our building options to create a space to help us achieve our learning outcomes. From a skyscraper to a castle – or even the furthest reaches of deep space – there are many different kinds of buildings to choose from in SL, and instructors can find, build, or buy pre-made, just about anything. For our purposes, we wanted to use a learning studio approach, a space where many different activities could take place simultaneously. To this end, we consulted with our in-world connections and partners, finding them willing to share transferable materials for buildings (prims), the skins for them (textures), and free advice, coaching us novice builders or volunteering to take on the work for free (Fig. 2).

We next made an informal analysis of the sims (Islands) of several colleges and universities in SL. Two of the schools we visited were Vassar College and St. Leo University, each with an extensive and utilized in-world presence. Other leading universities had only developing spaces, basic islands with no meaningful activity. In regard to the successful SL sites, we asked ourselves the following questions: What environment did these spaces create? Were these spaces traditional or different from real-world classrooms? Were these spaces used to facilitate learning or were they built for other purposes such as marketing and recruitment? What kinds of activities worked well in these spaces and how might they be improved upon? (Fig. 3).

Vassar was of particular interest as they had built a variety of usable spaces, traditional classrooms, and open space presentation areas (e.g., the "seminar swamp" is built in an amphitheater style). But their most unique space was a replica of the Sistine Chapel. Without traveling to Italy, anyone

Fig. 2. Jim Grenier Surveys the Middlesex SL Island.

Fig. 3. Jim Grenier Overlooks Middlesex SL Island.

can experience a virtual representation rendered in high resolution using their SL camera controls to pan and zoom, seeing Michelangelo's paintings in ways no causal tourist could. Through the magic of SL, visitors even can fly up to the ceiling itself and mingle with the angels for a close up view few human beings in history have had.

\In addition to the real-world institutions with an in-world presence, we looked at some fictional institutions. The *University of OxBridge* is one such in-world group which helps new SL users adjust to living and learning in SL. Many such in-world groups exist to teach technical and non-technical subjects ranging from HTML coding to philosophy, to SL-specific training such as buying land and running in-world businesses. You can find it all at Oxbridge.

Goals: Score One for the Team

Our initial goal was modest but important to create a safe, supportive space in which students and faculty could hold class, interact, and become comfortable with the virtual environment before launching further into it.

Other objectives included the following:

- Interact on the Middlesex Second Life Island using avatars they create from times and places convenient to them.
- Connect with others from the Middlesex community as well as experts from around the world.

- Participate in online events such as art exhibitions, concerts, virtual public lectures, and group meetings.
- Engage in learning activities that promote visualization and active, inquiry-based learning.

In the end, we decided that a variety of different learning spaces placed at intervals around the sim would suit our needs best. There is a central plaza where students may gather informally and serves as the main landing point for new visitors, and then, in no particular order: a traditional business conference room, a small out-door amphitheater, a music pavilion, an art gallery, a "solar powered" radio station, an in-world cybercafe, and Asian gardens. There is also, for those who wish to use it, a traditional classroom area with a whiteboard and desks. Some of these spaces have embedded multimedia presentation support, while others are simply open for students and faculty to interact via voice or instant message chat. We have left room for further development, including the in-process Asian gardens, and continue to solicit feedback from users about the environments that will meet their teaching and learning needs.

Second Life Case Studies

The following case studies are both from the Division of Business, Engineering, and Technology at Middlesex Community College. The division became involved with exploring SL in early 2008, when we did a survey to assess whether it would be suitable to use as a business simulator. While SL was not adopted widely at that time, involved faculty began to ask questions about how they might be able to expand on the work of colleagues in other divisions, and use virtual worlds to help our students learn in the 21st century.

Connection and Community

There is a vibrant music community within SL. Real-world musicians perform in SL by playing live in studios, spare rooms, and even live venues, streaming their music in-world. Disk jockeys, folk singers, and spoken word artists all thrive in an environment in which people enjoy live, interactive performances from the comfort of their own home computers. Fans choosing to follow performers may join a SL group and receive a specific URL landmark when they log in, making it easy for them to follow their favorites from virtual venue to virtual venue, often showing a level of dedication matched perhaps only by the followers of the Grateful Dead in the real-world.

Still, other musicians perform only in-world. Former touring performers who no longer wish to tour can enjoy the advantages of performing virtually and are still able to share their music and enjoy the community of a fan-base without having to face the rigors of the road. Still others, too shy to face down a club full of fans, can attend open mic nights or headline their own shows while they build their confidence and playing skills.

Therefore, it seemed logical for us to connect a Music Business class with the SL music scene, and we did this, surprisingly, by attending a virtual rave. From a Twitter feed, we found a DJ from Denmark who regularly performs in the trance and house clubs of Europe. On this occasion she was hosting a benefit dance on her SL Island. With students watching safely from their desks, the instructor Jim Grenier explained this background, as he logged in and the SL rave burst onto the classroom projection screen.

As students watched the live music and dancing, including Jim's avatar decked out in his black suit and sunglasses, they discussed the nature of the in-world environment as it related to musicians and performers, noting that the recording artists of today must use a battery of social media tools, the list of which grows constantly as communications technologies fall in and out of vogue. They realized the need for modern recording artists to use and mix multiple social media in order to reinforce their brand and expand their audience, as they saw how the music industry often intertwines with their daily lives through a very interactive process using the tools and technologies they themselves already favor – all of this to a steady backbeat of house music and dancing avatars.

Connection and Leadership

Managers in the early 21st century have to be able to communicate across virtual platforms with, often, globally remote teams, and SL provides an excellent opportunity for management students to practice these skills. This case study in a principles of management class used a lesson plan based on a modified web quest. After logging into the virtual conference space, the instructor introduced students to the basic technical skills for attending a virtual meeting. Next the students logged into the virtual conference room, similar to what they would experience in an actual corporate setting, complete with conference table, chairs, and PowerPoint projection screen.

Divided into small groups, students worked on a project in-world during class time, determining their roles, writing an agenda, and organizing synchronous meeting times to take place outside of class. The instructor also provided his contact information for struggling students and helpful links about common technical issues on the SL as well as user-made tutorials on YouTube. Using headsets with microphones and SL's instant messenger, students met independently in SL at various times to hold their meetings. At the next face-to-face class meeting, the instructor followed up to discuss what worked and what did not work with these virtual teams. Critical thinking and reflection about the experience was encouraged by asking:

- How did it feel to meet virtually?
- What aspects of the meeting were similar to or different from a traditional meeting?
- What elements of a face-to-face meeting seemed to be absent? How was communication different from a face-to-face meeting?
- What were the advantages and disadvantages to communicating simultaneously?

Students in these activities could experience a taste of the human dynamics involved in a corporate setting. Running a face-to-face meeting is not without challenges: people come to meetings with their own agendas with varying levels of attention, fail to read the agenda ahead of time, show up late, don't listen, look bored, and even fall asleep. These challenges also exist in the virtual world, and students of management need to run and participate in productive meetings in any environment, virtual or otherwise.

PART III: OUR NEXT STEPS

Through our efforts, Middlesex faculty and students have explored the benefits and application of virtual worlds in a wide variety of academic disciplines.

A Variety of Possibilities

Art: Early in the development of SL, we saw the potential to create and promote virtual museums where works of art could be seen and admired from all angles (Willis, 2007). From famous and not-so-famous reproductions of paintings or sculpture to digital photography, SL has it all.

History: As noted earlier, faculty at Middlesex have used a variety of historical simulations and virtual worlds, finding the ability to recreate historical epochs an undeniably powerful tool, for students experience time and place all while interacting and communicating. One such popular world is *Rome Reborn*, created by Virtual World Heritage Laboratory at the University of Virginia (http://vwhl.clas.virginia.edu/).

Language Learning: Of all the areas where virtual worlds can offer educational opportunities, no subject has such rich possibilities as foreign language acquisition (von der Emde, 2002). World language students at Middlesex regularly communicate in SL through text and speech with communities of native speakers around the world.

Mathematics: Geometry provides a rich and almost infinite field of possibilities in a virtual environment. Several software programs – such as 3D Construct (Kaufmann, Schmalstieg, & Wagner, 2000) – allow students to enter a virtual world math lab and construct 3D geometric models that they can observe from any angle – certainly a testament to how virtual labs overlap with simulations, thereby, reinforcing constructivist learning of mathematical concepts (Winn and Bricken, 1992).

Psychology and Health: Virtual worlds offer a particularly rich area for faculty and students of psychology, and those at Middlesex have been particularly active in the area of exploring the popular topics of interpersonal distance and gender roles (Yee, Bailenson, Urbanek, Chang, & Merget, 2007) as well as the effects of prolonged experience in online environments. Of interest is the journal, *Cyberpsychology, Behavior, and Social Networking*. In addition, building on the health education work of Boulos, Hetherington, and Wheeler (2007), Middlesex is exploring the possibility of using virtual worlds to provide mind-body relaxation training for veterans.

Science: In learning sciences, virtual worlds have been shown to appeal to learning styles and increase conceptual understanding. (Nelson and Ketelhut, 2007; Price, 2008; Trindade, Fiolhais, & Almeida, 2002). On the safety and budget side, storage and use of chemicals in conventional classrooms can be costly and often present dangers, so the use of virtual environments allows students to mix chemicals and view results without incurring any of the risks inherent in a traditional physical environment – no more emergency shower or eye wash stations!

PART IV: TURTLES ALL THE WAY DOWN

Despite our relatively long history with virtual worlds, sometimes the best-held beliefs must be challenged from unexpected directions, for just as

Stephen Hawking reminds us, it really is turtles all the way down (1988). At Middlesex, the basic concepts associated with virtual worlds have been expanded upon to create a flexible model that can be applied across disciplines. Two of the fundamental strengths of virtual worlds are that they support new kinds of community among students, providing leadership opportunities, and creating unique environments for self-examination through the exploration of multiple identities. This model, which was piloted in a spring of 2007 literature course and refined over ensuing semesters, was developed drawing from an interest of Asian philosophy, which provides a holistic integration of concepts through a cosmological lens (Fig. 4).

Our model provides a description of the *yin* and *yang* aspects of effective learning activities within virtual worlds. The opposed but still interconnected concepts are community versus leadership and identity construction versus self-examination. The best learning activities taking place in virtual worlds not only ask students to collaborate to achieve shared objectives but also give them opportunities to take on the role of leader, managing the work of others. More importantly, effective virtual world instruction leverages the unique ability to create avatars with different physical and psychological characteristics from their creators. The creation of a character, or multiple characters, is reflective of introspection into one's own identity and the understanding of multiple perspectives in "... an endless stream of always novel yet continuous situations" (Ames & Hall, 2003).

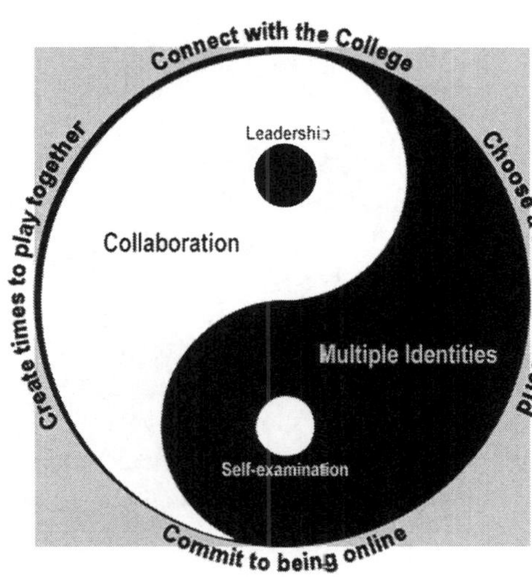

Fig. 4. Cady and Olson's Model for the Use of Virtual Worlds.

According to modern theories of learning, knowledge itself can only exist embedded in a participation framework. That is to say that learning can only truly be demonstrated in the context of the world, virtual or otherwise, as we interact with others in our lifelong journey. According to the social constructivists who base their ideas on the works of Vygotsky and Dewey among others, learning takes place in a sociocultural context, an idea that has been extended by Jean Lave and Etienne Wenger to situational learning as, "… the process of coming to be, of forging an identity in activity in the world" (Lave & Wenger, 1991).

As players, then, spend time in these worlds, they participate, form relationships, and make meaningful connections within the community that has its own participant structures, values, and goals (Steinkuehler, 2006). Through their interactions they come to understand the world and themselves from the perspective of that community. They learn who they are, who they are becoming through a participation framework, not in the individual mind (Lave & Wenger, 1991). "Changes in knowing become changes in being: through participation in communities of practice, an individual does more than merely acquire symbolic knowledge about the world; she or he is ontologically transformed by it" (Derry & Steinkuehler, 2003).

If we say, then, that virtual worlds are wholly immersive and that transformation is a continuous process, perhaps we should view virtual worlds through an Asian lens, for Asian philosophy tells us that we are all embedded in the context of our path through life. We are not separate from our journey; we are inextricably a part of it. Quite different from the Aristotelian mind–body dichotomy. According to Hans-Georg Moeller (2004), "new 'postmodern' theories are closer to ancient Chinese thought than they are to ancient Greek philosophy." This seems to have consistency with modern theories of learning that place knowledge – and therefore changing identity of self, connection, and community – into a participation framework. As much as we may feel we know something as an individual, our knowledge is actually contained within a social and cultural matrix, and only exists when put into use – field and focus. For, "persons are constituted by their relationships and these relationships are valorized and made real in the process of persons bringing their fields of experience into focus" (Ames, 2007). Henry Jenkins, Director of the Comparative Media Studies Program at MIT, agrees that the "ability to adopt alternative identities – to shift virtual identities – for the purpose of improvisational discovery is key to being able to interpret and construct dynamic models of real-world processes" (2008).

And so, change, connection, and community – are hallmarks both of virtual worlds and Asian philosophy – for it is "only by examining ourselves in different environments and exploring the different I's will we experience more connections" (Kohn, 2009).

There are, admittedly, many ways to use virtual worlds in instruction, but those educational experiences, as evidenced earlier in this chapter and developed using our model informed by Asian philosophy, take on a richer character, they promote deeper critical and integrative thinking required by the 21st century while providing a flexible framework to explore the collaborative and introspective aspects of virtual worlds that engage, connect, and educate.

CONCLUSION

Work with virtual worlds is, by information age standards, a long-standing tradition at Middlesex Community College, dating back to 2003. Over eight years the community of practice we established to nurture this work, called the VERG, has grown to include representatives from many disciplines and support areas across the college. Lessons learned over time have helped us to develop not only a rich set of instructional models and guidelines for using virtual worlds but also a culture of community and connection that supports and encourages creativity using virtual worlds in new ways with faculty members learning from each others' success and failures, adding to the growing knowledgebase of important extensions to the 21st century learning environment.

REFERENCES

Active Worlds in Education. (2011). Retrieved from www.activeworlds.com/edu

Aldrich, C. (2009). *Learning online with games, simulations, and virtual worlds: Strategies for online instruction*. San Francisco, CA.

Ames, R. (2007). The way is made in the walking: Responsibility as relational virtuosity. In: B. D. Smith (Ed.), *Responsibility* (pp. 41–61). Plymouth, UK: Lexington Books.

Ames, R., & Hall, D. (2003). *A philosophical translation Dao De Jing: "making this life significant"*. New York: Ballantine Books.

Boulos, M. N. K., Hetherington, L., & Wheeler, S. (2007). Second Life: An overview of the potential of 3-D virtual worlds in medical and health education. *Health Information & Libraries Journal*, *24*, 233–245.

Burgess, M. L., & Caverly, D. C. (2009). TechTalk: Second Life and developmental education. *Journal of Developmental Education*, *32*(3), 42–43.

Cady, D., Kalivas, D., Margulis, D., & Olson, M. (2006). Creating a community of practice to support technological innovation in the community college. *Community College Journal*, October/November 2006.

Campbell, J. (2008). *The hero with a thousand faces* (3rd ed). Novato, CA: New World Library.

Collins, C., & Jennings, N. (2007). Emerging best practices for campus builds in Second Life. In: D. Livingston & J. Kemp (Eds.), *Proceedings of the second life education workshop 2007: Part of the second life community convention 2007*, August 24–26, Chicago (pp. 78–81). Retrieved from http://cis.paisley.ac.uk/livi-ci0/slccedu2007rev2.doc.

Derry, S. J., & Steinkuehler, C. A. (2003). Cognitive and situative theories of learning and instruction. In: L. Nadel (Ed.), *Encyclopedia of cognitive science* (pp. 800–805). London: Nature Publishing Group.

deWintera, J., & Vie, S. (2008). Press enter to "say": Using Second Life to teach critical media literacy. *Computers and Composition*, *25*(3), 313–322.

Gee, J. P. (2003). *What video games have to teach us about learning and literacy*. New York, NY: Palgrave Macmillan.

Hawking, S. (1988). *A brief history of time*. New York, NY: Bantam.

Jenkins, H. (2008). *Confronting the challenges of participatory culture: Media education for the 21st century*. Boston, MA: MacArthur Foundation.

Kaufmann, H., Schmalstieg, D., & Wagner, M. (2000). Construct 3D: A virtual reality application for mathematics and geometry education. *Education and Information Technologies*, *5*(4), 263–278.

Kohn, L. (2009). *Introducing Daoism*. London: Routledge.

Lave, J., & Wenger, E. (1991). *Situated learning, legitimate peripheral participation*. Cambridge, UK: Cambridge University Press.

Moeller, H. (2004). *Daoism explained*. Chicago, IL: Open Court.

Nelson, B., & Ketelhut, D. (2007). Scientific inquiry in educational multi-user virtual environments. *Educational Psychology Review*, *19*(3), 265–283.

Putnam, R. (2000). *Bowling alone*. New York, NY: Simon and Schuster.

Price, C. (2008). Learning physics with the unreal tournament engine. *Physics Education*, *43*(3), 291–296.

Steinkuehler, C. (2006). Massively multiplayer online videogaming as participation in a discourse. *Mind, Culture & Activity*, *13*(1), 38–52.

Trindade, J., Fiolhais, C., & Almeida, L. (2002). Science learning in virtual environments: A descriptive study. *British Journal of Educational Technology*, *33*(4), 471–488.

Vincenti, G., & Braman, J. (Eds). (2011). *Multi-user virtual environments for the classroom: Practical approaches to teaching in virtual worlds*. Hershey, PA: Information Science Reference.

von der Emde, S. (2002). Technically speaking: Transforming language learning through virtual learning environments (MOOs). *Modern Language Journal*, *85*(2), 210.

Winn, W., & Bricken, W. (1992). Designing virtual worlds for use in mathematics education. Paper presented at the Annual Meeting of the American Educational Research Association, April, San Francisco. Retrieved from http://www.wbricken.com/pdfs/03words/03education/03iconic-math/07worlds-for-math.pdf

Willis, H. (2007). The unexamined Second Life isn't worth living: Virtual worlds and interactive art. *Afterimage*, *35*(2), 13.

Yee, N., Bailenson, J., Urbanek, M., Chang, F., & Merget, D. (2007). The unbearable likeness of being digital: The persistence of nonverbal social norms in online virtual environments. *CyberPsychology & Behavior*, *10*(1), 115–121.

LESSON PLAN: CITY OF HEROES – MISSION ARCHITECT ASSIGNMENT

This lesson using the CoH Architect MMORPG asks students to create their own adventures within the larger game structure. Through this assignment students gain experience writing for a new medium, reinforcing aspects of the narrative framework including plot, setting, character, point of view, symbol, and theme.

This assignment provides students with interactive experiences so they and/or their partners can craft and play their own interactive story-based missions that they share not only with their classmates but also with the rest of the CoH community. The narratives students create reflect one or more of the themes of the course reflecting the archetypal Hero's Journey.

OUTCOMES

Upon completion of this lesson the student will be able to

- Use the CoH Architect to design, write, and publish a mission to be played by students in this class
- Create and explore an alternative identity (avatar hero)
- Apply the narrative framework to the MMORPG genre
- Illustrate important course themes through their published narrative missions
- Collaborate to complete each other's missions
- Assume leadership roles within in the collaborative process.

PRELIMINARY ACTIVITIES

Introduction to Virtual Reality

Look at most descriptions of the future, and you'll find mention of *virtual reality* as an emerging technology that will impact our lives in many ways. Inventor and futurist Ray Kurzweil predicts that by 2019 you will be able to do anything with anybody regardless of where they are located physically. To acquaint you with this technology and its potential, we will be spending some time in virtual worlds this semester, primarily CoH. The specific assignments will follow below.

CITY OF HEROES ASSIGNMENT GETTING STARTED

1. Purchase a copy of CoH Architect online through the NC Soft website or another vendor. The list price of $19.95 provides the software and a month of online time. If you wish to test out the program before our assignment starts, you can download a free trial directly from NC Soft. Be sure to only buy a new copy; used copies will usually not provide you with a usable code for a new account and a month's use.
2. Create an account at NC Soft, using the code that comes with your purchase to gain access to the CoH virtual world. You will need to create a login name and password.
3. Install the program on your computer. We also will have some computers at the college that have the program installed that can be used for the assignment. We will create some lab hours for anyone who wants to make use of these computers. CoH runs on both Windows and Mac computers and should be able to run on most machines. If your computer is over four-year-old and very basic, the program might be sluggish. You can adjust the video settings to be less demanding if needed. You will need an Internet connection, preferably a broadband cable connection. Using a modem and phone line will probably not process data fast enough for a fluid experience.
4. Click on the startup icon. The first time you log in, the program will install any updates that might take 10–20 minutes depending on the speed of your connection. Select our class server, "Virtue."
5. Create your first character (avatar). Once you are connected to the Virtue server, you will be given the opportunity to create a character. Select a "hero" rather than a "villain." There are two parallel worlds included in your program: CoH and City of Villains (CoV). We will be using the CoH world. You have a rich set of tools to create the Superhero of your dreams. (Note: you can create multiple heroes if you wish to experiment with different looks and abilities.)
6. Select an Archetype – you will need to decide on the class of your character that will determine his or her abilities.
   - A *Tank* is a powerful hero that can take a licking and keep on ticking. They like to challenge their adversaries up close and personal and protect their friends by drawing attention to themselves.
   - A *Scrapper* prefers to deal damage rather than absorb it. They prefer to end any confrontation quickly. Think martial arts specialist.

- A *Controller* manages conflicts by controlling the odds, immobilizing certain adversaries so that their companions can take care of business without unpleasant interruptions.
- A *Defender* has the ability to heal and strengthen their allies and weaken their enemies.
- Finally, a *Blaster* prefers to deliver punishment from a distance – no sense getting your shiny new costume dirty.

7. Enter the world and complete the tutorial. Once you've created your character and selected a name, you can enter the world and be led through a tutorial that will introduce you to the interface and the basics of the world. After completing the tutorial, you'll be given a choice of starting points in the world. Select Atlas City for easy access to your fellow class members.

Once you've created a Super Hero and completed the tutorial, you will enter the world of Paragon City and its surroundings. To join our class group for communication and collaboration purposes, you'll want to become a member of our Super Group (think guilds), which is an online collaborative community within a virtual world. Our class Super Group is the Futurenauts. Send the name of your avatar to either of your professors and we will arrange a time to meet you in the world and invite you to our class group. Most of our online communication will take place in our Super Group chat. Once you become a member, you can chat with any members who are online without having to type in any commands.

TECHNICAL SUPPORT

While some of you may have had prior experience with virtual worlds, computer games and other online tools, we're aware that others may be new to this technology. It can be a bit confusing at first until you get familiar with the interface and controls. Don't be discouraged; it's a bit like learning to type or drive a car. After a while, the actions become automatic.

We'll attempt to provide you with plenty of support. Both faculty members will make themselves available online to assist you. Some of your fellow students should also prove to be of help to you once you've joined our Super Group and have access to our group chat. Finally, college technical support staff has created a character and will be available as technology support.

MISSION ARCHITECT ASSIGNMENT

Accepting Your Mission

When you first enter Paragon City, your character will have little to his/her name an their outfit and a few special abilities. Over time, your hero will gain experience by completing missions as you attempt to make the city safe for its inhabitants. As you gain experience, you will achieve different levels. Each level will provide you with additional benefits and powers. While it's possible to spend many hours improving your avatar's level (there are 50 available levels), that's not the primary focus of our classroom activity.

We suggest that you attain level 5 by completing the early missions (quests). It should not take you very long to reach that level, and it will give you a feeling for how missions are designed, the interface, and the nature of the world. At level 5 you will receive an invitation to visit the AE building (Mission Architect building) where you will be provided with information on how to use the mission architect tools. When you finish the tutorial, you are free to try some of the missions created by others, as well as use the mission architect editor to begin to create your own story-based mission.

Creating Your Own Mission

The primary assignment for our CoH experience is to create your own story-based mission using the Architect editor provided for you in the AE building. Choose a theme that relates to some of the future concepts from our course content. You might want to focus on robots, nanotechnology, or virtual worlds themselves. You might want to create a scenario around the dangers of technology that has gone out of control.

While you're designing your mission, you can invite other class members to test it and give you their suggestions and impressions. Missions can be short or long, single or multiple episodes. We will base our evaluation of your mission primarily on its thoughtfulness, creativity, quality, and connection with course material, rather than its length. You may submit more than one mission.

Ask for assistance if you need any help using the mission architect tool. While this tool is fairly intuitive to use and requires no special computer skills, it may be a bit confusing at first to some. If you jump in and experiment, you'll get the hang of it before long.

Once you are satisfied with your mission, you should publish it so that class members and the larger CoH community have access to it. Players can rate and make comments on available missions.

Mission Architect Assignment Requirements

To receive credit for your mission, complete the following steps:

1. After creating your mission in the editor, it should be published to the community once you are satisfied with your design.
2. Send us the name of your mission (via email or the discussion board), so we can try it out.
3. Ask at least two class members to attempt your mission and provide you with feedback. Provide us with their real or avatar name.
4. List the missions that you have played including your feedback. You should play at least three different missions.

That's it! You've now created digital content that can be experienced and enjoyed by others while assisting your classmates with their creations. You'll receive credit not only for this assignment, but your involvement can also contribute toward your overall class participation grade. See the CoH assignment rubric for specific grading criteria.

CITY OF HEROES ARCHITECT GRADING RUBRIC

Course Themes	**4 points**	**3 points**	**1 points**
	The game storyline reflects: Future consciousness and our role in its creation The qualities of a desirable or preferable future Common themes found in science fiction and fantasy literature	The game reflects some aspects of: Future consciousness and our role in its creation The qualities of a desirable or preferable future Common themes found in science fiction and fantasy literature	The game reflects limited aspects of: Future consciousness and our role in its creation The qualities of a desirable or preferable future Common themes found in science fiction and fantasy literature
Game Design	**3 points**	**2 points**	**0 points**
	Game design is challenging and interesting, addressing all of the following: Strong narrative framework including internal dialogue. Clear and detailed mission instructions. Challenging and interactive environment. Possibilities for solo as well as team play. Playable by characters at a range of levels.	Game design is somewhat challenging and interesting, addressing some of the following: Strong narrative framework including internal dialogue. Clear and detailed mission instructions. Challenging and interactive environment. Possibilities for solo as well as team play. Playable by characters at a range of levels.	Game design is difficult or uninteresting, addressing few of the following: Strong narrative framework including internal dialogue. Clear and detailed mission instructions. Challenging and interactive environment. Possibilities for solo as well as team play. Playable by characters at a range of levels.
Collaboration	**2 points**	**1 points**	**0 points**
	Student collaborates to complete the mission. Student takes on a leadership role.	Student collaborates to complete the mission but does not take on a leadership role.	Student does not collaborate or take on a leadership role.
Persistence	**1 point**	**0 point**	
	Student shows persistence, mastering technical aspects of game creation Student maintains positive attitude throughout game development process despite challenges.	Student gives up when challenged and does not complete game design. Student maintains a negative attitude throughout game development process.	

INSTRUCTIONAL DESIGN FRAMEWORKS FOR SECOND LIFE® VIRTUAL LEARNING

Scott J. Warren and Jenny S. Wakefield

ABSTRACT

This chapter discusses two instructional designs that sought to leverage the multiuser virtual environment Second Life to support learning and instruction with both undergraduate and graduate students at two different universities. We examine each of these curricular developments in depth and provide findings from research conducted with each. Using data collected from students and faculty, we describe 11 research-based virtual world design principles that emerged from each experience that include such suggestions as Create opportunities for sustaining virtual community beyond a task *and* Expect your learners to go off-task. *These principles may be used by readers to guide future designs that use virtual worlds to support learning.*

Keywords: Instructional design; Second Life; higher education; virtual worlds; multiuser virtual environment

Transforming Virtual World Learning
Cutting-edge Technologies in Higher Education, Volume 4, 113–161

ISSN: 2044-9968/doi:10.1108/S2044-9968(2011)0000004010

INTRODUCTION

The use of virtual and social online learning has increased at all educational levels in the United States ranging from K-12 to higher education and is further predicted to grow (U.S. Department of Education, 2010). Technology has, in many ways, become the vehicle that helps learners explore and create (Clemson University, 2010), and these technology tools are often available for free on the World Wide Web allowing educators and instructional designers the opportunity to design engaging learning, while also providing important technology training. Students can access tutorials, reading, podcasts, training, games, and simulations online, immersing in learning like never before – and when carefully designed, the instruction can accommodate each individual learner's specific need. This new classroom is not limited by the traditional brick and mortar walls (Fose & Mehl, 2007; Moore & Kearsley, 2005). It is fast, engaging, socially interactive, and often real-time.

> Many students' lives today are filled with technology that gives them mobile access to information and resources 24/7, enables them to create multimedia content and share it with the world, and allows them to participate in online social networks where people from all over the world share ideas, collaborate, and learn new things. Outside school, students are free to pursue their passions in their own way and at their own pace. The opportunities are limitless, borderless, and instantaneous. (U.S. Department of Education, 2010)

The online platform of the virtual world allows for social educational opportunities as well as new approaches to learning, communication, innovation, and entrepreneurship (Ondrejka, 2008). Experts in various fields may join efforts in virtual communities to share reusable documentation (Caprotti, Seppälä, & Pauna, 2007) and best practices. Educators and instructional designers collaborate with colleagues here, share ideas, assignments, and designs that work with the new generation of digital learners. Stiller and Dunbar (2007) have noted that an online participatory culture has evolved, claiming that a digital revolution has taken place.

One attempt to understand how far reaching this suggested revolution has spread took place at one university in the southwestern United States as three new islands in Linden Labs' Second Life (SL) were acquired in August 2009 as part of a University of Texas System grant under the Transforming Undergraduate Education (TUE) program. Each of the 16 universities and health institutions in the University of Texas System were provided three islands for the duration of a year – totaling 48 islands arranged in a virtual archipelago in order to provide visual interactive contiguity.

This chapter begins by examining how fostering a community of practice (CoP) was attempted using state-of-the-art instructional design strategies and models in a 3D virtual environment. Further, we review how this nascent program evolved in response to student, staff, and faculty needs by means of providing illuminative examples and a model for others to draw upon when developing immersive, collaborative learning environments. Our second model and example examines the designs and implementations of 3D learning modules utilized at both this university and at another local university where SL has been used with graduate students for learning and teaching.

EXAMPLE ONE: DESIGNING THE STUDENT SECOND LIFE SUCCESS PROGRAM

When designing the Student Second Life Success (SSLS) program – several learning theories were considered. The theoretical perspectives that guided the design and development of SSLS included social constructivism, communities of practice (CoPs), and Presence Pedagogy (P2). In addition, the designers examined other researchers' experiences and instructional designers with engaged learners who had designed both multiuser virtual environments (MUVE) for learning and online CoPs.

MUVE

Multiuser virtual environments are systems in which large number of online users may build digital spaces including the individual elements of the virtual world (i.e., buildings, vehicles, clothing), revising avatar appearance, and the development of other objects with which users can interact (i.e., notes, sales points, landscaping) (Warren & Jones, in press; Warren, Jones, & Trombley, 2011). In addition, these environments include communication tools to support coordination of in-world behaviors. For example, the open-access MUVE Second Life is one that has increasingly been the focus of research and is being employed at universities to support instruction and learning management systems (LMS) (De Lucia, Francese, Passero, & Tortora, 2009) and is commonly used as a supplementary communication and presentation tool. Some research indicates positive results at the postsecondary level related to increased student satisfaction, engagement, and overall enjoyment of a course (Jarmon, Traphagan, & Mayrath, 2008).

Other MUVEs, such as *ActiveWorlds*, have shown substantial promise to support learning, especially in K-12 environments. Three in particular have shown statistically significant results in terms of improving student learning for writing and science learning. These are *Anytown*, *River City*, and *Taiga* worlds, two of which were created under the auspices of the Quest Atlantis National Science Foundation project (Barab, Warren, & Ingram-Goble, 2008).

THEORETICAL FOUNDATION FOR THE STUDENT SECOND LIFE SUCCESS PROGRAM

Appalachian State University, an early adopter of 3D virtual worlds to support online instruction, developed a special pedagogy called Presence Pedagogy (P2). This pedagogy, based on social constructivism – a view in which "knowledge evolves through social negotiation and the viability of individual understandings" (Savery & Duffy, 1995, p. 2) – is one where learners actively, continuously, and as they become aware of one another, learn and grow together through knowledge sharing in a community. In this conception each learner becomes "a potential expert, instructor, peer, or novice" (Bronack et al., 2008).

In P2, the distinction between who is a teacher and who is a learner is blurred as each independently and all in concert contribute their specific knowledge to the collaborative community. Participatory learning and CoP were considered as the SSLS program was designed. Jenkins, Clinton, Purushotma, Robison, and Weigel (2006) defined participatory culture as "(one) with relatively low barriers to artistic expression and civic engagement, strong support for creating and sharing one's creations, and some type of informal mentorship whereby what is known by the most experienced is passed along to novices." In this conception, learning requires bringing about change through "experience and interaction between people and their environment" (Jones & Bronack, 2007, p. 93).

VIRTUAL COMMUNITIES OF PRACTICE

Second Life has several components in common with what has separately been suggested as supportive of CoPs (Lave & Wenger, 1991; Riel & Polin, 2004). Namely, this includes opportunities for legitimate peripheral participants (LPP) to witness or participate in activities, events, groups, and communities (Barab & Duffy, 2000; Barab, MaKinster, & Scheckler, 2004). Legitimate peripheral participation, as defined by Lave and Wenger (1991, p. 29), "provides a way to speak about the relations between newcomers and old-timers, and about activities, identities, artifacts, and communities of knowledge and practice."

In SL, residents engage in situated learning as they learn to create objects through building and scripting while observing and asking those more skilled (Ondrejka, 2008). Residents of virtual worlds are also encouraged to train one another, engage in knowledge sharing, communicate in real-time, and participate in synchronous discourse among both legitimate peripheral and core participants (Jones & Bronack, 2007, p. 92). However, as Barab et al. (2004) noted with the e-Inquiry Learning Forum (ILF), providing the technology tools alone is insufficient to establish a CoP and "that an online CoP requires a great deal more design up front than a face-to-face CoP (p. 22) … (t)here are literally thousands of design decisions that go into an online project as complex as the ILF and each of these decisions could be regarded as a limit – or a boon – to emergent community" (p. 23).

Therefore, the SSLS program was designed also with these practices and challenges in mind. To begin with, collaborative training was incorporated into the program, as well as weekly brown-bag lunches where avatars could meet in-world to train together and discuss project progress as a means of supporting participatory learning, also adding to the sense of community.

Schunk and Zimmerman (1998) suggest that seeing a successful model may encourage students in their belief that they can learn as well, helping build self-efficacy. Given that students entering the SSLS program would all be new to the SL environment, building opportunities for exposure to accurate models was especially important. These models may act as a form of simulation of skills and knowledge for the learners according to Aldrich (2003). The better they model reality, the better future student work and transfer of learned skills can be expected to be (Guetzkow, 1963; Horn, 1977).

CoPs often develop around specific activities or practices leading to completion of a task that matters to the community members (Jones & Bronack, 2007, p. 94). The small core development group consisted of the program coordinator, also trainer and instructional designer, and the volunteer students working toward a final showcase event, which presented the developed content designed for their clients (we shortly return to explain the student/client work). At the end of the program, the showcase was a way for the students to present, both to the larger university community and to the global community of SL, what they had accomplished. Thus, students were training and building skills on how to use the virtual environment with this showcase as a goal and means of presenting their materials for public critique, this last step having been shown necessary for CoPs to be sustained and be qualified as supporting education (Moore & Barab, 2002).

Baker (2008) states that for learning to take place in virtual spaces, students need to make connections and give the instructor feedback of their understanding. Therefore, the instructional design included weekly training sessions during which time the designer trained volunteer students in the use of SL building tools and strategies. In addition, the design included training from experts around the world who are experienced with teaching in this environment. They were invited to teach specific techniques to students and the larger university community. The built-in synchronous voice tool in SL allows for communication over a client-server Voice-over-IP (VoIP) system and therefore VoIP was included as a tool to support collaboration within the environment. It was chosen as a component both to provide the instructor with a means of communicating and conducting direct instruction and to aid students as they had questions and worked to help one another, supporting the fostering of a CoP centered on learning to use SL and using it to teach and learn (Fig. 1).

For an online community to become successful, its infrastructure administration needs to be considered (Butler, Sproull, Kiesler, & Kraut, 2002). This was considered when prototyping the program and involved installing and maintaining a group communication system. SL allows for the use of a variety of communication tools that are built into the user interface:

- local text-based chat
- private channel instant message (IM)
- group text chat
- voice calls

The voice feature can be used in the local environment as well as inside a channel with a group or between two residents privately. Using the voice and text tools, SL residents can communicate synchronously. The built-in synchronous voice tool in SL is powered by Vivox, and is used by 52% of SL residents as per Monty Sharma, marketing director of Vivox (personal communication, September 20, 2010). Voice makes a good tool for in-world interviews, in-world training, meetings, language practice, and presentations. For example, Henderson, Huang, Grant, and Henderson (2009) reported that students engaged in collaborative food-ordering activities using Mandarin language in a virtual Chinese restaurant, showed significant

Fig. 1. Students Learning Building Block Linking and Coloring from an Invited Instructor Using VoIP.

increase in their self-efficacy beliefs in using the language also in a real-world setting. In our study, we found that when using VoIP during training sessions feedback to students was made faster. Students did not have to wait for typed feedback and thereby "dead-time" was avoided. Students reported they felt very comfortable using voice as well as listening to the instructors using voice.

To support asynchronous communication, community network needs and social needs of in-world learners, special interest groups were used such as the "Development" group through which others within this specific community were reached by means of notifications. These notifications were used to cross-distribute information from within the virtual world to outside the system. Further, it is possible to reach group members' e-mail with, for example, event information. Interconnecting and reaching out to other educational community groups and networks through communication mechanisms can be done through building *social systems* in the virtual world (Dawley, 2009). Being part of educational groups other than the own group, and being able to use notifications in these other groups, is a way to reach out to other residents of the world in a viral way. Using these channels information sharing and announcements about upcoming SSLS events in-world was greatly facilitated.

The SSLS program was developed using rapid prototyping. This is a technique following the analysis, design, development, implementation, and evaluation steps included in the ADDIE instructional design model (Bichelmeyer, 2005; Molenda, 2003). However, the design and development in the rapid prototyping model are often concurrent rather than step-by-steps, therefore speeding up the design. In rapid prototyping, development is done early in the design process, toward the end of the analysis stage (Tripp & Bichelmeyer, 1990). Using this technique, it was possible to develop the entire program during the two-week winter break at the end of 2009 and for the program to be approved and immediately launched early January 2010 (Fig. 2).

While designing and developing, it was kept in mind that students, learning within the context of a virtual world and working for clients, must also learn important concepts of problem solving. Taking this approach allows learners to be immersed in the learning experience (Warren & Jones, 2008). The nascent program focused on volunteering students in a CoP collaborating with campus clients (Lave & Wenger, 1991). Each learns the emerging technology, engages in real-world projects, collaborates with clients (e.g., administrators, faculty, and staff), and builds virtual content. The campus clients were found in various departments of the university.

The instructional design included an infrastructure to support communicating information regarding events such as training sessions and presentations. In addition, these structures allowed for posting notifications on the official SL events listing website, Twitter, blogging, and mailing lists

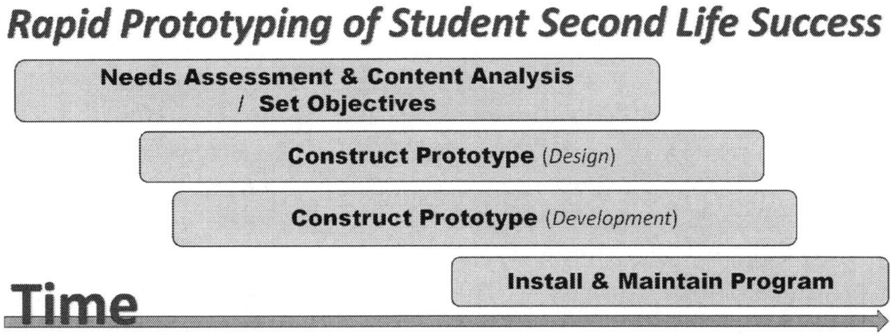

Fig. 2. Rapid Prototyping of Student Second Life Success.
Source: Adapted from Tripp and Bichelmeyer (1990).

such as Second Life Educators (SLED), Second Life Research List (SLRL), and a specially created Microsoft Outlook group for the campus participants and others who had expressed interest in being added. Notifications of larger events were posted to the university events calendar. These included:

- on-site presentations shared in-world
- streamed seminar
- final student showcase.

Using these communication systems and resources allowed participants from as far away as Australia to attend real-time virtual training sessions and presentations in Texas. Only the time difference provided an attendance obstacle for those far away.

Butler et al. (2002) state that active participation is necessary and that providing and consuming content is a must for sustaining online groups. Further, good community design takes into consideration the opinion from not only the community but also people outside of the community. To invite both "insiders" and "outsiders" in a dialog about what the community is to achieve and how the community can best be designed (Lave & Wenger, 1991), the instructional design included a website[1] for visibility featuring a timeline of offered activities. In addition, the design provided communication tools such as an e-mail list for the community, a Twitter feed, a Flickr account for image sharing, and Google Docs feedback forms. The last mentioned was linked to mailboxes on the virtual islands allowing visitors to send questions and provide feedback on their virtual island experience.

Skills classes in various topics, such as building, avatar management, scripting, and avatar animations, were offered at various days and times to meet diverse student needs. Several presentations were also intertwined on the timeline making professional development a part of the program and available to a larger audience. One such presenter was Dr. Robert J. Sternberg who presented at the university and was simultaneously streamed through his avatar to the university's virtual island auditorium. This presentation was attended by 22 people in-world, in addition to the filled campus auditorium. The SSLS website held information about all the offered programs and included the timeline of events. It supported the program with links both in the virtual (in-world) and with useful SL-related Internet resources. As the SSLS program launched, the designers believed that it was equipped with the blueprint necessary for building a successful community.

FINDINGS FROM ILLUMINATIVE EXAMPLE ONE

Gall, Gall, and Borg (2010) state that phenomenological studies require extensive data collection of the specific instance studied to exemplify an in-depth of the studied case. This phenomenological study focused on students' motivation in their volunteer work with campus clients while building community in the virtual environment and was approved by the institutional review board at the university. We sought to learn to what extent undergraduate students would be motivated and engaged to complete a volunteer technology-based program working with campus clients, and after completion, from their perspective, how successful they felt they were in the program. Further, we were interested to learn to what extent it would be possible to develop and sustain a CoP in the SSLS program that would roll on past the program completion and continue at the institution in the virtual setting.

The participants in this study were four volunteer undergraduate students interested in learning the emerging technology of virtual worlds, working with campus clients, and building their work portfolio. Students were recruited through an advertisement campaign on campus. Flyers were distributed and classroom visits were made where information about the program was shared. Three of the students were males from the computer science and engineering programs and one female was from the arts and humanities program. All four students were new to SL.

At the end of the program students were asked to take a post survey, participate in a post interview, and we also conducted field observations throughout the program as means of gathering data (Fig. 3).

Six differently designed flyers were distributed around campus to recruit participants to the program. One example is illustrated on the following page. The reverse side of the flyer held program information.

Students met both online and on campus with their respective clients on their individual projects. They also met with the trainer on building and scripting in the virtual learning techniques to use as they worked on their projects and in preparation for their showcase event. Training sessions were offered 19 times throughout the duration of the program and were more frequently held in the beginning of the program to build student skills early on and for them to later have more time to work on their respective projects. All four students felt the training sessions were appropriate for their individual needs while working for their clients. However, one of the students noted at the end of the program that he would have liked to have had a little bit more time between finishing his campus classes for the day

Fig. 3. Ad Campaign.

and attending workshops in-world. As it was, he had to rush home so that he wouldn't miss sessions. He commented: "I would have liked the SSLS program to start outside the school's semester and finished training before classes started. I felt like a bit off more than I could chew. The training sessions often conflicted with class attendance or class' homework."

This comment reminds us how important the audience analysis is when designing volunteer programs that are not otherwise tied to a student's class schedule.

Volunteering, actively participating people who are motivated to serve, feeling commitment to the community and the cause, are important ingredients of a community (Butler et al., 2002). Wenger, McDermott, and Snyder (2002) describe how CoPs are successful over time because they are made up of volunteers who together generate a "spark" or "aliveness." Wenger et al. say this comes from collaboratively generating excitement, relevance, and value – components not easily designed. Collins' study on efficacy in students (as cited in Bandura, 1997) shows that belief in own efficacy and positive attitudes toward the task at hand highly contributes to student success. We found that much can be accomplished with and by motivated and engaged volunteers. From the post survey and the interviews it was found that the students ranked themselves highly on motivation during the duration of the program – an average of 7.5 on a 10-point scale was noted. Three of the four students stated that the main reasons for joining the program was because they were interested in building portfolio as well as being interested in learning the technology. Fifty percent of the students listed the reasons for joining as "to challenge myself" and "wanted to experience working with campus clients." Though the number of students that participated in the program was low, it appears those that did so attended because they wanted to stretch themselves a bit further in their educational endeavor while also being able to work with real-world projects (for the campus clients) producing a piece of work they could add to their portfolio.

Students were all satisfied with the support they had received from their clients. In semi-structured interviews, all four students expressed that they felt their contributions significantly added to their respective portfolios. One student excitedly answered the question "Will the SSLS experience contribute to your portfolio?" with: "Yes, definitely. It's gonna' (sic) be pretty much like, a big part of it because I can say that I helped this project take off and at the end …I can say I participated in this, so that is really exciting!"

Another student was less certain as he felt his work had not been as significant as he would have liked it to be. He felt he had not put in as much time toward the end as he should have due to other obligations, leaving his final project somewhat unfinished.

Field observations further confirmed that the students were highly motivated and engaged in their work. For example, one of the students who was familiar with other virtual environments was quickly self-taught the skills he needed to work on the virtual assignment for his client. He only attended a couple of training sessions. The other three students attended sessions regularly even though these were not mandatory. All four students felt the training sessions were appropriate to what they were to work on for their clients. They also individually sought out and met with the instructional designer to get clarification on the building components of their client-stipulated assignment. All students reported positive attitudes toward their work in the virtual throughout the program, though toward the end of the program some exhaustion was noted. This was expected and planned for in the program design resulting in a requirement that the program to conclude two and half week before finals, so not to burden the volunteers, and help ensure their success with work completion.

While students had met in-world during workshops and training sessions, they only met in the physical world for the first time in an informal focus group toward the end of the program when preparing for the final showcase event. They all concurred that they would have liked to have met in the physical world earlier in the program to connect and "work more together" even though they did work on individual projects. It is suggested for future implementations of similar programs to include more "face-time" meetings to allow for students to informally talk to each other about their projects and thereby motivate each other as well as add to the sense of community.

One of the intentions of the SSLS program was to create a CoP (Wenger et al., 2002) that would continue and grow over time bringing faculty and more students onboard – the community that emerged, however, was in fact a hybrid of two community types described by Riel and Polin (2004) as *Task-Based Learning Community* and *Practice-Based Community*. In a Task-Based Community, Riel and Polin explain, members are often classroom students assigned to participate and may almost be seen as *tourists* (p. 26). Thus, according to Riel and Polin, they are not true members in the sense that they are part of a sustaining community; instead, they are working to create a finished product – and once the product is complete the community disbands (p. 33).

The SSLS group did indeed work toward a final goal – the showcase event – but unlike the members of a Task-Based Community, the SSLS community was made up of volunteers, bringing it closer to Riel and Polin's description of the volunteer-based Practice-Based Community and Wenger et al.'s (2002) CoP. In the Practice-Based Community, like in the SSLS community, members work and learn together through social activities such as meetings, training sessions, and discussions. In a sense, the SSLS community could have been a true CoP had the practice captured attention from more university students and faculty wanting to participate and contribute. Then the core of the group, the students and the trainer, also instructional designer, would have been able to provide the help and support needed for newcomers to seamlessly join. This did, however, not happen and the community disbanded. A recommendation for future community builders would be to heavily promote and advertise the new community and further build on the excitement around participation to allow it to grow throughout the initial implementation and past the critical start-up phase.

Lessons Learned

- *Principle One:* Create opportunities for sustaining virtual community beyond a task
- *Principle Two:* Provide social communication opportunities to participants
- *Principle Three:* Promote and advertise new community to leverage excitement
- *Principle Four:* Leverage participant experience with new technology to experiment

EXAMPLE TWO: DESIGNING SL 6100

In the second example, an assistant professor at another large university in the American Southwest redesigned a doctoral level course to include the use of SL as a means not only of delivering instruction, but also to interrogate the learning affordances present within SL. During the spring of 2010, the professor used the virtual tool for virtual office hours to support the distributed, online students in both the masters and doctoral program. This research study, however, focuses only on his construction of learning activities in support of his doctoral course "Theory and Practice of Distance Education." The course introduces students to the past, present, and the future of distance-delivered education including the use of virtual worlds, games, simulations, and social media tools.

Theoretical Framework for the Design

The first stage of design was to construct learning activities for the course that fit with the professor's personal view of teaching and learning similar to Savery and Duffy's (1995) view. Specifically, he believes that "knowledge evolves through social negotiation and the viability of individual understandings" (p. 2) where communication between student and peers as well as student and instructor is responsible for the construction of knowledge. Therefore, learning activities in a classroom or online setting must be geared toward generating learner dialogs. It is also only through the repeated study of discourse that emerges from such interactions among students and between students and instructor that allows understanding the acts of teaching and learning.

Social Constructivist Principles Guiding Design

The criteria used to guide the instructional design followed Savery and Duffy's (1995) instructional design principles. Specifically, these are:

- Anchor all learning activities to a larger task or problem.
- Support the learner in developing ownership for the overall problem or task.
- Design an authentic task.
- Design the task and the learning environment to reflect the complexity of the environment they should be able to function in at the end of learning.
- Give the learner ownership of the process used to develop a solution.
- Design the learning environment to support and challenge the learner's thinking.
- Encourage testing ideas against alternative views and alternative contexts.
- Provide opportunity for and support reflection on both the content learned and the learning process (pp. 3–6).

Within the doctoral level distributed learning course, students were immersed in SL as a means of challenging students from a critical thinking, problem solving, and design perspective. Problem solving, as defined by Smith and Ragan (2005) is "the ability to combine previously learned principles, procedures, declarative knowledge, and cognitive strategies in a unique way within a domain of content to solve previously un-encountered problems" (p. 218).

Ill-Structured Versus Well-Structured Problems

There is a difference between well-structured and ill-structured problems; namely, well-structured problem-solving exercises are best approached by the instructional designer using information processing theory while ill-structured problems best are approached with the model for ill-structured problem solving as well as constructivist and situated cognition (Jonassen, 1997, p. 65). Well-structured problems are textbook problems that only have one correct answer. Ill-structured problems are the everyday problems that have no correct answer or are in fact not a problem at all – only perceived as such. Faber, Mazlish, Nyberg, and Templeton (2003) point out that feedback and scaffolds provided along with the ill-structured problems help build self-efficacy and intrinsic motivation. This kind of learning develops students into self-regulatory learners with a much higher potential for learning problem solving as well as for transferring learning. It is important to keep in mind that ill-structured problems may provide as many answers as there are problem solvers depending on perception: "You give the same design problem to three different people and you get three different designs … (or,) you show your design to three different people, then you get three different evaluations of that design" (Jonassen, 2006).

Scaffolding Learning
Taking on what Clark Aldrich (2009, p. 88) calls a "tough-love" approach, the professor asks students to enter SL and to "figure it out themselves." However, where this design differed is that the professor also included embedded supports that Brush and Saye refer to as "hard scaffolds" (2001). Further, he was present with the students to provide what the same authors refer to as "soft scaffolds"; specifically, this meant additional direction, troubleshooting, help with the learning environment, and challenging poor knowledge constructions.

The two-week SL lesson design of the course was meant to have learners interrogate and analyze the usefulness of SL as a means of supporting distributed instruction. The large learning goal for the lesson was to have students synthesize what they had read and discussed in previous weeks and then analyze the digital tool from three different epistemic learning perspectives drawn from Prawat and Floden's (1994) constructivist constructs. This included the mechanistic, information processing view, the organismic, radical constructivist view, and the contextualist or social constructivist view.

DESIGNED LEARNING COMPONENTS

The overall experience included two main parts: *Orientation* and an *Experience of* SL. In the Orientation part, learners would be exposed through immersion in the SL Orientation constructed by Linden Labs. In the Experience of SL part, learners would be required to examine SL through Prawat and Floden's (1994) lenses to determine the learning affordances of the MUVE as they would support each perspective.

Orientation to the Virtual Environment

The first requirement for the course module was to download the SL viewer, sign up for an account, and go through the orientation at least a day ahead of a mandatory in-world meeting held on ISTE – International Society for Technology in Education – island (ISTE Island 144, 148, 26). During the meeting, students used voice and text chat with the instructor and peers and got an opportunity to ask questions about the assignment they were about to embark upon. Two opportunities to meet with the instructor (120–180 minutes each) were provided to accommodate student availability to participate in this introductory meeting. The specific learning goals, objectives, activities, and scaffolds for the Orientation activities are presented in Table 1.

Once students had completed the Orientation, the expectation was that each had the rudimentary skills needed to navigate through and communicate in SL. For the next learning experience, the students were given the directions as shown in Fig. 4.

Experience of Second Life Activity

There were three main components to the Experience of SL activity. Each was intended to challenge learners to think about the use of SL to support instructional and learning goals from the three main epistemic perspectives that have been described in the previous class meetings. These included the (1) mechanistic or Empiricist view, (2) contextualist view, and (3) relativist view.

Mechanistic View Activity

For the first Experience of SL activity, the main meta-learning goal was to ask learners to examine how SL could be used to support instruction and learning from a mechanistic, objectivist, or Empiricist epistemic view of learning in which knowledge is reified and something to be acquired as depicted by Sfard (1998). In order to support this goal, students were asked to experience learning from this perspective and then draw their own conclusions about how learning could be supported and instruction

Table 1. Orientation Goals, Objectives, Activities, and Scaffolds.

	Learning Goals	Sample Learning Objectives	Sample Learning Activities	Sample Learning Scaffolds
Orientation	The Learner will (TLW)	TLW locate HOME, END, PgUp, and PgDn buttons on the keyboard.		*Hard scaffold*: TxDLA Second Life essentials training manual.
	Be familiar with the user interface of Second Life.		TLW follow Orientation Island virtual sign directions in SL given to fly.	
		TLW select appropriate buttons to demonstrate ability to fly.		*Soft scaffold:* Instructor was present to give clarifying directions.
			TLW follow Orientation Island virtual sign directions in SL given to find different locations.	*Hard scaffold:* TXDLA Second Life essentials training manual.
		TLW identify keys on keyboard and UI controls for avatar movement.		
			TLW follow Orientation Island virtual sign directions in SL given to leave Orientation Island.	*Soft scaffold*: Instructor was present to lead students on virtual trail.
	TLW be competent with navigating in SL.	TLW demonstrate ability to move the avatar along the trail.		

Table 1. *(Continued)*

Learning Goals	Sample Learning Objectives	Sample Learning Activities	Sample Learning Scaffolds
	TLW identify and select UI button for in-world text chat.		
	TLW compose text in local chat.	TLW follow Orientation Island directions to reply to the trainer chat.	*Hard scaffold:* TXDLA Second Life essentials training manual.
TLW be competent with SL communication tools.			
	TLW respond to trainer chat.	TLW follow Orientation Island directions to reply to peers and instructor.	*Soft scaffold:* Instructor provided VoIP directions for students who could not communicate.
	TLW respond to classmates in local chat.		

designed. Table 2 presents the goals, objectives, and learning activities that were provided to learners which included framing using Bloom's Taxonomy to keep the perspective and constructions authentic.

Students were expected to examine the SL simulations with their specific media and learning affordances (Gibson, 1977) and challenges intact as any first-time user would experience them. Frustration was expected initially to be a part of the experience; however, this has been theorized by Savery and Duffy (1995) as necessary to allow the instructor to challenge poorly formed knowledge constructions. Further, it was found to be necessary to support student learning in problem-based learning environments such as the *Anytown* MUVE game (Warren, Dondlinger, Stein, & Barab, 2009) because it allows the designer to predict when students will have trouble with knowledge constructions or learning environment issues and provide hard

Tonight, you will have three separate activities, taking approximately 30 minutes each.
Begin at **EdTech Island**, since it's quiet.
Below this post are three sets of directions and I would like you to proceed through the designs in order:

1. Objectivist/Empiricist Designed Lesson
2. Subjectivist/social constructivist Designed Lesson
3. Relativist/radical constructivist Designed Lesson

Upon concluding the three lessons, head back to **EdTech Island**.
We'll have a brief 10-15 minute debrief afterwards.
Before next week, post your responses on the Forum as well and discuss there in more detail with your peers.

Fig. 4. Directions Given to Students Prior to Entering Second Life.

and soft scaffolds before they become a problem. Simulations are rarely perfect; therefore, it is important to allow students to figure things out themselves, which provides them the opportunity to think deeply about their experience. In addition, they may express their thoughts using available communication tools (Aldrich, 2009).

Contextualist View Activity

According to Cennamo and Kalk (2005), instructional design is never a process that happens in isolation but is a collaborative effort between the client and the designer, an interpersonal interaction where ideas and often ill-structured problems need be discussed and negotiated. The social interactions that take place in the teams, as students discuss the design they are immersed within at the different simulations, are designed to help students describe learning context in which they identify instructional problems, articulate thoughts, reflect on others' ideas, and negotiate the answers. Bonner (1998) points out that the core of "Instructional Design is about making learning relevant and efficient and about making teaching effective." Experiencing the design and using problem-solving methodologies within the simulation help students understand these concepts in a more real and immersed way and allows for close transfer of skills and knowledge to future student work (Warren & Dondlinger, 2008) and from design project to design project.

Though the assignment required searching and several hours of environment construction by the instructor to locate or build places for students to visit, Jones and Warren (2011, in press) state: "Constructivist

Table 2. Experience of Second Life Mechanistic Goals, Objectives, and Learning Activities.

	Learning Goals	Sample Learning Objectives	Sample Learning Activities
Experience of Second Life	The learner will (TLW) understand the basic features of a science simulation.	The learner will (TLW) understand and be able to recite the basic rules and norms/standing orders of the Star Trek simulation. The learner will locate and record Seven of Nine's data.	To begin, teleport to: http://slurl.com/secondlife/TovaDok%20II/25/211/35
			Wait until the sim loads completely. This is important as it may crash your SL instance if you do not.
			Activity 1: Find the "standing orders" in the room you first come upon. Write them down. How are these similar or different from those you might find in a school or other learning setting? Write that down as well. Post these in the Moodle LMS where it says: O1-Act-1.
	TLW analyze the structures of a complex simulation designed from an objectivist/Empiricist/mechanistic viewpoint that is set in an experiential learning mode.	The learner will understand basic concepts about physics explored in Star Trek.	*Activity 2*: Find Seven of Nine. If you don't know who she is, look her up on a search engine. Write down whatever she has to tell you. Post this information in Moodle LMS where it says: O1-Act-2.
			Activity 3: Locate the movie room showing "Star Trek with a Physicist." Watch the film and take notes on the content presented here. Post your notes in

Table 2. (*Continued*)

Learning Goals	Sample Learning Objectives	Sample Learning Activities
		Moodle where it says: O1-Act-3. Exit the building.
	The learner will be able to produce the correct answers to test questions.	*Assessment:* Take the test in the Moodle LMS regarding this content.
TLW be able to complete a brief assessment related to the information contained in the SL sim that they acquire during the three activities.		
		Answer the following questions: 1. What is the highest lettered enterprise? 2. The in-world presenter tool is slow. 3. The person doing the Star Trek sim is a physicist (true/false). 4. Can you go faster than the speed of light? 5. What simulation do you find near Seven of Nine and Picard? 6. (Bonus) What is the main form of instruction in the Star Trek sim?

environments … require certain amount of time in order to be successful." In this assignment, students are allowed to spend as much time as they deem necessary to complete the exercise removing any stress, as groups get to determine when they want to get together to complete the assignment. The instructor was present in the virtual environment to act as facilitator and

Table 3. Experience of Second Life Contextualist Activities and Scaffolds.

	Learning Goals	Constructivist Principles	Sample Learning Activities	Sample Learning Scaffolds
Experience of Second Life	Established by learner groups in response to the problem.	1. Give the learner ownership of the process used to develop a solution.	Directions for social constructivist lesson design experience. Teleport to: http://slurl.com/secondlife/Virtual%20NLM/130/145/25 You must self-organize into four person teams immediately. You have less than five minutes to do so.	*Soft scaffold:* Instructor was present to support self-organization.
		2. Anchor all learning activities to a larger task or problem.	Explore the region quickly and identify the major problems simulated here. How you do so is up to you.	*Soft scaffold:* Instructor was present to help students locate problems.
		3. Design the task and the learning environment to reflect the complexity of the environment they should be able to function in at the end of learning.		
		4. Provide opportunity for and support reflection on both the content learned and the learning process.	Given the serious challenges in this sim, choose one major problem. In your small group, generate a solution that would leverage a distance communication or	*Soft scaffold:* Instructor challenged group knowledge constructions.

Table 3. *(Continued)*

Learning Goals	Constructivist Principles	Sample Learning Activities	Sample Learning Scaffolds
		education solution that everyone agrees upon.	
	5. Design the learning environment to support and challenge the learner's thinking.	Meet back at the original entrance to the area at 10 PM.	
	6. Encourage testing ideas against alternative views and alternative contexts.	Each group will have two minutes to present their solution.	
	7. Design an authentic task.	After our session tonight, post it in the social constructivist solution forum of the Moodle LMS to continue the discussion and reflect on the experience in your blog.	
	8. Anchor all learning activities to a larger task or problem.		

coach, but not as a conveyor of reified knowledge to be acquired, as in the first activity (Table 3).

Team members were asked to choose a leader within the group to coordinate discourse regarding the questions and capture the discussion for further asynchronous discourse in the Moodle LMS. This was to support the idea that "Just as viewing the perspectives of others appears to be essential to the formulation of ill-structured problems, having one's proposed solutions challenged by others, and defending and revising them accordingly, is crucial to the problem resolution phase" (Murphy, 2004).

On the LMS, other groups were expected to challenge the posted solutions and knowledge constructions, further the discussion, and to compare experiences as a means of constructing socially validated knowledge.

Table 4. "Experience of Second Life" Relativist Constructivist Activities, and Scaffolds.

	Learning Goals	Sample Learning Activities	Sample Learning Scaffolds
Experience of Second Life	Established by the learner individually	What do you want to learn?	*Soft scaffold:* Instructor was present to support student learning information seeking.
		Do a search in Google and see if there is anything in SL related to it.	
		Write yourself two learning goals related to this topic.	*Soft scaffold:* Instructor was present to challenge construction of learning goals, objectives, and activities as well as the individual knowledge constructions that emerged from the completed activities.
		Write supporting learning objectives you would like to reach in support of the larger goals.	
		Describe 2–3 learning activities you will engage in within SL to learn.	

Table 4. *(Continued)*

	Learning Goals	Sample Learning Activities	Sample Learning Scaffolds
		Describe how you will evaluate your own learning success.	*Soft scaffold:* Instructor challenged learner individual knowledge constructions and evaluation methods.
		Complete these activities and write a § page description of your experience and evaluate your success.	
		Post this to the Moodle LMS where it says: My radical constructivist learning experience.	

For this particular experience, the National Library of Medicine simulation Tox Town (Tox Town, 129, 145, 25) was leveraged to allow students to explore ill-structured problems present in the simulation. The island provided examples of real-world problems such as a pile of burning car tires, a helicopter landing point next to a power line, a trash can with toxic waste on the beach, etc. Each problem posed within the sim has an information kiosk associated with it; that kiosk is clickable and provides additional information in addition to contributing visual context and immersive feel.

Relativist View Activity

For the last activity, learners were expected to examine the environment from a relativist or radical constructivist view. Namely, they were asked to enter the ill-structured environment and set their own learning goals, objectives, activities, and means of assessment. This was expected to give students the experience of attempting to design individualized learning experiences from this perspective while, at the same time, understanding the affordances of the environment that could be used to support learners from this challenging perspective. Table 4 shows the directions provided to the learners.

RESEARCH METHODS

As stated by Herring (2004), research should be motivated by a relevant question "based on prior observation" (p. 346). Further, she notes that a good question has four characteristics:

1. It is empirically answerable from the available data,
2. It is nontrivial,
3. It is motivated by a hypothesis, and
4. It is open-ended.

Therefore, the following research questions were generated:

- What challenges do first-time users of online virtual worlds face when seeking to use them for educational purposes?
- What supports are perceived by learners to be present in online virtual worlds that support student learning?

Participants and Setting

The participants that completed the assignments were all of the students in the doctoral course. Of the eight students, five were female and three were male. Demographically, the group included two Asian, one Kuwaiti, four white, and one student who classified herself as "other." Students ranged in age from 26 to 58 and two self-identified as being nonnative English speakers. Six of the eight had taught either in K-12 or college settings for at least 5 years, with two having taught for more than 15 years. Participants met online each of the weeks in Linden Labs' SL multiuser virtual environment (MUVE) and posted their thoughts and information in the course Moodle LMS asynchronous discussion forums. Due to the distributed nature of the course, each participant's physical location ranged from within the local city limits where the course is taught to one student being in California for the duration of the research.

Data Collection Methods

Data was collected by gathering student responses and reflections to the learning activities, which were posted to the asynchronous threaded LMS discussion forums. Data from a word processing document was then copied line-by-line into a spreadsheet. All data was gathered by the professor as part of the Scholarship of Teaching and Learning (Bass, 1999) in order to provide the professor with feedback on his instructional methods and student experiences with his instructional designs for future improvement of the course.

Data Analysis Methods

The collected utterances of the participants were analyzed following Herring's (2004) Computer-Mediated Discourse Analysis (CMDA) procedures. A three-person research team analyzed the computer-mediated communication (CMC) that occurred during the two-week collection period. Each researcher first conducted separate analyses of the discussion forum data following methods suggested by Boyatzis (1998) and Denzin and Lincoln (2003). The analysis took place using two raters who sought comprehensive agreement through constant-comparison of low-inference codes generated independently by each coder. The researchers then jointly built consensus by sharing their codes and reasoning with each other until agreement was reached. Codes were then consolidated into categories. These categories were analyzed by the group of researchers collectively to identify themes (Boyatzis, 1998). A third researcher reviewed the outcomes of the process and served to coordinate triangulation of the data and to ensure that rigor and trustworthiness were maintained. The codes were classified into larger categories. Those categories that had sufficient numerical support in terms of percentage of lines coded in support were then collapsed into larger themes generated by the entire group. Students have each been assigned code names for this research report.

FINDINGS FROM ILLUMINATIVE EXAMPLE TWO

Each major finding in this example includes a table with categories, codes, and overall themes in the form of guidelines for designers and instructors to be aware of when using SL with postsecondary students. In this case, however, we focus especially on older learners in graduate school settings.

From our Example One we earlier reported four emerging principles. Seven additional principles emerged here as a result of our Example Two analysis. All these principles may be used to help moderate any trouble instructors or students may face when leveraging this and other virtual worlds.

CODING SCHEME

A total of 179 lines were coded and 71 discrete codes emerged from student statements. Some lines included multiple codes with 597 separate instances being coded. A code with fewer than three lines associated with it was eliminated, leaving 47 validated codes and 573 separate instances in total. The codes ranged from technical challenges faced within the 3D world to suggestions for how the SL environment could better be used to support learning. These codes were then classified into categories agreed upon by the analysts.

FINDINGS

There were several categories that emerged from grouping the emergent codes. These five categories included (1) technical challenges, (2) benefits of virtual worlds, (3) learning and instruction challenges, (4) learning experience shared, and (5) informational. Each category with those codes that make it up is presented in Tables 5–9. Also provided in the tables is the number of instances counted for each code in order to produce the approximate percentage of the total number of instances coded that the category represents. In addition to the categories, explanations, and examples provided after each table, we also note one or more lessons learned from the experience from our research study. We discuss each category below and our discussion is followed by the principle that emerged from the analysis.

Category: Informational

The largest category included codes in which students engaged in *Exposition* or revealed their location through sharing of a Second Life URL (*SLURL*), with these two codes making up the bulk of the instances in this category.

Table 5. Informational Category with Codes and Total Instances.

Category	*Codes Included (10)*	*Count*
Informational		
	Content area shared	18
	Information (useful) present	26
	SLURL	15
	Exposition/location	71
	Information gathering activity	13
	Outside info	15
	How time is spent on activities in-world	18
	Speaker is ESL participant	4
	Humor	5
	External theory referenced	7
	Total instances coded for category	**192 (33.5)**

Table 6. Benefits of Virtual Worlds Category with Codes and Total Instances.

Category	*Code Included (11)*	*Count*
Benefits of VW		
	High value sim for learning	15
	Value of SL for distance learning (DL)	6
	Positive environmental design	10
	Positive experience	24
	Learned skill/knowledge	36
	Fun	3
	Teaching benefit	18
	Use of communication tools	10
	Successful exploration	13
	Suggested learning benefit of SL	16
	Immersive experience	12
	Total instances coded for category	**163 (28.5%)**

In addition, students made references to useful information they found, noted links to *outside information*, or gave general information about how they spent time in SL that was unrelated to the learning activities (*How time is spent on activities in-world*).

In some instances, students also referred to external theories to provide context for what they were discussing or making connections with for the

Table 7. Learning and Instruction Challenge Category with Codes and Total Instances.

Category	*Codes Included (12)*	*Count*
Learning and instruction challenges		
	Training needed	6
	Experience needed	7
	Instructor help	3
	Unsuccessful exploration	3
	Concerns about VW	9
	Teaching problem	4
	Empty SL/No people	3
	Follows instructor direction	3
	Navigation failure	5
	Comprehension problem	7
	Learning curve challenge	8
	Info gather fail	32
	Total instances coded for category	**90 (15.7%)**

Table 8. Learning Experience Shared Category with Codes and Total Instances.

Category	*Codes Included (8)*	*Count*
Learner experience shared		
	Justification by student	50
	Beginning XP	5
	XP comparison	4
	Navigation success	3
	Persistence for success	3
	Comparing FTF and VW	3
	Learning improvement suggestion	9
	Group work (negative value)	3
	Total instances coded for category	**80 (14.0%)**

course requirements. These codes provided context, but had the least impact on the learning activities.

Principle Five: Expect your learners to go off-task; be prepared for students to need to express nonrelevant information so that they can contextualize their own learning and make it meaningful to them.

Table 9. Technical Challenge Category with Codes and Total Instances.

Category	*Codes Included (6)*	*Count*
Technical challenge		
	User interface efficiency problem	10
	Technical problems	14
	Bandwidth problems	3
	Movement (in-world) problems	8
	Interaction problems	10
	Search problem	3
	Total instances coded for category	**48 (8.4%)**

Category: Benefits Of Virtual Worlds

This category includes the largest number of coded references that tied to the specific instructions that had been provided to the learners. These directions required student evaluation of the affordances of SL as a tool for learning and instruction. Students specifically discussed the benefits they perceived coming from SL as a whole as well as noting individual in-world SL tools (i.e., voice, text chat) they noted would be valuable for either instruction or independent learning. Also importantly, they reported *Fun* or *Positive Experiences* that could be leveraged for future instruction.

Both the *Teaching Benefit* and *Use of Communication Tools* codes are exemplified by Bill's statement that, "One good point to mention about Second Life is that users can hold a voice conversation which is a new feature that allows users to talk to each other." The largest number of codes fell under *learned skill/knowledge* and included particular knowledge and skills that students acquired during their experience in SL. For example, Jane noted that, "I searched economics as well but it was very disappointing" while Tara reported that, "I did learn how to land without falling on my face ...."

Some reports included learning in SL that was tied to larger concepts. These students connected to theoretical frames that the professor provided such as when Walter reported:

> On this island I experienced three of the four parts of Learning and Teaching as Communicative Action Theory: Strategic, Normative, and Dramaturgical. Strategic communication occurred for me every time I read a sign or followed directions that SL/island gave me. Constantive *(sic)* communication might have occurred for me if I would have scheduled an appointment for a tour. The environment of SL provides the user with

> the normative communication so that he/she understands what is acceptable and possible in on the island. Of course Second Life would not be successful if it was not for the Dramaturgical aspect of the communication experience.

Thus, the experience and use of the virtual world allowed Walter to connect theory and practice in a way that may not have easily occurred through other means. Tied to this positive experience, several students also conveyed *High value of* a particular SL sim for learning or otherwise had differing *Values SL for* distance learning (DL). For example, Walter followed his previous statement with, "I enjoyed the well thought design and how the different environments complimented each other" while John noted that "I think that learning could be scaled up with either student (me) training or more experience using the software … I had fun trying out the technology."

However, he also stated "It is easy to see how a teacher could lose students during class." Roger summed up his thinking that, "In Second Life, because of the space is persistent, virtual field trips, museums, and replicas and simulations of real-life places are all possible. Real-world physical handicaps are sometimes minimized, enabling equitable participation. In conclusion, I think Second Life can be used to mimic traditional educational environments; for example, classrooms or museums."

Principle Six: Virtual worlds allow for participation in learning activities that may not otherwise be possible; take advantage of those affordances to both innovate and replicate traditional instructional methods.

Category: Learning and Instruction Challenge

Codes falling within the *Learning and Instruction Challenge* category included those that impeded student learning or they viewed would cause difficulties for them when using SL for teaching.

One major challenge noted in this category included the *Learning curve* with learning to use SL as indicated by John, "I learned that this software has a learning curve just to be able to move around and interact with people or objects" and again by Tara who said that "I found the learning curve very steep for me since I am intimidated by games online in general."

A second major issue noted by students was their personal concerns about using virtual worlds for teaching and learning. Bill noted his concern, "I share the same thoughts with you regarding Second Life cannot be an excellent substitute for (face-to-face) classes, meeting in Second Life (sic) forces my attention to concentrate more on the text window rather on the discussed issue … I (also) had to quit the game and re-login again which make me miss parts of the discussion. Shana followed Bill's challenge with one about the visual nature of virtual worlds stating "I get a sense of being disoriented when I'm taking a look around a site and having to wait for visual reference points." Walter's concern was less practical and more related to concerns about the nature of virtual worlds for escapism when he said, "While I was there I spoke with other individuals that shared their ideas of Second Life. Most were there for recreation and spent and (sic) average of 20 hours a day on SL [their words] … (w)hich brings on the concerns of the artificial environment and escaping reality."

Each of these concerns stated by the students reflect their concerns about both teaching and learning in virtual worlds and some of the specific challenges that must be overcome before widespread adoption will take place.

Principle Seven: Be prepared to address learner and instructor practical and ethical concerns prior to using virtual worlds.

Principle Eight: Provide heavy supports and scaffolds for learners as they begin in virtual worlds. You are addressing not only technical issues but also differing worldviews. Some students just prefer face-to-face learning.

Category: Learner Experience Shared

In this category, students reflected upon their particular experiences in SL while specifically noting how and why they learned, as well as some barriers to learning when using SL.

The *Justification by student* code was the largest because students were expected as part of the instruction to explain how SL and particular locations within it could be used to support learning from the three major epistemic perspectives. For example, Walter noted that, "Bobcat Village, in Second Life (SL), is a campus tour of Texas State University. Other universities offer this virtual experience, but I found this one particularly nice. The island is very well built (from my experience) and you can set up "tours" of the campus. They also provide a YouTube tutorial to help perspective students."

In this instance, he is specifically discussing his experience in the location and justifying why it is useful from an instructional and learning perspective. Similarly, Roger went further and tied the space to particular instructional methods:

"Anyway, after I felt familiar with it, I realized that it can be very useful for instructional design when we know how to apply it for learning environment. For instance, when we are becoming accustomed to these worlds and expect to participate in them. Second Life can foster constructivist learning ([the instructor] created situations for us, then we questions and *(sic)* each other's assumptions)."

Principle Nine: Provide meaningful opportunities for learners to reflect on the experiences you provide them within the virtual world.

Other codes in this category such as *Comparing FTF and VW* and *Beginning XP* were instances in which students made particular comparisons between either their first and second SL experiences or the learning and instruction they encountered in face-to-face classrooms and those they experienced in SL. For example, John reflected upon the efficiency of using SL versus traditional classrooms, "The efficiency was low, when compared to face-to-face classroom, due to the over running of typed messages." Bill further noted that, "A (face-to-face classroom) is more competent and efficient that promotes learning and gives the opportunity to each participant to understand the discussion and then to participate in it."

Principle Ten: Be prepared for the idea that the virtual world experience will not always compare favorably with face-to-face instruction.

Category: Technical Challenge

Technical challenges represented less than 10% of the number of instances coded. It mainly focused on challenges faced due to computer problems such as graphics card failure, lack of bandwidth, and SL program issues.

However, all but two of the participants noted technical challenges, especially with bandwidth. For example, Shana noted, "My laptop has frozen up several times and SL can take a long time to load. I'm bothered that it sometimes takes a while for the graphics to load," while John reported that "(t)he technical problems that I saw were related to bandwidth or computer speed." Bill also noted the same crashing challenge as Shana, stating that "(a)nother problem I faced in Second Life is that the game kept crashing on me for several times." Despite these challenges, learners persevered and were successful at completing the learning task, which brings about the last lesson.

Principle Eleven: Expect technical challenges with virtual worlds just as with any other technology system; prepare your learners and set aside sufficient time to overcome them.

CONCLUSION

In this chapter, we examined the use of virtual learning using SL at the undergraduate and graduate levels at two universities. We examined how the framework for development of an attempted CoP was structured, within which volunteering students worked for campus clients building virtual presence. Further, they were expected to develop collaborative work skills while also adding technology expertise to their portfolios. We also looked at how the use of the virtual space can be used to help learners understand the implications of real-world technology implementation. We used SL to teach fundamentals of instructional design, ill-structured problem solving, and ill-structured problem assignments design.

What have we learned from designing instructional activities for virtual worlds? While we have just begun to touch the surface of the possibilities for using virtual worlds like SL, there emerge several lessons from the illuminative examples provided here. Specifically, we have generated 11 lessons and guidelines for preparing to bring your learners into virtual worlds. These principles can be applied regardless of your learner's educational level.

- Principle One: Create opportunities for sustaining virtual community beyond a task
- Principle Two: Provide social communication opportunities to participants
- Principle Three: Promote and advertise new community to leverage excitement
- Principle Four: Leverage participant experience with new technology to experiment
- Principle Five: Expect your learners to go off-task; be prepared for students to need to express nonrelevant information so that they can contextualize their own learning and make it meaningful to them
- Principle Six: Virtual worlds allow for participation in learning activities that may not otherwise be possible; take advantage of those affordances to both innovate and replicate traditional instructional methods
- Principle Seven: Be prepared to address learner and instructor practical and ethical concerns prior to using virtual worlds
- Principle Eight: Provide heavy supports and scaffolds for learners as they begin in virtual worlds. You are addressing not only technical issues but also differing worldviews. Some students just prefer face-to-face learning
- Principle Nine: Provide meaningful opportunities for learners to reflect on the experiences you provide them with in the virtual world

- Principle Ten: Be prepared for the idea that the virtual world experience will not always compare favorably with face-to-face instruction
- Principle Eleven: Expect technical challenges with virtual worlds just as with any other technology system; prepare your learners and set aside sufficient time to overcome them.

In his book *Teaching Digital Natives*, Prensky (2010) writes that the new generation of digital learners need to be taught through coaching and guidance, allowing students opportunity to work in groups with peers on group projects, allow students to make decisions and to share control, and connect with their peers and the world. In this chapter we have seen examples of how the use of the virtual environment can foster this new learning, making the learning engaging, immersive, effective, and fun – yet challenging enough to support true learning.

NOTE

1. utdallas.edu/gems/avatar

REFERENCES

Aldrich, C. (2003). *Simulations and the future of learning*. San Francisco, CA: Pfeiffer.

Aldrich, C. (2009). *Learning online with games, simulations, and virtual worlds. Strategies for online instruction*. San Francisco, CA: Wiley.

Baker, M. (2008). Merging technology and mathematics instruction: The case of virtual manipulatives and geometric concepts. In: C. Bonk, et al. (Eds.), *Proceedings of world conference on e-learning in corporate, government, healthcare, and higher education 2008* (pp. 566–573). Chesapeake, VA: AACE.

Bandura, A. (1997). Students cognitive self-efficacy. In: *Self-efficacy: The exercise of control* (pp. 214–215). New York, NY: W. H. Freeman.

Barab, S. A., & Duffy, T. M. (2000). From practice fields to communities of practice. In: D. Jonassen & S. Land (Eds.), *Theoretical foundations of learning environments* (pp. 25–26). Mahwah, NJ: Lawrence Erlbaum Associates.

Barab, S. A., MaKinster, J. G., & Scheckler, R. (2004). Designing system dualities: Characterizing an online professional development community. In: S. A. Barab, R. Kling & J. H. Gray (Eds.), *Designing for virtual communities in the service of learning* (pp. 53–90). Cambridge, UK: Cambridge University Press.

Barab, S., Warren, S., & Ingram-Goble, A. (2008). Conceptual play spaces. In R. Fertig (Ed.), *Handbook of research on effective electronic gaming in education*. Hershey, PA: Idea Group Reference: IGI Global.

Bass, R. (1999). The scholarship of teaching and learning: What's the problem? *Inventio*, *1*(1), 1–9.

Bichelmeyer, B. (2005). The ADDIE model: A metaphor for the lack of clarity in the field of IDT. *IDT Record* (AECT 2004 IDT Futures Group Presentations).

Bonner, J. (1998). Implications of cognitive theory for instructional design: Revisited. *Educational Communication and Technology Journal, 36*(1), 4–14.

Boyatzis, R. E. (1998). *Transforming qualitative information: Thematic analysis and code development*. Thousand Oaks, CA: Sage.

Bronack, S., Sanders, R., Cheney, A., Riedl, R., Tashner, J., & Matzen, N. (2008). Presence pedagogy: Teaching and learning in a 3D virtual immersive world. *International Journal of Teaching and Learning in Higher Education, 20*(1), 59–69.

Brush, T., & Saye, J. (2001). The use of embedded scaffolds with hypermedia-supported student-centered learning. *Journal of Educational Multimedia and Hypermedia, 10*(4), 333–356.

Butler, B., Sproull, L., Kiesler, S., & Kraut, R. (2002). Community efforts in online groups: Who does the work and why? In S. Weisband & L. Atwater (Eds.), *Leadership at a distance*. Retrieved from http://repository.cmu.edu/hcii/90

Caprotti, O., Seppälä, M, & Pauna, M. (2007). *Joining educational mathematics*. Retrieved from http://jem-thematic.net.

Cennamo, K., & Kalk, D. (2005). *Real world instructional design*. Belmont, CA: Thomson Wadsworth.

Clemson University. (2010). Educational technology. National Dropout Prevention Center/Network. Available at http://www.dropoutprevention.org/effective-strategies/educational-technology.

Dawley, L. (2009). Social network knowledge construction: Emerging virtual world pedagogy. *On the Horizon, 17*(2), 109–121.

De Lucia, A., Francese, R., Passero, I., & Tortora, G. (2009). Development and evaluation of a virtual campus on Second Life: The case of SecondDMI. *Computers & Education* (52), 220–233.

Denzin, N., & Lincoln, Y. (Eds). (2003). *The discipline and practice of qualitative research* (2nd ed.). Thousand Oaks, CA: Sage Publications.

Faber, A., Mazlish, E., Nyberg, L., & Templeton Anstine, R. (2003). *How to talk so kids can learn* (p. 180). New York, NY: Scribner.

Fose, L., & Mehl, M. (2007). Plugging into students' DNA: Five myths prohibiting proper podcasting pedagogy in the new classroom domain. *MERLOT Journal of Online Learning and Teaching*. Retrieved from http://jolt.merlot.org/vol3no3/mehl.htm

Gall, Gall, & Borg. (2010). *Applying educational research*. New York, NY: Pearson Education, Inc. ISBN-10: 0205596703.

Gibson, J. J. (1977). The theory of affordances. In: R. Shaw & J. Bransford (Eds.), *Perceiving, acting, and knowing: Toward on ecological psychology* (pp. 67–82). Hillsdale, NJ: Erlbaum and Associates.

Guetzkow, H. (1963). *Simulation in international relations*. Upper Saddle River, NJ: Prentice-Hall.

Henderson, M., Huang, H., Grant, S., & Henderson, L. (2009). Language acquisition in Second Life: Improving self-efficacy beliefs. In *Same places, different spaces. Proceedings ascilite. Auckland 2009*. Retrieved from http://www.ascilite.org.au/conferences/auckland09/procs/henderson.pdf

Herring, S. C. (2004). Computer-mediated discourse analysis: An approach to researching online behavior. In: S. A. Barab, R. Kling & J. H. Gray (Eds.), *Designing virtual communities in the service of learning* (pp. 338–376). Cambridge, UK: Cambridge University Press.

Horn, R. (Ed.) (1977). *The guide to simulations/games for education and training*. Crawford, NJ: Didactic Systems (Vol. 1).

Jarmon, L., Traphagan, T., & Mayrath, M. (2008). Understanding project-based learning in Second Life with a pedagogy, training, and assessment trio. Retrieved from http://bit.ly/96GwmU

Jenkins, H., Clinton, K., Purushotma, R., Robison, A. J., & Weigel, M. (2006). Confronting the challenges of participatory culture: Media education for the 21st century. *Building a field of digital media and learning*. Retrieved from http://digitallearning.macfound.org

Jonassen, D. H. (1997). Instructional design models for well-structured and ill-structured problem-solving learning outcomes. *Educational Technology, Research and Development*, *45*(1), 65–94.

Jonassen, D. H. (Speaker). (2006, February 16). Designing learning environments for troubleshooting. (iTunes podcast from TTU College of Education).

Jones, J. G., & Bronack, S. C. (2007). Rethinking cognition, representation, and processes in 3D online social learning environments. In D. Gibson, C. Aldrich & M. Prensky (Eds.), *Games and simulations in online learning. Research and development frameworks* (pp. 89–114). Hershey, PA: Idea Group, Inc.

Jones, J. G., & Warren, S. J. (2011). Issues and concerns of K-12 educators on 3D multi-user virtual environments in formal classroom settings. *International Journal of Games and Computer Mediated Systems*, *3*(1), 1–12.

Lave, J., & Wenger, E. (1991). *Situated learning: Legitimate peripheral participation*. Cambridge, UK: Cambridge University Press.

Molenda, M. (2003). The ADDIE model. In: A. Kovalchick & K. Dawson (Eds.), *Educational technology: An encyclopedia*. Santa Barbara, CA: ABC-Clio.

Moore, J., & Barab, S. (2002). The inquiry learning forum: A community of practice approach to online professional development. *Tech Trends*, *46*(3), 44–49.

Moore, M. G., & Kearsley, G. (2005). *Distance education: A systems view* (2nd ed.). Belmont, CA: Thomson Wadsworth.

Murphy, E. (2004). Identifying and measuring ill-structured problem formulation and resolution in online asynchronous discussions. *Canadian Journal of Learning and Technology*, *30*(1). Retrieved from http://www.cjlt.ca/index.php/cjlt/article/viewArticle/122/116

Ondrejka, C. (2008). Education unleashed: Participatory culture, education, and innovation in Second Life. Retrieved from http://papers.ssrn.com/sol3/papers.cfm?abstract_id = 1079245

Prawat, R. S., & Floden, R. (1994). Philosophical perspectives on constructivist views of learning. *Educational Psychologist*, *29*(Winter), 37–48.

Prensky, M. (2010). *Teaching digital natives: Partnering for real learning*. Thousand Oaks, CA: Corwin Sage.

Riel, M., & Polin, L. (2004). Online learning communities: Common ground and critical differences in designing technical environments. In: S. A. Barab, R. Kling & J. H. Gray (Eds.), *Designing for virtual communities in the service of learning* (pp. 16–50). Cambridge, UK: Cambridge University Press.

Savery, J. R., & Duffy, T. M. (1995). Problem based learning: An instructional model and its constructivist framework. *Educational Technology*, *35*, 31–38.

Schunk, D. H., & Zimmerman, B. J. (1998). *Self-regulated learning. From teaching to self-reflective practice* (p. 143). New York, NY: Guilford Press.

Sfard, A. (1998). On two metaphors for learning and the dangers of choosing just one. *Educational Researcher*, *27*(2), 4–13.

Smith, P. L., & Ragan, T. J. (2005). *Instructional design* (p. 218). Wiley.

Stiller, J., & Dunbar, R. (2007). Perspective-taking and memory capacity predict social network size. *Social Networks*, *29*(1), 93–104.

Tripp, S. D., & Bichelmeyer, B. A. (1990). Rapid prototyping: An alternative instructional design strategy. *Educational Technology Research & Development*, *38*(1), 31–44.

U.S. Department of Education. (2010, March 5). Office of Educational Technology transforming American education: Learning powered by technology. *National Educational Technology Plan 2010. Executive Summary*. Retrieved from http://www.ed.gov/sites/default/files/NETP-2010-exec-summary.pdf

Warren, S., & Dondlinger, M. (2008). Designing games for learning. In: R. Fertig (Ed.), *Handbook of research on effective electronic gaming in education*. Hershey, PA: Idea Group Reference: IGI Global.

Warren, S., Dondlinger, M., Stein, R., & Barab, S. (2009). Educational game as supplemental learning tool: Benefits, challenges, and tensions arising from use in an elementary school classroom. *Journal of Interactive Learning Research*, *20*(4), 295–301.

Warren, S., & Jones, G. (2008). Yokoi's theory of lateral innovation: Applications for learning game design. In Winston, J. (Ed.), *Journal of Educational Technology*, *5*(2), 32–43. I-manager's Publications.

Warren, S. J., & Jones, J. (in press). Supporting teachers, researchers, and emerging technologies: Evaluating games and simulations intended for learning. *Connexions*.

Warren, S., Jones, J., & Trombley, A. (2011). Skipping Pong and moving straight to World of Warcraft: The challenge of advancing educational game design models. *International Journal for Web-Based Communities*, *7*(2), 218–233.

Wenger, E., McDermott, R., & Snyder, W. (2002). *Cultivating communities of practice: A guide to managing knowledge*. Boston, MA: Harvard Business School.

LESSON PLAN 1: REAL WORLD AND VIRTUAL WORLD PROJECT-BASED COLLABORATION AND CONSTRUCTIVIST LEARNING

By Jenny S. Wakefield

OBJECTIVE

Facilitated by using collaborative and social constructivist learning theory, students learn to master cutting-edge technology, develop collaborative skills while working for real-world campus clients building campus presence in-world, and showcase their final designs for a global audience.

GRADE LEVEL

Undergraduate/Graduate

LEARNING OBJECTIVE

Using classification levels of Bloom's Taxonomy each student will:

Discuss [Comprehension] possible projects together with campus client, *decide on* [Evaluation] and *identify* [Analysis] for the student a suitable project.

Demonstrate [Application] ability to collaborate for project completion with the campus client both in the real world (in person) and in the virtual world (using avatar).

Participate in in-world training sessions with peers and *practice* [Application] necessary skills for virtual living and virtual content building.

Individually *apply* [Application] learned skills by *designing/developing* [Synthesis] presence for client and the university through in-world content building.

Experiment with [Analysis] and *solve* [Application] construction problems while building virtual content.

Prepare [Application], *summarize* [Synthesis] *and explain* [Evaluation] design projects during a showcase event open to assessment by a global audience. All students *discuss and explain* [Synthesis] verbally or in text, individual projects.

MATERIALS

- Access to SL for trainer and students (hardware, software, Internet connection).
- SL Parcel with building rights.
- Basic virtual world training materials for instructor.
- Campus clients with projects appropriate for showcasing and appropriately and challenging level for students.
- Access to website, e-mail, and various social media for announcing/posting training sessions and final showcase event information and receiving anonymous feedback.
- Student blogs (optional – see *Lesson Extension*).

PART I

Step 1

Set up SL parcel with building rights. Set up in-world group to facilitate in-world group announcements. Find campus clients interested in working with students. Set up a website with resources for students: Include in-world resources, a timeline with dates and times for training sessions, and project milestone dates.

Step 2

Team up students with campus clients that are ready to support learners and who will allow student develop ownership of the assigned project. Have each student set-up SL avatar accounts (and optional blogs). Go over available resources (website) and expectations with students.

Step 3

Conduct basic SL training session with all students.

PART II: WEEK 2 OR 3 AND BEYOND

Follow up with students and campus clients to ensure initial connections have been made for identification of suitable student projects. Have clients report any irregularities such as if a student is not working well, contact such student and discuss/suggest solutions or improvements if this happens.

Follow the timeline of scheduled in-world training sessions. Invite in-world instructors to guest-teach. Include informal socials where students can "hang-out" with their peers in-world (disco night, streamed music event, talk-show, group visit to in-world fun-fair, field trip to an interesting simulation, etc.) as these are fun and increase the feeling of community.

Provide weekly brown-bag lunches to give impromptu or scheduled mini-lessons to students if they are stuck on something in particular or need to informally ask questions. Find something to praise as you visit each student's build/project and focus on positive behaviors as these will increase collaborative behavior and project development.

If possible, hold a midterm campus get-together with all students on campus with refreshments where students can informally talk about their projects, connect in the real, and share their thoughts, successes, and frustrations. This will greatly contribute to community, create connections, and help students share ideas with one another if stuck on their projects (collaborative peer-learning).

Set the dates for the showcase events early so everyone can get it on their calendars and students have a deadline to work toward. Invite clients through special invitation as students appreciate their presence at the event. Advertise the one-hour showcase event on the campus event list, on the SL events listing, in-world through groups, other mailing lists, on appropriate Nings, blogs, Twitter, Facebook, website(s), bulletin boards, through flyers, etc.

Remind students to draft a summary of their projects in preparation for the showcase event presentations and hold a meeting with all students in preparation for the event to ensure everyone is ready to present. Allow students choose to present in voice or text depending on their comfort level. Provide feedback, support, and ideas.

Showcase – Students thoroughly enjoy this!

Wrap-up

Finish assessment of each student's work in concert with respective client and include in-world visitor comments and blog evaluations if applicable.

LESSON EXTENSION

Blogs may help the instructor ensure students are on track and allow the instructor to provide feedback to students helping them stay on course. It may also provide valuable ideas for program revisions. Whether or not they are assessed as part of a grade is optional.

ASSESS STUDENTS

Assessment of student collaborative skills and work is done mainly by campus client and the instructor in concert (preferably using a rubric, e.g., developed using Scholastic Rubric Maker). Visitor feedback from the showcase event can also be considered. Such can be accomplished when visitors are allowed to leave feedback through a comment box setup by each individual student's project in-world, linking to, for example, Google Docs surveys. If students are required to keep weekly blogs, these should also be analyzed and included in the assessment process.

ASSIGNMENTS

Students will primarily collaborate with campus clients working toward the final showcase event fulfilling their respective assignment. The number of in-world training sessions students are to attend may be mandated. No readings assigned, but resources provided on the program website to ensure student success with Project-Based Collaborative learning.

Students will participate at the final showcase event and present their work.

Blogs (if applicable).

EVALUATION

Use a survey form at the end of the semester to receive student feedback, review student blogs (if used), and/or interview students.

Suggested instructor resource: utdallas.edu/gems/avatar

LESSON PLAN 2: USING SECOND LIFE TO TEACH EPISTEMIC CONCEPTS FOR INSTRUCTIONAL DESIGN

By Scott J. Warren

OVERALL LEARNING GOAL

The goal of this lesson is to expose students to three major epistemic stances that can be used to guide instructional design: (1) objectivist/Empiricist/Positivist, (2) subjectivist/contextualist/social constructivist, and (3) relativist/radical constructivist through direct experience with immersive designs produced from each perspective.

INDIVIDUAL LEARNING GOALS

Each experience has different learning goals and, in respect to the relativist, the individual learners must set those goals. Instructor and groups may set goals through social negotiation in the contextualist/social constructivist activity.

Experience One (Positivist Stance) Includes the Following Goals

- The learner will (TLW) understand the basic features of a science simulation.
- The learner will (TLW) analyze the structures of a complex simulation designed from an objectivist/Empiricist viewpoint that is set in an experiential learning mode.
- The learner will (TLW) be able to complete a brief assessment related to the information contained in the simulation that they acquire during the three activities.

Experience Two (Contextualist Stance) Includes the Following Goals

In a small group, the learner will (TLW) identify and engage with an ill-structured problem with no single answer and develop a solution in conjunction with peers.

In a small group, the learner will (TLW) present and defend their solution to peers and instructor and revise it in response to feedback.

Experience Three (Relativist Stance) Includes the Following Goal:

- The learner will (TLW) work with the instructor to develop personal learning goals and objectives.
- The learner will (TLW) work with the instructor to develop their own learning activities to reach their goals and objectives.
- The learner will (TLW) develop specific activities intended to reach their learning goals and/or objectives.
- The learner will (TLW) develop specific means of assessing their learning of knowledge or skills.
- The learner will (TLW) develop an evaluation plan to determine whether they reached their learning goals and objectives.

INDIVIDUAL LEARNING OBJECTIVES

The learning objectives for Experiences Two and Three (contextualist and relativist) are set either through group negotiation in the first case or minor negotiation between instructor and learner in the second and therefore are not stated here. In contrast, there are separate objectives for the Positivist experience:

- The learner will (TLW) understand and be able to recite the basic rules and norms/standing orders of the Star Trek simulation.
- The learner will locate and record Seven of Nine's data.
- The learner will (TLW) understand basic concepts about physics explored in Star Trek.
- The learner will (TLW) be able to produce the correct answers to test questions.

GRADE LEVEL

Graduate/Doctoral

MATERIALS

- Access to SL for trainer and students (hardware, software, Internet connection)

- Microsoft Word
- Access to the Internet

PART I: OBJECTIVIST/EMPIRICIST/POSITIVIST LESSON

To begin, students should be directed to teleport to: http://slurl.com/secondlife/TovaDok%20II/25/211/35

Activity 1

Students are to find the "standing orders" in the room they first come upon. Write them down.

Students should answer the following question: How are these similar or different from those you might find in a school or other learning setting? Write that down as well.

Students should post these somewhere that the instructor can assess whether learning occurred.

Activity 2

Students are to find Seven of Nine. If they don't know who she is, they should be directed to look her up on a search engine. Write down whatever she has to tell you.

Students should post these somewhere so that the instructor can assess whether learning occurred.

Activity 3

Students should locate the movie room showing "Star Trek with a Physicist." They should be directed to watch the film and take notes on the content presented here.

Students should post these somewhere so that the instructor can assess whether learning occurred.

Test

Students should take an objective test regarding content included in this activity.

PART II: SOCIAL CONSTRUCTIVIST LESSON DESIGN EXPERIENCE

Teleport to: http://slurl.com/secondlife/Virtual%20NLM/130/145/25

Have students self-organize into four person teams immediately. They should be given less than five minutes to do so.

Students should explore the region quickly and identify major problems/ill-structured problems simulated there. How they do so is up to them.

Given the serious challenges in this simulation each group should choose one major problem. In their small groups, they should be asked to generate a solution that would leverage a distance communication or education solution that everyone agrees upon.

Students meet back at the original entrance to the area an hour or two later.

Each group is given two minutes to present their solution. Peer groups, instructor, and any available experts provide feedback on student solutions. The instructor challenges any poor knowledge constructions.

PART III: RELATIVIST/RADICAL CONSTRUCTIVIST LESSON

Students will individually define what they want to learn by exploring various locations in SL as they so choose. Provide them with the following:

- Search in Google and any other available research tools and see if there is any relevant information related to your topic.
- Write two learning goals related to this topic.
- Write supporting learning objectives for each goal.
- Write two or more outcomes of your learning you expect to reach.
- Describe two to three learning activities you will engage in within SL to learn.
- Create a means of assessing whether you learned what you wanted to learn in terms of knowledge or skills.
- Describe how you will evaluate your own learning success with respect to the goals and objectives you set for yourself.
- Complete these activities and write a half page description of your experience and evaluate your success.

WRAP-UP

Students should engage in a discussion of the three different experiences in SL, a discussion forum or face-to-face, reflecting specifically on how the three experiences differed and what that means for the design of instruction, learning, assessment, and evaluation.

LESSON EXTENSION

Students may engage in the design of instruction in SL according to each of these epistemic stances in order to show their clear comprehension of the differences among the perspectives and what instruction and learning are according to each.

ASSESS STUDENTS

Assessment can be done in several ways. The first may be done through peer evaluation of student reflections. Further, student reflections on each experience should be reviewed by the instructor of student knowledge constructions and their individual understandings of the different perspectives. Peers and the instructor should challenge poor knowledge constructions and students should revise their mental models accordingly.

EVALUATION

The instructor and at least two other reviewers should use a rubric aligned with the learning goals and objectives to determine whether students reached each. If all students mastered at least 85% of all goals and objectives, the learning experience instructional design may be considered a success. Any experience falling below this 85% mark should be followed up with 5–10 minute interviews with five or more students in order to identify weaknesses in the design or instruction.

USING THE COMMUNITY OF INQUIRY (COI) MODEL AND BLOOM'S REVISED TAXONOMY TO SUPPORT 21ST CENTURY TEACHING AND LEARNING IN MULTI-USER VIRTUAL ENVIRONMENTS

Melissa L. Burgess and Phil Ice

ABSTRACT

Online learning in higher education has, until most recently, been delivered primarily through learning management systems (LMS) such as BlackBoard, Moodle, and others. However, responding to budgetary concerns and burgeoning enrollments, delivery of online learning via multiple open source (free) formats, is quickly becoming an attractive and inexpensive option for online distance and learning programs. Multi-user virtual environments, or MUVEs, are one such option that provides an interactive and socially rich learning experience for learners. In this chapter, the authors propose a dually fused pedagogical framework that has the potential to provide both asynchronous and synchronous online

Transforming Virtual World Learning
Cutting-edge Technologies in Higher Education, Volume 4, 163–186

ISSN: 2044-9968/doi:10.1108/S2044-9968(2011)0000004011

learning activities the elicit critical thinking skills and that further align with additional skills twenty-first century learners and instructors need to compete in today's global society.

Keywords: Community of inquiry; Bloom's Revised taxonomy; multi-user virtual environments; 21st century teaching and learning; Second Life

INTRODUCTION

"As the artificial walls of our great universities come tumbling down through technology, and as electronic networks expand the reach of university campuses, the range of influence of higher education will increase ... The teaching of the best professors ... will be available ... to anyone who wants to learn." – Sculley (n.d.)

Although it may be some time before we can adequately predict in what ways higher educational institutions are going to be transformed, one thing is for certain, virtual spaces that support social learning are prompting educators at all levels to deeply reflect on where we are in our pedagogical practices and curriculum and where we need to be to support and engage our twenty-first-century learners. The restructuring of teaching and learning will not only be prerequisite to meet the needs of increasing enrollments in higher education but also to meet the learning needs of today's youth. Many higher education institutions are responding to this demand through online distance learning programs – where conversations continue on the design and delivery of quality instruction.

MULTI-USER VIRTUAL ENVIRONMENTS (MUVEs) AS AN ONLINE LEARNING PLATFORM

Online learning in higher education has, until most recently, been delivered primarily through learning management systems (LMS) such as Black-Board, WebCT, and others. However, responding to budgetary concerns and burgeoning enrollments, the notion of *blended learning* – delivery of online learning via multiple open source (free) formats – is quickly becoming an attractive and inexpensive option for online distance and learning programs (Garrison & Vaughan, 2008). Accompanying this notion are the ever-evolving knowledge and skills required in the workforce today – particularly in higher education.

In recent years researchers have primarily conducted studies in virtual learning platforms that are asynchronous. However, with the emergence of MUVEs, synchronous learning coupled with virtual *telepresence*, or the almost-like-being-there feeling, results in a potentially interactive and socially rich learning experience. In MUVEs, users, as 3D representations – commonly known as avatars – have the ability to communicate, move, fly, and interact with the environment and others, thus providing a real-life, synchronous experience. Telepresence adds a new dimension to virtual learning as it serves as a bridge between LMS (primarily asynchronous) and face-to-face classes (synchronous). *Second Life*® (SL) (Linden Labs, 2002) is one such MUVE where an avatar can create, collaborate, and engage in role-playing and simulated activities. Fig. 1 displays this unique environment as learners engage in discourse that is relevant, engaging, immersive, and conducive to higher-level cognitive capabilities (Figs. 1–3).

Designing instruction within this learning environment has prompted the attention of online designers and educators to carefully craft learning

Fig. 1. Learners Engage in Discourse During a Graduate-Level Class.

Fig. 2. Aerial View of Bearkat Island in Second Life.

Fig. 3. Graduate Students Gathering to Complete an Activity on Bearkat Island.

situations that elicit the establishment of social learning as a foundation toward the development of higher-level thinking. In this chapter, the authors have connected two educationally sound pedagogical foundations that online curriculum designers have used, individually, to develop and foster higher-level thinking skills and socially rich learning communities: (1) the Community of Inquiry (Garrison, Anderson, & Archer, 2000) and (2) Bloom's Revised Taxonomy (Anderson et al., 2001). The fusing of these instructional frameworks has the potential to provide both asynchronous and synchronous online learning activities that elicit critical thinking skills and that also align with additional skills twenty-first-century learners and instructors need to compete in today's global society.

TWENTY-FIRST-CENTURY SKILLS FOR TEACHING AND LEARNING IN MUVEs

Defining Distance/Virtual Education

Before defining what skills are necessary for teaching and learning in a MUVE, the authors stress the importance of distinguishing the term *distance education* to acknowledge and highlight the variations in delivery that have been associated with this term. A higher educational institutional board in the United States defines distance education as a "… course in which the majority of the instruction occurs when the students and the instructor are not in the same physical setting. A course is considered to be offered by distance education if students receive more than one-half of the instruction at a different location than the instructor. A distance education course can be delivered synchronously or asynchronously to any single or multiple location(s) through electronic, correspondence, or other means. The course may be formula-funded or offered through extension, and it may be delivered to on-campus students and those who do not take courses on the main campus" (Texas Higher Education Coordinating Board website, 2010). Although at first glance this definition would seem to apply to virtual environments, technically, it does not. When in a MUVE, users are indeed in the same physical, virtual location at the same time as the instructor. Therefore, this poses some implications for clearer definitions between *distance* and *virtual* in higher education.

Twenty-First-Century Skills for Teaching in MUVEs

Prior to teaching in a MUVE, an instructor should be prepared to explore and demonstrate particular skills that are vital when embarking in a MUVE. Churches (2008) provides an encompassing list of characteristics and skills that has applicability toward the overall concept of twenty-first-century teaching. The authors have adapted Churches' list by expanding the descriptions and offering more specificity with characteristics and skills in MUVEs.

The Adapter is able to have flexibility, diversity, and creativity toward instructional design through the use of MUVE tools (presentation viewers, video players, and multimedia tools, interactive tools) and activities (virtual field trips to other islands, invitation of guest speakers from anywhere in the world, create and distribute learning materials, scavenger hunts, group discussions).

- The Visionary is able to look at MUVEs and envision creative ways in which to deliver instruction and encourage ways.
- The Collaborator is able to actively engage in MUVE-related organizations, listservs, and professional learning networks as a form of modeling for learners.
- The Risk Taker is able to trust their own abilities to deliver instruction that supports digital native students and is not afraid to try various tools available within MUVEs.
- The Learner is a lifelong learner and models this commitment through the desire to participate in opportunities that allow for continual – yet experiential growth.
- The Communicator is able to communicate quickly, clearly, and effectively using tools such as in-world note cards, instant messaging, calling, text chat, or voice chat.
- The Model is able to model the same behaviors that are expected of students. Some of these behaviors include tolerance, acceptance, patience, global perspectives and awareness, and self-reflection.
- The Leader is able to lead student learning with MUVEs with clear objectives, vision, incentive, and action.

These characteristics are foundational toward executing the curricular change necessary at all educational levels and therefore vital to all learners. However, whether educators possess these twenty-first-century educator characteristics or not, there is a level of knowledge and skills necessary of both twenty-first-century skills and MUVEs to effectively establish learning environments that encompass both. Additionally, and perhaps even more important, are the intrinsic, or attitudinal characteristics underlying the twenty-first-century characteristics.

Twenty-First-Century Skills for Learning

Participating in a MUVE – whether for entertainment, socializing, curiosity, or educational reasons – requires certain prerequisite skills to be able to fully engage and immerse oneself in a virtual environment. One would assume technology skills would be at the top of the list; however, there are particular attitudinal characteristics that are at the core of learning these specific skills. Learners entering our colleges and universities are (a) technology literate and adept (able to troubleshoot and problem solve); (b) media savvy (able to utilize a variety of media); (c) digital multitaskers (are engaged in several technologies at one time); (d) communicators and collaborators (understand that through both face-to-face and digital social communication and working together, tasks get accomplished); (e) interactive and networked (belong to online social networks toward interacting with others; (f) reflective and critical (able to self-evaluate and use higher levels of cognition); (g) instant (need quick results and/or answers); creative, and adaptive (engage in endeavors that stretch creativity and allow for visionary thinking); (h) student-centric; (i) lifelong learners (understand that a higher educational degree is not only essential, but that to stay ahead of the competition they must continually be open to learning new things); (j) anywhere and anytime learners (do not allow barriers to learning); and (k) multimodal in their learning styles (visual, auditory, kinesthetic, etc.).

Foundational to keeping up with learning environments of any kind is the desire and genuine willingness to continually learn and adapt instruction to meet the needs of our learners – irregardless of the current era.

THE COMMUNITY OF INQUIRY MODEL

"Teaching must stop being a solo sport and become a community-based activity." – Simon (n.d.)

Within the last 15 years, online learning has advanced from an interesting experiment to "the new normal" (Davidson & Goldberg, 2009). With almost 4 million students enrolled in online courses in the United States alone, and a 12.9% growth rate in online enrollments, program growth is considered a priority at over 80% of major US institutions of higher education (Allen &

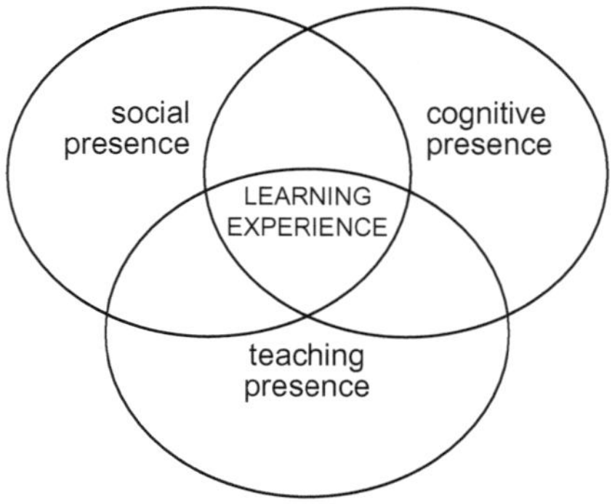

Fig. 4. Community of Inquiry Model (Garrison et al., 2000).

Seaman, 2010). However, understanding the foundational aspects of online learning is an area that is not yet fully developed. While several models have sought to address this issue, the one that has gained the most attention is the Community of Inquiry (CoI) framework (Garrison et al., 2000).

Based on a collaborative constructivist approach to learning, the CoI developers posit that optimal interactions in the online environment consist of three separate but overlapping elements: social, cognitive, and teaching presence. The underlying premise supporting this framework is that effective online learning requires the development of a learning community (Rovai, 2002; Shea, 2006; Thompson & MacDonald, 2005) that supports the meaningful inquiry and deep learning that is the hallmark of higher education (Dewey, 1938) (Fig. 4).

S*ocial presence* in a virtual environment can potentially develop rich, reflective student experiences, as students must be able to share and communicate their experiences with others by projecting themselves socially and emotionally, as in real life. The measure of effectiveness of this projection is the degree to which learners feel socially and emotionally connected with others in the virtual environment. Although the elements of social presence have been variously defined, in this chapter (and in the CoI survey it explores), we identify them as *affective* expression, where learners share personal expressions of emotion, feelings, beliefs, and values; *open communication*, where learners build and sustain a sense of group commitment; and *group cohesion,* where learners interact around common intellectual activities and tasks.

Perhaps because online learning was initially challenged on its ability to support social presence, the notion of social presence has attracted a good deal of research in the field. Indeed, contrary to initial challenges, that research has consistently shown that the social presence of others can be felt, often quite strongly, by participants in online discussions (Gunawardena, 1995; Richardson & Swan, 2003; Tu & McIsaac, 2002; Walther, 1993), and that participants in purely text-based discussions can project their feelings and personalities to others using verbal immediacy behaviors alone (Rourke, Anderson, Garrison, & Archer, 2001; Swan, 2003). Research suggests that perceptions of social presence vary depending on course design factors (Swan & Shih, 2005) and learner characteristics (Swan & Shih, 2005; Tu & McIsaac, 2002). Moreover, perceptions of social presence have been linked to student satisfaction in online courses (Gunawardena, Lowe, & Anderson, 1997; Richardson & Swan, 2003; Tu, 2002), as well as to students' perceived and actual learning from them (Gunawardena, 1995; Picciano, 2002; Richardson & Swan, 2003; Walther, 1993).

Indeed, research suggests that, while social presence alone will not ensure the development of critical discourse in online learning, it is extremely difficult for such discourse to develop without a foundation of social presence (Celani & Collins, 2005; Garrison & Cleveland-Innes, 2005; Molinari, 2004). However, there is little research linking social presence to either cognitive or teaching presence, and virtually no research, states Henri's (1992) groundbreaking, but difficult to apply, early work. However, initial work indicates that virtual environments may provide a rich context for increasing the likelihood that social presence will be enhanced.

Cognitive presence in a virtual environment encourages deep, critical thinking processes and can be attained by higher-level questioning derived from Bloom's Revised Taxonomy (Anderson et al., 2001). As conceptualized in the CoI framework, Bloom's taxonomy has its genesis in the work of John Dewey (1933) and his notion of scientific inquiry. For Dewey, inquiry was at the core of a worthwhile educational experience. The development of the cognitive presence constructed by Garrison, Anderson, and Archer (2001) is grounded in the critical thinking literature and operationalized by the Practical Inquiry Model (Fig. 3) that draws on and represents a slight truncation of Dewey's model.

The Practical Inquiry Model is defined by two axes. The vertical axis reflects the integration of thought and action, reflection, and discourse. The horizontal axis represents its interface. The extremes of the horizontal axis are analysis and synthesis. These are points of insight and understanding (Garrison et al., 2000). The model also distinguishes four phases of pragmatic inquiry – triggering, exploration, integration, and resolution – which the CoI model identifies as the elements of cognitive presence (Fig. 5).

As conceptualized in the CoI model, cognitive presence begins with a *triggering event* in the form of an issue, problem, or dilemma that needs

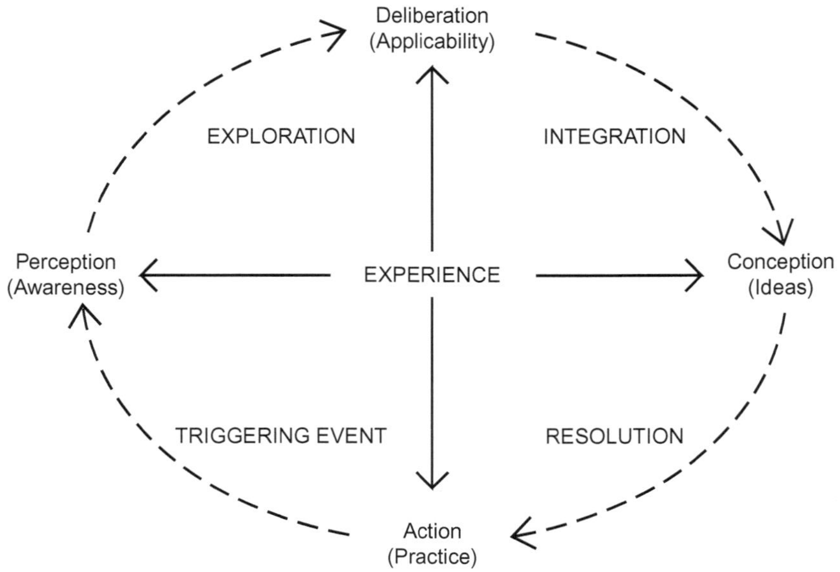

Fig. 5. Practical Inquiry Model (Garrison et al., 2001).

resolution. As a result of this event, there is a natural shift to *exploration*, the search for relevant information that can provide insight into the challenge at hand. As ideas crystallize, there is a move into the third phase, *integration*, in which connections are made and there is a search for a viable explanation. Finally, there is a selection and testing of ideas (through vicarious or direct application) leading to *resolution*. Consistent with Dewey's rejection of dualism, the phases should not be seen as discrete or linear. In an actual educational experience, they are very difficult to label, as those that have used this model to code transcripts will attest (Garrison et al., 2001).

In the CoI framework, cognitive presence is defined as the extent to which learners are able to construct and confirm meaning through sustained reflection and discourse (Garrison et al., 2001), and operationalized as through the four phases of practical inquiry. Researchers have found ample evidence of practical inquiry in online discussions; however, initial studies revealed that most postings in online discussion forums rarely moved beyond the exploration phase (Garrison & Arbaugh, 2007; Kanuka & Anderson, 1998; Luebeck & Bice, 2005; Meyer, 2003, 2004; Murphy, 2004; Shea et al., 2010). In other words, learners have been found to be effectively stimulated to engage in exploration and engage in exploration, but fail to move forward to integration and resolution.

Various explanations for the lack of integration and resolution in online discussions have been offered. One idea concerns the nature of the assignments and instructional direction provided (Akyol & Garrison, 2008; Garrison & Arbaugh, 2007). When students are challenged to resolve a problem, followed by continual and effective facilitation, the move toward integration and resolution is far more likely to occur (Meyer, 2003; Murphy, 2004; Shea & Bidjerano, 2008). Another explanation suggests that practical inquiry might be initiated in discussion, but reach integration and/or resolution in other parts of a course (Archer, 2010). With respect to technologically enhanced learning environments, work by Ice, Bain, and Stewart (2010) provides evidence that rich applications, as opposed to static content, can prove to be a catalyst for higher order learning outcomes. With respect to MUVEs, the ability to provide a richer basis for the emergence of cognitive presence has also be noted by Burgess and colleagues (Burgess, Slate, Rojas-LeBouef, & LaPrarie, 2010; Burgess & Caverly, 2009, 2011; Burgess & Ice, 2011).

Teaching presence is best described using the definition proposed by Anderson and colleagues (2001): "the design, facilitation, and direction of cognitive and social processes for the realization of personally meaningful and educationally worthwhile learning outcomes." In their model, teaching presence has three components: instructional design and organization, facilitating discourse, and direct instruction. These categories align well with others identified by researchers working on the roles of instructors in online environments, and the general conceptualization of teaching presence has been supported by other research (Coppola, Hiltz, & Rotter, 2002; LaPointe & Gunawardena, 2004; Stein, Wanstreet, Calvin, Overtoom, & Wheaton, 2005).

Instructional (Course) Design and Organization

Anderson et al. (2001) describe the design and organization aspect of teaching presence as the planning and design of the structure, process, interaction, and evaluation aspects of the online course. Some of the activities comprising this category of teaching presence include recreating PowerPoint presentations and lecture notes onto the course site, developing audio/video mini-lectures, providing personal insights into the course material, creating a desirable mix of and a schedule for individual and group activities, and providing guidelines on how to use the medium effectively. These are particularly important activities since clear and consistent course structure supporting engaged instructors and dynamic discussions have been found to be the most consistent predictors of successful online courses (Swan, 2002, 2003). Of the three components of teaching presence, this is the one most likely to be performed exclusively by the instructor (Swan et al., 2008). In a MUVE, establishing a teaching presence includes criteria such as avatar-as-teacher representation, facilitating time management for synchronous learning, preassessing a student's digital literacy knowledge, providing immediate feedback, facilitating social discourse that lends itself to higher levels of cognitive thinking, managing course content and materials, and implementing constructivist approaches within a synchronous virtual learning context.

Facilitating Discourse

Anderson et al. (2001) conceptualize facilitating discourse as the means by which students are engaged in interacting about and building upon the information provided in the course instructional materials. This role includes sharing meaning, identifying areas of agreement and disagreement, and seeking to reach consensus and understanding. Therefore, facilitating discourse requires the instructor to review and comment upon student comments, raise questions, and make observations to move discussions in a desired direction, keeping discussion moving efficiently, draw out inactive students, and limit the activity of dominating student contributions when they become detrimental to the learning of the group (Anderson et al., 2001; Brower, 2003; Coppola et al., 2002).

Direct Instruction

Anderson et al. (2001) contextualized direct instruction as the instructor provision of intellectual and scholarly leadership in part through the sharing of their subject matter knowledge with the students. Direct instruction is concerned with indicators that assess the discourse and the efficacy of the educational process. Instructor responsibilities are to facilitate reflection and discourse by presenting content and using various means of assessment and feedback. Explanatory feedback is crucial. This type of communication must be perceived to have a high level of social presence/instructor immediacy (Arbaugh, 2001; Baker, 2004; Gorham, 1988; Richardson & Swan, 2003) to be effective. In a MUVE in particular, instructors must have both content and pedagogical expertise to make links among contributed ideas, diagnose misperceptions, and immediately seek out knowledge from textbooks, articles, and web-based materials while immersed in a MUVE. The simultaneous roles of discussion facilitator and content expert within teaching presence go beyond early contentions that virtual instructors needed merely to transition from a role of knowledge disseminator to interaction facilitator (Swan et al., 2008). Teaching presence contends that for virtual learning to be effective, instructors must play both roles (Arbaugh & Hwang, 2006).

In a MUVE, a teacher who is engaged in students' interactions and is readily available for feedback, support, and guidance can potentially be more supportive as the environment offers a greater range of paralinguistic clues that is available in traditional LMS-oriented environments (Burgess et al., 2010; Mckerlich & Anderson, 2007). If so, then there is reason to believe that the teacher's role will be significantly enhanced in this setting, requiring some rethinking of the role of facilitation tasks from a pedagogical perspective.

BLOOM'S REVISED TAXONOMY

"Too often we give children answers to remember rather than problems to solve." – Lewin (n.d.)

Bloom's Revised Taxonomy (Anderson et al., 2001) takes into account emerging technologies and how virtual instruction and assessment can be supported using the varying levels of thinking skills. Implementation of these verbs (and their respective subcategories) into learning goals and objectives ensures high-quality instruction that reaches all types of learners (visual, auditory, and kinesthetic) while attaining levels in which they can develop and grow their knowledge base. The revised taxonomy represents qualitatively different cognitive processes that are supported through MUVEs. The lower-to-higher cognitive levels allow the learner to developmentally attain goals and objectives of a lesson through a variety of MUVE educational tools. One aspect of virtual learning is that these tools can be used by a learner to construct individual and personal knowledge. In MUVEs, understanding is attained through collaborative means. However, an increasing number of web-based applications are emerging that provide a means of collaboratively constructing an understanding. As in any technology integration into instruction, instructors must be mindful of the importance of supporting cognitive thinking using the tools instead of focusing on the tools themselves.

Aligning the taxonomic levels within a MUVE is, theoretically, not much different than aligning the levels in traditional face-to-face synchronous or asynchronous online learning. The instructional design, however, relies upon instructor knowledge of the various ways in which content can be provided through MUVE tools. Therefore, the development of instruction integrating Bloom's Revised Taxonomy within a MUVE should be carefully researched and constructed to account for the challenges (and opportunities) that are present (Dillenbourg & Jermann, 2010).

Remembering

The lower level cognitive process in this taxonomy is the storage of information or the passive viewing of displayed information. This utilization of virtual learning could be presented through MUVE tools such as note cards and presentational displays (text-based, image-based, audio, and video). This information can be saved into the avatar's inventory for later use. Instruction on this lower level in a MUVE can be interactive or passive.

Exploration

The second level of the taxonomy represents the active exploration gleaned from materials and ideas. At this level, the learner is engaged in the conscious pursuit of information that will lead to a better understanding of an existent issue, question, or concept. In a MUVE, exploration could be encouraged through in-world field trips whereby the learner could be required to explore other in-world locales toward discovering new information based upon the teacher-presented content. Another example might include the exploration of information on the Internet while simultaneously in-world. The cognitive process becomes more advanced and relevant as the learner is directing his/her own learning acquisition via in-world or outside sources. Collaborative learning can also be integrated toward exploration where knowledge is constructed via social discourse (IM, text chat, voice chat, or note cards).

Application

The application of new knowledge using a MUVE platform requires the learner to compare simulated situations to real-life situations and vice versa. Applying the concept in this manner allows the learner to reflect on its veracity and utility. For example, the knowledge of different components of an e-portfolio for preservice teachers presented in a MUVE can be applied via creative artifacts in-world or on the Internet through an electronic web developer.

Analysis

The use of MUVEs to allow individuals to analyze materials or ideas by manipulating them and organizing them.

Evaluation

The fifth level of the taxonomy represents the use of MUVEs to support the process of evaluation. This can be done in a number of ways. One way to engage students at this level is by compiling information, landmarks, and resources into an in-world digital repository that will allow learners to address issues of history or current events and to evaluate these resources. It can be facilitated by developing simulations that will immerse students in an environment that will help them evaluate relevant dimensions and solve the problems that are posed.

Creating

The highest level of Bloom's Revised Taxonomy involves the creating of an artifact that represents all of the previous learning levels. In a MUVE, this can be established through the in-world building tools that are available. Users can build objects, or prims toward establishing a virtual environment that includes associated learning objectives. Another example of creating in a MUVE could include the development of scripts toward creating animations and interactive objects, clothing design, and graphic design. Using a MUVE platform at this higher-level taxonomic level allows for limitless virtual creations.

The authors of this chapter posit that this taxonomy could be used by instructors to design learning experiences using emerging technologies, such as MUVEs. Further, instructors in MUVEs are reminded to examine contextual factors such as the aforementioned digital literacies, developmental learning levels, and the various learning modalities to guide assessment and to design instruction.

COI AND BLOOM'S REVISED TO DESIGN INSTRUCTION IN MUVEs

"Once a new technology rolls over you, if you're not part of the steamroller, you're part of the road." – Brand (2011)

As emphasized in both the CoI framework and the Bloom's Revised Taxonomic levels, design has a significant impact on the nature of the interaction and whether students approach learning in a deep and meaningful manner (Garrison & Cleveland-Innes, 2005). Although much of the literature exploring the design of online instruction has incorporated one framework or the other, no known literature exists for the combination of the two. The stakes are high regarding whether or not instruction in a traditional setting or in an online setting is well-designed (Duffy & Kirkley, 2004) as poorly designed learning environments of any kind typically yield poor educational experiences.

In a MUVE, planning and implementing rich learning experiences is equally paramount; however, designing instruction within this particular learning environment demands a culmination of collaborative, higher-level cognitive, and technical skills that are considerably different from an LMS. Therefore, through combining the two frameworks, more emphasis is placed upon the cognitive presence as a graduation of cognitive growth is the desired outcome. The CoI framework, with its emphasis on critical thinking and collaboration, provides a well-structured model and a set of guidelines to create effective learning communities in online and blended learning environments (Garrison & Anderson, 2003; Garrison & Vaughan, 2008). Moreover, Bloom's Revised Taxonomy provides the developmental levels of cognition needed to support higher-level thinking. With a focus on the cognitive construct in the CoI, embedding the Bloom's Revised Taxonomic levels within this construct heightens the potential of higher-level thinking in a MUVE.

To illustrate the applicability of CoI and Bloom's Revised Taxonomy within instruction, we have included a sample syllabus and lesson plan specifically highlighting components of each model as it appears in each. As a basis for design in MUVEs, educators should always focus on the objectives set forth in the course, and then proceed to outline the course using CoI and Bloom's Revised Taxonomy according to the objectives.

CONCLUSION

SL is an online teaching and learning platform that has been explored by many higher education institutions across the globe; however, little direction has emerged from the literature on how to develop activities that foster the above-mentioned skills. Instructional design using Bloom's Revised Taxonomy coupled with instructional implementation using the CoI will undoubtedly offer quality virtual instruction in an age where this particular type of learning is a *necessity* and not a choice.

REFERENCES

Akyol, Z., & Garrison, D. R. (2008). The development of a community of inquiry over time in an online course: Understanding the progression and integration of social, cognitive and teaching presence. *Journal of Asynchronous Learning Networks*, *12*(3-4), 3–22.

Allen, I. E., & Seaman, J. (2010). *Learning on demand: Online education in the United States 2009*. Wellesley, MA: Babson Survey Research Group.

Anderson, L., Krathwohl, R., Airasian, P., Cruikshank, K., Mayer, R., Pintrich, P., Raths, J., & Wittrock, M. (Eds). (2001). *Taxonomy for learning, teaching, and assessing: A revision of Bloom's taxonomy*. New York, NY: Longman.

Arbaugh, J. B. (2001). How instructor immediacy behaviors affect student satisfaction and learning in web-based courses. *Business Communication Quarterly*, *64*(4), 42–54.

Arbaugh, J. B., & Hwang, A. (2006). Does "teaching presence" exist in online MBA courses? *The Internet and Higher Education*, *9*(1), 9–21.

Archer, W. (2010). Beyond online discussion: Extending the community of inquiry framework to entire courses. *Internet and Higher Education*, *13*(1–2), 69.

Baker, J. D. (2004). An investigation of relationships among instructor immediacy and affective and cognitive learning in the online classroom. *Internet and Higher Education*, *7*, 1–13.

Brand, S. (2011). *Great-Quotes.com*. Retrieved from http://www.great-quotes.com/quote/922008

Brower, H. H. (2003). On emulating classroom discussion in a distance-delivered OBHR course: Creating an on-line learning community. *Academy of Management Learning and Education*, *24*(1), 22–37.

Burgess, M. L., & Caverly, D. (2009). Second life and developmental education. *Journal of Developmental Education*, *32*(3), 42–43.

Burgess, M. L., & Caverly, D. (2011). Techtalk: An online framework for developmental literacy. *Journal of Developmental Education*, *34*(1), 38–39.

Burgess, M. L., & Ice, P. (2011). Optimal experience in virtual environments among college level developmental readers. *Journal of Educational Computing Research*, *44*(4), 421–443.

Burgess, M. L., Slate, J. R., Rojas-LeBouef, & LaPrarie, K. (2010). Teaching and learning in Second Life: Using the community of inquiry (CoI) model to support online instruction with graduate students in instructional technology. *Internet and Higher Education*, *13*(1-2), 84–88.

Celani, M. A. A., & Collins, H. (2005). Critical thinking in reflective sessions and in online interactions. In: K. Rajagopalan (Ed.), *Applied linguistics in Latin America: AILA review* (Vol. 18, pp. 41–57). Amsterdam: John Benjamins Publishing.

Churches, A. (2008). *Bloom's digital taxonomy*. Retrieved from http://media.ccconline.cccs.edu/ccco/FacWiki/Blooms_Taxonomy_Tutorials/Churches_2008_DigitalBloomsTaxonomyGuide.pdf

Coppola, N., Hiltz, S., & Rotter, N. (2002). Becoming a virtual professor: Pedagogical roles and asynchronous learning networks. *Journal of Management Information Systems, 18*(4), 169–190.

Davidson, C. N., & Goldberg, D. T. (2009). *The future of learning institutions in a digital age*. Cambridge, MA: MIT Press.

Dewey, J. (1933). *How we think* (Rev. ed.). Boston, MA: D. C. Heath.

Dewey, J. (1938). New York, NY: Macmillan.

Dillenbourg, P., & Jermann, P. (2010). Technology for classroom orchestration. In: M. S. Khine & I. M. Saleh (Eds.), *New science of learning* (pp. 525–552). New York, NY: Springer Science + Business Media.

Duffy, T. M., & Kirkley, J. R. (2004). Learning theory and pedagogy applied in distance learning: The case of Cardean University. In: T. Duffy & J. Kirkley (Eds.), *Learner-centered theory and practice in distance education: Cases from higher education* (pp. 107–143). Mahwah, NJ: Lawrence Erlbaum.

Garrison, D. R., Anderson, T., & Archer, W. (2000). Critical inquiry in a text-based environment: Computer conferencing in higher education. *Internet and Higher Education, 2*, 87–105.

Garrison, D. R., Anderson, T., & Archer, W. (2001). Critical thinking, cognitive presence and computer conferencing in distance education. *American Journal of Distance Education, 15*(1), 7–23.

Garrison, D. R., & Arbaugh, J. B. (2007). Researching the community of inquiry framework: Review, issues, and future directions. *Internet and Higher Education, 10*(3), 157–172.

Garrison, D. R., & Anderson, T. (2003). *E–Learning in the 21st century: A framework for research and practice*. London: RoutledgeFalmer.

Garrison, D. R., & Cleveland-Innes, M. (2005). Facilitating cognitive presence in online learning: Interaction is not enough. *American Journal of Distance Education, 19*(3), 133–148.

Garrison, R., & Vaughan, H. (2008). *Blended learning in higher education: Framework, principles and guidelines*. San Francisco, CA: Jossey-Bass.

Gorham, J. (1988). The relationship between verbal teaching immediacy behaviors and student learning. *Communication Education, 17*, 40–53.

Gunawardena, C. N. (1995). Social presence theory and implications for interaction and collaborative learning in computer teleconferences. *International Journal of Educational Telecommunications, 1*, 147–166.

Gunawardena, C., Lowe, C., & Anderson, T. (1997). Analysis of global online debate and the development of an interaction analysis model for examining social construction of knowledge in computer conferencing. *Journal of Educational Computing Research, 17*(4), 397–431.

Henri, F. (1992). Computer conferencing and content analysis. In: A. R. Kaye (Ed.), *Collaborative learning through computer conferencing: The Najaden papers* (pp. 115–136). New York, NY: Springer.

Ice, P., Bain, B., & Stewart, M. (2010). Using the community of inquiry survey instrument to inform online learning outcomes. In: Z. Abas, I. Jung & J. Luca (Eds.), *Proceedings of Global Learn Asia Pacific 2010* (p. 455). AACE. Retrieved from http://www.editlib.org/p/34215.

Kanuka, H., & Anderson, T. (1998). Online social interchange, discord, and knowledge construction. *Journal of Distance Education, 13*(1), 57–75.

LaPointe, D. K., & Gunawardena, C. N. (2004). Developing, testing, and refining a model to understand the relationship between peer interaction and learning outcomes in computer-mediated conferencing. *Distance Education, 25*(1), 83–106.

Lewin, R. (n.d.). *Great-Quotes.com*. Retrieved from http://www.great-quotes.com/quote/

Linden Labs. (2002). *Second Life* [Online]. Retrieved from http://secondlife.com

Luebeck, J. L., & Bice, L. R. (2005). Online discussion as a mechanism of conceptual change among mathematics and science teachers. *Journal of Distance Education, 20*(2), 21–39.

McKerlich, R., & Anderson, T. (2007). Community of enquiry and learning in immersive environments. *Journal of Asynchronous Learning Networks, 11*(4), 35–52.

Meyer, K. A. (2003). Face-to-face versus threaded discussions: The role of time and higher-order thinking. *Journal of Asynchronous Learning Networks, 7*(3), 55–65.

Meyer, K. A. (2004). Evaluating online discussions: Four different frames of analysis. *Journal of Asynchronous Learning Networks, 8*(2), 101–114.

Molinari, D. L. (2004). The role of social comments in problem-solving groups in an online class. *American Journal of Distance Education, 18*(2), 89–101.

Murphy, E. (2004). Identifying and measuring ill-structured problem formulation and resolution in online asynchronous discussions. *Canadian Journal of Learning and Technology, 30*(1), 5–20.

Picciano, A. G. (2002). Beyond student perceptions: Issues of interaction, presence and performance in an online course. *Journal of Asynchronous Learning Networks, 6*(1), 21–40.

Richardson, J. C., & Swan, K. (2003). Examining social presence in online courses in relation to students' perceived learning and satisfaction. *Journal of Asynchronous Learning Networks, 7*(1). Retrieved from http://www.aln.org/publications/jaln/v7n1/index.asp

Rourke, L., Anderson, T., Garrison, D. R., & Archer, W. (2001). Methodological issues in the content analysis of computer conference transcripts. *International Journal of Artificial Intelligence in Education, 12*(1), 8–22.

Rovai, A. P. (2002). Development of an instrument to measure classroom community. *Internet and Higher Education, 5*, 197–211.

Sculley, J. (n.d.). *Great-Quotes.com*. Retrieved from http://www.great-quotes.com/quote/922008

Shea, P., & Bidjerano, T. (2008). Measures of quality in online education: An investigation of the community of inquiry model and the net generation. *Journal of Educational Computing Research, 39*, 339–336.

Shea, P., Hayes, S., Vickers, J., Gozza-Cohen, M., Uzuner, S., Mehta, R., Valchova, A., & Rangan, P. (2010). A re-examination of the community of inquiry framework: Social network and content analysis. *Internet and Higher Education, 13*(1-2), 10–21.

Shea, P. J. (2006). A study of students' sense of learning community in online learning environments. *Journal of Asynchronous Learning Networks, 10*(1). Retrieved from http://www.sloanc.org/publications/jaln/v10n1/v10n1_4shea_member.asp

Simon, H. (n.d.). *Great-Quotes.com*. Retrieved from http://www.great-quotes.com/quote

Stein, D. S., Wanstreet, C. E., Calvin, J., Overtoom, C., & Wheaton, J. E. (2005). Bridging the transactional distance gap in online learning environments. *American Journal of Distance Education, 19*(2), 105–118.

Swan, K. (2002). Building learning communities in online courses: The importance of interaction. *Education Communication and Information, 2*(1), 23–49.

Swan, K. (2003). Learning effectiveness: What the research tells us. In: J. Bourne & J. C. Moore (Eds.), *Elements of quality online education: Practice and direction* (pp. 13–45). Needham, MA: Sloan Consortium.

Swan, K., & Shih, L-F. (2005). On the nature and development of social presence in online course discussions. *Journal of Asynchronous Learning Networks*, *9*(3), 115–136.

Swan, K. P., Richardson, J. C., Ice, P., Garrison, D. R., Cleveland-Innes, M., & Arbaugh, J. B. (2008). Validating a measurement tool of presence in online communities of inquiry. *e-mentor*, *2*(24), 88–94. Retrieved from http://www.e-mentor.edu.pl/_pdf/ementor24.pdf

Texas Higher Education Coordinating Board. (2010). *2010 Progress Report on the long-range plan for technology 2006–2020*. Retrieved from http://www.tea.state.tx.us/index2.aspx?id=2147489836

Thompson, T. L., & MacDonald, C. J. (2005). Community building, emergent design and expecting the unexpected: Creating a quality eLearning experience. *Internet and Higher Education*, *8*, 233–249.

Tu, C-H., & McIsaac, M. (2002). The relationship of social presence and interaction in online classes. *The American Journal of Distance Education*, *16*(3), 131–150.

Walther, J. B. (1993). Impression development in computer-mediated interaction. *Western Journal of Communication*, *57*, 381–398.

LESSON PLAN: GRADUATE-LEVEL RESEARCH METHODS

Objective

The student will conduct a mini-study using the SL learning platform.

The study will include the major components of a research study that include the following:

- Identifying a problem/issue
- Writing research questions
- Synthesis of the literature
- Theoretical framework
- Methodology
- Data collection/data analysis
- Results
- Conclusion.

WEEK 2

Identify a problem/issue

Examples:

- Student Growth and development – citizenship, social responsibility, twenty-first-century skills/learning; STEM Programs at forefront (science, math, engineering, technology SL islands)
- Personnel – professional development in SL; recruitment in SL
- Community outreach – partnerships with universities (SL universities)
- Finances – how SL could be used to cut finances in schools.

(100 points) Write Research Question(s) based upon topic chosen.

Lecture in SL on the various types of research questions. Students will practice writing research questions and share them with the class with feedback from the instructor.

Homework: Write up at least three research questions based upon your topic.

WEEKS 3, 4

(100 points) Synthesis of the Literature based upon topic chosen.
Lecture in SL on researching, organizing, and synthesizing applicable research.
Homework: Research topic; devise an excel spreadsheet organizing the information; synthesize the literature.

WEEK 5

(100 points) Theoretical Framework (write-up)
Lecture in SL on Theoretical frameworks
Homework: Student will research and choose a theoretical framework to base their topic upon.

WEEKS 6, 7, 8

(500 points total) Methodology =
SL meeting attendance (100 points)

- participants, setting, instruments (100 points)
- data collection – observations (see Activity no. 1 below); interviews (see Activity no. 2 below) (200 points)
- data analysis (100 points)

Activity no. 1 (Class Meeting in SL on observations)

Based upon the objectives/goals you want them to know regarding observations, what I have below follows the "I" DO, "WE" DO, "YOU" DO Model and should also address the Community of Inquiry model: (1) teaching presence (PPT/lecture, you, and me to help guide/give feedback/answer questions etc., (2) cognitive presence (the PPT, lecture, activity-application of knowledge), and (3) social presence (debriefing and sharing what we found).

I will present a lecture on the different types of observations in SL (via PPT), and students can take notes based upon the PPT/supplemental handouts/textbook/readings prior to class, etc.

I will model how to observe using the different approaches (direct, unobtrusive). Perhaps everyone can go to a role-play island – somewhere on SL that's highly populated (e.g., Tombstone/Help Island). I will decide which observation type students will use, and then we will spread out and explore the various islands individually and take notes. We will meet back up at Bearkat Island at a designated time.

We can all share and debrief which observation type we used and share with each other some of our notes. We can also begin to extract common themes.

Homework (100/200 points above from the data collection assignment):

Students research various islands related to their topic (maybe give them a list of "safe" places to go within a variety of different islands) and choose one to observe for a period of time.

Again, based upon course objectives students will present to the next class (or maybe post to discussion board and have other students respond) such things like the following:

(1) Where they went?
(2) Why they chose to go there?
(3) Which observational approach did they use?
(4) How did they record the data?
(5) What did they see?
(6) What themes from the observations did they see begin to emerge?
(7) Write-up of information.

Activity no. 2 (Class Meeting in SL on interviews)

*Note: Prior to this activity, however, students will need to devise their own individual interview questions based upon a topic of their own choosing, or one that I choose.

Based upon the objectives/goals regarding observations, what I have below follows the "I" DO, "WE" DO, "YOU" DO Model and should also address the Community of Inquiry model: (1) teaching presence (PPT/lecture; Instructor), (2) cognitive presence (the PPT, lecture, activity-application of knowledge; Students), and (3) social presence (debriefing and sharing the interview experience).

(1) Students will present a lecture on interviewing in SL (via PPT) and students can take notes based upon your PPT/supplemental handouts/textbook/readings prior to class, etc.
(1) I will model different approaches on how to interview.
(2) Students will break up into groups and spread out to different buildings on Bearkat Island to conduct their interviews with each other. Prior to this activity, however, they will need to devise their own individual interview questions based upon a topic, and will need explicit directions on how to copy the text from the interview in SL and send to you.

Homework (100/200 points above for the data collection assignment):

(1) Extract themes
(2) Analyze
(3) Develop write-up.

WEEK 9

(200 points) School Improvement Development Plan. Based upon the information from the mini-study, students will create a school improvement plan.

PART III
TRANSFORMING VIRTUAL WORLD DEVELOPMENT

MARINETTA OMBRO: A CULTURE NOT A CLASSROOM

Owen Kelly

ABSTRACT

In 2002 Arcada began an experiment that aimed to develop a learning laboratory in the form of a virtual culture embodied in an online world. This chapter examines how and why this was attempted, the opportunities that it offered, and the reasons why the experiment was ended. It draws from interviews with staff and students, both during and after the project, as well as papers and reports written as the project evolved. Marinetta Ombro was designed to explore several possibilities inherent in online worlds, other than their use as "virtual classrooms" – possibilities that were intended to derive a pedagogical approach that drew from the core features of multiuser worlds, rather than ignoring them. These included the ever-present possibility of creative disruption. The chapter presents a case study that focuses on an approach to virtuality that was genuinely challenging and innovative. It offers practical and theoretical insights, including a sample learning plan, for educators wishing to explore virtual worlds as well as those wishing to reimagine their current work.

Keywords: Constructivism; networks; pedagogy; second life; virtuality

Transforming Virtual World Learning
Cutting-edge Technologies in Higher Education, Volume 4, 189–214

ISSN: 2044-9968/doi:10.1108/S2044-9968(2011)0000004012

INTRODUCTION

Marinetta Ombro was an experimental virtual world that was begun at Arcada University in early 2002, and maintained and developed by staff and students until late 2009. The chapter outlines the purposes for which this world was devised, looks briefly at its development, and describes a range of educational uses to which it was put. Lessons are drawn from these descriptions. Because of the nature of Arcada, and the nature of the virtual world that was created, it is necessary to begin by clarifying some of the background to the project.

ABOUT ARCADA

Arcada is a university of applied science, in Helsinki, Finland.[1] It is a relatively small institution with approximately 2,000 students. Its official languages are Swedish and English, and it has grown out of the amalgamation of four polytechnics. As a result its ethos is academic, but its bias is still vocationally directed.

Because of its size, teaching in Arcada takes place in groups that are small even by European standards. The four-year BA course in online media accepts 12 students each year, and the Film & Television School, of which it is a part, accepts a total of 38 students.

The unusually low teacher/student ratio affects the creation of course plans and lesson plans, the flexibility within courses, and the forms of assessment used. Many classes contain between 6 and 12 students, and thus class goals can often be supplemented, and in some cases completely replaced, by individual learning plans. Assessment is carried out primarily through project work, self-assessment, and discussion during and after courses. Although students are asked to fill in formal questionnaires the low numbers in each group mean that statistical analysis of the results of these exercises has a limited value.

ABOUT ARCADA'S EDUCATIONAL THEORY

From its inception Arcada has adopted an active learning, social constructivist approach to education, which recognizes that students are unique individuals, that learning is social, and that students learn through discovery. This is especially true within the Film & Television School, where first-year students begin making movies or web sites within a few weeks of enrolling. Instruction here complements ongoing practical work, and is specifically designed to challenge students by proceeding ahead of their development and alongside their current project, since constructivist theory suggests that learning occurs within a zone of proximal development, defined as "the distance between the actual developmental level as determined by independent problem solving and the level of potential development as determined through problem solving under … guidance, or in collaboration with more capable peers" (Vygotsky, 1978).

In practical terms the views of learning within the department draw upon those of John Holt (1978), expressed in his declaration that he never saw himself as practicing the cello, only as playing it badly in the hope of later playing it better. More formally, the department draws upon Lorin Anderson's revision of Bloom's taxonomy (Anderson & Krathwohl, 2001) where the original noun-based formulation is replaced by a set of verbs, with a consequent move from learning objects to learning processes.

At the time when the Marinetta Ombro project was first under discussion Tore Ståhl, a colleague at Arcada, was undertaking research into the relevance of the Bloom taxonomy to virtual learning environments. He concluded (Ståhl, 2004) that the optimal use of virtual learning environments would "require a dynamic and not necessarily a linear use of different spaces during different phases of the educational process, a strategy already used e.g. within problem-based learning."

In further developing this understanding the online media team has moved to a position close to the framework proposed by Andrew Churches (2007). This seeks to find a place within the work of Bloom and Anderson for the new (and typically digital) activities such as "bookmarking" and "podcasting" that have come to constitute important means within the taxonomy of learning processes. These, then, were the theoretical bases upon which Marinetta Ombro was conceived.

ABOUT MARINETTA OMBRO

In 2002 Arcada owned a cable channel in a small town outside Helsinki for which the television students had to produce programs each week. Even though the channel had very few viewers it shaped all the students' studies. Everything they did was both a learning exercise and a contribution toward the television schedule. Project deadlines were also an inflexible commitment to fill a certain time-slot on a certain date.

Students were encouraged to believe that they were not practicing, but rather making real programs for a tiny, little-known channel in the belief that one day they would be making programs for a large, publicly acknowledged channel. From the perspective of social constructivism, the complexity of the learning environment was designed to reflect "the complexity of the environment that the learner should be able to function in at the end of learning" (Knowles, Holton, & Swanson, 2006).

The television station acted as an overarching project-based environment for the film and television students, and in 2002 it was agreed that a similar learning environment should be established for the online media students. According to the initial project documentation (Kelly, 2010) this projected environment was "intended to act as a laboratory within which students could test their ideas; improve their planning, development and programming skills; and then watch as their experiments had real and lasting effects."

After consultation between staff and students it was decided that the learning environment should take the form of a virtual world. The precise nature of this world was the subject of a lengthy discussion (Kelly, 2006), at the end of which it was agreed that the virtual world should take the form of a small Mediterranean island, located approximately halfway between Malta and Crete, and that all those involved should act as though what was being created was the digital simulation of a real island.

The virtual island was named Rosario, and its native language was deemed to be derived from Ido.[2] The main village on the island was named Marinetta. The project itself was then titled Marinetta Ombro, which translates from Ido as "The Shadow of Marinetta."

MARINETTA OMBRO: PROJECT OVERVIEW

Marinetta Ombro was originated and supervised by Owen Kelly (2004b) and Camilla Lindeberg, who were the full-time lecturers for Arcada's online media course. We were responsible for leading and overseeing the project's development.

Our decision that all those involved in Marinetta Ombro should act as though what was being created was the digital simulation of a real island may at first seem overcomplicated, but it arose from our understanding of the term "virtual world." This understanding needs to be examined because it differs from, and is in direct contradiction to, a use that has become fashionable in some educational circles in the period since the Marinetta Ombro project began.

DEFINITIONS

The project began with the decision to create a virtual world. All the participants rapidly realized that this term was open to many interpretations. It was, however, a phrase that could usefully be pulled apart, examined, and then put back together again.

Richard Bartle (2003), the originator of the first MUD, had done just that. He defined the terms as follows:

"virtual: that which isn't, having the form or effect of that which is.
world: in this context, a world is an environment that its inhabitants regard as being self-contained. It doesn't have to mean an entire planet: It's used in the same sense as 'the Roman world' or 'the world of high finance'."

From this we drew a clear distinction between "virtual worlds" and "virtual spaces," and it is this distinction that lay behind many of the steps that were taken in the development of the project.

A virtual space is an illusion projected onto a computer screen by specialized software. This illusion provides a set of visual cues that enable a user to imagine that they are looking into, or are actually inside, a three dimensional (3D) environment. Usually this illusion is detailed enough to enable the viewer to describe this environment by reference to the real world, and to differentiate one such environment from another.

In 2011 this kind of virtual space is provided by companies such as Teleplace who promote the spaces as immersive alternatives to video conferencing. The spaces are generic in design and isolated from each other. Users can rent an office space, or a lecture theater, or an arena. Each space has been developed to appear realistic enough not to cause users any distraction. Users can interact, access media that has been uploaded, and, if the space has been subdivided, move from one virtual area to another. Users cannot usually leave the building, though, because the virtual space has no "outside" and is not part of anything larger than itself. It is isolated by design because its function is not exploration, but to facilitate purposeful interaction between a known group of people with a shared agenda.

A virtual world, on the other hand, is analogous to something like "the Roman world" or "the world of high finance," which is to say it cannot simply be defined by its geometry. The "world of fashion," for example, is not just a collection of clothes. The "world" evoked here includes interlocking sets of aspirations and attitudes, a wide range of actors from designers to models to journalists, as well as calendar events and the various venues at which these events are held.

From this perspective the reconstruction in Second Life of the Cite de l'Architecture at Place du Trocadero, one of the venues for the Paris Fashion Week, and the creation of suitable clothing, would not constitute the creation of a virtual "world of fashion." It would simply be a virtual space with a particular kind of decoration.

To create a "world of fashion" would be a much more complex operation, and one that many educators might feel irrelevant to their needs. It would involve creating or invoking a virtual culture within which the clothing, the events, and the venues made a self-contained sense (Kelly, 2004a).

That was precisely what was attempted at Arcada with the Marinetta Ombro project. We intended to create the culture of Marinetta, a culture in which the students would be foreigners, and to depict this immersively. We intended this virtual culture to be coherent (i.e., to make consistent sense once its axioms were accepted) and for students to engage within the world as they would in any new and unfamiliar environment.

We expected this "otherness" to be a key feature of the project, which was why we did not begin to develop or create a virtual space of any kind until our research had told us what we could expect to find there.

AIMS

The aim of the project was fourfold. We wished to provide:

- a new kind of environment for distance learning;
- a laboratory for cultural studies;
- a test bed for web applications;
- a framework for in-house apprenticeships.

Almost all the online environments that we had seen suffered from the fact that they were designed for one single purpose. Some were designed for distance learning; others were designed for entertainment such as role-playing games. The real world, however, never works like that. People walk the same streets and sit on the same train for very different reasons.

Arcada's intention was to create a multipurposed world – a world that was unpredictable because it was multipurposed and where learning online was just one of the possible activities taking place.

We believed that this would allow for spontaneous interactions that were unplanned yet fruitful. We also believed that if the environment that we created was rich enough then learning how people used the world and what people wanted from it would provide students with valuable experience in the fields of monitoring and marketing, as well as planning and design.

The project was premised on the idea of "creative interference" – a belief that single purpose institutions do not reflect how (or where) learning actually happens. We believed that by making the world genuinely open for almost any kind of use, residents would find that they were often and unexpectedly surprised and challenged; just as a tourist is surprised and challenged walking down the streets of a foreign city for the first time.

METHODOLOGY

At the beginning of the project we had a goal but no clear road map. We adopted the open-ended approach recommended by Albert Einstein (quoted in Murty, 2006), when he asserted that "if we knew what it was we were doing it would not be called research, would it?" We set an initial three-year period of exploration with the intention of conducting an assessment at the end of it.

We were aware when we began that in many educational institutions there "is little room in today's educational climate for technologies that do not either accelerate or greatly increase learning," and that "many learning games do not demonstrate a sound, efficient educational or instructional design" (Warren, Jones, & Lin, 2011). Fortunately the size and structure of Arcada meant that we were freer of these constraints than many of our colleagues. Thus, we were able to make the construction of the project a part of the project itself. Rather than creating a virtual world within which learning and instruction could take place we began by placing all the key aspects of the creation of a virtual world on the student curriculum.

The initial methodology for constructing the world consisted of aligning the term projects within existing classes in such a way that these projects could be aggregated into a larger whole. This was made possible by the project-based instruction at the heart of Arcada's programs. Since almost all classes would conclude with a practical project designed to demonstrate learning outcomes then our task was to devise projects that would progress one aspect or another of the emerging virtual world.

It is important to note that we did not begin with the software. We did not program a virtual space and then decided what to put in it, or how to act in it.

We did not have any world within which users could move and interact for the first 15 months of the project. Our methodology was founded upon asking questions in classes that ranged from media theory to foundations of Photoshop.

Initially, these questions focused on the difference between virtual spaces and virtual worlds, beginning with questions such as "where does the Parisness of Paris lie?" "what are the core elements of a sense of place?" and "how could these be depicted on a screen?" Later, as core decisions were made, the questions became more specific.

PROCEDURE

At the start of each academic year we established one or more annual goals. In the first year the goals had been to "discover the culture and history of Rosario" and to "research technologies for realizing the village of Marinetta on the internet." In the second year we moved onto visualizing the culture and building an online depiction of Marinetta using SCOL Technology, a promising French software that failed to gain support and subsequently faded away.[3]

We reviewed our goals twice a year, adjusting them where circumstances required. We established a staff/student forum that met at least once a month, and usually more often. The purpose of this was to generate ideas and feedback, and to give us early warning signs about likely problems or issues.

MILESTONES

Marinetta Ombro passed a series of milestones through which its progress could be measured. The following is a summary, given to provide the reader with a brief glimpse into the project's life. There are more detailed descriptions available elsewhere (Kelly, 2010).

We began the project with a year of research, during which we questioned, what we meant by "virtual world," explored mechanisms for creating a virtual culture, and then depicting it immersively on-screen. During this period we answered several key questions concerning history and geography. Crucially, we decided to adopt Ido as the language for all signs, displays, and public pronouncements.

In 2003, we launched the first online version of the world, using a SCOL Technology server and client software.

In 2004, we launched several related web sites. The first was a site that documented 2,000 years of the island's history in great detail. The second was La Voco, a newspaper-styled site that documented the development of the project as it happened. The third was a site posing as a genuine tourism site, providing details of the island's highlights.

We also published a set of five e-books containing a complete history of Rosario in terms of people, places, and events.

In October 2005, we bought private land in Second Life, where we launched the third version of the online world. This expanded to model the entire island of Rosario over nine sims.

In 2006, a three meter square model of Rosario was constructed by business and engineering students for an exhibition in Helsinki. This was used by the business students for a public presentation of the data collected in a project discussed later in this chapter.

In 2007, we held an open day, Semano Semano, in Second Life that attracted large crowds.

In 2008, as part of the celebrations for the Eurovision Song Contest in Helsinki, we created a set of machinima[4] that were broadcast on Finnish television and held a second Semano Semano that attracted over 800 visitors in 24 hours. This, too, is described below.

In 2009, we realized that the current project had gone as far as it could. The context within which we worked had changed dramatically since 2002, due to the advent of always-on mobile media, and we closed the project to regroup and think again.

LEARNING PROJECTS IN MARINETTA

This section looks at the role of Marinetta Ombro as an overarching environment for the online media students. During its lifespan it was used much more widely than we had planned. The business, computer technology, health care, television, and tourism courses all made use of it to enhance their instruction. This section describes a representative series of uses to which the virtual world was put, in approximate chronological order. The headings refer to the title of the class.

STRUCTURING INFORMATION

The first-year structuring information class were given an initial assignment when we began envisaging the virtual culture of Rosario. They worked under the guidance of a third-year student who intended to use the process as a research for his thesis.

Input

The students were told to develop strategies for inventing a logical and coherent history for the island. They were told that they had to allow for an unknown number of future contributors to be able to insert additions to the history, as they were needed; and that they had to provide a mechanism that would render these additions internally consistent and believable.

Action

The students decided that the most general historical and geographical information could be deduced by comparing the histories and geographies of Malta and Crete, with some reference to southern Italy and the history and geography of Libya, with some reference to Tunisia and Egypt. By averaging these, and then deciding at each point whether the island's development was affected most by Europe or Africa, the students produced a very general view of Rosario's development.

A detailed history was then compiled using a methodology that involved looking for genuine gaps in official records and then inserting Rosario into them. One student sought to find a reason for a link between Swedish culture and Rosario. His work illustrates the approach that the group developed.

He found that in "859 a Viking expedition under the command the sons of the legendary Ragnar Lodbrok, left Sweden for the Mediterranean Sea with 62 ships. At first they were beaten by Christian and Moorish armies, but at Gibraltar their luck turned and they plundered the city of Algericas and then continued to the Moroccan coast and Balearerna ... They returned to Sweden in 862, after further battles, with only 20 of the 62 ships remaining" (Weckström, 2004).

There is an 18-month gap in the historical record where the Vikings' activities are unrecorded. Using this historical fact he wrote Swedish culture into Rosarian history in a way that would be completely convincing if Rosario actually existed.

Outcomes

The insights gained during the course were broadened through references to other scenarios where this technique might be professionally useful. The group looked at material relating to the development of Star Trek, Hill Street Blues, and other television series set in consistent, but entirely fictitious, locales.

Critical thinking was encouraged as the group assessed each other's ideas in relation to group-developed notions concerning the boundaries of believability. First-year students learnt to work in teams as they were forced to champion their ideas, while being prepared to drop them when they were successfully challenged.

The third-year student decided to devote his thesis entirely to the issue of creating believable backstories and environments for online virtual worlds (Weckström, 2004).

CONCEPT DESIGN AND BRANDING

In Autumn 2003, a group of third-year students began a course on brand development. The aim of this course was to examine the ontology of brands, and the ways in which packaging, advertising, web sites, and other media can be made to reflect the look, feel, and "values" embodied in a brand.

This was the first course to be taught entirely within the framework of Rosarian culture (Lindeberg, 2004).

Input

In previous years students had been told to invent an imaginary brand (a cola or toothpaste), create a package for it, and make a presentation explaining its brand values. This time the students had to work within a complex framework. In addition to the previous year's tasks students also had to create a display in Marinetta in the form of hoardings, shop fronts, or vehicles designs.

Action

The students had to survey what had already been done, and then decide what was possible on the island; what was wanted by the island's consumers;

and what the company's competition would be, based on the existing records.

Students created brand names and slogans in Ido in addition to creating packages using Adobe Photoshop and Illustrator. They created in-world advertising campaigns. Finally, they made 15-minute presentations in English, as though they were pitching ideas for a campaign in a foreign country, with all the explanations of ideas, idioms, and language involved in such a process.

Outcomes

As the students explored the documentation created in the previous year, the feedback loops in the project became clear to both staff and students. Some students found that the information they felt they required did not exist, and so it had to be created before they could access it.

The need to create slogans in Ido forced them to consider the sounds and shapes, as well as the meanings, of the text. Freed from the (often unnoticed) inhibitions of being amusing in their mother tongue they were able to focus on their slogans as pictograms and music as well as meaningful utterances.

RESEARCH METHODS FOR HEALTH CARE

Staff in other departments at Arcada became interested in the project, but initially they were more enthusiastic about the conceptual framework than its manifestation on the web. Many departments had been using primitive simulations of different kinds in their teaching and several members of staff recognized that there could be significant benefits in finding ways of incorporating these into the narrative of Rosario.

In spring 2005, a lecturer in health care approached us about using Marinetta in a class concerning research methodology for *Public Health Nursing*. In this class students were set a group assignment during which they were provided with sets of statistics for a (fictitious) locality in Finland and told to create a district health plan from them.

Input

In previous years the staff took the figures from an undisclosed Finnish city and altered them a little before giving them to the students. Every year the brighter students guessed what kind of city the figures related to, and often what city. They then reverse-engineered their reports by studying the actual public health plans of the city they had guessed and altering the figures a little. This year the students were told to create a district health plan for the town of Marinetta.

Action

Staff and students sat down and created population data, in the form that the exercise required. To do this we followed the procedure previously laid down by the students in the structuring information course – we gathered data from the surrounding areas, averaged it, adjusted it according to an agreed formula, and based our estimates on this, taking into account certain (previously invented) special factors.

The students received two lectures on the history and culture of Rosario, as an introduction to the class. These included discussions on employment patterns and leisure activities.

The students then began their calculations. They were allowed to email and ask for more figures, or for more details regarding the figures they had already been given. They did this several times, and we sat and generated the figures they had asked for, using the same formulae each time.

Outcomes

The project was enthusiastically received by the students. The trainee nurses had to research health issues on comparable (real) Mediterranean islands, and they had found this an interesting and engaging starting point for what they felt might otherwise have been a rather dry exercise. One said that "it was useful to be forced to look at health care in other parts of the world and to have to think about problems that are not the same as Helsinki problems." Another said simply that "we should have more assignments like this."[5]

The staff members involved also regarded the project as a success, and later expanded the idea to include health plans for all the nine villages on the island.

ENTREPRENEURSHIP STUDIES

In 2005, a member of staff suggested a collaboration with the international business course. He had been running an assignment based around a simulation in the form of a turn-based game where students created and managed a company. He sent them a set of financial data that they analyzed before making decisions, and returning a list of actions to him. He would then run these through a spreadsheet before sending out the next set of data. He wished to set these companies on Rosario and have the students use the history, geography, and statistical data as background material for the assignment.

Input

The lecturer began by suggesting additions to the data we had amassed about Rosario. He was interested in the island's natural resources, and about what industry already existed. Together the staff created a detailed economic history for the island. This included an overview of the Rosarian industrial revolution and a timeline of companies that had succeeded and companies that had failed.

Action

For the 2005 course the students listened to a short series of lectures about Rosario before being told that they were to consider themselves international entrepreneurs with a set amount of capital. They had been told that Rosario was a market they should target. Their task was to devise a detailed business plan to establish a company in Rosario, and to ask whatever questions they wanted, if they felt that they needed further background information.

Outcomes

Not only were the students highly enthusiastic about the assignment, they pushed us to create a more and more detailed picture of the island. It was no surprise that they demanded more economic information. However, they also asked a range of questions regarding the trustworthiness of the local people, their attitude to work, whether they were socially adventurous or conservative, and the amount of immigration compared to emigration.

Finally, they persuaded a group of engineering students to help them construct a three meter square scale model of the island, with detailed models of the various refineries and factories they had projected in their business plans. This was used on several occasions as part of public presentations at conferences and exhibitions.

This clearly demonstrated that, educationally, the virtual culture of Rosario was as powerful as the virtual landscape that was explorable on-screen. The ideas were proving as interesting as the furniture.

FOUNDATIONS OF PHOTOSHOP

The skills required to make clothing in Second Life are almost exactly the same as the skills that students learn in the Photoshop foundations class – an understanding of channels, transparency, layers, layer masks, and file formats. In 2006, we combined the two in an assignment where students made and gave away clothing on Rosario.

Input

Students were challenged to explore Second Life for a week in order to understand the current fashions and crazes; to pick something from these and then to design a range of clothing using the Photoshop skills they were learning.

Action

The course began as usual, with introductory sessions looking at the toolbox. The students' initial project was based around the creation of a range of postcards. In this course the source material was created by the students using screenshots from Second Life.

The final project brought together the skills they had learned through creating a range of clothing. A free clothing store, where each student had one or more vending machines, was established in Marinetta and advertised within Second Life. The decision to make the clothes "freebies" was deliberate, and designed to reduce the complexity of the assignment. Forcing the students to guess a market value for their clothes was irrelevant to the assignment.

For their final presentation the students had to show the clothes they had made, explain how many they had been able to give away, and offer a self-critique of the process. Put (over)simply: if you had not managed to give away any clothes then you had a lot of explaining to do!

Outcomes

Most students enjoyed the assignment, and the majority felt that it was technically challenging. However, a few students refused to accept that the assignment had much bearing on what they were supposed to be learning because the outcome was not one that they regarded as useful professionally.

The course concluded with a heated debate about the relevance of Second Life to the class. This ended when one of the students announced that they had been commissioned for a (small) amount of real money to make some uniforms for an avatar they had met while exploring.

We learned that we were naive to assume that students would automatically find Second Life fascinating and enjoyable. From that point on, we made certain that we always introduced the Marinetta project by linking it to wider topics such as the unpredictable growth of the web and the surprising ways in which businesses become successful online.

Providing a preliminary contextual presentation helped to minimize the number of future occasions in which students become hostile to the idea of learning in-world.

TOURISM AND MEDIA

Arcada offers a degree in tourism management, and several of the courses concern strategies for the use of media. In 2006 staff decided that two classes, one containing students of tourism, and one containing online media students would work on a long joint project.

It was decided that Rosario would celebrate Semano Semano (which, literally, means Week Week in Ido), an annual festival that the history on the web site claimed was held each May.

Input

In Arcada's first year in Second Life a number of students attempted to start a club on the island, but it never worked. Although the club had visitors, it failed to attract or retain a regular crowd. It was therefore decided that we would have one or two large public events each year that could be organized in the same way as film productions.

Action

After a period of exploration and familiarization the online media students built a festival site, while the tourism students determined the festival program. Then both groups created and staffed the festival itself.

Initially, small groups of students set off to explore Second Life, document their explorations, and make presentations to the rest of the group. Their brief was to seek out what was popular and then devise ways in which the festival could tap into that popularity for one weekend. Over eight weeks, the suggestions were refined into a potential program. At each stage the groups had to consider not only whether what was being suggested would be popular but also whether it would be feasible.

For the multimedia students the second phase became a series of design and programming tasks, which called for them to bring their specialist knowledge and experience to bear. For the tourism students, this phase involved deciding how they could generalize from the course in which they had made a marketing plan for a holiday resort and apply it to a virtual world that did not have mass media of the kind they were used to.

Outcomes

Both groups were forced to think at length about why people were spending time in Second Life, and they reached an interesting set of conclusions. Most people spend time in there doing rather than watching; being active rather than passive. They decided that, for the majority of residents, these activities could be divided into four primary groups: showing off (shopping and dressing up), socializing (at clubs, beaches, and malls), playing (parachuting, windsurfing, and so on), and creating (building and scripting).

The result of these deliberations was a 24-hour festival that consisted of treasure hunts and games; with a festival beach club, and a row of shops giving away a range of free Rosarian clothes and accessories. The event attracted approximately 150 residents. Both groups of students were impressed with the outcome. Organizing a successful virtual event had given them real satisfaction.

The tourism students were convinced that the work flow they had been through was directly comparable to that involved in running a real festival. One said, "I did not view the exercise as virtual at all. We were trying to attract real people during a real weekend and even if we were attracting them to a computer game we still had to attract the real them."

CROSS MEDIA PRODUCTION

In May 2007, Helsinki was due to host the Eurovision Song Contest, a huge media event that has been broadcast annually across Europe since 1956. It was decided at Arcada to expand the model of Semano Semano for the occasion.

It was also decided that this would be the final production for the cross media production class, and that it would be led by a student team consisting of three students from Helsinki and four exchange students from the Institute of Technology Tallaght (ITT), in Dublin, with additional help from several avatars that we knew only from meetings in Second Life.

Input

We explained to the team what had happened the previous year. The group then decided to organize a nighttime festival that would last for 12 consecutive nights. However, because Second Life has four-hour days/night cycles, this meant that, in reality, Semano Semano would last for 12 one-hour sessions, taking place every four hours for two days.

Action

The whole team worked for six weeks conceiving, building, designing, and scripting the objects needed to transform a bare valley on the island into a festival site, with a lot of activities and a lot of "freebies."

We had, for example, a synchronized national dance in full Rosarian national costume. We also had a machinima of the banned Rosarian entry for the Eurovison Song Contest – a song (sung in Ido) called Al Dek Manto.

Students recorded and edited videos from inside SL. These proved to be very useful for the television students running live television feeds for

Arcada's cable channel, which broadcast 24 hours a day during the Eurovision week. The team was able to provide them with quirky content that they could drop into gaps in the schedules, and reuse whenever they needed to.

Nonstop television broadcasts were streamed live into La Moyena Valo, the festival valley in Rosario. Video taken in the valley was streamed out and broadcast on television in Helsinki, on the web, and over Finnish mobile phone networks.

During the 12 sessions of Semano Semano approximately 700 people participated in some sort of in-world activity. The numbers varied wildly from session to session; partly because we failed to appeal to as many American residents as we would have liked, and (judging from conversations we had) partly depending on what else was, or was not, happening in Second Life at the same time. Social gaming activities such as Terra Z races and skydiving were popular, though, every time we hosted them.

The 11th session took place the hour before the contest itself began, and was almost full from the outset. Because nobody wanted to leave, it simply carried on throughout the three hour televised contest. During this unplanned five-hour party there were never less than 30 people in La Moyena Valo, and we estimated that over 100 people were there for at least 15 or 20 minutes.

Outcomes

The involvement of the Irish students sparked a collaboration between ITT in Dublin and Arcada in Helsinki that continues to this day.

The use of Rosario as material for us on television and mobile phone suggested a number of possibilities. During the debriefing that followed the project it was decided that some of these could better be explored outside the framework of Rosario. It was therefore agreed the project would be ended after one more year, which would be devoted to documentation and technical experimentation in preparation for the launch of another unifying project.

This period saw the production of one more student thesis addressing the issue of building an environment to house and reflect a virtual culture (Gröndahl, 2010).

LESSONS LEARNED

The Marinetta Ombro project was conceived as an environment that would, through its every design, present learning opportunities. For this reason it was created as a virtual culture presented within an online "world." Our approach was one of immersion not augmentation, and the fictitious history of the island was as important for the possibility of learning as its virtual geometry.

Our plans were deliberately open-ended at the outset and allowed to develop freely. The reason for this was clear. In 2002 we did not know what opportunities a virtual world might present as a learning laboratory, and we did not believe that anyone else did either. Because the institution allowed us, we adopted an exploratory approach, and, as a result, Marinetta expanded in directions that we could not have predicted.

The arguments in favor of adopting an "official" language (Kelly, 2003) were neither imposed nor preplanned. They were developed by students as the project was developed, out of perceived needs that grew organically. In this Marinetta Ombro was successful. It demonstrated the value of allowing learners to own the learning tools, and making the design and upgrading of those tools part of the curriculum.

However, there were areas where the project was less obviously successful. The small size of the staff and student team made for efficient development. If the cohort had been one or two hundred there would have been a need for much more formalized procedures. However, once the island was created the small number of students became a disadvantage. There were never enough people involved at any time to create the significant mass that would have been needed to make the island of Rosario a phenomenon that was recognized throughout Second Life. If the island had been "inhabited" by several hundred students then our efforts to draw in other users would have had more impact.

Although it is outside the scope of this chapter, it should be noted that there were other groups of people using Rosario, ranging from a group of "furries" who set up a colony in a disused corner to a group of Australian artists who set up and managed a gallery for several years. This creative interference was useful at several levels. First the existence of skilled builders spurred the students on. Second the sense of in-world community that developed gave the island a flavor that was not institutional or rule-bound.

Finally, we discovered that the project had a lifespan that proved difficult to ignore. Lars Lundsten, a media philosopher, had warned us at the beginning that the initial excitement that the project generated would be difficult to sustain. He warned that within a few years students would arrive at Arcada and see Marinetta as an established routine into which they were supposed to fit. An analysis of the final cross media project clearly showed that the Irish students, who had arrived without any knowledge of Marinetta, had galvanized the other students. Their enthusiasm had encouraged the Finnish students to reclaim ownership of the project's narrative.

The project was put into hibernation in large part because we recognized that this prediction had come true. Circumstances had indeed changed, but one of the changes was that Marinetta Ombro had become a part of the curriculum rather than a challenge to it.

It was decided that the online media course should focus on augmentation for three years, as it applies to mobile media as well as the web, before looking again at immersion, the models and documentation created during the seven years of the Marinetta Ombro project.

CONCLUSIONS

The project raised three issues that seem worthy of further detailed research. The first of these concerned the use of the term "virtual worlds" in education. Used loosely this can often obscure differences that have important pedagogical consequences. It can bundle together projects that have different goals and different outcomes. There is a need for a taxonomy of virtuality that clearly spells out the possible spectrum from virtual spaces that can be used as controlled environments for problem-based learning to virtual worlds where learning takes within a larger in-world culture. This issue was raised by Henrik Bennetsen (2006) in an influential paper on immersion versus augmentation. There is much that needs to be studied and tested in this field, if educationalists are to consider, not just how virtuality might be used for learning, but how learning might be changed through exposure to virtuality.

The second issue concerns the nature of the relationship between what is modeled in virtuality and what is perceived in the real world. The Marinetta Ombro project suggested that this is a far from straightforward relationship, and certainly not one that should be taken for granted. Kenneth Ketner has suggested a fruitful approach to this problem in his writings about Charles Sanders Peirce's method of diagrammatic inquiry (Ketner & Percy, 1995). The propositions that "we schematise our perceptions diagrammatically," and that "virtuality presents us with a powerful diagramming tool whether we notice it or not," point toward areas that call for detailed exploration (Kelly, 2011).

If we accept that much learning occurs through processes of diagramming then a third issue arises concerning the extent to which skills are gained merely through prolonged experience in a virtual environment, and the extent to which these skills are themselves transferable to the physical world. Beck and Wade (2006) have demonstrated the educational power such background effects can have even when they are unintended.

These three issues spring from the same belief that, during the Marinetta Ombro project, we were swimming tentatively in the shallow end of a very deep stream, and that it was the depths that warranted detailed research.

NOTES

1. See http://www.arcada.fi/en
2. Ido was an artificial language created in 1906 as an intended replacement for Esperanto. From an outline history of the language see http://en.wikipedia.org/wiki/Ido
3. As of the time of writing SCOL Technology continues to exist as a small hobbyist group, who can be found on the web at http://www.scolring.org/
4. The use of 3D graphics software to make movies. See http://en.wikipedia.org/wiki/Machinima
5. Comments here and subsequently taken from, as yet, unpublished project records.

REFERENCES

Anderson, L. W., & Krathwohl, D. R. (Eds.). (2001). *A taxonomy for learning, teaching, and assessing: A revision of Bloom's taxonomy of educational objectives*. Boston, MA: Allyn & Bacon.

Bartle, R. (2003). *Designing virtual worlds*. Indianapolis, IN: New Riders Publishing.

Beck, J. C., & Wade, M. (2006). *The kids are alright*. Boston, MA: Harvard Business School Press.

Bennetsen, H. (2006). Immersion versus Augmentation. Retrieved from http://slcreativity.org/wiki/index.php?title=Augmentation_vs_Immersion on 12/12/2010

Churches, A. (2007). Bloom's & ICT Tools. Retrieved from https://edorigami.wikispaces.com/Bloom's+and+ICT+tools

Gröndahl, C. (2010). *Developing virtual environments for educational use*. Degree thesis, Arcada University of Applied Science, Helsinki, Finland.

Holt, J. C. (1978). *Never too late*. New York, NY: Delacorte.

Kelly, O. (2003). Possibilities of virtual cultures. *Presented at the 5th annual phenomenology & media conference* (May), Arcada University, Sweden.

Kelly, O. (2004a). Ghost towns & virtual worlds. *Presented at the 6th annual phenomenology & media conference* (May), Brigham Young University, Provo, UT.
Kelly, O. (2004b). Unifying the curriculum in a digital playground. Presented at the Society for Information Technology & Teacher Education international conference, Atlanta, USA.
Kelly, O. (2006). *Logic, structure & real virtuality* (Presented at league of worlds, October 3). Boone, NC: Appalachain State University.
Kelly, O. (2010). Sexton Blake and the virtual culture of Rosario: A Biji. In: S. Sonvilla-Weiss (Ed.), *Mashup cultures* (pp. 120–135). NewYork, NY: Springer.
Kelly, O. (2011). Diagrammatic inquiry. In: L. Annetta & S. Bronack (Eds.), *Serious educational game assessment 2010*. Boston, MA: Sense Publishers.
Ketner, K. L., & Percy, W. (1995). *A thief of Peirce*. Oxford, MS: University Press of Mississippi.
Knowles, M. S., Holton, E. F., & Swanson, R. A. (2006). *The adult learner* (6th ed.). Boston, MA: Elsevier.
Lindeberg, C. (2004). Concept development in a virtual world. Presented at Ed-Media, Lugano.
Murty, K. K. (2006). *Spice in science: The best of science funnies*. Delhi: Pustak Mahal.
Ståhl, T. (2004). Pedagogical conditions for course design in network supported learning. In: L. Cantoni & C. Mcloughlin (Eds.), *Proceedings of world conference on educational multimedia, hypermedia and telecommunications*, AACE, Chesapeake, VA (pp. 3773–3776).
Vygotsky, L. S. (1978). *Mind and society: The development of higher psychological processes*. Cambridge, MA: Harvard University Press.
Warren, S., Jones, G., & Lin, L. (2011). Usability and play testing. In: L. Annetta & S. Bronack (Eds.), *Serious educational game assessment* (pp. 131–146). Boston, MA: Sense Publishers.
Weckström, N. (2004). Finding "reality" in virtual environments. Degree thesis, Arcada University, Sweden.

LESSON PLAN: PHOTOSHOP FOUNDATIONS

This is the learning plan for the Photoshop foundations class described in this chapter. The key terms are derived from Andrew Churches' (2007) reworking of Bloom's taxonomy.

AIM

During the class students will learn how to use imagery software for professional needs, to apply their skills to a variety of situations, and to develop effective working routines.

GENERAL OUTCOME

At the end of the course the student will be expected to be able to deliver graphical material for web productions in a timely manner and to a professional standard.

The emphasis is on practical work done within given deadlines. Absence without notifying the teacher will affect the grading even if all tasks are finished within the given timetable.

COURSE CONTENT

1. Working with pictures
2. Graphic design for the web
3. Practical work.

Session 1

Activities: Introduction to Photoshop, the interface, and the toolbox. Introduction to file formats. Introduction to Second Life.
Assignment: Exploration of Second Life. Creation of a simple hoarding/billboard with user-created textures. Search the web and bookmark useful online references and tutorials for independent learning.
Key terms: Searching, bookmarking, categorizing, tagging, locating, finding

Session 2

Activities: Presentation of individual bookmarks and compilation into group list. The nature of color in Photoshop. Channels and Layers. Colorizing a grayscale image using channels and the selection tool. Saving selections.
Assignment: Take a self-portrait and desaturate it. Now create three colorized versions: one realistic, one that looks like a Warhol print, and one that displays a dramatically heightened mood.
Key terms: Locating, finding, inferring, paraphrasing, classifying, comparing, explaining

Session 3

Activities: Use of filters. Text in Photoshop. Filter and text.
Assignment: Take each of the three images from the previous week and turn them into book covers.

Session 4 and 5

Activities: Montage and the combination of images. Working with layers. Taking images in Second Life.
Assignment: The creation of e-cards for use on the Marinetta web site. Explore Rosario in Second Life and take photographs on the island. Using these make a set of four e-cards that can be used by the IT students when they program the e-card service on the site in the next period.
Key terms: Locating, finding, implementing, editing, uploading, sharing

Session 6

Activities: Color palettes and design choice.
Assignment: A large self-portrait that has been desaturated and then colorized to simulate the airbrushed perfection in an advertisement for cosmetics. You must look perfect, but realistically perfect!
Key terms: Finding, classifying, comparing, deconstructing, implementing, editing

Session 7

Activities: Scaling and skewing. Correcting perspective. Realism in montage: shadows, lighting, and blurring.
Assignment: The creation of a landscape in which several clones of you appear in ways that appear completely natural.
Key terms: Experimenting, critiquing, judging, testing, implementing

Session 8

Activities: How are clothes made in Second Life? An introduction to multilayered templates using transparency. An overview of uploading and testing clothes. An overview of creating 2D images intended to be projected in 3D.
Assignment: The creation of clothing for distribution in Second Life.
Key terms: Planning, producing, inventing, devising, testing, implementing

Session 9

Activities: Continuation of assignment. Discussion of techniques for displaying clothes (images vs. demonstrations).
Assignment: The creation of clothing for distribution in Second Life.
Key terms: Planning, producing, inventing, devising, testing, implementing

Session 10

Activities: Student reports on exercise, including demonstration of clothes made, discussion of choices, and "sales" figures. They must have previously uploaded all the relevant material to the class site.
Key terms: Reflecting, summarizing, explaining, publishing
Note: Arcada does not usually create lesson plans because classes are small enough to move smoothly between planned lessons and individual study plans. Instead, learning plans are created for each 10-week class. Typically, these provide an overall structure for the class, overall aims and expected outcomes, topics and assignments for each session, and outcomes for each assignment.

ENHANCING GRADUATE COURSES THROUGH EDUCATIONAL VIRTUAL TOURS

Irena Bojanova and Les Pang

ABSTRACT

An innovative approach for enhancing college courses using virtual worlds was developed to raise the students' level of engagement, promote critical thinking, and meet pedagogical objectives. Reaching to a new level of teaching delivery, this approach involves conducting tours of rich and exciting virtual world venues and assigning students' reflective assignments during and after the tour. In this chapter, the procedures for conducting virtual educational tours are presented, descriptions of explored virtual demonstrations and simulations are provided, findings from the learning experiences are discussed, and students' reactions to the technologies based on comprehensive surveys are shared. Furthermore, key lessons learned and recommended teaching strategies are provided and future plans for application of cutting-edge technologies to education are described.

Keywords: Virtual worlds; Second Life; Web 2.0; Web 3.0; avatars; cloud computing; innovative teaching; virtual tours

Transforming Virtual World Learning
Cutting-edge Technologies in Higher Education, Volume 4, 215–239

ISSN: 2044-9968/doi:10.1108/S2044-9968(2011)0000004013

INTRODUCTION

Field trips to different venues provide an engaging and fun learning experience for students. However, this is difficult if not impossible to accomplish for online classes. One alternative that is suitable for the online environment is for students to participate in virtual educational tours using modern technologies such as virtual worlds.

Virtual worlds provide a venue for supporting social networking, entertainment, collaboration, business activities, and education. Although virtual worlds appear to be like video games, in fact they are not since there could be physical world consequences to the activities undertaken in these worlds such as generating income. Virtual environments allow members to build their own worlds, create social relationships, and participate in a virtual economy using its currency. These worlds create unique opportunities for users to pursue economic, social, fantasy, and physical activities such as learning (Mennecke et al., 2008). Virtual worlds offer a new dimension in learning in a fun and provocative environment – students can develop their own persona in the form of avatars, experience new modes of movement such as flying, and discover new worlds of wonder.

Second Life® was selected as the learning platform for the virtual educational tours. It is a popular web-based world created by Linden Lab that provides for virtual business, education, and entertainment opportunities. Many businesses and universities have established a virtual presence in Second Life. It is also the most promising virtual platform for supporting collaborative online learning (Tsiatsos, Konstantinidis, Ioannidis, & Tseloudi, 2009). There is no fee to obtain an account in Second Life or to visit the virtual locations, but there is a charge for a higher level of technical support, virtual goods, and acquiring an island for building purposes.

Going on guided tours in Second Life, students can explore new educational sites, interact and communicate with other users' avatars, participate in interactive demonstrations and simulations, and attend informative virtual meetings and conferences. During several semesters, virtual tours were organized for University of Maryland University College (UMUC) students attending the following graduate-level online courses: ITEC 610 (Information Technology Foundations) and ITEC 620 (Information Technology Infrastructure).

Participation in these tours was voluntary, but strongly encouraged by program directors and often by their instructors. Educational venues were selected based on their relevance to the ITEC 610 and 620 course objectives. Students were able to reinforce the concepts learned in the classroom with the virtual demonstrations and simulations experienced during the tours.

The ITEC 610 course objectives, which are relevant to the virtual tours and listed below, were attained by introducing a novel perspective on how data and information can be delivered, demonstrating how emerging technologies can support learning, and having students discover a new social-economic order for study and discussion. The technologies also reflected recent developments in the IT field.

- Analyze the underlying nature of data and information such as its digital measure, characteristics, formats, and processing.
- Demonstrate how the components of IT fit together to form useful systems that are responsive to organizational needs.
- Assess the utility of IT in the operations, decision making, and investment of organizations.
- Identify and appraise the principal economic, social, and cultural issues raised by the applications of IT.
- Show currency with events and developments in the IT field.
- Assess the relevance of current events and developments in the IT field to management practices and significance to social change.

The ITEC 620 course objectives, which are supported by the tour and listed below, were attained through interactive virtual demonstrations, presentations, and simulations on distributed data processing, and computer hardware and architectures. Students could relate the online experience to business applications as well as trends in information technology.

- Describe fundamental functions, architectures, and applications of distributed data processing.
- Define, evaluate, and compare major IT components: computer hardware, operating systems, and communication networks.
- Identify and delineate modern computer architectures and the concepts involved in designing input/output devices and memory systems.
- Apply concepts and techniques to business applications.
- Evaluate trends in IT and their impact on the future developments.

This chapter is organized as follows. First, the general approach and procedures used for conducting the virtual educational tours are discussed. Next, the educational demonstrations and simulations at the visited locations in Second Life are described in detail so that the reader should be able to teleport him/herself and a class to experience the venues. Further, findings are presented in the form of students' learning experiences and their reactions based on comprehensive surveys. Consequently, recommended teaching strategies based on lessons learned from the tours are presented, and future plans on using Second Life in teaching and learning are shared. Finally, conclusions summarizing authors' reflections of this innovative approach are provided.

APPROACH

During each semester, students were invited to participate in the tour approximately mid-semester of their course. The following is a typical invitation:

Subject: The ITEC Virtual Learning Tour – Summer 2010

You are invited to go on a tour of Web 2.0, Web 3.0 (Virtual Worlds and Avatars), and cloud computing venues. After some prep work, you will virtually meet with other ITEC610 and ITEC620 students on the evening of July 28 at 7:00 pm EDT to attend a short presentation on the utilized technologies and do the tour in real time, guided by two faculty members.

As a "tourist" you will need to first get familiar with Second Life (this represents Web 3.0), Twitter and Twibes (these are Web 2.0 applications) and Google Docs (this is an example of cloud computing) using our user-friendly "Getting Started" tour guides, available at http://polaris.umuc.edu/~ibojanov/GSMT/Events/VirtualTour-Summer2010/Overview.htm. In case the link does not open from here, please copy and paste the URL in your browser.

Once you create your Second Life account, do not forget to sign up here http://www.surveymonkey.com/s/TTH9ZYX to be granted access to the UMUC's Second Life Island (Linden Lab, 2011b).

This promises to be a fun and fascinating learning experience in the emerging world of Web 2.0/3.0 and cloud computing![1]

Students are instructed to perform specific preparation activities prior to the start of each tour. In particular, they are required to review specially developed user tutorials (Bojanova & Pang, 2009–2010), the UMUC Code of Student Conduct (University of Maryland, 2011), and the Second Life security guidelines (Linden Lab, 2011c). This assures the time during the tours should be used for visiting education sites and not on basic preparatory procedures.

Students are also required to create their own Second Life accounts. The tutorials provide general guidance on account procedures and instructions on basic interface and navigational features. They contain also descriptions of the Second Life locations to be visited and their SLURLs (Second Life URLs) to help students teleport from venue to venue.

On the evening of a tour, students gather in one of the UMUC virtual classrooms in Second Life for a short presentation on technologies used during the tour. Students are asked to take snapshots during the tour using the Second Life viewer and download them to their computers. Later they are required to post these images in a collaborative presentation. Students are requested also to tweet to a Twitter site if they are having technical issues or just want to share their immediate observations.

After a tour is complete, students are asked to provide feedback about their tour experiences through an online survey application. The survey gathers information on students' opinion about the use of Second Life, the sites visited, and the value of the experience. Some of the key survey findings are discussed in a later section.

VIRTUAL DEMONSTRATIONS AND SIMULATIONS

This section provides a representative sample of educational virtual demonstrations and simulations students experienced during our ITEC virtual learning tours. Teleporting and navigational instructions are provided for each site to allow the reader visit it on their own. Note that because of the fluid nature of the Second Life content, the availability of these venues may vary in the future.

Mainframe and Servers Demonstrations

The IBM Systems EduCenter Island explores ways to use virtual worlds for improving and enhancing user experience. For example, at the IBM Server Tower (Fig. 1), students can individually watch educational sessions about the System Z10 mainframe, the Power 595 processor, and the IBM blade server center. The interactive environment allows each student to open the mainframe computer doors and explore its parts. After the educational

Fig. 1. Mainframe and Servers Demonstrations.

experience, the students can have complimentary espressos and lattes, and use the comfortable chairs and sofas to relax.

- Teleport to the IBM Systems EduCenter (http://slurl.com/secondlife/IBM%20Systems%20Educenter/150/110/30/).
- When you arrive to the IBM EduCenter site, you will see a plaza with a nice fountain. Spin around until you see four blue signs on a post. Right-click on the "IBM Server Tower" sign to teleport in-world to that exact location.
- Head straight ahead and click on the big green arrow to watch the video about IBM System Z10 mainframe. Make sure to touch the doors to open them and explore the details. Do not forget to take snapshots to document your tour.
- Next, go to the left and watch the video about IBM Power 595 processor.
- Finally, go to the right and watch the video about IBM BladeCenter.
- While in the same area, find the espresso machine and have a complimentary espresso or latte. After you select "Keep," go to your inventory, right-click on the espresso and select "Wear." Then sit on the comfortable white couch (right-click the sofa and choose "Sit Here") to drink the espresso and relax.

Blade Server Simulations

At the IBM Systems EduCenter Island, students can explore also the BladeCenter Serviceability Pavilion (Fig. 2). Through virtual simulations, they are able to learn how to add a blade to an IBM BladeCenter and how to replace a faulty dual in-line memory module in an IBM BladeCenter S Chassis Server. During these visits, students appreciate the simplicity of the modern designs of server architecture by actually performing the technical procedure needed to maintain them. Similar experiences are difficult to offer to students and replicate in real life.

- Teleport to the IBM Systems EduCenter – Technology Island (http://slurl.com/secondlife/IBM%20Systems%20Educenter/150/110/30).
- At the fountain plaza spin around to find the teleport blue signs and click on the "IBM Blade Server Interactive Demo" sign to teleport in-world to that exact location.
- Head straight ahead and click on each of the big green arrows.
- Learn through a virtual simulation how to add a Blade to an IBM BladeCenter.
- Learn through another virtual simulation how to replace a faulty memory module in a BladeCenter S Chassis Server.

Fig. 2. Blade Server Simulations.

Evolving Datacenter Demonstration

The Sun Microsystems Public Sim Island hosts interactive exhibits for educational purposes. For example, students can be introduced to the evolving datacenter (Fig. 3) and the challenges in migrating from a legacy datacenter to one built on future technologies. The virtual demonstrations show dynamically the various scenarios by which such an evolution can be achieved. Students can observe the substantial energy waves generated by the datacenter and be motivated to discuss the importance of green computing nowadays.

- Teleport to the Sun Microsystems Public Sim (http://slurl.com/secondlife/Oracle%20Corporation%201/185/128/23).
- Spin around until you face the Sun Bookstore.
- Turn to the left and you will see a ramp across a stream.
- Cross the ramp and on your left will be stairs with a sign "Evolving the Datacenter – Sun POD Architecture Interactive Demonstration."
- Click where it says "Touch for Notecard." Keep the card, read in the window the explanations about the demonstration. Close the window when done.
- Proceed up the stairs and head for the first panel at the far end.

Fig. 3. Evolving Datacenter Demonstration.

- Click on each panel that interests you and note what is happened behind the panels.
- Observe the red and blue waves demonstrating the heating and cooling energy used for all the servers.

Particle Accelerator and Tram Riding Simulations

The U.S. Department of Energy's (DOE) Island is a gateway for providing department information, media, and interactivity. Students can find information about current and future energy policies and explore interactive features such as being inside a giant particle accelerator and on a train (Fig. 4). So, they can look at the variety of DOE informational resources, smash into their friends as subatomic particles and take a tour of a super collider. Seeing how lush and verdant the island is, students can be reminded of how energy consumption affects the ecosystem around us.

- Teleport to the Sun Microsystems Public Sim (http://slurl.com/secondlife/Energy/130/141/46).
- Spin around until you see the front entrance and walk out of the building through that entrance.

Fig. 4. Particle Accelerator and Tram Simulations.

- We want you to experience the particle accelerator. Look for a three floating interconnected balls (or a ghost-like white blob) floating in air (this is called a proton). Get close and click on the proton.
- A window will appear. Immediately click on the "Let's Go" button.
- Enjoy a spectacular ride in a particle accelerator!
- After your ride, head back to where you started from – inside the building. Look for the globe with a sign below it displaying "Energy Planet" and "Energy Revolution." Click the "Play" button.
- If you saw trams moving along the bridges throughout the complex, you can ride one of these trams. Go up to the second floor (stairs are behind the front desk). Find the "Board Here" sign (it is on the ocean-side of the building). Wait for the next tram and sit in it when it arrives. It makes stops but stay on the vehicle to return to the main building.

Skydiving Simulation

The U.S. Military Veterans Center is created by and for U.S. military veterans, active duty and families, bridging the gap between generations for all services, Army, Navy, Marines, Air Force, Coast Guard, and others. Students can see how Second Life serves veterans who are incapacitated and/or homebound, an opportunity to be highly mobile and interactive in this environment. Students can also have virtual skydiving experiences (Fig. 5).

- Teleport to the US Military Veterans Center – Patriot Island (http://slurl.com/secondlife/Patriot%20Island/157/124/29).
- Look for a tall building that looks like a hangar.
- Walk through the building and proceed to the opposite entrance.
- On the right side, look for the skydiving pod (circular multi seat vehicle).
- Click the cube to get a Terra E-Chute simple parachute.
- Keep the chute.
- Review the note and discard.
- Click the Inventory button.
- Select and drag the Terra E-Chute 2.2 in the inventory to the pelvis of your avatar. (There should be a plus sign on your arrow as your drag it.)
- A small wrapped chute should appear on your avatar.
- Right-click a seat and select Skydive!
- Click Start.
- Enjoy your jump!
- You can guide your landing spot with the arrow keys.

Fig. 5. Skydiving Simulation.

Genome Scavenger Hunt Simulation

The Genome Island is designed to support genetics classes for biology students, but is also a technological experience useful to students from other disciplines. Among the places to visit is the Gene Tower (Fig. 6), which includes in its multi-story structure information and activities on genes, chromosomes, and DNA strands. Some of the activities involve exploring the inherited traits that can occur from generation to generation. Students can gain valuable learning experiences through exploration and self-discovery and, in particular, conduct virtual genetic experimentation that in the real world takes years to accomplish.

- Teleport to the Genome Island (http://slurl.com/secondlife/Genome/118/144/54). (Note: The following scavenger hunt takes a while to complete.)
- Click on the spinning yellow cube to begin the Genome Island Scavenger Hunt.
- Keep the card and review it.

Fig. 6. Genome Scavenger Hunt Simulation.

- Click the mini-map button to orient yourself. Spin until you are heading northwest then walk to the Gene Tower Office.
- A building with a ramp appears.
- Touch the spinning yellow cube with the "1" on it. Keep the card and review it. If you want the shirt follow the instructions. Discard the card.
- Touch the glass door to open it. Go up the ramp.
- Walk up each level of the building while looking for the next spinning cube numbered "2." (It is next to the multicolored DNA strand). Check out some of the interesting exhibits along the way.
- Continue your scavenger hunt by looking for each task described on the spinning yellow cube.

Conference Keynotes, Panel Discussions, and Technical Chats

The Cisco Live Conference is an education and training event for IT, networking, and communications professionals, which in 2009 was held both in real life in San Francisco and virtually in Second Life. At the Cisco Live Video Center (Fig. 7), students can watch the conference keynotes and highlights, panel discussions on education in virtual worlds and on sensor

Fig. 7. Conference Keynotes, Panel Discussions, and Technical Chats.

networks, and experts' technical chats on wide area network services, products for the remote workforce, and secure unified communications. Students can also be amused by visiting the gift center and picking up wizard hats and boxed gifts.

- Teleport to the Cisco Live Virtual Conference (http://slurl.com/secondlife/Cisco%20systems%204/104/151/28).
- When you arrive to the Cisco Live Conference site, you will see the "Cisco Life!" sign in concentric red to yellow circles and the "Knowledge is Power" sign on the flour.
- Read the two panes in front of you and then play the Cisco Life invitation.
- Next, go to the left, to visit the "Gift Center" and click on a box below a hat to take one of the Cisco Live Wizard Hats. After you accept the hat, go to your Inventory, right-click the hat, and select "Wear." Take some of the other gifts, too.
- Then, go to the Cisco Live Video Center, step on a pad, and click the "Play movie" button to watch a panel discussion or a tech chat. Do not forget to take snapshots to document your tour.
- Finally, on your way back go to the left and to the "Bandwidth Stage Teleport," right-click the stage and experience one more teleport.

Meteorological Simulations

The U.S. National Oceanic and Atmospheric Administration (NOAA) Island serves as another demonstration on how Second Life can be used as a rich educational tool. It features simulations and activities related to the agency's roles and responsibilities. Students can fly above a real-time weather map, hang from an ascending weather balloon, observe the life cycle of glaciers, and experience being on a beach when a tsunami hits (Fig. 8).

- Teleport to the NOAA Meteora Island (http://slurl.com/secondlife/Meteora/177/161/27).
- When you arrive at the NOAA Meteora site, you will be in the NOAA/ESRL plaza. Spin around until you see the map on the post. It should show the layout of the island.
- It is suggested that you visit the following sites:
  - Real-Time Weather Map
  - Balloon Ride
  - Glacier Exhibit
  - Submarine
  - Tsunami.

Fig. 8. Meteorological Simulations.

- Turn directly around and head for the Real-Time Weather Map. In the building you will see the actual weather conditions across the country. Exit the building and go into the swirling cloud.
- Climb the stairs on the left and at the top right-click the weather balloon – select Hang On. Up you go! Click "Stand up" you will fall back to the earth. Return to the plaza.
- Look for the Glacier Exhibit sign (left of the cloudy entrance). Past the overhead sign, climb the hill and head for the sign at the end of the wharf. Face the glacier and click the "Animate" button and watch the show.
- Backtrack to the Glacier sign. Go past the "Science as a Sphere" building and look for the Submarine and Tsunami sign. Head for the submarine first.
- At the end of the wharf, follow the instructions to ride the submarine. (Click the down arrow to get a broader look.) You can select "Stand up" to get out.
- Fly and head for the Submarine and Tsunami sign you saw earlier (head east – Southeast). Go to the Tsunami. Click the sign.
- Do you hear the siren? Click the sign again. Does the water recede? Click the sign again. Did you get wet?

Manufacturing Design Simulation

The Siemens Innovation Connection Center reflects the activities of Europe's largest engineering conglomerate that focuses on manufacturing, energy, and health care. Students can be exposed to innovations in each of these areas – for example, they can experience designing and creating rocket-propelled scooters that their avatars will be able to fly in the sky (Fig. 9).

- Teleport to the Siemens Innovation Connection (http://slurl.com/secondlife/Siemens%20innovation%20Connection/168/157/22).
- When you arrive to the Siemens Innovation Center, you will be on the PLM platform.
- Look for the cube on the table and get a Siemens shirt. Be sure to check "Wear clothing now."
- Next, head out on the dark ramp to the "Solid Edge" sign and sit on the chair in front of the transparent screen (right-click the chair and choose sit). Create a scooter using the design objects offered. When done, click the "Manufacture" button. A message will ask if you want to keep the

Fig. 9. Manufacturing Design Simulation.

object and keep it. You can find your scooter by clicking your Inventory button on the bottom of your screen and selecting Razor.

- Drag the razor item from the list onto the screen. Right-click the scooter and choose "Scoot!" Have fun zooming around!
- Roam around and view the other exhibits.

FINDINGS

The findings listed in this section are based on comprehensive surveys and reflect students' learning experiences and reactions to the applied technologies.

The conducted course enhancement activities were found academically challenging and stimulating students' curiosity, sense of discovery, critical thinking, and problem solving. The knowledge gained through the tours expands with each new semester and students generated ideas about new tour locations and experiences related to course learning objectives.

Table 1 shows an overview of the accumulated survey results from the ITEC virtual educational tours.

The student population represented the following demographics: 78% male, 74% with average technical level, 85% working full time; 11% in the 16–25 age frame, 33% in the 26–35 age frame, 30% in the 36–45 age frame, 22% in 46–55 age frame, and 4% in 56–65 age frame. Students found the preparation time reasonable – between half an hour and five hours. They were at the tour sites on their own on average for two hours. The integrated technologies helped students learn about virtual worlds at a 77% response rate.

Table 2 focused on student reactions to the use of Second Life.

Seventy-nine percent of the students found that Second Life enhanced the standard online classroom. They enjoyed teleporting (one comment was "cloud teleport-real cool") and found that the virtual simulations enhance the course objectives (67%).

Table 1. Overview of the Virtual Tours Survey Results.

Question Topic	Definitely Not (%)	No (%)	Maybe (%)	Yes (%)	Definitely Yes (%)
Engaging and interactive	0	3.4	6.9	**58.6**	31.0
Supports collaboration	0	6.9	10.3	**41.4**	**41.4**
Provokes curiosity and sense of discovery	0	3.4	3.4	**55.2**	37.9
Provokes critical thinking and problem solving	0	3.4	17.2	**58.6**	20.7
Academically challenging	0	13.8	24.1	**37.9**	24.1
Fun experience	0	10.3	10.3	34.5	**44.8**

Note: Boldfaced figures represent maximum values for each response.

Table 2. Overview of *Second Life (Virtual Environments)* Survey Results.

Question Topic	Definitely Not (%)	No (%)	Somewhat (%)	Yes (%)	Definitely Yes (%)
Liked using Second Life	7.1	14.3	14.3	**32.1**	**32.1**
Helped learn about Web 3.0	0.0	10.7	14.3	**42.9**	32.1
Second Life enhanced online classroom	3.6	3.6	14.3	**39.3**	**39.3**
Teleporting was easy	0.0	3.6	28.6	**39.3**	28.6
Simulations enhanced course objectives	0.0	10.7	14.3	**50.0**	17.9

Note: Boldfaced figures represent maximum values for each response.

The students listed as the most valuable aspects of the tours the exposure to new technologies ("experience … I would not have otherwise attempted,") the online collaboration and communication, Second Life ("heard about it but never looked into using it before.") Although most of the students stated they could not think of any nonvaluable aspects, some would prefer that this time-consuming activity be for credit. Some of the comments at the end of the survey are as follows: "This technology has a tremendous upside for educational purposes"; "It is a fun way of learning"; "Really amazing virtual experience"; "I can see the value in virtual worlds for meetings, training, and problem analysis"; "Especially useful when a group is geographically dispersed in the physical world"; "Definitely the potential for a new way of interacting with instructors and students – especially where physical presence is limited. I was very impressed with this technological approach to learning … By creating an avatar and actually attending a classroom you are fully engaged"; "While sitting in SL for the lecture, my initial thoughts where that this would be an excellent extension to our learning environment. To date our online learning is all text based and being able to get in a room with the professor and ask questions and listen to a lecture was both helpful and enlightening"; "I showed SL to my daughter who now wants me to show her it nightly. She likes to see me fly. I would like to learn more about SL."

LESSONS LEARNED AND RECOMMENDED TEACHING STRATEGIES

Preparation

While preparing for the activities, it is important to select virtual world sites based on educational value and interactive activities. The locations must be directly relevant to the course objectives and yet be interactive and engaging. This ensures an experience above that of a traditional online classroom. The preparation of clearly written activity tutorials is essential, as students lost in virtual worlds may delay the tour while facilitators search for them. A navigation guide would help students explore sites that often do not have clear maps or guideposts. All students have to check hardware requirements for adequacy. Second Life (Linden Lab, 2011a) requires use of a recently manufactured computer with a relatively powerful graphics card. Students with older computers will experience accessibility issues.

Before joining an activity, the students have to check their system audio and video readiness, and ensure a high bandwidth connection. It is important to ensure also students are prepared for the activities. The start of an actual virtual tour or colloquium is not the time for students to do account setups or avatar design, check audio and video functionality, or provide registration information. The preparation has to be done beforehand if the focus is to be on the learning experiences. It is appropriate to use the virtual activities to expose students to emerging technologies. Second Life itself is an example application of the next-generation Internet. It is a relatively new social and cultural community that has its own citizens, economy, and social norms. Second Life applications represent an emerging architecture for computing and managing data and information. Through these activities a global perspective can be provided. During a virtual tour, students can interact with avatars from other countries and visit sites created by foreign entities. In virtual worlds, students participate in discussions with industry professionals from around the world. These experiences provide broad exposure to foreign concepts and ideas and establish international collaborative opportunities.

Activity

During the activity, multiple facilitators should be involved. Some students can be laggards, others can be aggressive explorers; some may experience technical issues, and others may engage in unacceptable behavior. Thus, the activity facilitators, who typically are faculty members, must closely monitor participants. As a rule of thumb, each activity requires at least two main facilitators and for virtual tours one active "avatar herder" for each dozen of students.

It is important to use proper tools for student–instructor and student–student communication. Avatars can communicate in Second Life through text-based chat or voice via microphone. In these virtual worlds, voice communication was found to be much more efficient. However, if many participants have their voice devices on, unwanted sound effects may occur. In these situations, it is recommended that only activity facilitators use voice at all times, while the tourists or attendees communicate mainly through text-based chat. The integrated technologies should be creatively utilized. For example, use Twitter to direct students lost in Second Life to the current group location through direct teleport SLURLs.

During the tours, it is essential to monitor the elapsed time. Virtual tours were scheduled to last one hour. However, the tours often lasted for hours. Students become easily engrossed in the virtual environment, the fascinating tour sites, and the engaging interactions. Thus, the facilitators have to know when and how to conclude an activity.

Post-Activity

As a post-activity, a reflective assignment on the virtual world tour should be provided, as it is critical, after the virtual activity, to reinforce the connection between the learning experience and the course content. One way to achieve this is through reflective assignments, which document highlights of the activities and measure the level of learning gained by the students. IT is important also to integrate the experience with the rest of the course activities. Encourage faculty to reference the activity during subsequent lessons, conduct follow-up class discussion sessions, and include questions about the virtual world activity in quizzes and examinations.

FUTURE PLANS

Some future steps for the application of virtual tours to education are as follows: Explore new exciting virtual sites that are relevant to course objectives and reflect today's dynamic world. Look into sites that can effectively supplement course materials. Investigate the use of mobile devices, such as iPad and iPhone, for tweeting in parallel to using a computer to navigate in Second Life. Be aware of the technical and human pitfalls, such as the need for powerful graphics cards and managing students' curiosity. Identify security and privacy issues that surround the use of Second Life and how it impacts the conduct of virtual tours. Research ways for virtualized access to Second Life to facilitate students who lack the appropriate hardware. Locate efficient tools for recording virtual tours to be shared with other students and faculty. Explore the effectiveness of recording virtual world sessions with the WebEx recorder. Study reasons for resistance to the use of virtual worlds based on the student surveys and identify strategies to overcome them. Further develop the demonstrated ideas on integrating virtual worlds with emerging technologies for enhancing teaching and learning. Look for promising new tools and technologies that would support virtual educational activities.

CONCLUSIONS

The presented innovative approach for enhancing course objectives and teaching emerging IT topics reinforces the fact that the UMUC is at the forefront of online educational technologies. The virtual educational tours have proven to provide a novel, rich, and effective extension to the current educational platform. The utilized technologies represent a quantum leap over the use of traditional online delivery techniques, such as learning management systems and presentation slides. The conducted virtual activities meet the pedagogical objectives of being engaging, interactive, and supportive of student experiences reflection.

One key challenge in implementing the approach is that teaching professionals will need to become familiar and comfortable with utilized technologies and learn how to implement them effectively in their courses. To address this challenge, educators need to have "buy-in" into the concept by understanding the benefits from utilizing emerging technologies. As supported by the tours' survey results, students truly enjoy their experiences in the presented novel environment and want to return and learn more new concepts and ideas. This innovative and engaging approach is conducive to a higher order of learning and is clearly warranted for the future.

This challenge can be overcome also through displayed acceptance and commitment by upper-level institutional managers and their providing moral and financial support toward the utilization of these technologies. In addition, adequate training, resources, and incentives should be provided to instructors who are interested in implementing these cutting-edge technologies. The expected reward from such a commitment is a clear return on investment such as raised pedagogical standards, increased student satisfaction and retention rates, and enhanced institutional reputation in terms of innovation.

NOTE

1. For more information, please do not hesitate to contact Dr. Irena Bojanova at ibojanova@umuc.edu or Dr. Les Pang at lpang@umuc.edu.

REFERENCES

Bojanova, I., & Pang, L. (2009–2010). *Descriptions, tutorials, links to Twibes accounts and Google Docs presentations, and demo recordings of conducted virtual tours*. Retrieved from http://polaris.umuc.edu/~ibojanov/Demos/Virtual Tours. Accessed on September 1, 2010.

Linden Lab. (2011a). *System requirements.* Retrieved from http://secondlife.com/support/system-requirements

Linden Lab. (2011b). *UMUC Second Life Island.* Retrieved from http://maps.secondlife.com/secondlife/UMUC/226/98/31

Linden Lab. (2011c). *Linden Lab Official: Online Safety Guidelines.* San Francisco: Linden Lab. Retrieved from http://wiki.secondlife.com/wiki/Linden_Lab_Official:Online_Safety_Guidelines

Mennecke, B., McNeill, D., Ganis, M., Roche, E., Bray, D. A., Konsynski, B., Townsend, A., & Lester, J. (2008). Second Life and other virtual worlds: A roadmap for research. *Communications of the Association for Information Systems, 18*(28). Follow-Up Article to the 2007 International Conference on Information Systems Panel.

Tsiatsos, T., Konstantinidis, A., Ioannidis, L., & Tseloudi, C. (2009). Implementing collaborative e-Learning techniques in collaborative virtual environments: The case of Second Life. In: C. Douligeris, D. Stamatis, P. Kefalas, & IEEE Computer Society (Eds.), *Proceedings of the 2009 Fourth Balkan Conference in Informatics: 17-19 September 2009, Thessaloniki, Greece* (pp. 181–186). Los Alamitos, CA: IEEE Computer Society.

University of Maryland University College, University Registrar and Vice Provost, Student Affairs. (2011). *UMUC policies.* Adelphi, MD: UMUC. Retrieved from http://umuc.edu/policy/student/stud15100.shtml

LESSON PLAN: INTEGRATION OF VIRTUAL ENVIRONMENT, WEB 2.0, AND CLOUD COMPUTING TECHNOLOGIES

Grade Level: Higher Education, Graduate School

Subjects
Information Technology Foundations
Information Technology Infrastructure
Duration: One hour

DESCRIPTION

The students utilize the virtual world Second Life to visit and explore virtual educational sites. During the tour, the students use the Web 2.0 applications Twitter and Twibes to capture their experiences as well as to summon assistance. At the end of the tour, the students utilize the cloud computing application Google Docs to document and present their experiences at the visited virtual sites.

GOALS

- Introduce students to the emerging technologies that will lead to the next-generation Internet: Virtual worlds, Web 2.0, and cloud computing.
- Provide students with opportunities to explore complex, abstract concepts and ideas, and observe or participate in potentially expensive or precarious activities not restricted by the limitations and risks of the real world.
- Enhance the course learning objectives of the first two core courses in the ITS graduate program, ITEC610 Information Technology Foundations, and ITEC620 Information Technology Infrastructure.

OBJECTIVES

- Students will be able to use Second Life, Twitter/Twibes, and Google Docs to gain learning experiences in a virtual environment.

- Students will learn through virtual demonstrations and simulations about distributed data processing, modern computer architectures, and current trends in technology.
- Students will gain a global perspective on the state of telecommunications and information technology today.

MATERIALS

- Activity overview and guidelines
- Application and account setup tutorials
- Computer with a state-of-the-art video card and Internet access
- Second Life viewer and accounts for all instructors and students
- Twitter accounts for all instructors and students
- Twibe account and membership in the Virtual Tour twibe
- Google Docs account and access to the class presentation file
- Instructor-prepared PowerPoint presentation for the briefing in Second Life that introduces utilized technologies and overviews tour locations, activities, and procedures
- Feedback survey: http://www.surveymonkey.com/s/RS8ZT7H

PROCEDURES

1. Students examine an overview on the planned virtual tour activities and tutorials on utilized applications. They also read the UMUC Code of Student Conduct (http://www.umuc.edu/policy/student/stud15100.shtml), the Second Life online security guidelines (http://secondlife.com/policy/security/), and the Twitter rules of conduct (http://support.twitter.com/groups/33-report-a-violation/topics/121-guidelines-best-practices/articles/18311-the-twitter-rules).
2. Days before the tour, students create accounts for the applications used for the tour. In Second Life, each student creates his/her own avatar.
3. At a designated time, students meet at the UMUC Island for a PowerPoint briefing on the planned tour activities. Typically, two faculty members serve as tour directors.
4. Students teleport to three or four different virtual locations in Second Life to view and explore virtual demonstrations and participate in

simulations and interactive skills development activities. Students take snapshots of places they visit using the camera feature in Second life capture their experiences. They also use Twitter and Twibes to share immediate impressions and summon assistance if needed.

5. After the tour, students work together to prepare a collaborative presentation in Google Docs reflecting what they observed, experiences, and learned.

ASSESSMENT

The students' Google Docs presentations are not graded.

USEFUL INTERNET RESOURCES

- Second Life: www.secondlife.com
- Twitter: www.twitter.com
- Twibes: www.twibes.com
- Google Docs: www.docs.google.com

USING PROBLEM-BASED LEARNING WITHIN 3D VIRTUAL WORLDS

Vanessa Parson and Simon Bignell

ABSTRACT

Immersive and collaborative virtual worlds can offer educationalists a future-focused solution to enhancing the learning experience they provide. Problem-based learning (PBL) is one option by which virtual worlds can provide a creative solution to providing physical-world experience within a safe and controlled environment free from the consequences associated with typical physical-world experiences. This collaborative approach to teaching and learning can be run synchronously or asynchronously and is based on sound pedagogical principles. PBL within virtual worlds can be used to provide an active and engaging learning experience that enables individuals to learn safely and effectively within a complex and realistic environment, allowing the student to be at the centre of, and in relative control of, their own learning experience.

Keywords: Virtual worlds; Second Life; problem-based learning; enquiry-based learning; learning; pedagogy; case study

Transforming Virtual World Learning
Cutting-edge Technologies in Higher Education, Volume 4, 241–261

ISSN: 2044-9968/doi:10.1108/S2044-9968(2011)0000004014

INTRODUCTION

The sense of immersion experienced within multi-user virtual environments can provide educators and students with the ability to connect and communicate in ways that greatly enhance the learning experience, even when attending a lecture or seminar in person is not possible, practical, or desirable. Virtual worlds offer the potential to provide students with a customised and safe environment to learn, which provides a controlled virtual space that can be adapted to the needs of individual educators and courses. Using virtual worlds as a method of teaching takes the innovative approach of placing the students at the centre of their own learning by directly involving them in the experience itself.

It has long been established that problem-based learning (PBL) leads to a deeper approach to learning (Newble & Clarke, 1986), and there is ample evidence for the value of active and cooperative learning (Johnson, Johnson, & Smith, 1991). An emphasis on team skills and the ability to work with others are highly prized by future employers. Students and non-students alike, of all disciplines, require the ability to define problems, gather and evaluate information and develop solutions: it is the ability to use these skills to address problems in a complex real-world setting that is one of the key enduring assets of using PBL within virtual worlds.

The ability to use these skills to address problems in a complex real-world setting is one of the key enduring assets that undergraduates can take with them beyond university. Immersive collaborative tutorials provide an engaging and future-focused way of providing technology-enhanced learning. Using PBL within virtual worlds offers the educator the option of using both synchronous and asynchronous learning to enhance learning on their courses. The use of virtual worlds adds a different dimension to the teaching and enlivens the education for the student: increasing learning through enhanced immersive collaborative learning. The process of learning becomes active, rather than simply being passive learning. The immersive nature affords activity and group work is often rewarding for the learner who forms part of a cohesive PBL group.

Teachers need to acquire specific skills in order to run effective learning and teaching using these virtual learning platforms. Existing pedagogies may not be sufficient to inform good practice in these settings, so this chapter outlines a theoretical framework for understanding how to develop the link between the tools, techniques and technology used in learning, and support and research in these evolving virtual spaces specifically using PBL. Examples are drawn from the PREVIEW-Psych project, a JISC-funded collaboration between University of Derby, Aston University and The Higher Education Academy, along with related projects such as a recent HEA-funded project that investigates the 'Education for Sustainable Development' agenda within Second Life. The authors outline the development of interactive PBL scenarios in the virtual world, including their experiences of developing a computer reproduction of a family house featuring 'intelligent avatars' that replicate the social interactions and symptoms of people with clinical conditions such as depression, dementia, schizophrenia and anorexia nervosa. The project has now expanded to include other subject groups and has provided training for academics and developers across the UK, examples of which are given in this chapter.

WHY USE PBL IN 3D VIRTUAL WORLDS?

Virtual worlds offer the potential to carry out synchronous and asynchronous learning. As a persistent 3D learning environment the content placed 'in world' by educators remains there for students to access in their own time or to use as part of live teaching sessions. Virtual worlds can facilitate learning in many ways and can be a very effective teaching method in the virtual learning space. PBL is a way of using planned scenarios, such as case studies, to aid learning in a multi-disciplinary or multi-skill context. It is an active way for students to learn basic problem-solving skills and acquire knowledge through interaction with others, a key skill demanded within every workplace. Students learn within small self-directed groups to define and carry out the specific tasks, either real-life or study-based. The principles of problem-based learning are well established and for an in-depth guide to these and the use of PBL online Savin-Baden provides excellent examples (Savin-Baden, 2007; Savin-Baden & Wilkie, 2006).

The PBL teaching method shifts the focus of learning from the teacher to the student, with the student in control of his or her own learning under the guidance of the teacher. PBL takes place within the context of structured tasks aligned with courses or real-world scenarios linked with course material. A carefully crafted problem is initially posed, which contains minimal information needed for its solution, and from this all learning is triggered through student-centred knowledge finding and information assimilation – all within a collaborative framework. Students are not simply passive learners; the whole experience is active, engaging students with their learning.

Students benefit post-university if they can learn how to solve novel problems by thinking creatively and to communicate and collaborate with others. In learning how to work with others, it enables them to acquire knowledge for themselves. PBL helps students to integrate knowledge and skills from a range of subjects and modules whilst developing their problem-solving skills. In addition, these techniques can encourage self-motivation, thinking and analytical skills with the aim of making learning an interactive and enjoyable experience. This can be achieved by encouraging flexible and creative thinking and juggling of multiple sources of information in order to solve novel problems. Ideally, within a PBL scenario students learn all of these, providing them with important transferable skills for the workplace, as well as improving their subject knowledge and therefore their performance while studying.

CONDUCTING PBL IN VIRTUAL WORLDS

There are several ways of conducting PBL, and as long as the core concepts are followed it is a flexible method for learning which is driven by the teacher, and can be used to directly target particular topics, as well as for more general scenarios of general knowledge acquisition. Table 1 shows an extended version of the 7-step approach, an order by which PBL could be carried out.

Table 1. PBL core concepts and structure.

1. Define the problem clearly.
2. Explain clearly and in detail exactly what is required of the students.
3. Explain any core concepts, statements or unknown wording.
4. Form groups (can be tutor-driven or student-driven).
5. Brainstorm and try to analyse the problem.
6. Ensure there is a time limit and more information than can be gathered for any one individual. Students will then have to co-operate and divide the labour of evidence gathering between them.
7. Systematically gather evidence.
8. Re-gather to discuss evidence and develop strategies for gathering remaining information needed.
9. Within the group develop an answer for the problem posed.
10. Individually students then fill in an assessment form and produce a written piece of work detailing the problem and the subsequent solution.

Within virtual worlds, PBL needs to be particularly well defined and explained, as there is less scope for individuals to refer to teachers for additional help, even within synchronous sessions. This can be done using detailed instructions in various locations, along with strategically placed arrows directing individuals to those instructions and various strategic aspects of content for the PBL scenario. Brainstorming is another area which needs additional instructions as communicating in a virtual world is somewhat different than a real-life scenario, even when headsets are employed to allow for voice communication. Ideally instructions on using 'world chat' in preference to 'private' chat need to be visible and communicated to individuals using the scenarios.

METHODS OF RUNNING PBL SCENARIOS IN SECOND LIFE

Problem-based learning in the context of virtual world learning takes the form of a user-focused approach. In virtual world teaching, these scenarios most usually take the form of either avatar-driven scenarios or information-driven scenarios. Educators are typically involved in preparing materials as immersive tutorials, using interactive virtual scenarios in virtual worlds. Learners interact with these, usually in small groups of around 5–8 students.

Avatar-driven scenarios are typically used after the students have formed groups and been given the PBL problem scenario; the student starts by entering the virtual world learning area (parcel) and asks programmed chatbots/avatars questions that elicit ordered replies. A chatbot, or intelligent avatar, is an automated computer program in the form of a virtual world avatar that provides realistic text-based conversational responses and information when approached. These replies are triggered by keywords written into the programming of the chatbot. This information is used to direct the student to different locations and on different 'fact-finding' missions to obtain the information required to solve the problem scenario. Students then are required to work together to plan how to find and use this information to solve the problem provided. These scenarios entail students interacting with an intelligent avatar or chatbot. Often this can be direct communication, but teachers can also use chatbots to guide the story of a PBL scenario. Typically the chatbots act out the story in front of the students who are faced with making decisions based on these events. This type of scenario is more labour intensive for the teacher initially, but more interesting and exciting from the students' point of view.

Information-driven scenarios are characterised by scenarios in which the learning is led by students exploring their virtual surroundings within virtual worlds. Students have to search for information within virtual worlds, relating to the PBL problem scenario provided by the teacher. They typically search within an area in the virtual world the teacher has pre-defined and in which is placed sufficient information to solve the problem given. They search for material for the relevant problem, much as they would in the real-world applications of PBL scenarios. This type of scenario requires more division of labour from the students and is a better method for teaching collaboration, management and communication skills.

A typical method of running an information-driven scenario initially provides instructions about the PBL problem scenario in the virtual world pre-defined study area: usually within easy sight upon entry to the area. Students then form groups and use the clues located around the area to find out relevant information and solve the problem scenario. The clues are made up from materials uploaded into the virtual world by the teacher or from books/wider internet that the teacher directs them to, either through notices within the virtual world or on the handout containing the initial PBL problem scenario. This information is assimilated by the students and they collaborate to use this information and solve the PBL problem scenario provided.

The case study on the PREVIEW-Psych project shown in Table 2 details how PBL was utilised within Second Life in a Psychology-based scenario. The overall aim of the project was to validate, transfer and disseminate materials developed from the PREVIEW-Psych project at Coventry University to the wider academic community. The system of immersive collaborative tutorials provided an engaging and future-focused way of providing technology-enhanced learning initiated by a real-world problem. The PREVIEW-Psych project created a fictional family within Second Life to look at how well this technology coped with the PBL mechanism for learning. A complex of virtual buildings was created, including a house, office area and information area. Materials provided within the complex were audio files, note cards, posters, web links, interactive notice board, postbox (for posting answers to teachers) and a receptionist avatar to provide instructions.

Table 2. Case study: The PREVIEW-Psych project.

In the PREVIEW-Psych project Psychology undergraduates collaborated on interactive problem-based learning scenarios in the virtual world. A replication of a family house features 'intelligent avatars' that replicate the social interactions and symptoms of people with clinical conditions such as depression, schizophrenia and anorexia nervosa. Students work in teams with a faculty member to find out more about the virtual family as they interact with the evolving 3D scenarios to construct a report from the perspective of a social worker who is visiting the house.

Psychology undergraduates worked in groups to find and use appropriate resources towards a solution to the problem. The module content and learning outcomes were incorporated into the scenarios to encourage group discussion and higher order thinking. In this way, learning was active, integrated, cumulative, and connected. The students' task was to work in small groups to find out what was wrong with the family in the virtual house on this location. Their task was to find the characters in the house and work out from the materials provided the following:

- How the family fits together. What is wrong with each family member?
- Information about these disorders (from objects in the house).
- What treatment might be recommended to the individuals?
- What the long-term prognoses are for each family member.
- The model of psychology that best fits when explaining each set of issues.
- How the model works.
- What the starting point for treatment is.

Students entered the house and grounds twice as a group during each scenario. Each scenario was loaded separately and took about 20 minutes. Before each trip students had to decide what their approach would be and ensure that everyone knew what to do. The learning objectives of the project were to gain knowledge of clinical disorders and to gain skills of critical analysis relating to mental health.

Students reported feeling more engaged with the module content and having ownership of their learning. Group dynamics complimented the way that each of the members of the groups preferred to learn. Some took a more reflective analytical role whilst some preferred to lead the group.

Feedback from student experiences indicates that these new techniques of teaching and activity-based learning methods offer a sense of presence and interactivity that leads to deeper understanding of psychological content. Student statements taken from feedback on the PREVIEW-Psych project:

- "We worked as a team ... this seemed much more valuable than just writing an essay or having a discussion."
- "It gave me a chance to interact with case studies in a virtual mock-up of real life."
- " ... the content was easy to access and the tasks very enjoyable."
- "I was thinking more about the real-life Psychology because the avatars represented real people with real psychological problems."

THE ROLE OF THE TEACHER IN VIRTUAL WORLD EDUCATION

In problem-based learning (specific teaching), the key aspect of problem-based learning is allowing the students to direct their own learning process through the exploration, integration and assimilation of information they acquire themselves. Students identify the knowledge and skills required to solve the problem and identify the learning issues and goals. Students then assess their own competency to facilitate this and engage in self-directed learning, returning to the group periodically to assess progress, and identify new goals and issues. This process continues until the problem is resolved and explained. The teacher is simply a facilitator for students to learn: learning outcomes and knowledge acquisition are produced by the student. The onus in this teaching method is on providing sufficient instruction and material for the students to achieve the desired outcomes and knowledge acquisition without directly providing them. As long as instructions are sufficiently detailed about the PBL scenario and the demands required of the students, the students learn for themselves: using their own initiative to find out information they require to solve the problem provided. Other forms of learning require different techniques and skills and these can be effective when blended with problem-based teaching methods. For example, traditional teaching relies on the learners to passively listen to a teacher and then most often engage in some learning activity related to the topic at hand. A blended approach that mixes experiential and taught elements can provide a reliable framework to scaffold both confidence and knowledge.

There are two methods for helping students during this process: asynchronous and synchronous learning – or e-learning when referring to teaching within virtual worlds. In both instances, the aim of the teacher is to make sure the students facilitate the learning for themselves and, in the first instance, attempt to resolve any group issues independently. The teacher maintains the role of mediator and addresses issues only when they become problematic for the group as a whole.

Asynchronous e-learning is facilitated at a distance, through email, discussion boards, blogs and other online devices. This enables students and teachers to be online at different times. It is a method of learning which ensures that students spend more time reflecting on their communications, refining and specifying more directly the issues and ideas. Hrastinski (2008) found that more than 90 per cent of asynchronous communications were content-related, compared with around 60 per cent of synchronous communications. The cognitive model of media choice by Robert and

Dennis (2005) theorises that asynchronous learning increases the ability to process information as the receiver has more time to comprehend a message due to the fact that immediate response being unnecessary. Asynchronous learning is best used when reflection is required and when time constraints mean learning must take place over times when not all participants are available. Distance learning courses are an ideal method for using asynchronous PBL teaching within virtual worlds: the courses are already asynchronous and the virtual world experience provides students with an opportunity to interact more fully with their fellow students and enhance their entire learning experience.

Synchronous e-learning is a little different from asynchronous e-learning. The teacher and learner inhabit the same learning space at the same time. Learning is facilitated through use of media and chat facilities within the virtual world. This method of e-learning is a more dynamic and social method of learning, enabling students to feel like participants in the learning process rather than isolated individuals. It also helps students feel like they are not alone in the learning experience, that there is expert help should they need it. The teacher becomes a reassuring safety net for students, allowing them to explore and interact with confidence they might not otherwise have had. Synchronous e-learning is also useful when topics that are more difficult are being covered, as the teacher is able to steer the students towards the information which is relevant.

The cognitive model of media choice by Robert and Dennis (2005) predicts that synchronous learning increases motivation. This may well be because learners are participating in an ongoing exercise where reactions are required to further the process of task completion. A downside to this motivated process is that there is an over-focus on quantity rather than quality of communication, as learners want to respond quickly so as not to disrupt the flow of conversation. Synchronous learning is best used when complex issues need discussion and in the planning of tasks. Within Second Life it is possible to use asynchronous learning and avoid the pitfalls of isolated learning as students work in groups synchronously and the teacher can move between synchronous and asynchronous learning as best suits the students.

JUGGLING THE ROLES OF LEARNING DIRECTOR AND LEARNING FACILITATOR

In the classroom and in Second Life, teachers using PBL in virtual worlds have to multi-task and split their time between the real-world classroom setting and the virtual world their students are using. This is the case with synchronous PBL rather than asynchronous PBL; students have no need to congregate within classrooms when doing asynchronous learning. Classroom-based roles are more directive than facilitative, when using the virtual world as the teaching resource: what the students need in the classroom is technical assistance and verbal nudges to stay on task and limit noise disruptions. Giving the students headsets to use while performing the task in-world can limit real-world interaction and promote immersion within the virtual world: enhancing engagement with the material to be learned.

Fielding questions can happen in the virtual world and in the classroom: it is often helpful to have technical assistance during synchronous teaching time so that students experiencing technical difficulties can get assistance without this interrupting the learning of the other students. In addition, technical aspects of Second Life may need demonstrating to students so they can complete the tasks. To be visible within the virtual world enables students to have questions answered in-world; in addition there is the benefit of making sure students remain on task. Juggling the in-world and classroom roles takes practice, but most skilled educators should find this straightforward enough. A useful tip when juggling these roles is to make sure that the teacher's status is set to "busy" so that students within Second Life know they may have to wait.

Instructions are a key tool to helping students explore the virtual environment and complete the task independently: leading to maximum learning potential for the students and increased smoothness to the running of teaching sessions for the teacher. Exploration of virtual learning areas is crucial to completion of PBL tasks within virtual worlds, as it is likely that there is material important to the task placed there. Instructions placed in-world have to be clear and detailed, well laid out and clearly signposted, enabling the students to work as independent groups rather than as students dependent on teacher leadership: something which contradicts the premise of PBL itself. However, with the best intentions and clearest instructions in the world, there will always be some students who do not understand what to do. It is easy for the process of answering questions to translate into detailed additional instructions and pointers, in particular when groups of students require help, finding the balance between hinting and leading directly to the answer is tricky. Leading group discussions is a critical aspect of the learning process for the students learning experience for both the PBL aspect of the task and the virtual scenarios within which it is embedded.

THE VIRTUAL CLASSROOM

Access to the educational environment within the virtual world is a paramount consideration. Teachers can choose to keep an area of virtual land, and therefore tasks, open to the whole virtual world community, or keep the area private just for the students involved. This access can be restricted either permanently or temporarily. One method of doing this is to protect the teaching area from everyone except those in the designated group for the teaching session. The virtual land parcel settings can be changed to 'Group Access only' via land settings menu by adding avatar names in advance to a group (e.g. Group 1). Alternatively, teachers can leave an area as open access but ban individual avatars if they are causing disruption: in Second Life this simply involves right clicking on the unwanted avatar and selecting 'Ban'. However, it is courteous to warn individuals with the individual messaging (IM) function before taking such action.

Materials located within the virtual world for educational purposes have a point and purpose to them. Superfluous materials serve to distract students from the task and lead to delays in successful completion of PBL scenario projects. Input of materials into the virtual world is an intuitive balance of sufficient but not excessive information. Insufficient materials and information lead to confusion among students and problems completing tasks. However, excessive information reduces the value of the learning outcomes, reducing the quality of the PBL task itself.

Groups form an important part of the organisational management of the teaching space. It is part of the role of the teacher to monitor group dynamics within any PBL scenario, and can be one of the more demanding elements of time management during tasks. This process can be easier when teaching within virtual worlds. In Second Life you can use the mini-map to monitor how many 'green dots', i.e. students, are in any place at any one time. You can also, if students are added to the teacher's 'Contacts List', see if students are online or not. This is necessary during synchronous PBL teaching to ensure that less motivated individuals do not hold back progress on the task for their groups. Keeping track of students can prove problematic in virtual worlds; however, independent learning is a feature of PBL, so continual monitoring of student locations is not necessary. When conducting synchronous PBL, it can be beneficial to add students to the 'Contacts List' of the teacher; this can ensure that all students are online and active in the task.

Communication happens in three main ways within virtual worlds: voice, general text, and private chat. Headsets are an effective solution to the problem of in-world communication in a busy classroom or computer lab. It is also possible to get a more immersive experience of the virtual world when using headsets as a means of communication. Learning to take turns speaking is more problematic when not using the text functions. However, this is another aspect of learning using PBL scenarios. Students may disrupt conversations and interfere with the thought processes of their group if they have been on 'fact finding missions' relating to the task; but as they do more PBL scenarios they become more adept at constructively contributing to the group thought processes, so this is only a problem in early PBL sessions. In synchronous PBL the teacher can intervene where excessive disruption is being caused, playing the role of mediator where necessary. A negative aspect to headsets involves the actual computers being used by the students: computers with lower specifications will refresh more slowly and this can lead to disjointed conversations and confusion relating to this. One solution to this problem is to ensure synchronous PBL sessions are run in university laboratories where all the computers have the same specifications. For asynchronous PBL sessions, the students have to manage for themselves: but this provides an additional learning aspect to the session – they must learn to cooperate with fellow group members and acquire patience when communicating with those on lower specification machines.

Text communication is familiar to the vast majority of individuals, thanks to the proliferation of messenger programs and social networking sites. These do not provide such an immersive experience as does the addition of voice into the virtual world, but still provide a more than adequate method of communication, and one that does not require accurate spelling for comprehension. For this reason, the chat communication facility is often preferred when working in-world: with the additional benefits that individuals can follow the conversation and computers of all specifications can cope with rapid text communication easily. However, during synchronous PBL sessions, teachers should monitor how much conversation is occurring through private chat mechanisms. This is, unfortunately, a very simple method for groups to splinter: if too much discussion is occurring in private chat, other members of the group will be at a disadvantage through no fault of their own, as they will not be aware of discussions taking place. This is an aspect that students should monitor themselves, however, in early synchronous PBL sessions the teacher is best placed to monitor this and points out the disadvantages to students getting sidetracked by this method of communication.

TECHNICAL ASPECTS OF PBL IN VIRTUAL WORLDS

The *Second Life Client* is the program that users run Second Life from on their desktop computers. Higher Education institutions sometimes have a pre-installed version mirrored to multiple desktop PCs. However, this method is not recommended for running teaching sessions as problems of shared caching of temporary file information can lead to program crashes when multiple avatars are being run from computers in close network proximity. Our recommendation is that facilitators of Second Life teaching sessions invest in a handful of high-speed USB memory sticks (1–2 gigabytes) from which to run the Second Life client. The SanDisk Cruzer© range of USB memory sticks work well and the desktop client can be downloaded from http://secondlife.com/support/downloads/ and run directly from the stick. The advantage of this method, rather than running the client from the PC's hard drive, is that the client will read/write files to the memory stick; a technique we have found much more reliable. Check with your technician if this is a viable method before trying it and that local network firewall permits using Second Life. As with all technology-based teaching, it is essential to plan ahead and test configuration before each session. Ideally this involves having multiple *Alts* (alternative avatar accounts) to test the virtual teaching environment before running a live session.

Avatars and user accounts must be provided or pre-registered for each student before each teaching session. Each user account is associated with unique avatar names and users log-in with their avatar name (First Name/ Last Name) and a password. Avatars can be registered for free at https:// join.secondlife.com/ and the process takes about five minutes. One issue that has proved troublesome for many educational institutions is a limit placed on the number of registrations possible from a single institution. This is governed by Linden Lab, the creators of Second Life, and can be resolved in advance by contacting them to negotiate 'White List' status. This effectively allows multiple user accounts (avatars) to be registered from within the institution's computer suites and prevents the need for students to pre-register an account off campus. Once again, a little planning can ensure that potential problems are solved before live sessions start. We recommend having a number of teaching Alts in reserve to use for students who have not pre-registered their own avatar accounts.

The ***user-interface*** of Second Life has changed continually over recent years with successive updates of the client. Generally the user interface is intuitive but it is recommended that students become familiar with the interface before taking part in a live teaching session. There are a number of excellent inductions within Second Life that will ease the initial period of acclimatisation that many users can face. Experience shows that it takes about an average of 20 minutes to become accustomed to the controls for the typical user. Group facilitators should ensure that students are familiar with the navigation and communication controls before they take part in a PBL session. We provide links to a number of popular inductions within Second Life at the end of the chapter.

Space in Second Life is divided in several different ways and is most often described as a 3D virtual environment, not just a tool for teaching. The 'grid' represents all of Second Life, which is composed of the 'mainland' and private 'Sims' (Simulators) otherwise known as Islands. The mainland is virtual land sold to individuals; the private islands are often joined into expanses of land and rented out or developed for specific purposes. Most educational land comprises private Sims that have been specifically developed for the purpose of teaching. From time to time virtual 'land' is made available by charitable organisations and universities for those wishing to become involved in virtual teaching and learning. A search of educational institutions in Second Life will often reveal these and they are ideal for educationalists new to teaching in Second Life. Examples of virtual spaces dedicated to PBL and virtual lectures and seminars can be found at University of Derby's virtual campus and across many other education providers within the Second Life.

Lag and performance issues of the Second Life client can be incapacitating to teaching and learning. Lag is a symptom where the result of an action appears later than expected. This is caused by many different reasons but the result is that moving and communications are spoilt. Often the reason is local and caused by an under-specification computer or a slow network connection. There are three main types of lag, (i) client-side lag, (ii) network lag and (iii) server-side lag. Lag is often caused by an overloading of the servers that manage the information traffic or by too many people in the same area on Second Life. The result is that everything slows down, most noticeable frame rates and movement across the virtual world. It can turn an enthralling learning session or demonstration into a painfully slow experience.

More than once we have seen an engaging session spoilt by technical issues that could have been avoided. It is in everyone's interest to avoid lag. Image frame rates (frames per second,fps) are not equivalent to contemporary computer games because Second Life generally uses different technology to produce 3D images. Because of the complexity required to render a 3D virtual world, the technology is more similar to a 3D graphics modelling program than a typical video game. You should aim for the best frame rates and a good network connection; you can check the statistics bar within the Second Life client. Typically you should get an average of 10–15 fps or better when teaching; fewer than 10 fps and you'll notice an impact on the smoothness and visual quality of the virtual world around your avatar. Table 3 gives six tips for avoiding lag during teaching sessions.

For the technical aspects of Second Life, setting up and fielding student questions, there are two options for teachers to take. Firstly, teachers can learn the technical side themselves, and secondly teachers can enlist the help of technical support staff from within their institution to help them with this side of the process. If teachers are sufficiently technologically competent then first option is the better approach, as it is easier to help students solve problems and complete tasks in situ.

Table 3. Six tips for avoiding lag during teaching sessions.

1. Turn down the graphics quality and performance settings from within Preferences. Also, turn down your 'draw distance'. This will help reduce the number one cause of problems by placing less demand on the computer's graphics card.
2. Upgrade your computer and ensure you use a fast broadband connection. The key is to have a good graphics card (GPU) and a fast processor (CPU). Although Second Life will usually run adequately on older computers, generally newer equipment is better. Also, try turning off unnecessary background programs.
3. Reduce the number of avatars on the 'Island' that you are teaching on. Sometimes this is not possible but high numbers of avatars (30 or more) can substantially slow down the Second Life servers and the network connection causing disruption to your teaching session. Teaching on a 'mainland' region for this reason is not recommended.
4. Remove 'prim-based' attachments on your avatar and advise students to limit theirs. These can take the form of virtual jewellery or clothes but mainly are high prim-count hair worn as an attachment. Using the standard attachable avatar hair and clothing from the inventory library during teaching can considerably improve performance.
5. Schedule your teaching sessions out of peak-hour traffic and turn off music and videos. Avoid using Second Life when lots of people are surfing the web at your institution or when your computer labs are busiest. These practices will help reduce network congestion.
6. Ensure you use an appropriately built educational Sim 'Island'. Unfortunately, many Sims intended for teaching are not designed from the ground up for lag reduction. Large textures, lots of sculpted prims and complex 'scripting' are a major cause of lag. Add to this mix lots of avatars and teaching sessions can quickly grind to a halt.

However, second option can be a very rewarding alternative as the technical aspects are relatively simple for any member of technical support staff, and it leaves the teacher free to monitor and direct the subject-specific learning. Academic staff should not spend a disproportionate amount of their time correcting problems in PBL sessions; they are there to direct the pedagogical aspects of the task, not the technical. It is beneficial, however, that the academic staff involved with virtual world teaching are the ones who set up and maintain the resources in-world. Relying on technical staff to develop resources within virtual worlds saves time but is less advantageous to the aims of PBL scenarios, as academics are best placed to know what is necessary and how things need to work in-world.

CONCLUSIONS

The potential for using Second Life within education is clearly evident: Second Life is an immersive and engaging environment which, whilst intrinsically entertaining, can facilitate learning and extend the time students spend positively engaging with educational content. The focus is on facilitating learning rather than directed teaching per se. In particular, problem-based learning appears to be an ideal tool for aiding learning within this immersive virtual environment. Virtual worlds are a potentially valuable resource for those involved with online and distance learning: providing the additional interactive benefits alongside the educational ones. The potential challenges for teaching within any virtual world remain the technological ones. However, once the local issues such as network congestion and familiarity with the user interface are resolved, virtual worlds such as Second Life can equip the educationalist with a formidable contemporary learning tool.

HELPFUL RESOURCES

To find out more about our problem-based learning projects and using Second Life for teaching please visit the PREVIEW-Psych website for more information: http://www.previewpsych.org. You can also visit us in Second Life here: http://slurl.com/secondlife/Derby%20University/185/96/22. Click this link after you have Second Life installed on your computer to 'teleport' to the PREVIEW-Psych project. The Quick Start for academics display is where you can find out more about teaching in virtual worlds. You can also 'teleport' direct to the project and virtual buildings to try out some of the problem-based learning scenarios for yourself by using the link http://tinyurl.com/6qx2uj.

There are also a number of excellent resources available online for starting out using problem-based learning in Second Life. Below is a list of a few of our favourite online resources for getting you up and running.

- Best Practices in Virtual Worlds Teaching: A guide to using problem-based learning in Second Life. This 40+ page publication covers a lot of ground in an easy to understand way. It's available as a free download of a little more than 6 MB in PDF format (http://previewpsych.org/BPD2.0.pdf).
- Coventry University, Kingston University and University of London St. George's problem-based learning collaboration blog offers an excellent insights and demonstrations into avatar-based scenarios in Second Life (http://www.elu.sgul.ac.uk/preview/blog/).
- The enthusiastic Torley Linden is your host, taking you on a tour through tips, tricks, and techniques that will increase your confidence with his video tutorials. You will be asked to log-in with your Second Life account (http://bit.ly/vidtut).
- This guide will help you get started fast, by explaining how to complete some of the most common tasks you will need to get the most out of your Second Life experience (http://secondlife.com/support/quickstart/basic).

REFERENCES

Hrastinski, S. (2008). Asynchronous & synchronous e-learning. *Eduserv Quarterly*, *4*, 51–55.

Johnson, D. W., Johnson, R. T., & Smith, K. A. (1991). Cooperative Learning: Increasing College Faculty Instructional Productivity. *ASHE-ERIC Higher Education Report No. 4*. Washington, D.C.: School of Education and Human Development, George Washington University. Retrieved from http://www.eric.ed.gov/PDFS/ED343465.pdf, 03/11/11, 13.55 GMT

Newble, D. I., & Clarke, R. M. (1986). The approaches to learning of students in a traditional and in an innovative problem-based medical school. *Medical Education*, *20*(4), 267–273.

Robert, L., & Dennis, A. (2005). Paradox of richness: a cognitive model of media choice. *IEEE Transactions on Professional Communication*, *48*(1), 10–21.

Savin-Baden, M. (2007). *A Practical Guide to Problem-based Learning Online*. London: Routledge.

Savin-Baden, M., & Wilkie, K. (2006). *Problem-based learning online*. Maidenhead, UK: Open University Press.

LESSON PLAN: VIRTUAL WORLD PROBLEM-BASED LEARNING

Sessions should ideally be run about a week apart so that students have time to gather information and assimilate it effectively. The minimum time between sessions should be 2 days. In between sessions, students are expected to search for information by themselves. As they experience more PBL, their search methods improve and become more focused; they should become better at deciphering wanted from unwanted information. This lesson plan can be adapted for synchronous or asynchronous PBL.

Session	Teachers' Role	Students' Role
Prior to Session 1	1. Run students through an induction for the virtual world to be used. 2. Ensure all students are able to function competently within the environment. 3. Provide students with the location of the PBL scenarios. For example, the Second Life 'SLURL' link. 4. Show students around PBL area within your virtual world. This can often be achieved by a series of 'screen grab' images or a virtual tour of the facilities.	1. Learn how to maneuver, communicate and interact with the virtual world. 2. Locate the PBL scenario area and make a note of where the necessary resources are.
Session 1 (1–1.5 hours)	1. Explain the task and the problem being set: ensure this is in enough detail for novice PBL students to know what they are meant to be doing. Once students become accustomed to this approach to learning, this step can be skipped and the students simply presented with the problem. 2. The 'Scenario Sheet' should be given to the students. 3. Explain concepts and answer questions regarding wording: clear up any ambiguities at the start so that there is no confusion later on. 4. Define the problem.	In Groups: 1. Find the information which is available in the virtual world. 2. Visit the virtual house and the information area. 3. Look at what information is available and use that to search for information about the family. 4. Brainstorm the problem set. 5. List relevant aspects and explanations they have found. 6. List explanations known/unknown and alternative explanations.

	5. Form groups by student choice or by selecting groups for the students, whichever method works best for your students.	7. Problem analysis: Work out what exactly the problem is requiring them to do. 8. Classify ideas into themes. 9. Create links between themes and explanations. 10. Highlight what is clear/unclear. 11. Formulate learning objectives: What they need to achieve by the end. 12. On the basis of what knowledge is lacking. 13. Create a link with the problem posed. 14. Create a clear, unambiguous and well defined list of what is to be learned from this problem (what it is precisely that they want to find out and learn). 15. Assign roles and divide tasks. 16. Divide up aspects of the problem to be researched.
After session 1	1. Be available to answer questions regarding the topic area. 2. Ensure you are available to be in-world for around an hour per day to field questions from students while they are in-world.	1. Additional evidence gathering. 2. Selecting relevant information: the theoretical background. 3. Critically studying the sources of information and assessing its value towards solving the problem defined. 4. Preparing details of relevant information that directly links to the problem and its impending solution: linking the information directly with the learning objectives. 5. Reconvene to discuss evidence and develop strategies for gathering remaining information needed. 6. Ideally in the virtual world; however, meetings can occur in the real world as well depending on the group locations, dynamics and technological skills. 7. Gather more evidence as needed.

Session	Teachers' Role	Students' Role
Session 2 and beyond (1–1.5 hours)	1. Check on the progress of all the groups within the virtual world. 2. Steer students back onto the correct course of action as needed. 3. Ask questions on areas or angles they may not have considered rather than state information. 4. Provide additional basic information as required – but allow students to think about in depth rather than being provided with information. 5. Assess whether the learning objectives have been met and the problem solved for each group. 6. Ensure that sufficient depth of information has been gathered by each group. 7. Critically test the new knowledge of the students' research through questions to individual groups and during the presentation phase. 8. Examine depth of knowledge. 9. Look at the strength of relationships students have formed between areas of the topic. 10. Look at the breadth of knowledge. 11. Assess the level to which the information has been critically examined. 12. Ensure that students are clear on what the report entails and how to complete it.	1. Reconvene in virtual world and discuss evidence obtained and how it addresses the problem posed. 2. Make links with discussions, evidence and learning objectives. 3. Translate information gathered into an answer for the problem posed. 4. Answer the problem as a group. 5. Provide evidence and formulate answer in preparation for presentation. 6. Present problem solution to the remaining groups. 7. Discuss and ask questions to fellow students. 8. Clarify and resolve questions. 9. Produce written evidence and rationale for solution. 10. Produce a report with details of the problem and how it has been solved. 11. The learning objectives should be clearly included and evidence should be provided of their successful attainment. 12. Evidence for the problem and its solution should be provided critically rather than descriptively.

PROBLEM-BASED LEARNING IN A VIRTUAL WORLD

SCENARIO SHEET: APPROACHES IN PSYCHOLOGY

There are various approaches in psychology for studying how people interact and function in their daily lives. These approaches allow us to interpret disorders, enabling specific treatment for any individual who may not be able to function without help. Some common problems which people experience are easily treatable and enable them to have a normal life. Some problems are more difficult and require more extensive treatment, possibly preventing individuals from living life without support and preventing them from caring for others.

Social workers and psychologists routinely have to evaluate families to assess normality of functioning. They have to look at what might be wrong with each family member and whether this treatment appears to be effective at helping them to lead a normal life. However, the most effective way is usually through observation rather than asking questions. Something many social workers and psychologists would like to have is a view of how a family functions on a daily basis. This option is provided in Second Life, in a house containing a virtual family. This family is in need of assessment and all the members are currently being treated for some form of disorder.

As far as social workers are concerned, families which are not able to care for a child should receive additional help to care for their child. As a psychologist you know that the best option for the child is to be cared for by their own family, and give them help should they need it, rather than taking a child into care. Whether you can manage a disorder depends on the approach taken to treat it, and on the success of that treatment in the long term.

Instructions and information are provided in the Preview-Psych area

PREVIEW-Psych Info Area, Derby University (170, 100, 21)
http://slurl.com/secondlife/Derby%20University/185/96/22

You should go to this location within Second Life and explore the area for information, the family and their virtual home. There is more information about the task and details how to write and submit your report with the Second Life PBL area.

PART IV
TRANSFORMING VIRTUAL WORLD DEPLOYMENT

INTERCULTURAL COLLABORATIVE LEARNING IN VIRTUAL WORLDS

Béatrice S. Hasler

ABSTRACT

This chapter evaluates the potential of virtual worlds for intercultural collaborative learning. A case study of a global lecture series is presented that used a virtual world as a platform for intercultural student collaboration. Students' subjective reports served as a basis for exploring cross-cultural differences in the perceived usefulness of virtual worlds for intercultural collaboration, and to examine what they have learned from working in an intercultural virtual team, what problems occurred, and how they resolved them. Based on the evaluation results, suggestions are provided for a culture-aware design of virtual worlds to facilitate intercultural collaborative learning and the development of intercultural literacy.

Keywords: Virtual worlds; global virtual teams; cultural differences; intercultural literacy; culture-aware design

INTRODUCTION

Globalization has profoundly affected work and education in the 21st century. Universities have adopted their missions in response to the demands of

Transforming Virtual World Learning
Cutting-edge Technologies in Higher Education, Volume 4, 265–304

ISSN: 2044-9968/doi:10.1108/S2044-9968(2011)0000004015

globalized workplaces, and aim to produce "global citizens" with "global competencies" (Altenbach, Reisberg, & Rumbley, 2009). Intercultural literacy has become one of the core competencies in today's globalized world, and its development has been incorporated in many educational programs (e.g., the Bologna Declaration in Europe[1]). A growing number of universities are offering intercultural learning experiences to students by means of Internet-based distance education (Buchanan, Wilson, & Gopal, 2008; Chia, Poe, & Singh, 2008; Dorazio & Corey, 2007; Liu & Hannafin, 2010). The effective use of information and communication technologies is crucial for members of global virtual teams who collaborate from remote locations. Intercultural literacy and technological literacy are therefore equally important; and they are closely connected as any cultural discourse is directly or indirectly influenced by the essence of its technology (McMinn, 2009).

The chapter explores the potential of virtual worlds – in particular the role of embodiment in a shared three-dimensional (3D) virtual space as its essential component – to support intercultural collaborative learning. The first part of the chapter provides a conceptual definition of "intercultural collaborative learning" and "intercultural literacy," and discusses the core elements of virtual worlds from a cross-cultural perspective. In the second part, a case study of a global lecture series is presented that used a virtual world as a platform for intercultural collaboration between students from 18 universities worldwide. As part of this large-scale international field study, cross-cultural differences are examined between Asian, European, and Arab students regarding their perceptions of avatar-based collaboration in virtual worlds. These findings serve as a basis to derive suggestions for a culture-aware design of virtual worlds as intercultural learning environments. In addition, students' reports are analyzed on what they have learned from working in an intercultural virtual team, what problems occurred, and how they resolved them. These evaluation results lead to a discussion of what needs to be considered in designing virtual worlds for intercultural student collaboration as an effective platform to foster intercultural literacy.

INTERCULTURAL LITERACY AND INTERCULTURAL COLLABORATIVE LEARNING

Intercultural Literacy

Heyward (2002) defines intercultural literacy as a multidimensional construct including the competencies, understandings, attitudes, language proficiencies, participation, and identities that are necessary for successful living and working in a cross-cultural environment. According to Heyward (2002), the interculturally literate person is able to effectively "read a second culture, to interpret its symbols and negotiate its meanings in a practical day-to-day context" (p. 10). Lack of intercultural literacy, on the other hand, leads to "misunderstandings and intercultural blunders that can be extremely costly to both individuals and organizations" (p. 10). Table 1 shows Heyward's (2002) developmental model of intercultural literacy with descriptors of its lowest and highest levels.

Intercultural Learning

The development of intercultural literacy requires the individual to learn what culture is by reflecting on his or her own culture, by learning about other cultures, and how to engage successfully with members of other cultures in various social contexts. Thus, intercultural learning takes place

Table 1. Heyward's (2002) Model of Intercultural Literacy.

	Descriptions	
Dimension	Lowest level	Highest level
Understandings	Unaware of own culture or of the significance of culture in human affairs.	Aware of how cultures feel and operate from the standpoint of the insider.
Competencies	No significant intercultural competencies.	Competencies include mindfulness, empathy, perspective taking, tolerance, and communication.
Attitudes	Assumes that all groups share similar values and traits.	Attitudes are differentiated, dynamic, and realistic, and demonstrate an overall respect for integrity of cultures.
Participation	No significant participation and unawareness of cultural dimension of contact.	Well-established cross-cultural friendships and/or working relationships.
Language proficiencies	No significant second language competencies.	Bilingual or multilingual understanding and proficiencies.
Identities	Unformed cultural identity.	Identities are bicultural, transcultural, or global; ability to consciously shift between multiple cultural identities.

through the experience of confronting oneself in a cross-cultural situation (Heyward, 2002). Intercultural learning environments need to be designed in a way that will enable equal participation of members from different cultures, in order to make students aware of their own and foreign cultures, to increase their understanding, to give them the opportunity to develop competencies, to increase their language proficiencies, and to eventually form transcultural or global identities.

Collaborative Learning

A collaborative learning approach appears to be most suitable to provide students with the opportunity to practice effective collaboration in culturally diverse groups. Collaborative learning can be best understood by its distinction from cooperative learning: Learning in cooperative groups takes place individually and involves mostly asynchronous group activities. Group members divide their work, complete subtasks individually, and assemble the partial results into a final group output. In contrast, collaborative learning occurs in coordinated, synchronous activities in which group members collaboratively construct knowledge through negotiation and sharing (Dillenbourg, 1999; Stahl, Koschmann, & Suthers, 2006). Dillenbourg (1999) explains collaborative learning in terms of four critical aspects: situation, interactions, processes, and effects, with bidirectional links among them. For instance, he defines the collaborative situation as a kind of *social contract* between individuals, which specifies the conditions under which some types of interactions *may* take place, yet there is no guarantee that they will actually occur. Hence, the general concern in collaborative learning is to trigger learning mechanisms and to increase the probability for desired types of interaction and positive learning outcomes to occur.

Intercultural Collaborative Learning

If we integrate the above definitions, intercultural collaborative learning refers to intercultural *situations*, in which members from different cultures *interact* in coordinated, synchronous activities with joint efforts and common goals. The *process* in which individuals negotiate and share meanings is expected to lead to positive *effects* regarding the above-mentioned dimensions of intercultural literacy. In contrast to cross-cultural trainings in which the development of intercultural literacy is the main learning goal, it could emerge as a side effect in intercultural collaboration, which in turn may primarily focus on other (academic) subjects. While this definition of intercultural collaborative learning leaves it open whether the interaction takes place face-to-face (FTF) or computer-mediated, the focus of the chapter lies on cross-cultural interactions in virtual worlds.

POTENTIAL OF VIRTUAL WORLDS FOR INTERCULTURAL COLLABORATIVE LEARNING

Virtual worlds provide new ways for individuals to meet and collaborate from remote locations using graphical representations of themselves (i.e., avatars) in a shared virtual environment. Users can design the appearance of their avatar (e.g., by modifying gender, ethnicity, body shape, hair, and clothes), move their virtual bodies, and jointly look at and manipulate objects in a shared 3D virtual space. They can communicate verbally via text and voice chat, and display nonverbal behaviors by changing the position of their avatar, and choosing from a set of postures, gestures, and facial expressions. These analogies to FTF communication are assumed to create a sense of copresence among interacting users, that is, a feeling of "being there together" in a virtual room (Schroeder, 2006). In addition, there are various features that go beyond the simulation of FTF communication, and enable us to overcome the restrictions of the physical world; for example, cultural identity switch by changing one's avatar appearance, or interaction with nonplayer characters controlled by artificial intelligence. These characteristics of virtual worlds open interesting new opportunities for cross-cultural training and intercultural collaborative learning.

Up to the present, only a few case studies on intercultural learning in virtual worlds have been published (Prasolova-Førland & Wyeld, 2008; Wyeld, Prasolova-Førland, & Chang, 2006). Other approaches to cross-cultural trainings in 3D virtual environments can be found in the "serious games" literature (Ogan, Aleven, Kim, & Jones, 2010; Warren, Sutton, Diller, Leung, & Ferguson, 2005), some of which described the use of nonplayer characters for cross-cultural role-playing scenarios (Sims, 2007; Zielke et al., 2009). Only one study had been found, which evaluated the development of intercultural literacy in cross-cultural encounters in virtual worlds. Diehl and Prins (2008) applied Heyward's (2002) model of intercultural literacy to interview responses of participants in cross-cultural language learning activities in *Second Life*. The authors conclude that such activities enhanced intercultural literacy in terms of "fostering use of multiple languages, cross-cultural encounters and friendships, greater awareness of insider cultural perspectives, and openness towards new viewpoints" (p. 101). They also observed that participants modified their avatar appearance in order to construct and shift cultural identities.

Although the potential of virtual worlds for cross-cultural training has been recognized, it is still unclear how virtual worlds need to be designed in order to enhance the intercultural collaborative learning experience, and to foster sustainable, positive learning outcomes. As a first step in this direction, we need to take a closer look at the core elements of virtual worlds from a cross-cultural perspective.

Virtual Space and Place Metaphors

Three-dimensional virtual spaces provide a more vivid and realistic environment compared to 2D representations, and facilitate the creation of a more correct and complete mental model of a collaborative task at hand (Chittaro & Serra, 2004). In line with this assumption, Wyeld et al. (2006) found that the 3D aspect led to more active social involvement and concretization of the performed activities in an intercultural collaboration task in a virtual world.

Virtual architecture always serves – whether intentionally or unintentionally – as a place metaphor and provokes specific types of social behavior. For example, a virtual room that is designed like a lecture hall is likely to trigger similar social norms as in a physical lecture hall, whereas a very different type of social behavior is expected in a virtual space designed as a leisure park. Prasolova-Førland (2008) provides a framework for analyzing place metaphors in virtual worlds for different educational goals, including the factors of appearance (e.g., real vs. abstract), structure (e.g., relationships between different parts of the environment), and roles (e.g., meeting or information place). The framework has been applied in case studies that evaluated place metaphors of a 3D virtual campus (Prasolova-Førland, 2008), and a 3D "virtual stage" for educational role-play and socialization (Prasolova-Førland & Wyeld, 2008; Wyeld et al., 2006).

Cross-cultural meetings in the real world always take place in a specific cultural environment, which determines the social conventions and rules that visitors are expected to follow. Similar effects may be found in virtual worlds that are designed according to physical-world models. In contrast to the physical world, virtual worlds offer the possibility to design culture-neutral spaces. Whether a virtual space is designed in a culture-specific or culture-neutral way, should be a conscious decision of the virtual world designer depending on the purpose of the cross-cultural meeting. It remains unclear whether cultural distances diminish in a culture-neutral virtual world and become more salient in a culture-(stereo) typical virtual world, and how the design of the environment influences the process and outcome of cross-cultural meetings. Another question that has yet to be investigated is how individuals with different cultural backgrounds would collaboratively create a 3D virtual space, and how world design issues would be negotiated in such an intercultural collaborative design process. Initial findings in this direction are reported by Wyeld et al. (2006). The authors note that "students found they could not assume that their remote counterpart would understand how to use the spaces they had constructed or interpret their actions. Methods needed to be developed that offered 'universal' communication metaphors" (p. 1076).

Avatar–Environment Interaction

As for the design of the virtual space, we have the option of designing the interaction of avatars with the virtual world either as a simulation of the interaction between humans and their physical environment or to introduce new forms of interactions that are not possible in the physical world, which Bowman, Kruijff, LaViola, and Poupyrev (2001) refer to as "the magic approach." Interactions with the virtual environment include how avatars orient themselves, navigate through it, and manipulate objects. In particular, the use of "magic" interaction designs (e.g., pointers to open a virtual door) may be intuitively understood by one culture, but interpreted differently by another culture. Several studies have been published on culture-aware web interface design. These studies investigated cultural preferences, conventions, and interpretation of 2D visual representations, such as icons and graphics (Marcus & Gould, 2000; Mushtaha & De Troyer, 2007; Teasley, Leventhal, Blumenthal, Istone, & Stone, 1994; Zahir, Dobing, & Hunter, 2002). While some cultural differences, such as the meaning of colors (Aslam, 2006; Madden, Hewett, & Roth, 2000), can be expected to apply equally in a 3D virtual space, other cultural differences in the use and perception of the 3D user interface have yet to be evaluated in cross-cultural interaction design studies.

Avatar Appearance and Identity Tourism

The use of avatars as a virtual representation of interacting individuals has been claimed to be of great pedagogical value. Wyeld et al. (2006) found that students across all cultures rated the notion of being able to "hide" behind their avatar as a "liberating and empowering" experience, especially for those who may not have "spoken out" in a cross-cultural FTF encounter. Moreover, virtual worlds provide its users with the freedom of defining their virtual appearance and identity. Visible signs of ethnicity can be used as "decorative features" in the creation of avatars, which can be attached or detached at will (González, 2000). Ethnicity can also be transmitted by choosing an avatar name with ethnic connotations or masked by a neutral avatar name. Identity swapping in virtual worlds makes it possible to experience rather than merely observe what it feels like to be the opposite gender, to have a different race, or no race or gender at all. While gender-swapping is a common phenomenon in cyberspace (Bruckman, 1999; Huh & Williams, 2010; Hussain & Griffiths, 2008), race-swapping is relatively rare (Kolko, Nakamura, & Rodman, 2000).

Such "identity tourism" – to borrow a term introduced by Nakamura (2000) – has consequences for human interaction as it changes the way we behave and perceive each other. It has been found that experiences made in a virtual body that is different from one's real-life appearance can lead to transformed social behavior with transfer effects to real-world behavior, which is known as the "Proteus Effect" (Yee & Bailenson, 2007). It has been suggested to use manipulation and elimination of visual differences among group members as a strategy in virtual world collaboration, as the vividness or salience of group diversity is expected to influence group dynamics (Kahai, Carroll, & Jestice, 2007). This malleability of self-representation in a virtual world could be used to create an unbiased cultural experience (Prasolova-Førland & Wyeld, 2008), and might result in a redeployment of mass-mediated stereotypes (Boellstorff, 2008).

Another issue is concerned with the ability of individuals to identify with their avatar. It might be a hindrance for the intercultural learning experience if avatar customization limits the means for expression of one's identity and belonging (Prasolova-Førland, 2008). We can also expect cultural differences regarding what attributes of avatar appearance are considered as relevant or desirable. According to Hofstede (1991, 2001), cultures differ in the dimension of collectivism versus individualism. Collectivistic cultures, such as those of Asian and Arab countries, place an emphasis on the interdependence of every individual in a collective group, and group goals have priority over individual goals. In individualistic cultures, such as the United States and Western Europe, personal achievement has priority over group goals, resulting in a strong sense of competition. While individualistic cultures may experience a stronger need to express individual characteristics in their avatar appearance, collectivistic cultures may be more satisfied when being able to display attributes that signalize belonging to a certain group instead of visualizing individual differences among group members.

Ducheneaut, Wen, Yee, and Wadley's (2009) study on preferences in avatar personalization of US Americans provides partial support for this assumption. They found that participants tended to create avatars as idealized versions of themselves, which reflect what would be considered as "improvements" in Western popular culture. Participants tended to create thinner, younger, and more fashionable versions of themselves. The authors note that many scales of avatar customization systems were hardly used, and that they should be optimized for the "perfect body" range, in which users from Western cultures prefer to design their avatars.

Similarly, we can interpret a call from the Arabic world to take the "Islamic perspective" in the design of virtual worlds into account (Yusof & Zakaria, 2007). The authors claim that "if the virtual world platform is going to be useful, effective, and attractive for international collaboration, issues of cultural compatibility must be considered in their systems design" (p. 101). They raise the question of how an identity and image can be created in a virtual world, which would reflect Islamic values. For instance, they request for "virtual burqas," and argue that designers "need to highly consider the image and identity (e.g., clothing) of the female players in particular. For Islamic women, they need to cover their heads with scarf and appropriate piece of cloth and the costumes also need to cover the whole body. As it is now, in all the virtual games, the women seemed to dress in a varied form of costumes, sometimes more exposed, which are not deemed as appropriate for the Muslim female audience" (p. 102).

At this point we may have to reconsider the design of culture-neutral avatars, and think carefully about the consequences. If cultural differences are to be erased, Barwell and Bowles (2000) aptly ask the question, "whose cultures precisely will be lost?" (p. 702).

Interaction between Avatars: The Role of Nonverbal Communication

Virtual worlds support rich behavioral interactions between avatars, which resemble FTF communication. Individuals can use their virtual bodies for nonverbal communication (NVC) in addition to the exchange of verbal messages via text and audio channels. NVC serves important functions in FTF communication (Feldman & Rimé, 1991). These functions include (a) transmission of meaning to interpret the often subtle meaning behind verbal messages; (b) conversational management to regulate the flow of communication by signalizing who speaks when (i.e., turn taking) and to whom; (c) back-channel responses to provide feedback about the listener's level of comprehension or agreement; and (d) expression of affect to provide information about emotional states and attitudes in order to build an accurate understanding of the social situation.

According to Hall (1976), cultures differ in the extent to which they rely on contextual and nonverbal cues in communication. High-context cultures, including many Asian and Arab nations, use more implicit communication in which meaning and intention are emphasized through the context (e.g., environment, situation, and parties involved) and nonverbal channels. Low-context cultures, such as the United States and most European countries, use more explicit communication in which meaning and intention are emphasized through explicit verbal messages. NVC is therefore of particular importance in intercultural interactions. In addition to hindrances that culturally diverse groups may encounter due to language barriers, individuals must be able to encode and decode nonverbal cues appropriately in order to avoid misunderstandings. However, it is still unclear how these cultural differences in the reliance on NVC are reflected in intercultural interactions in virtual worlds.

The display of NVC in virtual worlds is very different from NVC in FTF interactions. In most virtual worlds, NVC is generated automatically by the software without any user inputs. Avatars try to appear natural, for example, by moving their lips when they are talking, or swinging arms and hips when walking. Most virtual worlds also provide a set of gestures, postures, and facial expressions that users can choose from. For instance, users have the option to wave, laugh, nod, or shake their avatar's head through keyboard commands or by selecting the respective nonverbal behavior from a menu. While nonverbal behaviors contain many nuances and subtleties in FTF communication, virtual worlds typically offer only a limited, predefined set of nonverbal behaviors. NVC displayed by avatars has (at least in current virtual world technologies) no relation to the user's actual nonverbal behavior. It is therefore not surprising that they are relatively rarely used in virtual world interactions (Becker & Mark, 1998, 2002).

However, people often use their virtual bodies as a means of NVC by volitional movement and placement of their avatar in the virtual environment. It has been found that social conventions regarding spatial behavior that can be observed in real-world situations are transferred into the virtual world. For example, interacting avatars are typically facing one another and respect others' personal space (Bailenson, Blascovich, Beall, & Loomis, 2001; Yee, Bailenson, Urbanek, Chang, & Merget, 2007). The same effect has been found for cultural differences in spatial behavior of avatar dyads in a virtual world (Hasler & Friedman, 2011). Asian dyads interacted at larger interpersonal distances than European dyads, which is what we would expect in an equivalent physical-world setting. It is important to note that this effect was based on participants' actual cultural backgrounds, which were visualized by avatar names with ethnic connotations. The majority used a culture-neutral cartoon-style avatar that was identical for all participants. Those who customized their avatars were mostly European participants. These results indicate that cultural norms regarding NVC matter in avatar-based interactions, and that it deserves special consideration in virtual worlds designed for intercultural collaborative learning.

Although there are some universal consistencies in facial expressions of emotion (Ekman, 1989), cultures vary considerably in the degree of accuracy in their recognition of emotions based on facial expressions (Matsumoto, 1992, 2007). This also has consequences on how emotions are expressed and interpreted based on NVC in Internet-mediated interactions. For example, it has been found that cultures differ in the use of textual expression of moods or emotions (i.e., emoticons) in text-based computer-mediated communication (Kayan, Fussell, & Setlock, 2006). There are also cultural differences regarding the text-strings that are used to compose emoticons (see Takagi (2010) for a collection of Japanese emoticons). Such cultural differences have also been found in the interpretation of avatar facial expressions (Bartneck, Takahashi, & Katagiri, 2004; Koda, 2007; Koda, Rehm, & André, 2008; Yun, Deng, & Hiscock, 2009).

Although the field of research on culture-sensitive design of virtual worlds is beginning to emerge, it has yet to be examined which features of avatar appearance and aspects of NVC are considered as useful, and how they are being used across different cultures. Likewise, more research is needed on how to support cross-cultural meetings in virtual worlds in order to enhance the intercultural learning experience, and to facilitate the development of intercultural literacy. The exploration of these factors is the main goal of the case study, which is presented in the following part.

CASE STUDY

The ShanghAI Lectures: A Global Virtual Education Initiative

The case study was carried out in the context of a global lecture series, called "The ShanghAI Lectures,"[2] on embodied – natural and artificial –

intelligence. The lecture series by the Artificial Intelligence Lab of the University of Zurich was presented in fall term 2009 from Shanghai Jiao Tong University, connecting 18 universities worldwide via videoconference. In addition to global knowledge dissemination on the subject matter, the ShanghAI Lectures aimed to create a platform for the development of intercultural literacy in a global learning and collaboration context, and the conditions for practicing of the effective use of novel collaboration technologies in order to prepare students for a work environment across national borders. In order to comply with these educational goals, a virtual world named "UNIworld" was designed to facilitate intercultural student collaboration. The ShanghAI Lectures also served as a research platform as it provided a unique opportunity to study various aspects of cross-cultural team collaboration and learning in virtual worlds, involving a large, culturally diverse group of students. The case study presented here is part of a broader research agenda in the context of the ShanghAI Lectures (see Hasler, 2010; Hasler, Buecheler, & Pfeifer, 2009).

METHOD

Participants

Participants were 86 (65 male, 21 female) students[3] who volunteered to take part in the research project in the context of the ShanghAI Lectures. They were graduate, postgraduate, and doctoral students majoring in computer science and engineering. Mean age was 24.59 years ($SD = 3.10$). Forty-three students were Asian (40 Chinese, 1 South Korean, 1 Japanese, and 1 Mongolian), 32 students were European (17 Swiss, 5 German, 3 Polish, 2 Estonian, 1 Czech, 1 Hungarian, 1 Swedish, 1 Albanian, and 1 Italian), and 11 students were from Arab countries (9 Algerian, 1 Kuwaiti, and 1 Iraqi). All participants were nonnative English speakers.

Materials

Virtual world
Students collaborated as avatars in a virtual world named "UNIworld," which was developed based on *Open Wonderland*[4] (version 0.5). Eighteen instances of UNIworld were used, each of which consisted of five virtual team rooms and a public meeting area (see Fig. 1). UNIworld offered public and private text chat, and "spatial audio" communication (i.e., automatic

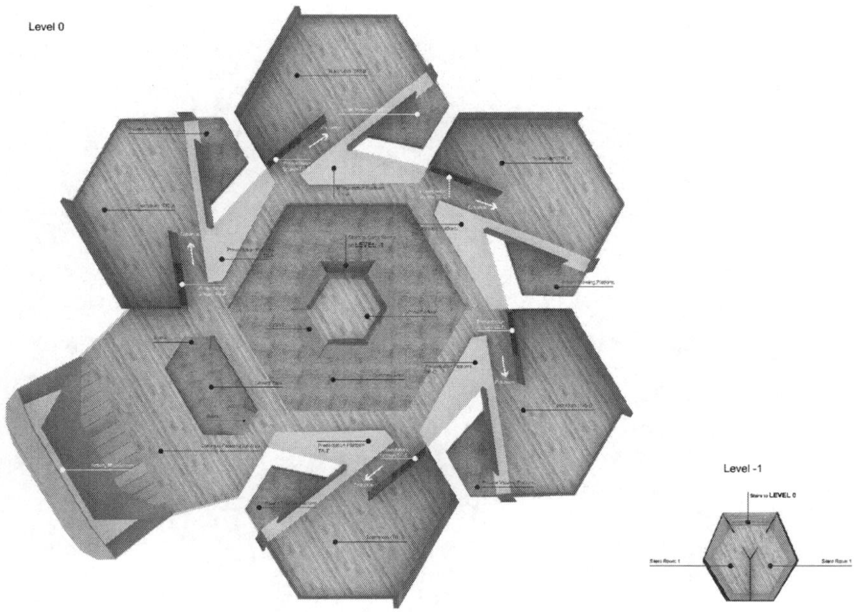

Fig. 1. Architectural Design of UNIworld. (Design by *Henn Architekten*, Munich).

volume adjustment according to the distance between avatars). Collaborative work was supported by in-world application sharing tools, such as web browsers, video-players, PDF viewers, text editors, and whiteboards. The interdisciplinary approach to the design of the UNIworld architecture and collaboration experiences is described in Schmeil et al. (2010).

Avatar appearance

In comparison to other virtual world applications, such as *Second Life*, the freedom to customize avatar appearance was limited in UNIworld. Participants began with a culture-neutral cartoon-style avatar, and were able to customize gender, clothing accessories, and color of skin, hair, pants, shirt, and shoes. These customizations were categorical and did not allow for gradual changes. Fig. 2 shows a group meeting of participants who used default avatars (standing on the right side) and customized avatars (standing on the left side).

Nonverbal communication

UNIworld provides a set of 14 basic postures (e.g., "sit" and "stand") and gestures (e.g., "wave," "raise hand," and "nod") that students could

Fig. 2. Group meeting in UNIworld. (Copyright by Henn Architekten).

perform with their avatars using keyboard commands or by clicking the corresponding buttons. Fig. 2 shows the available set of NVC. UNIworld does not support any user-controlled facial expressions.

Measures

Students were asked to respond to four free-text questions in an online questionnaire. All responses were categorized by two raters. Any disagreements between the two raters were resolved by consensus.

Cross-cultural differences

Two questions were asked to evaluate the perceived usefulness of avatars: "Do you think the deployment and appearance of avatars was significant for the virtual collaboration experience?," and NVC: "Did you notice others using means of NVC, such as gestures? Do you consider them useful in this setting?" In order to explore cross-cultural differences, the responses were analyzed separately for Asian, European, and Arab students.

Intercultural learning
Two questions were asked to evaluate learning effects: "What did you learn from working in an international (cross-cultural) team?," and problems and solutions: "What problems occurred in your international teamwork and how did you resolve them?" Responses to these questions were categorized using Heyward's (2002) dimensions of intercultural literacy.

PROCEDURE

Upon registration for the lectures, the students were requested to choose an avatar name and to fill in a profile page on the course website. The online registration form contained a description of the purpose of the research project, the kind of data that will be collected, and the privacy protection procedures. The students were also required to read and respond to an informed consent form. Participation in the research project was an optional part of the lectures, which had no bearing on their academic evaluation. Students were then assigned to international virtual teams of four to five members each, in which they collaborated on group assignments over the course of the semester.[5] Each university provided two to four teaching assistants who graded the student assignments according to standardized instructions and example solutions. The teaching assistants were randomly assigned to five or six international student teams. UNIworld was offered as a collaboration platform, but the teams were free to use additional media to schedule their meetings and to coordinate their tasks. An online questionnaire was administered after the last group exercise, containing the questions that are considered in the current case study.

RESULTS

Cross-Cultural Evaluation of Avatars and Nonverbal Communication in Virtual Worlds

Perceived usefulness of avatars
Fig. 3 shows a comparison between Asian, Arab, and European students regarding their perceived usefulness of avatars for collaboration in virtual

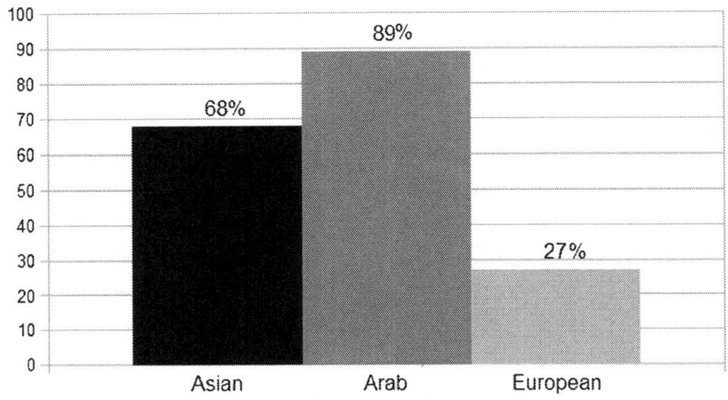

Fig. 3. Cross-Cultural Comparison of Perceived Usefulness of Avatars for Collaboration.

worlds. The bars represent the percentage of statements for each cultural group that expressed usefulness of avatars.

Asian and Arab students perceived avatars more often as useful than useless, while the opposite was the case for European students. A Chi-square test could only be performed for a comparison of ratings by Asian and European students due to the small number of responses from Arab students. The difference in perceived usefulness of avatars between Asian and European students was statistically significant, $\chi^2(1) = 8.72$, $p = .003$. Table 2 shows example statements of the reasons provided for perceived usefulness versus uselessness of avatars for virtual world collaboration by each of the three cultural groups.

Only a few European students clearly indicated that they perceived avatars as useful for remote collaboration, and most of their statements contained some reservations. The most frequent critique was the limited degree of freedom in avatar customization. These statements regarding the importance of individualization in avatar appearance can be interpreted as an indicator of individualistic values in Western cultures (Hofstede, 1991, 2001). Other European students mentioned that traditional 2D communication tools, such as email or chat, were sufficient for effective collaboration. They further mentioned that avatars distracted from the collaboration tasks, and that their handling was too time consuming. Those who perceived avatars as useful mentioned that it made the experience more interesting, and that it facilitated communication. Similar reasons were mentioned by Asian and Arab students for perceived usefulness of avatars.

Table 2. Example Statements of Perceived Usefulness versus Uselessness of Avatars for Collaboration in Virtual Worlds.

Culture	Rating	Example Statements
European	Useful	"Yes. It focused attention in a spatial location. I think that's important for good thinking – to use your body and your senses in a somewhat coordinated fashion. Without avatars, sight wanders off and the attention does too"
		"For this particular experience, sure. I mean it wouldn't have been this experience without, would it?"
	Useless	"No it wasn't especially as it was nearly impossible to individualize the avatars."
		"No, a simple shared whiteboard with audio and chat would be easier to use and much less time consuming."
Asian	Useful	"Yes it's very important. It can help us communicate."
		"Yes of course. You can see the character from the character (^-^)"
	Useless	"No, we all use the same avatar, and we do not care about the appearance."
		"No, it is not very important. Just an avatar having the ability to represent some person will be OK."
Arab	Useful	"Of course, because it represents a simulation about its user, on other hand, I can imagine the user ..."
		"Yes I think because it give you a comfortable feeling especially if it's a bit comical"
	Useless	"Deployment, yes. Appearance, not really. Maybe it would be case if I and other member have customized avatar appearance!"

They mentioned that avatars provide information about the user, and create a sense of presence in a virtual space. Arab students also criticized the limitations in avatar customization, whereas Asian students noted that individual appearance does not matter. These statements could be interpreted as an indicator of collectivistic values in Asian cultures (Hofstede 1991, 2001). Although Arab nations are also considered as collectivistic cultures, the statements of Arab students did not contain any indicators regarding the values associated with collectivism.

Perceived usefulness of NVC

Fig. 4 shows a comparison between Asian, Arab, and European students regarding their perceived usefulness of NVC for collaboration in virtual worlds. The bars represent the percentage of statements for each cultural group that expressed usefulness of NVC.

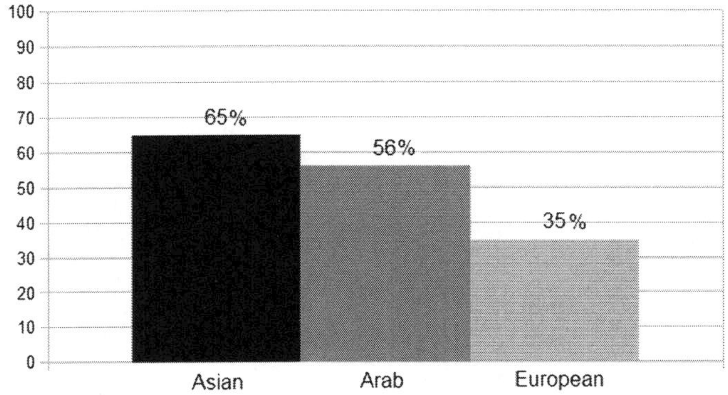

Fig. 4. Cross-Cultural Comparison of Perceived Usefulness of Avatar-Based Nonverbal Communication for Collaboration.

Asian and Arab students perceived NVC more often as useful than useless, while the opposite was the case for European students. A Chi-square test could only be performed for a comparison of Asian and European students due to the small number of responses from Arab students. The difference in perceived usefulness of NVC between Asian and European students was statistically significant, $\chi^2(1) = 3.96$, $p = .047$. Table 3 shows example statements of reasons provided for perceived usefulness versus uselessness of NVC in virtual worlds by each of the three cultural groups.

Students across all cultures who perceived NVC as useful for collaboration mentioned that NVC had the same functions in the virtual world as in the real world (e.g., to express emotions). However, there were cultural differences regarding the relevance and purpose of NVC, which reflect the differences between high-context and low-context cultures (Hall, 1976). While European students saw the main purpose of avatar-based NVC as "enhancing the experience," Asian and Arab students emphasized that NVC facilitates understanding in that it supplies additional information to the verbal communication channel. Asian students mainly noted the limited set of nonverbal behaviors as a reason why NVC was not perceived as a useful feature in avatar-based collaboration. These statements reflect the importance of NVC in high-context cultures. In contrast, most European students argued that there is no need for NVC in virtual worlds because verbal communication was sufficient for effective collaboration. These statements can be interpreted as an indicator of the lower reliance on NVC in low-context cultures. Some European students also mentioned that NVC would only be useful in virtual worlds if it was intuitive, and used in the same way by all participants as the meaning would be difficult to interpret otherwise.

Evaluation of Intercultural Collaborative Learning in Virtual Worlds

Learning effects

Table 4 shows example statements of students' reports on what they have learned from collaborating with an intercultural virtual team. The statements were classified according to the dimensions of Heyward's (2002) developmental model of intercultural literacy. None of the statements indicated aspects of cultural identity, or the development of transcultural or global identities. The "identity" dimension is therefore not considered in this analysis.

Out of a total number of 72 statements about learning effects from intercultural team collaboration, most were concerned with participation (26 mentions). The majority of students increased their awareness that contact between people from different countries is crucial for an intercultural discourse, and stressed the importance of team working skills and "team spirit". However, only a few students mentioned actual skill improvements regarding how to collaborate across geographical borders and time zones. Nineteen statements were classified as indicators for increased competencies. The students stated that they learned how to communicate with others who have different cultural backgrounds, and to see things from their perspective. While some reported actual skill improvement, others mentioned an increased awareness of the competencies needed for successful intercultural communication and collaboration. Twelve statements were concerned with a better understanding of other cultures and techniques (e.g., active listening, being patient) to improve understanding in the process of intercultural teamwork. Ten statements were concerned with attitudes as they showed an increased awareness of cultural differences regarding values and viewpoints. The least frequently counted dimension was language proficiencies (five mentions), which included the awareness of difficulties in intercultural communication due to language barriers, and an improvement in foreign language skills.

Seven out of 86 students mentioned that they did not learn anything new from working in an intercultural team during the ShanghAI Lectures. As the

Table 3. Example Statements of Perceived Usefulness versus Uselessness of Nonverbal Communication for Collaboration in Virtual Worlds.

Culture	Rating	Statements
European	Useful	"I think they are useful but first we must ensure that we are all using gestures with the same meaning."
		"Well, yes. I think it is useful, because one can show how he feels and can make the atmosphere while working better."
	Useless	"No, because we either used chat or voice. We tried gestures like pointing to an object once but it was too confusing what the other person wanted to express."
		"I never saw anybody using gestures. And honestly they didn't even work with me, if I tried to use them ... I think they would have about the same effect as emoticons in chat programs, but be less useful because you can already guess the opponents mood to a large extend by his voice alone."
Asian	Useful	"It's useful sometimes, because when there is no proper ways to describe your idea, maybe the gestures can help us."
		"Using gestures is very useful and important because it makes others understand your ideas more easily."
	Useless	"No, very hard to identify"
		"No, there's not much gestures I can show with the avatar, so I always use words."
Arab	Useful	"Yes. For instance turning around, and over oneself when getting bored, or when waiting a response from other members. Or moving to inform other members that you should change place to have a right perspective of 3D objects and to show how to use it. Yes, it is useful and their interpretation is contextual and easy."
		"I think it is very nice to use gesture for communicating because it gives you a sense that the other one has accepted you and respected you."
	Useless	"Not at all time. Express idea by writing is very useful."
		"Not very much."

main reasons, they mentioned that they already worked in international teams before or that they were familiar with other cultures because they studied abroad. One student noted that his team "seldom got over basic, task-related communication. This seldom got us into real cross-cultural experiences."

Table 4. Example Statements of Intercultural Learning Effects.

Dimensions	Example Statements
Participation	"I've learned to arrange virtual meetings over different time zones."
	"Meeting is difficult, but meeting helps a lot in order to build up a group."
Competencies	"I learned to respect others and to be friendly and considerate."
	"How to communicate with people with different culture."
Understandings	"We should know more about the culture of each other"
	"It is very important to listen and respond."
Attitudes	"That everybody has different work ethics when being in a multicultural class."
	"It reaffirmed my opinion of the fact that people are just as diverse in the same culture as they are between cultures."
Language proficiencies	"Some knowledge about how to communicate with foreign students in English."
	"It happens very fast that there are conflicts, which cannot be resolved because there are language barriers."

Problems

Students' statements about the problems that occurred in their intercultural virtual teamwork were categorized according to Heyward's (2002) model in order to identify issues that may hinder the development of intercultural literacy. Out of a total number of 82 statements, most were concerned with participation issues (48 mentions). Participation included situational factors (e.g., time zones) that influenced students' possibility to meet and collaborate synchronously, as well as personal factors (e.g., commitment and level of contribution) that reflected students' willingness to meet and collaborate. The fact that participation issues are mentioned most frequently is also reflected in the evaluation of intercultural learning effects. As participation was the main issue, it also influenced students' awareness of the importance of being able to (synchronously) meet and collaborate. Twelve statements indicated problems that occurred due to differences between team members regarding their attitudes toward the team, the collaboration tasks, or the distribution of workload. Misunderstandings due to different cultural backgrounds were categorized as understanding issues (10 mentions). Eight statements indicated issues regarding lack of language proficiencies. An inverted frequency of positive learning outcomes and the number of problems was observed for statements regarding competencies. Only four statements were concerned with missing competencies that hindered efficient collaboration with members that have different (educational and cultural) backgrounds. In contrast, the improvement in competencies was mentioned as a frequent learning outcome. It is also important to note that 12 statements indicated that no problems occurred in intercultural virtual teamwork.

Students' solutions

Table 5 summarizes students' solutions to overcome the issues that they encountered during the intercultural virtual team collaboration. The most frequently mentioned issue was the possibility to meet for synchronous collaboration due to time differences. Although the students tried to resolve this issue by showing more flexibility regarding meeting times, some teams split up and worked individually. It remains unclear whether the often-criticized lack of willingness to collaborate is a consequence of the time zone issue or did in fact rely on students' motivation. The other solutions to overcome issues associated with different attitudes, misunderstandings, lack of language skills, and missing competencies do not appear to require further explanation.

Table 5. Example Statements of Students' Solutions to Improve Intercultural Virtual Teamwork.

Issues Regarding ...	Solutions Suggested by Students
Participation	Situational factors: Try to find meeting dates/be flexible (16), distribute tasks and work asynchronously (13) Personal factors: Work with active team members only (13), try to insist and encourage contribution/contact members once more (3), people need to know/get to know their team members in order to be willing to contribute (1), report inactive team members to the teachers (1), reduce expectancies and just do the minimum (1)
Attitudes	Address problems and discuss in team (3), express arguments and opinions (2), accept cultural differences (2), explain your expectations (1), be friendly, accept/respect different values/customs/habits (1), find agreements (1), develop new working schemes (1), somebody makes a decision (1)
Understandings	Interact/communicate more (4), explain things more clearly (2), explain once more (1), try to understand each other in their way (1), discussions, invest more time (1), be patient (1)
Language proficiencies	Improve English skills (4), use written chat instead of audio (2), be patient (2)
Competencies	Share knowledge (1), learn to think from different perspectives (1), bring to the group what you have (1), those who know more should contribute more (1)

DISCUSSION OF A CULTURE-AWARE DESIGN OF VIRTUAL WORLDS

The case study explored cross-cultural differences between individualistic, low-context cultures (i.e., European countries) and collectivistic, high-context cultures (i.e., Asian and Arab countries) regarding the perceived usefulness of avatars and NVC for collaboration in virtual worlds. Based on the evaluation results, possible solutions are derived for a culture-aware design of virtual worlds, which is considered as a prerequisite for effective intercultural collaborative learning. Future research directions are discussed under the perspective of current technological developments.

Avatar Design

European students showed a preference for individualized avatars, which were less important to Asian students who perceived avatars merely as a representation of the user in the virtual space but did not stress the significance of individualistic appearance. This finding indicates that values of individualistic and collectivistic cultures are transferred into the virtual world. As Mushtaha and De Troyer (2007) stated, the perception of our (real and virtual) environment is founded in the very nature of culture: "Culture affects who we are, how we think, how we behave, and how we respond to our environment. Above all, it determines how we learn. A person's cultural background is learned, not inherited and is made up of experiences gained when growing up in his or her culture. Therefore, cultural background is used in understanding the 'virtual' world on the screen" (p. 164).

The evaluation results stress the importance for the design of culture-aware virtual worlds that take cultural preferences in avatar design into account by offering more flexibility in avatar customization. In addition to providing means to transfer "real-world" identities into the virtual world, we need to make it possible to create new transcultural identities of a global, virtual community that is free of visible signs of gender, race, ethnicity, and class, where other attributes rather than real-world appearance become salient, or alternative, nonhuman representations or hybrid characters can be chosen.

Avatar-Based Nonverbal Communication

Asian and Arab students stressed the importance of NVC, and requested more advanced options to perform nonverbal behavior in avatar-based collaboration. NVC was of less importance to European students who stated that verbal communication was sufficient for effective collaboration. This finding provides evidence for the relevance of cultural dimensions (e.g., high-context vs. low-context cultures) in virtual world design. Cultures not only differ regarding their reliance on NVC in FTF settings but also transfer their communication styles into the virtual world. The ability to appropriately encode and decode nonverbal cues is crucial in intercultural communication. Virtual worlds provide an additional challenge for appropriate encoding of nonverbal behaviors. While NVC is mostly unconscious to people while interacting FTF, it requires a volitional act in virtual worlds (e.g., keyboard commands). The way user-controlled nonverbal behaviors are currently performed in virtual worlds is neither natural nor intuitive. The fact that nonverbal behavior of avatars is not related to the users' actual behavior places additional demands on the appropriate decoding of nonverbal cues in virtual worlds. If NVC in virtual worlds is used in similar ways as emoticons in text chat (i.e., with cultural variations), we can also expect cultural differences in the intended meaning and interpretation of NVC in avatar-based collaboration.

Current Technological Developments

The avatar customization systems that are integrated in the common virtual worlds are often limited to the design of anthropomorphic avatars, while the design of nonhuman or hybrid characters often requires some creative workarounds (Ventrella, 2011). This places some limitations to the design of culture-neutral avatars to foster transcultural identities, as proposed above. The trend toward more (photo-)realistic human-like avatars, on the other hand, is supported by a number of sophisticated (external) avatar design systems, such as *FaceGen*[6] or *evolver*.[7] However, the import of the digital 3D models that can be created with these systems based on photographs is still not supported by every virtual world. Nevertheless, we are witnessing how the borders between synthetic 3D and video are blurring. We might soon be able to cross the "uncanny valley," in which negative psychological effects are expected when creating virtual humans that almost, but not perfectly, look like actual humans (Seyama & Nagayama, 2007). An important factor that should not be neglected in this development is the behavioral realism of avatars, in which the natural expression of nonverbal behaviors plays a crucial role (Bailenson, Yee, Merget, & Schroeder, 2006; see also Ventrella's

(2011) discussion of the "uncanny valley of expression" and his proposition of a "gestural Turing test").

For an effective use of avatar-based NVC in intercultural collaboration, we need to find new ways of how avatar gestures, postures, and facial expressions can be performed more naturally and intuitively. Amarakeerthi, Ranaweera, Cohen, and Nagel (2009) describe a feature developed for *Open Wonderland* that triggers avatar gestures based on keywords in a text-chat. For example, an avatar would automatically be displayed as laughing when the user types ":D." A similar approach uses speech input to create avatar gestures based on speaking style (Neff, Kipp, Albrecht, & Seidel, 2008). These text and voice puppeteering methods are described in more detail in Ventrella (2011), and are illustrated on the author's website.[8] Others utilize new techniques for real-time mapping of facial expressions onto avatars using video image, which has previously only been possible by attaching markers on the participant's face (Bailenson et al., 2006). There are also approaches that combine different speech- and video-based methods for real-time multimodal human–avatar interaction (Yun, Renxiang, Huang, & Danielsen, 2008). Probably the most promising development in natural human–avatar interfaces is controller-free gaming devices, such as *Microsoft's Kinect*, which has recently become commercially available. Such ubiquitous tracking technologies make it possible to map a user's body movement in real time onto his or her avatar. Many research labs are currently experimenting with these novel technologies, and are developing interesting new ways of expressing nonverbal behaviors in virtual worlds. For example, researchers at the Institute for Creative Technologies of the University of Southern California used *Kinect* and the *OpenNI* toolkit[9] to trigger predefined avatar animations in *Second Life* through natural body movement (Institute for Creative Technologies (ICT), 2011). Natural human–avatar interfaces will certainly revolutionize the way we interact with avatars in virtual worlds in the near future.

Future Research Directions

Many avatar customization systems are designed and optimized for a specific culture, which limits the possibilities to express and explore different cultural identities in a virtual environment. In order to design more flexible avatar customization systems, more research is required about which attributes in avatar appearance are considered as relevant across different cultures, and which nuances are requested by different cultures in which range of the respective attributes (Ducheneaut et al., 2009). Recent empirical studies investigated "cultural identity switching" in virtual worlds as a method to foster perspective taking in cross-cultural encounters. However, the results are inconsistent regarding the direction of the effect. Some found a decrease in racist attitudes when White participants were represented by Black avatars (Gonzales, Falisi, & Hancock, 2010), while others found the opposite effect in that being transformed into a Black avatar resulted in activation of negative stereotypes and greater racial bias (Groom, Bailenson, & Nass, 2009). Thus, the psychological consequences of "cultural identity tourism" in virtual worlds, and the conditions under which it may result in positive or negative outcomes, require further research.

Another line of research investigates the impact of salient group identity on normative behavior, which can easily be manipulated in avatar appearance. Kim (2011) describes two differential effects of uniform virtual appearance (i.e., group members being represented by identical avatars) as a means of "surpassing individuals' social or cultural differences" (p. 248). A clear visual distinction between one's own group (i.e., in-group) and an opposing group (i.e., out-group) resulted in increased willingness to agree with in-group members' opinions. At the same time some participants perceived a threat to their uniqueness if all in-group members were represented by the same avatar, which in turn resulted in participants' need to diverge from their in-group members' opinion in order to restore their uniqueness. Hence, as for the use of (stereo-) typical avatars as a means of cultural identity tourism and perspective taking, the impact of the utilization of culture-neutral (or identical) avatars as a technique to "neutralize" or eliminate cultural differences in virtual worlds requires careful consideration and a better understanding of the respective consequences.

As for the perceived usefulness of avatars and preferences regarding avatar appearance, cultural differences appear to be an important factor to consider in avatar-based NVC. However, possibly due to the limited expression of nonverbal behaviors in the currently available virtual world technologies, social scientists have not paid much research attention to NVC in virtual worlds yet; except for a small number of studies on virtual proxemics; that is, the distance at which avatars interact in virtual worlds (Hasler & Friedman, 2011; Yee et al., 2007). The study of NVC in virtual worlds is expected to become more interesting and relevant considering the current development in natural human–avatar interfaces, which bear a high potential for enhanced, mediated cross-cultural encounters. Researchers at the Advanced Virtuality Lab of the Interdisciplinary Center Herzliya are currently developing a translator of NVC for avatar-based cross-cultural interactions in using body tracking systems, similar to translation systems that exist for verbal communication (Hasler, 2011). Whenever the NVC translator recognizes a cultural difference in a gesture performed by one participant, it translates the intended meaning depending on the other participants' cultural background, and replaces this transformed avatar gesture in real time.

While the current evaluation was focused on cross-cultural differences in the perceived usefulness and preferences for avatar appearance and NVC, there are other factors that have yet to be investigated, such as cross-cultural differences in the interpretation of place metaphors, and cultural preferences in avatar–environment interaction. Cultural dimensions (e.g., high vs. low-context cultures and individualism vs. collectivism) provide a useful framework for exploring cross-cultural differences. However, such "sophisticated stereotyping" (Osland & Bird, 2000) has to be interpreted with caution as these dimensions do not convey the complexity found within cultures. In addition to cross-cultural differences, other factors (e.g., personality and gender) need to be examined regarding preferences in the design of virtual worlds.

LESSONS LEARNED ABOUT INTERCULTURAL COLLABORATIVE LEARNING

How to Facilitate Intercultural Collaborative Learning in Virtual Worlds

One of the goals of the ShanghAI Lectures was to facilitate intercultural collaborative learning, and to explore whether virtual worlds can be used as an effective platform for the development of intercultural literacy. Students' reports were analyzed regarding what they have learned from working in an intercultural virtual team, what problems occurred, and how they resolved them. The evaluation results indicated that virtual worlds have the potential to effectively support intercultural collaborative learning, and to foster the development of intercultural literacy under certain conditions. The students reported various learning effects in terms of an increased awareness and skill improvement regarding Heyward's (2002) dimensions of intercultural literacy. They were able to overcome many of the problems that they were facing during their intercultural team collaboration (see Table 5). However, some of the issues could be (at least partly) reduced by those who are involved in the design and administration of a global virtual education project (including the lecturers, teaching assistants, and the designers of the virtual world and collaboration tasks).

Participation

Possibility and willingness to attend synchronous team meetings in the virtual world were mentioned as the most frequent issue in intercultural collaboration. If different time zones hinder team members to work synchronously on their tasks, additional tools need to be provided that support asynchronous teamwork (e.g., backboards, discussion forums, file sharing, and collaborative text editing tools). Although many tools are available for free that support asynchronous teamwork, only a few teams made use of them. The students reported that most of their asynchronous work was coordinated via email. A collection of different tools that supplement one another has also been recommended based on the lessons learned from another cross-cultural education project, which used a virtual world as the main (synchronous) collaboration platform (Wyeld et al., 2006). The authors further noted that some tools were more appropriate for different phases of the collaboration process.

Future virtual student collaboration projects that use virtual worlds as a collaboration platform should also consider more advanced in-world collaboration tools. For example, *Open Wonderland* offers a variety of modules that can be installed as extensions to the standard in-world collaboration tools.[10] The active open-source community is constantly extending and adding modules, which include avatars (e.g., import functions for photo-realistic *evolver* avatars or scripts for nonplayer characters), collaboration tools (e.g., group chat, presentation features, meeting organizers, and screen sharer), world models (e.g., auditorium and gallery), multimedia elements (e.g., microphone for speakers, movie recorder, music player, and photo album), simulations (e.g., educational simulations of machines or computer algorithms, and a feature to drag and drop animations into the virtual world). The use of more advanced in-world collaboration tools may not only improve teamwork efficiency but also increase students' motivation to participate in synchronous team meetings in virtual worlds.

However, many of the currently available virtual world modules that were designed to facilitate collaborative work are merely a copy of techniques that are commonly used to support teamwork in FTF settings or "two-dimensional" collaboration tools, such as whiteboards and text editors. There is a need for more advanced group work technologies that are suitable and specifically designed for a virtual 3D environment. Such advanced collaboration features should go beyond importing "2D tools" into a 3D virtual world. Interesting approaches in this direction have been reported by researchers at the MIT Media Lab who developed tools for real-time visualizations of group interaction processes in virtual worlds (Drew, 2008;

Drew & Donath, 2008). Especially the dynamic visualization of affective processes could be highly beneficial for mutual understanding in multi-cultural virtual teams.

Attitudes, understanding, and competencies
In order to foster an intercultural discourse, students should be encouraged not only to meet for task-related work but also to socialize with their team members and other participants. The teams in the ShanghAI Lectures were not provided with any cross-cultural training because intercultural learning effects were expected to emerge as a side effect. However, trust and relationship building is crucial for effective collaboration, especially in global virtual teams composed of members with different cultural backgrounds (Jarvenpaa & Leidner, 1999). This process should be supported by team building and icebreaker tasks at the beginning of a collaboration phase. Although such "get acquainted" tasks have not been used in the ShanghAI Lectures, they can be expected to positively influence students' attitude toward their members, and reduce conflicts in the subsequent work-related group tasks. Furthermore, the role of the teaching assistants needs to be reconsidered. They were mainly instructed to provide the student teams that they have been assigned to with feedback on their group tasks. This feedback was usually given by email, and the teaching assistants did not have direct (i.e., synchronous) contact with their teams. In future projects of this kind, the teaching assistants should supervise their teams also in other (social) aspects, and meet them on a regular basis as avatars in the virtual world. Those students who encountered problems with their teams mostly reported them to their local lecturers. However, the local teaching staff at each participating university could often only offer "local solutions" for individual team members. It might be beneficial if the students are requested to work out solutions within their team with the support of teaching assistants as mediators.

How to Evaluate Intercultural Collaborative Learning Effects

The evaluation of the learning effects and the problems that occurred in the intercultural virtual teamwork was based on students' subjective reports collected at the end of the course. In order to determine whether or not students increased their intercultural literacy, future cross-cultural education projects should include pre- and post-course measurements. Standardized instruments are available that can be used to measure different dimensions of intercultural literacy, for example, the Intercultural Sensitivity Scale (Chen & Starosta, 2000), the Behavioral Assessment Scale for Intercultural Communication Effectiveness (Koester & Olebe, 1988), or acceptance of social stereotyping (Carter, Hall, Carney, & Rosip, 2006).

Additional insights could be gained by an objective evaluation of intercultural learning effects and possible conflicts, which requires observation of actual team behavior over time. Virtual environments make it possible to automatically collect data on the users' behavior in an unobtrusive way. A behavioral tracking and visualization system developed for detailed analysis of avatar behavior in *Open Wonderland* is described in Hasler (2010). Future cross-cultural education projects should also evaluate long-term effects regarding the sustainability of intercultural relationships, as well as transfer effects from the virtual collaborative learning experience to real-world behavior.

NOTES

1. The Bologna Declaration (1999), retrieved from http://ec.europa.eu/education/policies/educ/bologna/bologna.pdf on May 1, 2011; see Altenbach et al. (2009) for a review of other international education programs.
2. More information on the ShanghAI Lectures project and participating universities can be found at http://shanghailectures.org
3. In total 282 students participated in the ShanghAI Lectures. The sample of 86 participants only includes students from Asia, Europe, and Arab countries who filled in the surveys used in the current case study. Other nationalities were not considered in this case study due to their small number.
4. http://openwonderland.org
5. The group exercises are described in more detail in Schmeil, Eppler, and de Freitas' chapter in another Hinrichs and Wankel book, called *Engaging the Avatar*, soon to be released by Information Age
6. http://www.facegen.com
7. http://www.evolver.com
8. http://www.avatarpuppeteering.com
9. http://www.openni.org
10. http://openwonderland.org/module-warehouse/module-warehouse

ACKNOWLEDGMENTS

This work has been supported by the Swiss National Science Foundation (Grant No. PBZH1-130971), the European Union (Grant No. PIEF-GA-2009-254277), and the Education Authority of the Principality of

Liechtenstein. The author gratefully acknowledges the ShanghAI Lectures team, especially Rolf Pfeifer, Thierry Buecheler, Hanspeter Kunz, Nathan Labhart, Andy Zbinden, Bo Chen, and Andreas Schmeil, for their support in the organization of this global education project. The author would also like to thank Anat Brovman and Ady Nae O'Malley for their comments on the manuscript and their assistance in analyzing the data.

REFERENCES

Altenbach, P. G., Reisberg, L., & Rumbley, L. E. (2009). *Trends in global higher education: Tracking an academic revolution*. A report prepared for the *UNESCO 2009 World Conference on Higher Education*. United Nations Educational, Scientific and Cultural Organization, Paris.

Amarakeerthi, S., Ranaweera, R., Cohen, M., & Nagel, N. (2009). Mapping selected emotions to avatar gesture. In: *Proceedings of the 1st International Workshop on Aware Computing*, Aizu-Wakamatsu, Japan, September 17–18.

Aslam, M. M. (2006). Are you selling the right colour? A cross-cultural review of colour as a marketing cue. *Journal of Marketing Communications*, *12*, 15–30.

Bailenson, J. N., Blascovich, J. J., Beall, A. C., & Loomis, J. M. (2001). Equilibrium theory revisited: Mutual gaze and personal space in virtual environments. *Presence*, *10*, 583–598.

Bailenson, J. N., Yee, N., Merget, D., & Schroeder, R. (2006). The effect of behavioral realism and form realism of real-time avatar faces on verbal disclosure, nonverbal disclosure, emotion recognition, and copresence in dyadic interaction. *Presence*, *15*, 359–372.

Bartneck, C., Takahashi, T., & Katagiri, Y. (2004). Cross-cultural study of expressive avatars. In: *Proceedings of the Social Intelligence Design*, University of Twente, Enschede, the Netherlands (pp. 21–27), July 5–7.

Barwell, G., & Bowles, K. (2000). Border crossings: The Internet and the dislocation of citizenship. In: D. Bell & B. M. Kennedy (Eds.), *The cybercultures reader* (pp. 702–711). London: Routledge.

Becker, B., & Mark, G. (1998). Social conventions in collaborative virtual environments. In: *Proceedings of CVE'98*, University of Manchester, UK, June 17–19.

Becker, B., & Mark, G. (2002). Social conventions in computer-mediated communication: A comparison of three online shared virtual environments. In: R. Schroeder (Ed.), *The social life of avatars* (pp. 19–39). London: Springer.

Boellstorff, T. (2008). *Coming of age in Second Life: An anthropologist explores the virtual human*. Princeton, NJ: Princeton University Press.

Bowman, D. A., Kruijff, E., LaViola, J. J., & Poupyrev, I. (2001). An introduction to 3-D user interface design. *Presence*, *10*, 96–108.

Bruckman, A. S. (1999). Gender swapping on the Internet. In: P. Ludlow (Ed.), *High noon on the electronic frontier. Conceptual issues in cyberspace* (pp. 317–325). Cambridge, MA: MIT Press.

Buchanan, J., Wilson, S. T., & Gopal, N. (2008). A cross cultural virtual learning environment for students to explore the issue of racism: A case study involving the UK, USA and SA. *Social Work Education: The International Journal*, *27*, 671–682.

Carter, J. D., Hall, J. A., Carney, D. R., & Rosip, J. C. (2006). Individual differences in the acceptance of stereotyping. *Journal of Research in Personality*, *40*, 1103–1118.

Chen, G. M., & Starosta, W. J. (2000). The development and validation of the intercultural communication sensitivity scale. *Human Communication*, *3*, 1–15.

Chia, R. C., Poe, E., & Singh, P. (2008). An interactive virtual global cultural course: Building a real time cost effective global collaborative learning environment. *Journal of Educational Technology Systems*, *3*, 32–35.

Chittaro, L., & Serra, M. (2004). A brief introduction to Web3D technologies in education: Motivations, issues, opportunities. In: *Proceedings of the 1st International Workshop on Web3D Technologies in Learning, Education, and Training*, Udine, Italy (pp. 3–7), September 30–October 1.

Diehl, W. C., & Prins, E. (2008). Unintended outcomes in *Second Life*: Intercultural literacy and cultural identity in a virtual world. *Language and Intercultural Communication*, *8*, 101–118.

Dillenbourg, P. (1999). What do you mean by 'collaborative learning'? In: P. Dillenbourg (Ed.), *Collaborative learning: Cognitive and computational approaches* (pp. 1–19). Oxford: Elsevier.

Dorazio, P., & Corey, H. (2007). Modeling the global workplace using emerging technologies. *Journal of Educational Technology Systems*, *36*, 157–170.

Drew, H. (2008). *Algorithmic architecture in virtual spaces*. Master thesis, Massachusetts Institute of Technology, Cambridge, MA.

Drew, H., & Donath, J. (2008). Information spaces – Building meeting rooms in virtual environments. In: *Proceedings of the 26th Annual SIGCHI Conference on Human Factors in Computing Systems*, Florence, Italy, April 5–10.

Ducheneaut, N., Wen, M.-H., Yee, N., & Wadley, G. (2009). Body and mind: A study of avatar personalization in three virtual worlds. In: *Proceedings of the 27th International Conference on Human Factors in Computing Systems*, Boston, MA (pp. 1151–1160), April 4–9.

Ekman, P. (1989). The argument and evidence about universals in facial expressions of emotion. In: H. Wagner & A. Manstead (Eds.), *Handbook of social psychophysiology* (pp. 143–164). Chichester, UK: Wiley.

Feldman, R. S., & Rimé, B. (Eds.). (1991). *Fundamentals of nonverbal behavior*. Cambridge, UK: Cambridge University Press.

Gonzales, A. L., Falisi, A., & Hancock, J. T. (2010). Decreasing racist attitudes through virtual play: Evidence of verbal perspective taking by white students when playing black avatars in *Second Life* chat. Paper presented at the *2010 Annual Convention of the National Communication Association*, San Francisco, CA.

González, J. (2000). The appended subject: Race and identity as digital assemblage. In: B. Kolko, L. Nakamura & G. Rodman (Eds.), *Race in cyberspace* (pp. 27–50). New York, NY: Routledge.

Groom, V., Bailenson, J. N., & Nass, C. (2009). The influence of racial embodiment on racial bias in immersive virtual environments. *Social Influence*, *4*, 231–248.

Hall, E. T. (1976). *Beyond culture*. New York, NY: Doubleday.

Hasler, B. S. (2010). Report on research and evaluation. In: T. Buecheler, N. Labhart, & B. Rowland (Eds.), *The ShanghAI Lectures 2009: How to conduct a global technology-supported academic lecture. Final project report* (pp. 61–81). Zurich: Artificial Intelligence Laboratory, University of Zurich. Available at http://shanghailectures.org/images/stories/shail2009-finalreport_web.pdf. Retrieved on May 1, 2011.

Hasler, B. S. (2011). Intelligent transformation of multicultural nonverbal communication. Presentation at the *Symposium on "Human-machine Confluence"*, Interdisciplinary Center Herzliya, Israel, April 17.

Hasler, B. S., Buecheler, T., & Pfeifer, R. (2009). Collaborative work in 3D virtual environments: A research agenda and operational framework. In: A. A. Ozok & P. Zaphiris (Eds.), *Online communities* (LNCS 5621, pp. 23–32). Berlin: Springer.

Hasler, B. S., & Friedman, D. A. (2011). Spatial behavior in virtual worlds: Two field studies on inter-avatar distance. Paper presented at the *2011 Conference of the International Communication Association*, Boston, MA, May 26–30.

Heyward, M. (2002). From international to intercultural. Redefining the international school for a globalized world. *Journal of Research in International Education, 1*, 9–32.

Hofstede, G. (1991). *Cultures and organizations: Software of the mind.* London: McGraw-Hill.

Hofstede, G. (2001). *Culture's consequences: Comparing values, behaviors, institutions, and organizations across nations* (2nd ed.). Thousand Oaks, CA: Sage.

Huh, S., & Williams, D. (2010). Dude looks like a lady: Gender swapping in an online game. In: W. S. Bainbraidge (Ed.), *Online worlds: Convergence of the real and the virtual.* London: Springer.

Hussain, Z., & Griffiths, M. D. (2008). Gender swapping and socializing in cyberspace: An exploratory study. *CyberPsychology and Behavior, 11*, 47–53.

Institute for Creative Technologies (ICT). (2011). *Using Kinect and OpenNI to embody an avatar in Second Life: Gesture & emotion transference.* Project Report, University of Southern California. Available at http://ict.usc.edu/projects/gesture_emotion_transference_using_microsoft_kinect_and_second_life_avatars/ Retrieved on May 1, 2011.

Jarvenpaa, S., & Leidner, D. (1999). Communication and trust in global virtual teams. *Organization Science, 10*, 791–815.

Kahai, S. S., Carroll, E., & Jestice, R. (2007). Team collaboration in virtual worlds. *The DATA BASE for Advances in Information Systems, 38*, 61–68.

Kayan, S., Fussell, S. R., & Setlock, L. D. (2006). Cultural differences in the use of instant messaging in Asia and North America. In: *Proceedings of the 20th Anniversary Conference on Computer-supported Collaborative Work*, Alberta, Canada (pp. 525–528), November 4–8.

Kim, J-H. (2011). Two routes leading to conformity intention in computer-mediated groups: Matching versus mismatching virtual representations. *Journal of Computer-Mediated Communication, 16*, 271–287.

Koda, T. (2007). Cross-cultural study of avatars' facial expressions and design considerations within Asian countries. In: T. Ishida, S. R. Fussell & P. T. J. M. Vossen (Eds.), *Intercultural collaboration* (pp. 207–220). Berlin: Springer.

Koda, T., Rehm, M., & André, E. (2008). Cross-cultural evaluations of avatar facial expressions designed by Western designers. In: H. Prendinger, J. Lester, & M. Ishizuka (Eds.), *Intelligent virtual agents* (LNCS 5208, pp. 245–252). Berlin: Springer.

Koester, J., & Olebe, M. (1988). The behavioral assessment scale for intercultural communication effectiveness. *International Journal of Intercultural Relations, 12*, 233–246.

Kolko, B. E., Nakamura, L., & Rodman, G. B. (Eds.). (2000). *Race in cyberspace.* New York, NY: Routledge.

Liu, Y., & Hannafin, R. D. (2010). Exploring student identity in an intercultural web-assisted scientific inquiry project. *Journal of Research in International Education, 9*, 124–140.

Madden, T. J., Hewett, K., & Roth, M. S. (2000). Managing images in different cultures: A cross-national study of color meanings and preferences. *Journal of International Marketing*, *8*, 90–170.

Marcus, A., & Gould, E. (2000). Crosscurrents: Cultural dimensions and global Web user-interface design. *ACM Interactions*, *2*, 32–46.

Matsumoto, D. (1992). American-Japanese cultural differences in the recognition of universal facial expressions. *Journal of Cross-Cultural Psychology*, *23*, 72–84.

Matsumoto, D. (2007). Playing catch with emotions. *Journal of Intercultural Communication*, *10*, 39–49.

McMinn, S. W. J. (2009). Knowing culture in Second Life: International literacy and the technological know how in a virtual world. In: *Proceedings of the 5th international conference on multimedia and information and communication technologies in education*, Lisbon, Portugal, April 22–24.

Mushtaha, A., & De Troyer, O. (2007). Cross-cultural understanding of the content and interface in the context of e-learning systems. In: N. Aykin (Ed.), *Usability and internationalization: HCI and culture* (pp. 164–173). Berlin: Springer.

Nakamura, L. (2000). Race in/for cyberspace: Identity tourism and racial passing on the Internet. In: D. Bell & B. M. Kennedy (Eds.), *The cybercultures reader* (pp. 712–720). London: Routledge.

Neff, M., Kipp, M., Albrecht, I., & Seidel, H.-P. (2008). Gesture modeling and animation based on a probabilistic re-creation of speaker style. *ACM Transactions on Graphics*, *27*, 1–24.

Ogan, A., Aleven, V., Kim, J., & Jones, C. (2010). Intercultural negotiation with virtual humans: The effect of social goals on gameplay and learning. In: *Proceedings of the 10th international conference on intelligent tutoring systems: Bridges to learning*, Pittsburgh, PA, June 14–18.

Osland, J. S., & Bird, A. (2000). Beyond sophisticated stereotyping: Cultural sensemaking in context. *Academy of Management Executive*, *14*, 65–76.

Prasolova-Førland, E. (2008). Analyzing place metaphors in 3D educational collaborative virtual environments. *Computers in Human Behavior*, *24*, 185–204.

Prasolova-Førland, E., & Wyeld, T. (2008). The place metaphor in 3D CVEs: A pedagogical case study of the virtual stage. *International Journal of Emerging Technologies in Learning*, *3*, 54–60.

Schmeil, A., Steinbusch, M., Jost, A., Henn, M., Jacobi, M., Schwitalla, M., & Hasler, B. (2010). A refined workflow for designing virtual worlds for collaborative learning. In: *Proceedings of VS-Games 2010*, Braga, Portugal, March 25–26.

Schroeder, R. (2006). Being there together and the future of connected presence. *Presence*, *15*, 438–454.

Seyama, J., & Nagayama, R. S. (2007). The uncanny valley: Effect of realism on the impression of artificial human faces. *Presence*, *16*, 337–351.

Sims, E. M. (2007). Reusable, lifelike virtual humans for mentoring and role-playing. *Computers & Education*, *49*, 75–92.

Stahl, G., Koschmann, T., & Suthers, D. (2006). Computer-supported collaborative learning: An historical perspective. In: R. K. Sawyer (Ed.), *Cambridge handbook of the learning sciences* (pp. 409–426). Cambridge, UK: Cambridge University Press.

Takagi, H. (2010). *Japanese Emoticons Dictionary*. Available at http://club.pep.ne.jp/~hiroette/en/facemarks/body.html. Retrieved on May 1, 2011.

Teasley, B., Leventhal, L., Blumenthal, B., Istone, K., & Stone, D. (1994). Cultural diversity in user interface design: Are intuitions enough? *ACM SIGCHI Bulletin*, *26*, 36–40.

Ventrella, J. (2011). *Virtual body language. The history and future of avatars: How nonverbal expression is evolving on the Internet*. S.I.: Eyebrain Books.

Warren, R., Sutton, J. L., Diller, D. E., Leung, A., & Ferguson, W. (2005). Simulating scenarios for research on culture and cognition using a commercial role-play game. In: *Proceedings of the 37th Winter Simulation Conference*, Orlando (pp. 1109–1117), December 4–7.

Wyeld, T. G., Prasolova-Førland, E., & Chang, T.-W. (2006). Virtually collaborating across cultures: Theatrical performance in a 3DCVE spanning three continents. In: *Proceedings of the 6th IEEE International Conference on Advanced Learning Technologies*, Kerkrade, the Netherlands (pp. 1076–1078), July 5–7.

Yee, N., & Bailenson, J. (2007). The Proteus effect: The effect of transformed self-representation on behavior. *Human Communication Research*, *33*, 271–290.

Yee, N., Bailenson, J. N., Urbanek, M., Chang, F., & Merget, D. (2007). The unbearable likeness of being digital: The persistence of nonverbal social norms in online virtual environments. *CyberPsychology & Behavior*, *10*, 115–121.

Yun, C., Deng, Z., & Hiscock, M. (2009). Can local avatars satisfy a global audience? A case study of high-fidelity 3D facial avatar animation in subject identification and emotion perception by US and international groups. *Computers in Entertainment*, *7*(2).

Yun, F., Renxiang, L., Huang, T. S., & Danielsen, M. (2008). Real-time multimodal human-avatar interaction. *IEEE Transactions on Circuits and Systems for Video Technology*, *18*, 467–477.

Yusof, S. A. M., & Zakaria, N. (2007). Islamic perspective: Virtual worlds as a western-centric technology. *The DATA BASE for Advances in Information Systems*, *38*, 100–103.

Zahir, S., Dobing, B., & Hunter, M. G. (2002). Cross-cultural dimensions of Internet portals. *Internet Research*, *12*, 210–220.

Zielke, M. A., Evans, M. J., Dufour, F., Christopher, T. V., Donahue, J. K., Johnson, P., Jennings, E. B., Friedman, B. S., Ounekeo, P. L., & Flores, R. (2009). Serious games for immersive cultural training: Creating a living world. *IEEE Computer Graphics and Applications*, *29*, 49–60.

LESSON PLAN: GOALS OF THE SHANGHAI LECTURES

This lesson plan provides an example of how lectures can be given to a global audience with attendees and speakers from various locations, and to create an international collaborative learning environment on a particular academic topic. The case study presented in the chapter is based on the ShanghAI Lectures, a global digitally mediated course on "Embodied Intelligence", given to more than 250 students worldwide in approximately 20 universities. The lectures are presented by international experts and broadcast via videoconference. In addition, the students collaborate in interdisciplinary, multicultural teams on exercises in a 3D virtual environment. The course is intended for students with little or no computer science background.

Learning goals are formulated for both students and instructors as participants in a globally connected academic community:

- *Content-related learning goals*: Students become familiar with the far-reaching implications of embodiment for the development of intelligent behavior, and learn about the basic concepts, methods, techniques, and major issues in the study of intelligent natural and artificial systems that will enable them to understand, design, and build such systems. Instructors learn how to design exercises in this particular subject area in a way that exploits the potential of a virtual world, and is intelligible for an interdisciplinary, multicultural audience.
- *Intercultural learning goals*: Students increase their intercultural literacy by working in multicultural virtual teams (e.g., increasing their awareness of cultural differences and learning how to resolve conflicts in a culturally diverse team) in order to prepare them for a global workplace. Instructors learn how to effectively support cross-cultural teamwork in mediated environments by providing guidance and feedback in a culturally adept way.
- *Technological learning goals*: Both faculty and students gain first-hand experience of avatar-based collaboration, learn about its potentials and shortcomings, and can master virtual world technology effectively as a novel collaborative environment.

CONTENT OF THE LECTURES

The lectures are about natural and artificial intelligence, with a focus on the concept of embodiment ("Embodied Intelligence"). While in the classical approach "intelligence" was viewed essentially as information processing taking place in the brain, more recently the notion of embodiment (i.e., the idea that intelligence is emerging from a complete organism interacting with the real world) has been gaining increasing acceptance. As a consequence, intelligence is not longer a matter of the brain only, but of the interplay of brain, body (morphology and materials), and the environment.

The implications of an embodied view on intelligence are not only of a scientific nature but also lead to a completely different way of how we view ourselves and the world around us. Examples and illustrations are taken from humans, animals, engineering (robotics in particular), and business. Using the method of "understanding by building", the lectures provide a set of design principles that on the one hand enable a better understanding of biological systems, and on the other provide heuristics for how to design artificial ones, in particular robots.

COURSE PROGRAM

Week 1	VC	Welcome, site presentations, overview.
Week 2	VC	Intelligence: Artificial Intelligence and its landscape.
Week 3	CVE	Discussion session, exercises.
Week 4	VC	Prerequisites for a Theory of Intelligence.
Week 5	CVE	Discussion session, exercises.
Week 6	VC	Intelligence: Properties, Principles, and Development.
Week 7	CVE	Discussion session, exercises.
Week 8	VC	Evolution: Cognition from Scratch.
Week 9	CVE	Discussion session, exercises.
Week 10	VC	Collective/Modular Robotics, Intelligent Companies.
Week 11	CVE	Discussion session, exercises.
Week 12	VC	Intelligence in Ubiquitous Systems and Interfaces.
Week 13	CVE	Discussion session, student presentations.

VC, Videoconferene; CVE, Collaborative Virtual Environment ("UNIworld").

MODES OF PARTICIPATION

As universities have different requirements or preferences regarding the presentation style of lectures, several participation modes should be offered.

Making real-time attendance (of the lectures and discussion sessions) optional is important due to time zone considerations.

	Lectures (Videoconference)	Discussions (Virtual World)	Exercises (Virtual World)
A	Active participation	Active participation	Active participation
B	Connect, but watch/listen only	Optional	Active participation
C	Watch only recordings	Optional	Active participation

TECHNICAL COMPONENTS AND MATERIALS

Lectures (Videoconference). The lecture series is broadcast via videoconference, connecting local (physical) lecture halls around the world. In order to create an intercultural discourse, we recommend to include presentations from the various sites that demonstrate their own perspectives on the subject matter. Varying the broadcast location of the lectures also provides students with the ability to experience intercultural differences in presentation. It has further been found to be crucial for an increased awareness and sense of presence of a global community that participants not only meet as avatars but also see the "real" people with various cultural identities in the videoconference sessions.

Reading Assignments (Textbook). The lectures are supplemented by reading assignments (book chapters and papers; two hours per week). The textbook *How the Body Shapes the Way We Think – A New View of Intelligence* by Rolf Pfeifer and Josh Bongard, MIT Press, 2007, is used as compulsory reading material and provides the "backbone" of the lecture series. This is a nontechnical book that does not require prior training in any special discipline. Additional materials, in particular scientific papers, are provided during the course.

Discussion Sessions (Virtual World). Experience has shown that students rarely speak up during a globally connected videoconference lecture of this size. In order to increase the level of interactivity between students and lecturers, and to facilitate students' active participation, we introduced international discussion sessions held within the virtual world. Every second week, instead of a videoconference lecture, participants log in as avatars and discuss the topics that have been introduced in the previous week. They are requested to submit their questions to the lecturer beforehand by email.

Virtual worlds provide a safe environment that increases students' confidence to raise their hands due to an "equalizing effect" (i.e., visual anonymity). Being represented as an avatar leads to a reduced (i.e., less visually salient) hierarchy between students and lecturers. Another advantage of holding discussion sessions in a virtual world is the possibility of multiple comments at the same time using text-chat. Especially students with poor English skills feel more comfortable to formulate questions in text format than using voice chat. However, voice chat has been shown to be an essential feature, which should be used by the lecturer who leads the discussion, and for technical staff to provide help in case of technical problems. In order to avoid disturbing background noise, all participants are advised to mute their microphones when not speaking.

In addition to text and voice communication, several tools are available in a virtual world that can be used to make discussions more interactive, such as whiteboards or sticky notes for idea generation (i.e., collective brainstorming) in which each participant can become active and edit the shared notes. Since multimedia works effectively in the virtual world, any website, wiki site, blog site, or other Internet interface can become part of the environment. Also, conversations can be cut and pasted onto note cards and handed out through objects that are clicked on by the students. Students are not confined to a particular time slot to review presentation materials because the content can persist in the environment as long as the faculty leaves their presentations.

Group Exercises (Virtual World). In addition to attending the lectures and discussion sessions, students are required to work in international virtual teams on exercises that are designed to deepen the understanding of the materials presented (two hours per week). Each team is assigned to a team room in the virtual world where they meet and collaborate on the group exercises. Teaching assistants who are recruited from the participating universities supervise four to five international student teams, which they have been randomly assigned to. They are the main contact person for the students if they encounter any problems during their virtual teamwork, and are also responsible for grading students' work. Example solutions and detailed instructions are provided to the teaching assistants in order to assure a standardized grading of the exercises.

Virtual worlds are particularly useful for demonstration of 3D simulations, demonstration of objects interacting with each other, and visualizations in general. The instructions to the virtual world exercises used in the ShanghAI Lectures are available to registered users on the course website (http://shanghailectures.org).

Projects Assignments (Different Collaboration Media). In addition to the group exercises, students are requested to choose a project that they work on with their international team. A collection of projects along the typical steps of research in Artificial Intelligence (AI) is offered. The projects contain different elements of AI research to give students an impression of the tasks that scientists in this field are currently working on. While the exercises are specifically designed to be completed in the virtual world, students are advised to use different tools to collaborate on their projects. The virtual world was offered as a collaboration platform during the ShanghAI Lectures, providing each student team with their own virtual team room, and a group chat feature, which made it possible to work "quietly" (i.e., having private group conversations). However, most student teams used traditional chat tools (e.g., Skype and MSN) and email to coordinate their project work. Virtual worlds provide an interesting option for creating virtual galleries of students' project work. Students can display the process and outcome of their projects in the virtual world using poster signs or links to web pages.

Web-Based Resource (Course Website). Recordings of the lectures, guest talks, discussion sessions, as well as additional study materials, instructions to exercises, and announcement of project assignments were published on the course website, and remain available for registered users (http://shanghailectures.org). The course website is also used as a community platform, which requested each participant to create a profile page. We found it important that each participant has the possibility to show who they are in the physical world, and optionally upload photos. This is particularly important in an intercultural learning environment in which students collaborate with team members who they have never met before, and do not have the possibility to meet face-to-face. Adding physical-life information/photos adds a personal dimension to an otherwise anonymous mediated contact.

Assessment/Evaluation (Virtual World and Online Survey Tools). In order to assess students' AI-related knowledge, traditional (paper-based) exams are administered locally at each university. Feedback on the technology and intercultural teamwork experience is collected via online surveys. In addition, we used an integrated tracking system, which unobtrusively tracks participants' behavior in the virtual world. Such observational data of actual group processes have been found to be highly valuable to increase our understanding of cross-cultural collaboration in virtual worlds.

ALICE'S ADVENTURES IN PROGRAMMING NARRATIVES

Reneta D. Lansiquot and Candido Cabo

ABSTRACT

This chapter describes our innovative approach to the teaching of computer programming and writing; professors worked with students across classes united by a theme of narrative. A year-long study examined if using Alice, a three-dimensional microworld programming software that allows users to create interactive narratives, was more effective than Visual Basic (VB) in developing problem-solving abilities in first-year college students in introductory computer programming courses. Results revealed that although both the Alice and VB group showed a statistically significant ($p<0.05$) increase in performance for problem-solving questions related to computer programming, only the Alice group showed a significant increase in problem-solving abilities not directly related to computer programming, and an increase in student retention.

Keywords: Alice; composition; computer programming; interdisciplinary studies; narratives

INTRODUCTION

All the world's a stage, and all the men and women merely players ...
– William Shakespeare, *As You Like It*

Transforming Virtual World Learning
Cutting-edge Technologies in Higher Education, Volume 4, 305–325

ISSN: 2044-9968/doi:10.1108/S2044-9968(2011)0000004016

The power of narrative is not new to English composition. College first-years around the country frequently go through a rite of passage where they must make connections to a literary canon, which at first may seem distant or foreign. At a public university in New York City, computer systems technology majors used the theme of narrative to make the lessons of Aristotle relevant in a 3D environment. In their English composition class, students prepared original video game narratives, and, in their computer programming class, they actually programmed these stories. The approach taken by this "learning community" is unique because traditional writing composition is taught in a way that must connect to other courses first-years take. Therefore, in this case, traditional texts of composition such as Aristotle's *Poetics* had to be taught to students in ways that related the texts to a computer programming curriculum. Collaboration, in-person, and online peer review were important components of this learning community. Such technologically enabled collaboration enables communities and their members to explore, define, and express a common identity; foster sustained mutual engagement around a practice; and support an experience of togetherness that makes the community a social container for learning together (Wenger, White, & Smith, 2009).

In their English composition course, students start by reading Aristotle's *Poetics* and they focus on his six elements of drama: plot, what happens in the play or the order of events; theme, what the play means or the main idea within the play; character, the personality or the part an actor represents in a play or a role played by an actor in a play; dialogue, the word choices made by the playwright and the enunciation of the actors delivering the lines; rhythm, the sound or melody of the speeches; and spectacle, the visual elements of the productions of a play, the scenery, costumes, and special effects in production. Sophocles (1991) *Oedipus Rex* is used as an exploration of these elements, not only because Aristotle was a great admirer of this Greek playwright, but also Oedipus is a perfect fit to Aristotle's ideal tragic hero; he follows all the rules. As this outline has become a guideline for many playwrights throughout history and is also emphasized in the works of Shakespeare (1990), students then read Shakespeare's *Macbeth* and analyzed this standard five-act play using Freytag's Triangle: Exposition, Rising Action, Climax, Falling Action, and Resolution.[1]

Students also read short stories such as Kate Chopin's "The Story of an Hour," William Faulkner's "A Rose for Emily," Liam O'Flaherty's "The Sniper," and Stephen King's "Strawberry Spring" to understand situational irony first introduced in *Oedipus Rex*. After reading Richard Connell (2006/1924) "The Most Dangerous Game," they begin to see that Freytag's analysis was intended to apply not to modern drama, but rather to ancient Greek and Shakespearean drama because more modern works, for example, may have no resolution because of a quick or surprise ending, or no ending such as the open ending in Frank Richard Stockton (1890) "The Lady, or the Tiger?" This title is also the question that the reader is left to ponder, and this gives students a chance to write an alternate ending. Students are then presented with the linear three-act structure used in film: the first act includes a plot point, an event that turns the story in another direction; the second act includes the confrontation, which includes the second plot point and almost always a turning point in the middle; finally, act three includes the resolution.

From the triangle of drama to the straight-line plot structure of film, students are finally introduced to Joseph Campbell's idea of the mythic hero and the hero's journey. This theory has been applied to many movies such as George Lucas' *Star Wars* (1977) and now to video games. Instead of a triangle or straight line, the hero's journey can be depicted as a circle. It begins at the tip of the circle with the ordinary world then moves counterclockwise through a series of stages – a call to adventure; the refusal of the call; meeting the mentor; crossing the threshold; tests, allies and enemies; approach the inmost cave, the ordeal; reward; the road back; resurrection; return with the elixir – and eventually returns to the ordinary world (Campbell, 1949/2008).

At this point, the connection to video game narratives is made and the importance of an engaging protagonist is emphasized. Students use the hero's journey to create their video game, plot outlines and, eventually, collaborate to create nonlinear narratives (see Appendix; Bateman, 2007). When given the chance to work on a meaningful project of their own choosing, students collaboratively created innovative video game narratives. The social nature of virtual worlds was used to engage students. After all, with virtual worlds, the playing field is open.

In a response to the growing need for a technologically savvy means of facilitating student learning, Stein (1998) called for rethinking the conceptual model that teaches students computer programming as computation and calculation, reconceptualizing pedagogy with a model of computer programs as embedded in, and interacting with a dynamic environment. A decade later, Zyda (2009) provided a reminder that ignoring the transition from the information age to the conceptual age has contributed to a drop in student interest in computer programming. Play supports learning, and learners can construct knowledge through interaction with objects (Piaget, 1973). As students play within microworlds, existing cognitive structures can be modified based on new knowledge learned by creating and interacting within the programming environment (Robertson & Kenton, 2010).

A phenomenographical study of introductory programmers revealed that students learn programming in any of five different ways: by (1) following, (2) coding, (3) understanding and integrating, (4) problem solving, and (5) participating or enculturation (Bruce et al., 2004). Although students experienced learning in these ways, we decided to focus on problem solving, as this requires students to discover the means to solve a problem using declarative knowledge (specific facts, concepts, and principles) and procedural knowledge (use of a declarative knowledge base) (Palumbo, 1990).

PHASE ONE: WHERE WE STARTED

Although a larger study was conducted that examined students' writing improvements and peer feedback, this chapter focuses on the aspect of the study that explored whether using an education software that teaches students computer programming in a 3D environment called Alice[2] is more effective than using previous methods in developing problem-solving skills in first-year computer systems technology majors. In English composition classes, the students prepared original video game narratives, and then, in their computer programming class, they actually programmed working prototypes of their games. Each prototype included a sample game world, characters, their interactions with their setting, and a nonlinear narrative.

Our research contributes to the work of Cooper, Dann, and Pausch (2003), who found an objects-first approach to computer programming to be the best way to help students understand complex foundations. Programming constructs like objects, properties, and methods, as well as selection structures and repetition loops were used. Consequently, focusing on problems easily understood by students (e.g., stories created by student teams, instead of temperature conversions or other mathematical applications) facilitated learning of computer programming.

The impetus for the subsequent research study is an article published in the *Communications of the ACM,* titled "Learning to Program and Learning to Think: What's the Connection?" by Mayer, Dyck, and Vilberg (1986). In this article, the authors contended that "focusing on thinking skills that are cognitive components of programming – rather than on intellectual ability – can illuminate the relationship between learning a programming language and learning more about thinking processes" (p. 605). They pointed out that the search for methods to teach problem solving has been elusive, citing the failed Latin School Movement as one of the first large-scale efforts to teach students to read, write, and speak Latin, as well as to teach some Greek and geometry, in order to build logical and disciplined minds. The negative results of educational research studies helped bring on the demise of the Latin Schools. Thorndike (1923) classic "transfer to training" studies also found that learning Latin did not produce strong transfer to other domains. Similar failures to produce transfer have been observed for modern curricula aimed at teaching general problem-solving abilities. Transfer is even rare when students have learned problem-solving strategies within one domain and are asked to solve formally identical problems presented within different domains. It is from this historical context that Mayer et al. concluded that there is no convincing evidence that learning a program enhances students' general intellectual ability, or that programming is any more successful than Latin for teaching "proper habits of mind."

Problem Solving with Computer Programming (CST 1101) is a required course for incoming students and is a prerequisite for all other courses in the major. Many students who pass the course have trouble succeeding in more advanced programming courses. After taking CST 1101, some students develop an aversion to computer programming, and they either change their major or decide to concentrate in areas of computer systems less computer-programming intensive, such as networking or system administration.

Based on student observations, when Visual Basic (VB) is used with introductory computer programming courses, several problematic areas for our students are apparent. First, students have difficulty translating word problems into a computer algorithm. Second, most problems proposed to students are closely related to mathematics and accounting, and our students are not well prepared in mathematics. Third, the syntax of computer programming languages is often overwhelming to first-year students who get distracted from solving the problems by the obscurity of the statements. Finally, students do not easily understand data types (e.g., numbers and strings). After the decision was made to switch from VB to Alice, it became clear that the effectiveness of this new approach required careful empirical research.

Our year-long, mixed-methodology study used a pre and post comparison group design. Results from phase one showed that students who used Alice increased performance in problem-solving based on the Mayer et al. (1986) problem-solving test with statistical significance (Fig. 1). Implementing a computer program in Alice required students to drag and drop the necessary components, resulting in a more enjoyable and less frustrating programming experience. Accordingly, they shared

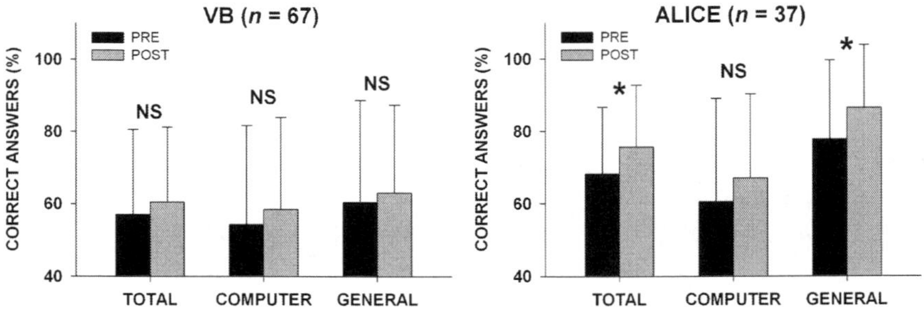

Fig. 1. Results of the pre and post problem-solving questionnaires for the Alice and VB groups.

objects with their group, and, when their program did not perform as they envisioned it would, the visual nature of Alice allowed them to pinpoint the exact location of the problem. We observed that students who used Alice were able to understand why the problem occurred; they spent time debugging their code with an interest, which was missing in the comparison group (Lansiquot & Cabo, 2010).

We used a problem-solving questionnaire based on the questions proposed in Mayer et al. (1986), and later used by Evans and Simkin (1989). The questionnaire consisted of 10 questions. Five questions were related to problem-solving abilities commonly applied to computer programming, such as word-problem translations, word-problem solutions, and following directions and procedures. None of the five questions were specifically related to programming constructs in Alice or VB. The other five questions were related to general problem-solving abilities not necessarily applied to computer programming, but important in other areas such as logical reasoning and spatial and verbal ability.

The Alice group showed a statistically significant ($p<0.05$) increase in performance for all questions (TOTAL), whereas the VB showed a non-significant (NS) increase. Interestingly, for the subset of questions relating to computer problem-solving skills (COMPUTER), there was a NS increase in both groups, the Alice group having a larger although NS increase. For the subset of questions that related to general problem-solving skills (GENERAL), there was a significant increase in the Alice group, whereas the VB group showed a NS increase. In the pre questionnaire, the performance of the Alice group was significantly higher than the VB in the set of GENERAL questions, but not in the COMPUTER questions.

PHASE TWO: WHERE WE WENT

Alice, a teaching tool for introductory computer programming, has been designed to circumvent the problems that we, and others before us (e.g., Cooper et al., 2003; Mullins, Whitfield, & Conlon, 2009; Sykes, 2007), have identified as the main problems encountered by computer programming students in introductory classes. Students use computer programming constructs like objects, properties, and methods, as well as selection structures and repetition loops to implement stories in a computer. The expectation is that focusing on problems easily understood by students (i.e., student-generated proposed scenarios or narratives) will facilitate the learning of computer programming, and play in this microworld can be used to engage students.

Using object-oriented programming for video games helps students see and act on the world in a new way, collaborate, develop resources for future learning and problem solving, and think about design spaces (Gee, 2003). To this end, storytelling in Alice lends itself to play and to students creating a shared finished product (Bishop-Clark, Courte, & Howard, 2006). This play involves critical thinking, iterative problem solving, interactive design and programming, as well as writing and storytelling (Flower, 1993; Salen, 2007).

Because students in the first semester who used Alice so clearly outperformed the group that did not, the second phase of our study, which again examined student problem-solving abilities, included all computer systems technology majors. The goal of this phase of our year-long study was to expand our investigation into whether Alice was more effective than VB as a tool for first-year students to develop problem-solving abilities in an introductory course in computer programming (Lansiquot & Cabo, 2010). Accordingly, in the subsequent semester, a total of 104 first-year students participated in this study in Fall 2009 (VB group), and a total of 136 students in Spring 2010 (Alice group). Students completed a problem-solving questionnaire in 10 sections in which Alice was used and in all nine sections in which VB was used. The same questionnaires were completed in the first week of class (pre) for all sections, and in the last week of class (post). Only students who completed both questionnaires were included in the analysis.

In the pre questionnaire, the performance of the VB and Alice groups were not different for the TOTAL, COMPUTER, and GENERAL groups, indicating that there were no significant differences in performance at the beginning of the study. Fig. 2 shows the average of the correct answers for

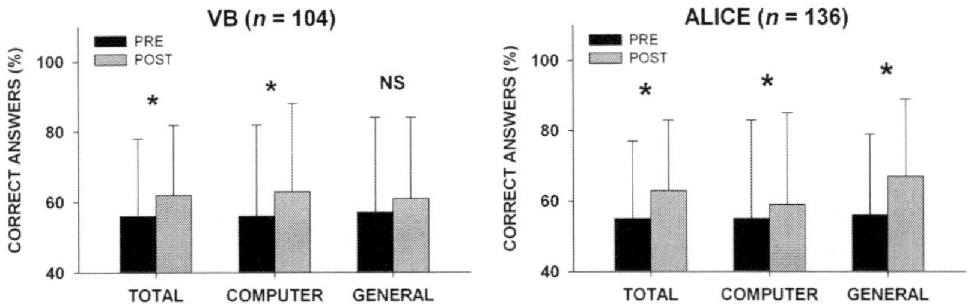

Fig. 2. Results of the pre and post problem-solving questionnaires for the Alice and VB groups. *, statistical significance ($p < 0.05$).

all students in each group. Both the VB and Alice groups showed a statistically significant ($p < 0.05$) increase in performance for all questions (TOTAL), with the Alice group showing a greater increase. For the subset of questions related to computer problem-solving abilities (COMPUTER), there was a significant increase in both groups, the VB group having a larger increase. For the subset of questions related to general problem-solving abilities (GENERAL), there was a significant increase in the Alice group, whereas the VB group showed a NS increase. Therefore, while VB (as expected) is effective at developing computer problem-solving abilities but not general problem-solving abilities, a narrative computing environment using Alice is effective in developing both computer and general problem-solving abilities.

Fig. 3 shows the percentage of students who answered correctly each of the 10 questions for the VB and Alice groups. Overall, the percentage of students who answered correctly in the post questionnaire (empty circles, solid line) is equal or better than the percentage of students who answered correctly in the pre questionnaire (filled circles, dashed line). Pre and post changes, although significant for some questions, were not dramatic, with improvements always below 0.2 ($\sim$20%). It is also apparent from the data that students in the VB group developed a different set of abilities (significant improvement in the responses to questions 1 and 3e) than students in the Alice group (significant improvement in the responses to questions 5, 8, 9, and 10). This is consistent with the fact that VB increases computer problem-solving abilities, whereas Alice increases not only general problem-solving abilities, but also computer problem-solving abilities (question 5: We can create a secret code by assigning to each letter of a word the letter that follows in the alphabet. For example, the word HOME could be coded as IPNF. What is the English word that is coded

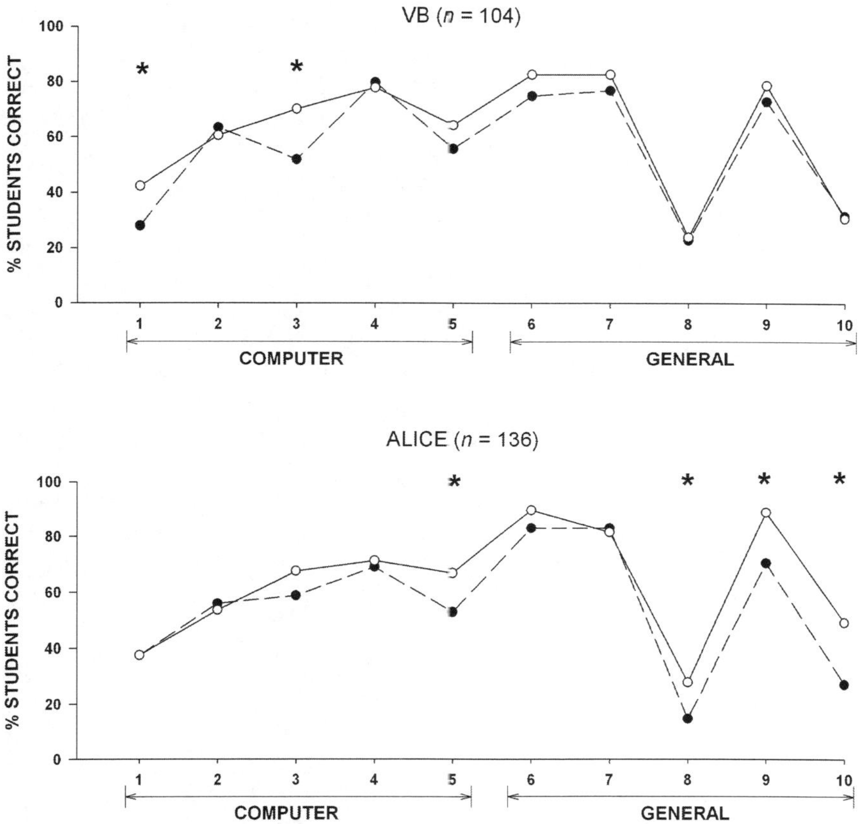

Fig. 3. Percentage of students who responded correctly to the specific questions of the pre (*filled circles*) and post (*open circles*) questionnaire. *, statistical significance ($p<0.05$).

as FODZDMPQFEJB?). It seems that while VB only improves problem-solving abilities in a narrow category, Alice improves problem-solving abilities more broadly. It should also be noted that the percentage of student who answered questions two and four correctly did not change in both groups.

To further investigate the relationship between the development of general and computer problem-solving abilities, we plotted the improvement in general problem-solving abilities (ΔGEN) versus the improvement in computer problem-solving abilities (ΔCOMP) for each individual student

(Fig. 4). A negative value indicates that there was no improvement or that the student performed worse in the questionnaire for the given skill. Statistical analysis shows that the slope of the regression line for the VB group is not statistically different from zero ($p = 0.18$), indicating that an improvement in computer problem-solving abilities does not lead to an improvement in general problem-solving abilities. In contrast, the slope of the regression line in the Alice group is different from zero ($p = 0.01$). Two conclusions can be extracted from the results in Fig. 4. First, in the Alice group, an improvement in computer problem-solving abilities is accompanied by an improvement in general problem-solving abilities, indicating a relationship between general and computer problem-solving abilities, which does not occur in the VB group. Second, in the Alice group, which has a regression slope different from zero, the correlation between both groups of abilities is not as strong as indicated by the small regression slope (0.20) and $R^2 = 0.05$.

Fig. 4 shows that although some students improved their performance in the problem-solving questionnaire at the end of the semester, other students did not (students with negative or zero ΔCOMP and/or ΔGEN). Fig. 5 shows the percentage of students whose performance increased, did not

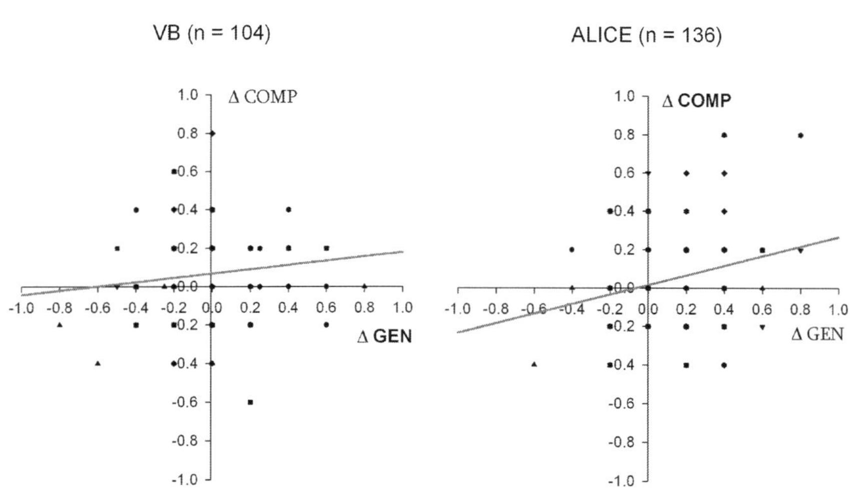

Fig. 4. Improvement in computer problem-solving abilities (ΔCOMP) versus general problem-solving abilities (ΔGEN) for every student in the VB and Alice groups. Each point in the graph may represent more than one value.

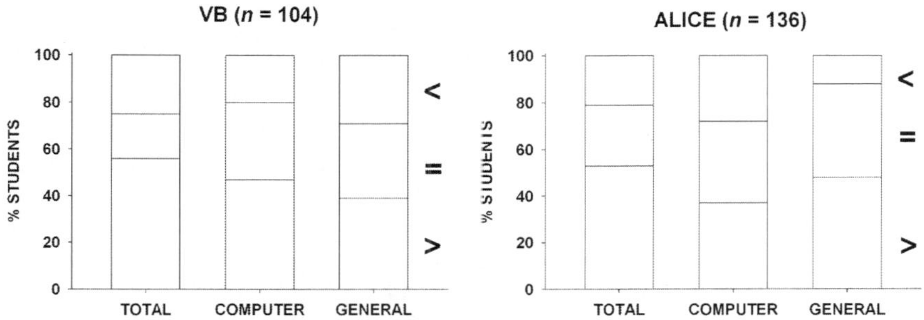

Fig. 5. Percentage of students whose performance increased (>), did not change (=), or decreased (<) in the different problem-solving skill areas for the two groups.

change, or decreased for the different problem-solving skill areas (TOTAL, COMPUTER, GENERAL) for the VB and Alice groups. Overall improvement in computer problem-solving abilities (COMPUTER) shown in Figs. 1 and 2 is the result of the effort of 47% of the students in the VB group and of the 37% of the students in the Alice group who improved their performance in that category. About 33% in the VB group and 35% in the Alice group did not change their performance, and 20% (VB) and 28% (Alice) actually decreased their performance. Similarly, the overall improvement in performance in general problem-solving abilities (GENERAL) in the Alice group was the result of the effort of 48% of the students who improved their performance in that category. Forty percent students in the same group did not change their performance in GENERAL, whereas only 12% showed a decrease in their performance.

We estimated retention in both groups by quantifying the percentage of students who officially dropped the course by the official deadline (W grade) plus the percentage of students who stopped attending (WU grade). In the VB group, 25% of the students withdrew from the course either officially or unofficially. In the Alice group, 16% of the students withdrew. This indicates that retention was higher for the Alice group than for the VB group.

Our study concludes that computer programming using VB improves computer problem-solving abilities, but not general problem-solving abilities. However, Alice improves both computer and general problem-solving abilities. Although within the Alice group both problem-solving areas are improved, the relationship (correlation) is not strong and there is no correlation between both areas in the VB group. However, as only 50%

of students showed improvement in problem-solving abilities in both groups, further research clearly remains to be conducted.

PHASE THREE: WHERE TO GO FROM HERE

During the previous academic year, primary data were gained from student responses to a problem-solving questionnaire (as well as from a computer programming self-efficacy survey). Results from the problem-solving questionnaire revealed that Alice improves both computer and general problem-solving abilities. Overall, Alice provides a significantly better environment for the development of problem-solving abilities in first-year students taking an introductory course in computer programming, which, in turn, improves student retention. Since Alice also improves performance in general problem solving, it would also be a more appropriate environment for an introductory course in computing for non-majors and an effective way to promote problem-solving across the curriculum. However, further research remains to be conducted, since, although overall student problem-solving abilities significantly improved, only half of all students enrolled in the introductory programming course represented this change.

Further research will focus on the language of the problem-solving questionnaire. Because students indicated being confused by the language of the problem-solving questionnaire, a new area of research will be on the questionnaire itself. The questionnaire will be revised. Students in the learning community will be recruited to participate in a focus group, along with members of the student computer club at the college, to help clarify and revise the problem-solving test questions to make them more relevant to all students. These new problem-solving test questions will ensure that culturally diverse students are able to easily understand and analyze data from the test that will be administered to students in all problem solving with computer programming sections.

Furthermore, students' perceptions of self-efficacy (Bong, 2002; Bong, 2004) tend to decrease during the semester both for students in the Alice and VB groups. Self-efficacy surveys were assessed at the beginning and the end of the semester. We used a survey with five questions adapted from the Motivated Strategies for Learning Questionnaire (Pintrich & De Groot, 1990) and the Patterns of Adaptive Learning Survey (Roeser, Midgley, & Urdan, 1996). There were no significant differences between the self-efficacy measures at the beginning and the end of the semester for each group or between the Alice and VB groups (Two-factor Analysis of Variance). It is interesting that while there is a clear improvement in student performance during the semester, as measured by the problem-solving questionnaire, especially for the Alice group (see Figs. 1 and 2), students' perceptions of their own abilities in problem solving and computer programming tend to decrease. In retrospect, this result is not surprising. Over the years, many of us have observed that, in general, students know more than what they think they know and could benefit greatly from a stronger sense of self-efficacy. A weak performance could be the result of a weak motivation and not necessarily lack of ability. Since both motivation and ability are important traits to be a good problem solver, it is important to understand their relationship.

In contrast to our findings, a large body of literature points to a correlation between a strong sense of self-efficacy and student performance (e.g., Bandura, 1997; Ramalingam, LaBelle, & Wiedenbeck, 2004). It is possible that the relationship between perceptions of self-efficacy and performance are discipline- or problem-specific (Bong, 2002). Therefore, the relationship between self-efficacy and student performance in the context of problem solving and computer programming deserves further investigation.

CONCLUSION

Alice seems to be as effective as VB in developing problem-solving abilities relating to computer programming. However, it seems clear that Alice improves performance in general problem-solving abilities, whereas VB does not. Students in the Alice group completed the course in greater numbers than in the VB group. Therefore, we can suggest that, overall, Alice provides a better computing environment for the development of problem-solving abilities in first-year students taking an introductory course in computer programming, which, in turn, improves student retention. Since Alice also improves performance in general problem solving, we suggest that Alice would also be a more appropriate environment for an introductory course in computing for non-majors.

NOTES

1. Freytag (1863), in his book *Die Technik des Dramas* (1863), outlined a method of analyzing plots based on Aristotle (1997) concept of unity of action.
2. Alice. (2010). Retrieved from http://www.alice.org.

REFERENCES

Aristotle. (1997). *Poetics*. (M. Heath, Trans.). New York: Penguin.

Bandura, A. (1997). *Self-efficacy: The exercise of control*. New York: W.H. Freeman.

Bateman, C. (Ed.) (2007). *Game writing: Narrative skills for videogames*. Boston: Charles River Media.

Bishop-Clark, C., Courte, J., & Howard, E. V. (2006). Programming in pairs with Alice to improve confidence, enjoyment, and achievement. *Journal of Educational Computing Research, 34*(2), 213–328.

Bong, M. (2002). Predictive utility of subject-, task-, and problem-specific self-efficacy judgments for immediate and delayed academic performance. *Journal of Experimental Education, 70*(2), 133–162.

Bong, M. (2004). Academic motivation in self-efficacy, task value, achievement goal orientations, and attributional beliefs. *Journal of Educational Research, 97*(6), 287–297.

Bruce, C., Buckingham, L., Hynd, J., McMahon, C., Roggenkamp, M., & Stoodley, I. (2004). Ways of experiencing the act of learning to program: A phenomenographical study of introductory programming students at university. *Journal of Information Technology Education, 3*, 143–158.

Campbell, J. (1949/2008). *The hero with a thousand faces* (Original work published 1949). Novato, CA: New World Library.

Connell, R. (2006/1924). *The most dangerous game* (Original work published 1924). Whitefish, MT: Kessinger Publishing.

Cooper, S., Dann W., & Pausch, R. (2003, February). Teaching objects-first in introductory computer science. In: S. Grissom (Chair), *ACM SIGCSE* – The Special Interest Group in Computer Science Education. Symposium conducted at the meeting of the Technical Conference of ACM SIGCSE, Reno, Nevada.

Evans, G. E., & Simkin, M. G. (1989). What best predicts computer proficiency? *Communications of the ACM, 32*(11), 1322–1327.

Flower, L. (1993). *Problem-solving strategies for writing* (4th ed.). New York: Harcourt Brace Jovanovich.

Freytag, G. (1863). *Freytag's Technique of the drama: An exposition of dramatic composition and art*. (E. J. MacEwan, Trans.). Chicago: Scott, Foresman and Company.

Gee, J. P. (2003). *What video games have to teach us about learning and literacy*. New York: Palgrave.

Lansiquot, R., & Cabo, C. (2010). The narrative of computing. In: *Proceedings of World Conference on Educational Multimedia, Hypermedia and Telecommunications 2010* (pp. 3655–3660). Chesapeake, VA: AACE.

Mayer, R. E., Dyck, J. L., & Vilberg, W. (1986). Learning to program and learning to think: What's the connection? *Communications of the ACM, 29*(7), 605–610.

Mullins, P., Whitfield, D., & Conlon, M. (2009). Using Alice 2.0 as a first language. *Journal of Computing Sciences in Colleges, 24*(3), 136–143.

Palumbo, D. B. (1990). Programming language/problem-solving research: A review of relevant issues. *Review of Educational Research, 60*(1), 65–89.

Piaget, J. (1973). *To understand is to invent: The future of education*. New York: Grossman.

Pintrich, P. R., & De Groot, E. V. (1990). Motivational and self-regulated learning components of classroom academic performance. *Journal of Educational Psychology, 82*(1), 33–40.

Ramalingam, V., LaBelle, D., & Wiedenbeck, S. (2004). Self-efficacy and mental models in learning to program. *ACM SIGCSE Bulletin*, *36*(3), 171–175.

Robertson, J., & Kenton, J. (2010). Microworlds to improve learning in introductory computer programming courses. In: D. Gibson & B. Dodge (Eds), *Proceedings of Society for Information Technology & Teacher Education International Conference 2010* (pp. 3348–3355). Chesapeake, VA: AACE.

Roeser, R. W., Midgley, C. M., & Urdan, T. C. (1996). Perception of the school psychological environment and early adolescents' psychological and behavioral functioning in school: The mediating role of goals and belonging. *Journal of Educational Psychology*, *88*, 408–422.

Salen, K. (2007). Gaming literacies: A game design study in action. *Journal of Educational Multimedia and Hypermedia*, *16*(3), 300–322.

Shakespeare, W. (1990). *Macbeth*. (N. Booke, Ed.). Oxford: Oxford University Press.

Sophocles. (1991). *Oedipus rex*. (G. Young, Trans.). New York: Dover Publications.

Stein, L. A. (1998). What we swept under the rug: Radically rethinking CS1. *Computer Science Education*, *8*(2), 118–129.

Stockton, F. R. (1890). The lady, or the tiger? In: *The lady, or the tiger? And other stories* (pp. 1–10). New York: Charles Scribner's Sons.

Sykes, E. R. (2007). Determining the effectiveness of the 3D Alice programming environment at the computer science I level. *Journal of Educational Computing Research*, *36*(2), 223–244.

Thorndike, E. L. (1923). The influence of first-year Latin upon the ability to read English. *School Sociology*, *17*, 165–168.

Wenger, E., White, N., & Smith, J. D. (2009). *Digital habitats: Stewarding technology for communities*. Portland, OR: CPsquare.

Zyda, M. (2009). Computer science in the conceptual age. *Communications of the ACM*, *52*(12), 66–72.

APPENDIX. SCARLET SWORD: THE PLAN

Carlos Farje

Shinzo dashes to Kobayashi's mansion, where he hopes to settle his score with his former boss. As he traverses the busy streets of Roppongi, Shinzo notices a dark figure tailing him. The crowd of people slowly dissipates, until no form of life can be seen in the area. Shinzo stops and draws his sword, surveying his surroundings to make sure he is not at a disadvantage. A fire breaks out in the neighborhood; smoke and flame begin to rush out of all the buildings on the block. The sky – having transformed from a clear, warm blue – now tints everything an evil orange. The greenery in the area wilts and rots, and ash flies viciously through the air. A man whose grey skin and shiny armor are the inverse of Shinzo's pale appearance and tattered apparel confronts Shinzo. They battle; each swings his sword mightily at the other. As the fight progresses, their swords glow brighter, and Shinzo begins to feel a surge within his body. He goes into shock and collapses on the floor, leaving him defenseless. Using his sword, Shinzo tries to get back on his feet, but to no avail. He falls again and is rendered unconscious. The mysterious man sheathes his sword and vanishes into the fire.

When Shinzo regains his strength, he reawakens to find himself in a desolate forest. The fires, the orange sky, the ash have all but disappeared. As he gets back to his feet, he sees Hanzo walk towards him. He tells Shinzo about the mysterious man from earlier. "The sword is slowly taking over your soul, Shinzo. As your thirst for vengeance grows, your thirst for blood grows with it. These emotions feed the sword. The man you were fighting before is merely yourself. To be precise, it is the 'you' that you will become if you do not clear the darkness in your heart. As the sword grows stronger, you will begin to see that dark world more often. If you continue down the path of revenge, those delusions will become your reality and your soul will never find peace."

"Kobayashi must die by my sword!" Shinzo angrily yells.

"The key lies not in killing Kobayashi, but within his enemies," Hanzo replies. In the blink of an eye, Hanzo disappears from Shinzo's sight. He realizes now that manipulating Kobayashi's main rivals, Takahashi and Masuda, will lead to an all-out war for power within the yakuza. It would also mark the end of the syndicate's reign over Japan. Shinzo goes to Shinjuku, the location of the yakuza's drug warehouse.

At the warehouse, Shinzo spots numerous yakuza thugs guarding the entrance as a truck exits the driveway. He also sees Masuda, the yakuza captain in charge of the syndicate's drug operations, entering the warehouse by himself. Rather than attack head on, he uses his invisibility technique to drop in unnoticed through one of the windows. Now inside, Shinzo finds the yakuza captain and quietly apprehends him, tying him to a chair and binding his mouth closed with rope. He tells Masuda that he will be taking the drugs with him and that Masuda will pay for thinking he could take Kobayashi's place as yakuza boss. Shinzo unbinds Masuda's mouth and severs both of his hands, freeing him from the chair. In extreme agony, Masuda yells for help, and Shinzo is promptly faced with dozens of yakuza. He swiftly outmaneuvers them all, making his way outside to the truck, where he kills the truck's driver and takes control of the wheel, driving off with the drugs. Masuda's henchmen enter their vehicles and chase after Shinzo.

Shinzo drives to Ginza to find Takahashi, the yakuza's second in command. He exits the truck and enters Takahashi's penthouse and finds Takahashi in his bedroom with a pair of prostitutes. Shinzo warns him that Kobayashi's men are coming to kill him and that he should escape immediately. As Shinzo is speaking, Masuda's men have caught up and exit their cars outside. Without a word, Takahashi hurriedly dresses himself, grabs his sword, and runs out of the penthouse, driving off on his motorcycle. Half of Masuda's men follow Takahashi, and the other half enter the penthouse. They surround Shinzo, who quickly kills the first wave of thugs and allows the others to pursue him outside. Shinzo gets back into the truck and drives off. This time, Shinzo heads straight to Kobayashi's mansion. With Masuda's men still on his tail and Takahashi thinking Kobayashi is targeting his life, Shinzo's plan slowly begins to unfold.

LESSON PLAN 1: ENGLISH COMPOSITION I: UNDERSTANDING AND CREATING GAME CHARACTERS

Goal: To Introduce Students to the Different Types of Game Characters

Objectives: At the end of the lesson students will be able to:

- Describe game characters in standard academic prose;
- Identify the similarities and differences between game characters;
- List character traits of their favorite video game character and compare these to traits of their favorite character from a different media genre;
- Write clear compare-and-contrast paragraphs;
- Conduct peer review based on grammar and logic and suggest additions and changes;
- Revise what they have written based on feedback provided.

Motivation

Before students can write a character background story and create this character in the problem solving with computer programming class, they need to understand the characteristics of protagonists, antagonists, and additional archetype characters. The exemplary characters that they review and vocabulary they learn will help them develop a more realistic and engaging character.

Time: 1 hour and 15 minutes

Required Materials

The lesson should be conducted in a computer lab so that every student has online access. Alice (www.alice.org) should be installed on all computers. Students will be given handouts on descriptive adjectives for character traits and creating game characters.

Prerequisite knowledge: At the beginning of the session, students should be able to:

- Identify the steps in the hero's journey;
- Search online for an image of their favorite video game character and post it on the course discussion board;

- Describe the physical appearance of their favorite character;
- Articulate the personality traits of this character.

Activities

- The instructor will introduce character archetypes as well as the difference between player and nonplayer game characters (10 minutes).
- Referring to the "Game Characters" and "Character Traits Descriptive Adjectives" handouts, students will jot down the characteristics of their favorite video game characters and share these with their partners, then complete a Venn diagram showing how their characters are similar to and different from their partners' characters (10 minutes).
- Students will list traits of their favorite video game character along with traits of their favorite character from film or literature (10 minutes).
- Students will draft a paragraph about their favorite video game character and another paragraph on a character from a different media genre that the video game character reminds them of (20 minutes).
- Students will review what they have written with their partners and ask them to listen to and rate their grammar and logic and identify a sentence that should be added or changed (10 minutes).
- Students will revise what they have written and show their paragraph to another classmate, then post their completed handout on the class discussion board online (10 minutes).
- Students will brainstorm characteristics of their own game characters with the class, noting why they believe their idea for a game character will be engaging, providing examples discussed with their classmates earlier (5 minutes).

Assessment

Successful completion of the "Game Characters" handout and the quality of the compare-and-contrast paragraph will be used to assess students' understanding of character types, characteristics, and the revision process.

Follow-Up

In the following class, all students will present their videogame plot outlines to the class, and the best ideas will be chosen to proceed.

LESSON PLAN 2: PROBLEM SOLVING WITH COMPUTER PROGRAMMING: UNDERSTANDING AND CREATING OBJECTS IN ALICE

Goal: To introduce the concept of classes and objects in computer programming.

Objectives: At the end of the lesson students will be able to:

- Demonstrate an understanding of the difference between classes and objects;
- Explain the difference between the properties and the methods of an object;
- Demonstrate an understanding of the concept of composite objects and how complex objects consist of simpler objects;
- Give examples of objects in the real world and define their components (i.e., properties and methods);
- Add a predefined object from the local or Web gallery library to an existing Alice world and identify the properties and methods of the object;
- Create a video game character using the He/She Builder tool in Alice.

Motivation

After students create a character for their video game prototype in their English composition I class, they will use Alice in this class to implement the setting and characters of their story in a 3D computer environment. The concepts they will learn and the skills they will develop will be helpful in more advanced computer programming courses.

Time: 1 hour and 40 minutes

Required Materials

The lesson should be conducted in a computer lab so that every student has access to a computer. Alice (www.alice.org) should be installed on all computers.

Prior knowledge: At the beginning of the lecture students should be able to:

- Start Alice in the computer;
- Identify the different elements of the Alice environment (toolbar, object tree panel, details panel, world view window, events editor and methods editor);
- Open and play an existing Alice world.

Activities

- The instructor will introduce the concepts of classes and objects as well as the different components of an object: properties and methods (15 minutes).
- Each student will orally give an example of objects of the real world and will identify the object components as well as their properties and methods (15 minutes).
- Each student will reflect and write a "minute paper" explaining in writing the concepts of class, instantiated object, composite object, properties, and methods, giving examples (15 minutes).
- Students will add predefined objects to an Alice world and save that world, then identify in the Alice environment the object elements, properties, and methods of the added object (15 minutes).
- Students will engage in group discussions (in the groups developing the game prototypes) that focus on their characters as programming objects and will identify their object components as well as their properties and methods (10 minutes).
- Students will use the He/She Builder tool in Alice to create and save their story characters (30 minutes).

Assessment

The "minute paper" and the oral responses will be used to assess students' conceptual understanding of classes, objects, instantiation, properties, methods, and composite objects. The hands-on computer work with Alice will be used to assess students' skills in creating and manipulating objects in a 3 D computer programming environment.

TEACHING HIGHER EDUCATION STUDENTS WITH DIVERSE LEARNING OUTCOMES IN THE VIRTUAL WORLD OF SECOND LIFE®

Sue Gregory

ABSTRACT

This chapter explores how Jass Easterman (the author's avatar name) teaches education students concurrently, both pre-service teachers and postgraduate, in Second Life. It discusses how a virtual world can be a valuable teaching and learning tool for the whole group even though they have a variety of overall goals and learning outcomes. Jass brings distant university students located around the world studying at the one institution together to liaise with each other in Second Life. She has created an innovative tutorial model where students go on virtual tours, visit other educational institutions, attend guest lectures, undertake role play activities, and go on Web quests and learn basic building and scripting skills, all from their own homes. Adult learning theories and communities of practice, in a virtual world, underpin all activities. Why Second Life was chosen for these students and what the students say about this type of learning are discussed in this chapter. The value of this

Transforming Virtual World Learning
Cutting-edge Technologies in Higher Education, Volume 4, 327–356

ISSN: 2044-9968/doi:10.1108/S2044-9968(2011)0000004017

tutorial model will be explored and reflected upon and conclusions made of its efficacy.

Keywords: Virtual worlds; Second Life; engagement; role-play; virtual tours; virtual lectures

INTRODUCTION

Studying from a distance, also known as correspondence or off-campus, was once a very lonely existence. Paper-based study materials would arrive by the mail delivery service, and assignments were written on paper and returned by the same method. The turnaround time for feedback was a considerably long time. Often feedback would arrive after the next assessment task was due, leaving little or no time for learning and reflection. With the advent of the Internet and use of Web 2.0 tools, feedback has been reduced dramatically and the loneliness that existed for distance study is almost removed. In this context, Web 2.0 tools are online interactive tools such as blogs, wikis, chat rooms and discussion boards that can be used to interact in peer to peer, or peer to educator, dialogue. Delays in feedback have been removed due to the availability of this technology though the Internet. Nowadays, studying by distance has a new meaning if the educator uses the online tools for interaction with students. Some tools provide asynchronous interaction, where people interact at a different time, such as discussion board postings where one person posts a message and another responds at a later time, or synchronous interaction, at the same time, such as talking to someone in a chat room where the conversation is in 'real time', 'live' (Dabbagh & Bannan-Ritland, 2005). Virtual worlds can provide this interaction.

A virtual world is a three-dimensional online environment that imitates real life in the form of a personal presence through someone's avatar (the alter ego which is a graphical representation of themselves in the virtual world). Lee (2010) supports this definition with his version of virtual worlds, 'A computer-based, simulated environment in which users are able to immerse themselves, and within which they are able to, through their avatars … experience, manipulate, interact with and/or create virtual objects and places that are graphically depicted in three dimensions' (p. 2).

Currently, the Gartner Hype Cycle (Stamford, 2010a, 2010b) indicates that public virtual worlds are at the bottom of the 'Trough of

Disillusionment' just before the 'Slope of Enlightenment'; however, as many higher education institutions have been using virtual worlds for over 5 years, they are already on the 'Plateau of Productivity'. This chapter highlights how higher education institutions are using virtual worlds for productivity. They are incorporating learning in a virtual world into student study materials (Lester, 2008). Virtual worlds are being used in the higher education sector where these models are using virtual worlds for lectures, workshops, simulations, skill building and teaching cohorts of students from the one subject, enabling specific learning outcomes to be taught. When virtual worlds were introduced at higher education institution in 2008, two subjects were used as a trial. One subject was a core for postgraduate education students and the other for later year education students of an undergraduate degree. As the possibility of learning in a virtual world was

Fig. 1. The author's avatar, Jass Easterman.

only being introduced to these students for the first time, and this was something very foreign to these students, the number of uptake for this learning was going to be low. For both subjects, the choice of using a virtual world was an optional assessment task. This chapter outlines the experiences of teaching and learning in a virtual world with different cohorts of students who have different learning outcomes (skills and knowledge to achieve from their studies), introducing an innovative tutorial model.

Jass Easterman (the author's avatar name), Fig. 1, is an academic in information communication technology (ICT) education in a regional higher education institution in Australia. She also works as a research fellow investigating the efficacy of virtual worlds as a teaching and learning tool. Jass introduces an innovative tutorial model that could be implemented into any study program regardless of what students were studying. Students provide feedback on this method of teaching and learning in a virtual world to reinforce the notion that a virtual world can be used by any discipline using this model of teaching.

BACKGROUND

This institution is situated in regional NSW, Australia where approximately 80% of students study in off-campus mode where they receive their study materials via a learning management system (LMS) on the Internet. Traditionally, students received their study materials via paper where they worked with little or no interaction with their peers or their educator. With the onset of technology, universities are utilising the Web 2.0 tools available in an LMS, including the ability to download study materials to provide students with their learning resources. Learning management systems are used to provide interactive tools to students. Many of the Web 2.0 tools can be embedded in the LMS so that students can use these tools from the one portal.

Another option to immerse students in their learning is through the use of a virtual world such as Second Life where students can come together in a context that feels like face-to-face lectures and workshops from their own home. Jass was created in 2007 with the objective of teaching students in a virtual world in the later part of 2008. She set about learning how to function in a virtual world. Being a non-gamer, this proved difficult and time-consuming. However, after a couple of months, she was right to start constructing the learning space for her students. She attended several courses in Second Life and acquired a small parcel of land that she could make secure, just for her students, known as Education Online Headquarters (Fig. 2).

Jass also had to learn what virtual worlds were and what they had to offer. As a priority, the learning outcomes for the two subjects that were going to offer virtual worlds as a component of their study had to be addressed. How were these outcomes going to be learnt in a virtual world?

The learning outcomes had to be taken into consideration with the planning of this learning space for students. The virtual world component was voluntary, that is students could choose to study this or they could choose another topic. Learning outcomes for the two subjects related to the virtual world component were to

1. plan for the integration of social computing technologies as tools for learning in an educational setting
2. display an understanding of innovations in ICT and their potential for enhancing student learning.

A virtual world was an appropriate tool to ensure students acquired these learning outcomes. Jass began teaching students and an innovative tutorial model was established, which is discussed later in this chapter. As the model was very successful and student numbers grew, several more subjects were incorporated into the sessions in 2010. Because of the increase in numbers,

Fig. 2. Education Online Headquarters in Second Life.

Fig. 3. Second Life classroom and playground.

another space was created for students where more diverse activities could be undertaken. A Second Life classroom and a playground were created with a variety of meeting spaces and educational resources. Fig. 3 shows the Second Life classroom and playground that are utilised more often as that caters for more students at the one time.

WHO ARE THE STUDENTS?

All students were studying education subjects in off-campus mode. In 2010, more students were invited to participate. There were a variety of students, some first year pre-service teachers, others in their later years of the pre-service courses, and some were studying higher degrees in education. In 2008, twelve students participated in the Second Life sessions; in 2009, twenty students; in 2010, ninety-six students; and in the first half of 2011, one hundred eighty-eight students have registered to participate in these sessions.

When more students were invited to participate, the model was already esablished and not changed to accommodate the new cohorts of students; however, their learning outcomes were reviewed to ensure that this was appropriate. The learning outcomes from all the newly added subjects that included the virtual world component were to

- investigate trends in the use of technology in learning contexts to inform the understanding of e-learning environments
- discuss the use of emerging tools in the context of technology development, educational paradigms, usage by various social groups, innovation and adoption by social groups
- use a range of ICT (wikis, blogs, podcasts and other Web 2.0 applications) for own learning in collaborative online environments and evaluate their relevance and use in e-learning environments
- apply a range of technologies to the design of e-learning environments relevant to own social environment/context and professional work
- analyse the role that new technology can play in enhancing learning
- evaluate the potential for using ICT in their profession
- use and evaluate software suitable for classroom use, including social networking and computing tools.

Although the learning outcomes covered a variety of subjects, the model outlined could be used to achieve them. As this was a combined class, all students received their own learning outcomes including many others that were a requirement for different subjects.

As Second Life is an immersive and engaging virtual world created by the users where features are put in context (Constance, 2007), it was decided to make use of this environment by using what others had created. This included using the space and experience of educators whose students were from specific discipline areas. Students enrolled in the education subjects at this institution were studying to become primary school teachers, high school teachers or specialist educators in a variety of fields including commercial and government. The only common feature was that they wanted to become educators. They could have been in educators primary, science, business, mathematics, languages, fire safety, the professions or almost any discipline that one could think of. Because of this, specific lessons could not be conducted for these students on how to use the virtual world in their particular context or key learning area (KLA).

ADULTS' LEARNING IN A VIRTUAL WORLD

Adult learners choose to participate in formal learning activities either by choice or because it is required of them by employment or institutional establishments. There is no definitive theory on how adults learn in a virtual world, and it is almost impossible to describe a unifying framework or theoretical model to fit all the ways in which adults learn (Cranton, 1992). The four major adult learning theories that are considered here on how adults learn in a virtual world are andragogy, transformative, consctructivist and connectivism theories.

Andragogy was introduced by Knowles in 1968 and developed for the self-directed adult learner (Cranton, 1992; Knowles, 1984). Adult learners are volunteers and therefore take responsibility for the decisions they make (Green, 1998). They usually do so because they want to learn or make changes to their life (Green, 1998). Adults are mature. They increase their knowledge reservoir and are ready to learn, engage more in problem-based learning and become more motivated (Cranton, 1992; Knowles, 1984; Smith, 2002). Learning in a virtual world is for highly motivated students as they engage in their learning to experience the potential of a virtual world as a teaching and learning tool, in this context, voluntarily. Adult learners require their learning to focus on the process rather than the content and are best taught by role-playing, simulations and self-evaluation (Kearsley, 2009a), all of which lend themselves to a learning in a virtual world as they can be undertaken anonymously and in context.

Transformative theory is where adults focus on learning through task-oriented problem solving to determine cause and effect relationships and communicating individual's feelings, needs and desires (Kearsley, 2009b). It is the process of reflection and action (Cranton, 1992). Transformation occurs when one critically reflects actions and pays particular attention to when these critical reflections take place (Finger & Asun, 2001). At the end of each session in a virtual world, students were asked to reflect on discussions and activities that had taken place. Transformative theory relies on adult learners to be critically self-reflective of their learning. It is an extension of andragogy but includes psychological change, where values and beliefs are challenged and self-concepts are threatened (Cranton, 1992). Learning in a virtual world uses elements of transformative learning. Students are continuously challenged and reflecting on what they have learnt in a virtual world to be able to transfer these skills to real life.

New ideas or concepts are constructed based on one's current or past knowledge, known as the constructivist theory (Kearsley, 2009c). 'Knowledge is constructed in the mind of the learner' (Bodner, 1986, p. 873) by the learner's internalising knowledge. Knowledge already acquired is built on. Knowledge is user constructed and students integrate new experiences into their knowledge base over time in a virtual world (Slone, 2009).

Finally, Siemens esablished the need for another theory, connectivism, because knowledge is growing exponentially (Siemens, 2008) and theories should take into consideration changes due to the digital age (Siemens, 2004). Knowledge grows exponentially in a virtual world, where teachers and students are learning new things that only a short period before would not have percieved as being possible.

If a range of pedagogical approaches are used when educating in a virtual world, then student education will be enhanced (Hollins & Robbins, 2008). There will be variations amongst educators depending on educator's level of expertise in educating in a virtual world (Gregory, Reiners, & Tynan, 2010). To cater for learners in a virtual world, a new model of pedagogy is required so that learners have greater opportunities for social–experiential learning, autonomy and connectivity (McLoughlin & Lee, 2008). This new model is presented here.

EDUCATION ONLINE HEADQUARTERS, SECOND LIFE CLASSROOM AND PLAYGROUND IN SECOND LIFE

Two meeting places have been created for students at this institution. They were created so that students had a starting point for their virtual world sessions in Second Life. Students met at Education Online Headquarters or the Second Life classroom and playground at the beginning of each session to discuss issues they were having, assessment tasks and general discussions around the efficacy of using a virtual world as a teaching and learning tool. These spaces were also used to debrief at the end of a session. After sessions were complete, students would return to one of the spaces to discuss the session that they had just participated in.

Education Online Headquarters is a two storey meeting place, in the sky, consisting of an outdoor area with picnic tables, logs around a fire and cushions to sit on. On the top floor is an indoor area with traditional lounges, and chairs around a conference table. When given a choice of places to return to, the conference area was the place of preference. This is possibly due to sitting in close proximity around a table so that it was easier to see everyone.

The second space, the SL Classroom and Playground, on the island known as Australis4Learning (Reiners, 2010), was created for role-play activities with pre-service teachers. The classroom is a replica of classrooms that are found in small schools in rural or regional Australia, except more windows were included. Interactive equipment was placed in the school classroom and playground so that students could engage with the environment as if they were in a real school or playground. The space also incorporates a staffroom, a science lab and a library, and elevated approximately 300 meters in the sky are resources of educational tools available in Second Life.

In 2010 and 2011 when more students were invited to participate in the virtual world sessions, Austalis4Learning was used more often as it was capable of admitting more students. The space where meetings are held is dictated by the size of the group. It is valuable to start and finish at the same place each time over the semester. In the first semester of each academic year, Australis4Learning is used predominantly with the students, as it is a larger space that can take more students. In the second semester, Education Online Headquarters is used with the much smaller cohort of students.

THE STATE OF PLAY OF SECOND LIFE IN HIGHER EDUCATION INSTITUTIONS

There is a growing community of educators worldwide that report their usage of how virtual worlds, in particular Second Life, are being used by their higher education institutions. There are over 200 virtual worlds from which to choose, Second Life being but one (Gregory, et al., 2010). Linden Lab, the proprietors of Second Life, released Second Life to the public in 2003 (Jennings & Collins, 2007) to create an environment where members could inhabit and build their own virtual world (Linden Research, 2008). Calonge (2007) stated there were more than 250 universities using Second Life as an educational tool; however, in 2008, John Lester, former academic program manager of Linden Lab, maintains it was difficult to accurately state but believed there were more than 1,000 educational institutions using Second Life. Cummings (2010a), manager of strategy and customer insights at Linden Lab, claims there are as many as 750 educational institutions using their own sim (large parcel of land). Warburton (2009) states that Second Life is the 'most mature of the social virtual world platforms and the high usage figures compared with other competing platforms reflect this dominance within the educational world' (p. 416). This is supported in a report compiled by 21 Australian higher education institutions (Gregory et al., 2010) out of a possible 39 Australia wide that state that they are using

Second Life as a teaching and learning tool with their students. However, with the removal of educational discounts in 2011 (Nelson, 2010), this figure could decrease as educational institutions reassess their standings.

The Horizon Reports 2007 and 2008 from the United States (Johnson, Levine & Smith, 2008; New Media Consortium, 2007) were at the forefront of research in virtual worlds where they stated in their original report of 2007 that virtual worlds would impact on higher education in the next 2 or 3 years. In the 2008 edition, Australia–New Zealand version, they reported that virtual worlds were a technology to watch with an adoption time of up to a year.

Research in the United Kingdom by Minocha and Reeves (2010) looked at the learning spaces that had been created in virtual worlds. They found that many spaces had been created based on real-life places so that students using the spaces would be familiar with the setting to 'relate to their expectations and mental models from real life' (p. 117). However, as more students choose to study by distance and have not physically visited their institution, this is becoming a more obsolete reason for creating spaces in this way. They also found that learning and teaching in a virtual world supported active learning – learning through doing, reflection and role-playing. More virtual worlds are being 'designed creatively to foster socialisation, information learning, exploratory and experiential learning' (p. 133).

In a report commissioned by the Joint Information System Committee (JISC) on serious virtual worlds in the British training industry, de Freitas (2008) provided examples of ways in which virtual worlds are being used for learning, mentoring, activities, trails and quests, role-play and skill practice. The report states that virtual worlds support cross-disciplinary collaborative research and learning.

Research by Hew and Cheung (2010) on education settings internationally found that there were three main purposes for using virtual worlds: communication spaces, simulation space, and experiential spaces. Lee (2009) conducted an analysis of virtual worlds used by education institutions and stated there was an emphasis on collaboration. Gregory and Smith (2009), Gregory and Tynan (2009) and Gregory and Masters (2010b) analysed virtual worlds in relation to choice of e-learning tools, engagement and role-play in higher education institutions.

Collins (2008) outlines many uses of virtual worlds for higher education institutions, such as cost-saving techniques by leveraging the collaborative capabilities they have to offer. Virtual worlds provide spaces for collaboration and meetings to accommodate different needs of academics and students not requiring constrains of proximity and facilities and had access to experts from around the world (Gregory et al., 2010). Higher education institutions are using Second Life for almost any discipline one can think of (Robbins, 2007), which includes social interaction, collaboration, creative construction, awareness raising, information resource, data visualisation, and simple simulation in a teaching and learning environment (Kovela, 2008).

Twenty-one Australian institutions that provided a snapshot of how they were using virtual worlds confirm that many institutions have adopted virtual worlds as a teaching and learning tool in Australia (Gregory et al., 2010). Some of the institutions have been teaching in virtual worlds for more than 5 years but many have only introduced this mode of education in the past 1–2 years. These institutions report a range of learning activities that are being undertaken with students including meetings, discussions, Web quests, guest lecturers, role-play, simulations, scientific investigation, business modelling, art, music, drama, language classes, ethics, task-based learning, near-authentic experiences, curriculum-specific work, platform for students with disabilities, blended simulations, inquiry learning, assessment, modelling, groups, communities and organisations. Students at these institutions are studying a variety of disciplines, including education, languages, criminology, law, computing, arts, nursing, international studies, business, accounting, auditing, history, English, librarianship, information management, information systems, ethics, humanities, research and research supervision.

ALTERNATIVE METHODS OF EDUCATING STUDENTS

By incorporating the use of a virtual world into a student's repertoire of study materials, the educator is creating a sustainable model of teaching. Authentic learning experiences can occur with the use of a virtual world where real-life costs and consequences are avoided. For example, using chemicals for an experiment can be replicated in a virtual world where the results are the same as in a real-life experiment without the cost, damage or consequences of the experiment. Medical or health students can practice attending to patients without the need of a real person and therefore the consequences of their actions do not have an impact on a real person. Students can practice their learning with bots (non-player characters) in their own time so that they can repeat their learning experience until they are satisfied that they can replicate the correct mode in real life. People with disabilities can learn in a virtual world without experiencing the discrimination that they may face in a real-life scenario. A level playing field is created for these students.

WHAT IS THIS INNOVATIVE MODEL?

The innovative model is simple in its nature and execution. Specific instruction relating to student KLA was impossible. The original plan was that students would research the virtual world relevant to their own KLA. Initially, students were asked their preferred model of learning. Did they want to learn how to use the virtual world themselves in their own time and receive tasks to undertake individually (asynchronously) or, did they want synchronous sessions to learning how to use the virtual world as a group enabling group tasks and discussions to occur? The overall consensus was that all students wanted to partake in synchronous activities on a weekly basis. The students decided they wanted to meet regularly with their peers, even though they were not enrolled in the same subject or studying the same KLA. It was established that everyone meets one evening a week for 2 hours. This suited most people even though some would come in late after other 'real-life' commitments.

Students met on a weekly basis over the semester, even when Jass could not be there. They even met during university vacation. All sessions began with round-table discussions. Students were given a topic that they had to discuss, or they were given leading statements or questions to resolve. Each week began at one of the meeting spaces. Issues were discussed in relation to Second Life, how to do various things, teaching and learning in, and the efficacy of, virtual worlds. Individual needs were addressed or discussions undertaken as directed. The following are the types of leading statements and/or questions asked:

1. What are the implications of using Second Life in an educational setting?
2. What is the educational purpose of a virtual world?
3. Why would you use Second Life as a teaching and learning tool?
4. What are the pros and cons of using a virtual world or Second Life in particular?
5. If you were to have input from anyone else, what sort of input would you want and where would you get this assistance?

As discussed, the learning outcomes for the students were very broad and as the students were studying different subjects and at different levels, tasks specific to their assessments could not be taught. Therefore, a more general approach was taken to educate the students. It has been so successful it has now been repeated four times. Also, past students return even though they are no longer enrolled in the subject, course and, in some instances, the university.

It was decided to give the students the type of experience they could receive if they are able to attend a face-to-face session. However, there was a vast difference. Because of the nature of a virtual world, these students were going to receive a more immersive and engaging experience that was not possible in a face-to-face session, from their own home. Over each semester, the first session was always an introductory session where students got to know each other and learnt how to control their avatar in Second Life. They were given a list of educational places to visit, were given instructions on how to change their appearance, and organise their inventory and a glossary of common terms used in Second Life. The first session always concluded with a shopping expedition so that students could change the appearance of their avatar so that they did not all look the same. The model had variety each week including going on virtual excursions, listening to guest lecturers, undertaking role-play activities, going on Web quests and learning basic building and scripting skills.

Virtual Excursions

Students participated in virtual excursions that could not be achieved in real life due to time and money constraints or were actually impossible to do in real life. As the students were either current or future educators, they were able to see how they could take students on any excursion they desired, without the usual time and monetary constraints they faced in real teaching environments. They explored a variety of locations, which is changed from year to year, to provide variety for returning students. There are three spaces that are always visited due to the immersive and engaging nature these spaces provide. These are:

1. NASA (SLURL: http://maps.secondlife.com/secondlife/NASA%20CoLab/128/128/2): This space has been developed for astronauts to practice piloting rockets where atmospheric and other real life situations are incorporated into the training without the expense and consequences (Lester, 2008). Fig. 4 is an image of NASA in Second Life.

Fig. 4. NASA Colab.

2. A virtual excursion to the Sistine Chapel (SLURL: http://maps.secondlife.com/secondlife/Vassar/182/91/25) always evokes student responses such as: 'As an Italian teacher I am impressed!' which is why we return every semester to view the artwork of Michelangelo.
3. Finally, the space known as Jokaydia (SLURL: http://maps.secondlife.com/secondlife/jokaydia/113/150/24) is one where students gain knowledge of what is happening in a more local context as this space is owned and managed by an Australian educator.

Students are taken on virtual excursions around the world and to places that do not even exist in the real world. At the click of button, students can visit a number of places to receive their education. Costs that would normally be incurred are minimal such as computer Internet connection, as opposed to travel, food, accommodation and entry fees incurred on real-life excursions. They explore places that have been created purely for educational purposes, such as walking through a model of a computer or heart, visiting a planet, or walking on the floor of the ocean. As students in this learning context are exploring virtual worlds as an alternate to conventional real-life learning environments, educators are able to further student's exposure through excursions in virtual worlds where time and money would prevent them from doing so in real life. Virtual excursions can occur in real-life educational settings using video conferencing equipment but require synchronous connection with the presenter elsewhere. Virtual world excursions can be conducted at any time and any place.

Expert Virtual Guest Lectures

Where else but in a virtual world can students attend lectures given by experts worldwide from their own home yet get the experience of really being there? Over the semester students regularly attend guest lectures to learn of their experiences of using a virtual world with their own cohort of students. This variety provides the students with different perspectives, ideas and ways in which they can ponder on their future teaching.

The guest lecturers from Australian and international universities and educational institutions use a variety of tools during their presentation. They have used traditional methods with screens to display videos or presentations. They have taken the students on tours of their institution to demonstrate how they teach in the virtual world. They showcase their own students' work. Some change their avatar's appearance to take on the persona of the person presenting, such as a judge at a courthouse or a Buddhist monk. They demonstrate the use of gravity in their spaces and use things that are not available in real life (e.g., sitting on a mushroom for discussions, or in a building that in real life would defy gravity and collapse). They have also given demonstrations that in real life would have dire consequences but are able to be changed back by the click of a button. They demonstrate holodecks, which are scene changers. That is, they could be sitting in a lecture theatre, then a workshop area, then an outdoor space, just by clicking a button. None of these are achievable in real-life presentations. They have demonstrated that you can fly from lecture to lecture or use bots to interact with to undertake the required learning. Interactive surveys can be undertaken where results are e-mailed to the educator. The possibilities are only limited by the imagination of the educator (Keesey, 2007).

Role-Play Scenarios

Role-play exercises can be carried out effectively in a virtual world. Virtual worlds are particularly advantageous for breakout groups where the students can be in the same room, but can only hear members of their group. Collaboration occurs more readily in a virtual world where people want to work with others to achieve an outcome. Tasks set for groups work well because students can go to different locations but be in synchronous contact. As they use the group chat method of communication, they can still talk to each other. Students learn well from their peers and when someone wants to know how to do something, there is usually another student willing and able to assist. Undertaking various role-play activities are easier to do in a virtual world as the avatar can instantly change clothes to take on the role they have been given or even change their avatar's appearance.

Basic Building/Scripting Lessons

Students always want to learn how the virtual world is created. Every semester there is at least one session for students to learn how to build and script in Second Life. Building in Second Life is similar to desktop publishing. Objects in a virtual world are created using similar techniques. Scripting is used to make objects undertake certain tasks, for example making a car drive or an automatic note to be given to people. Scripting enables interactivity to occur between objects and avatars. Information on how to build and script can be found on the author's website at: http://www.virtualclassrooms.info/howto.

Virtual World Web Quests

When Jass is unable to attend virtual world sessions, students are given Web quests to complete. They are given tasks where they are asked to find the locations of certain places and they have to send Jass the location (landmark) of the place they have found. They also have to send Jass a photo of places they visit. By undertaking these tasks, the students are learning many techniques, including ability to search using criteria given to them and create a landmark or photo to share with someone. Usually these tasks are undertaken as a group, so collaboration occurs between team members.

STUDENT PERCEPTIONS OF THEIR LEARNING IN A VIRTUAL WORLD

To understand the immersion and engagement students felt when participating in sessions in a virtual world, below are some of the student perceptions. The first were on anonymity when learning in a virtual world. Only the educator knows the identity of the student and those who they have chosen to share their identity with.

- People will say things if they feel there will be no knowledge that it was them that said it.
- Anonymity is a big drawcard.
- I believe that they are engaging because of the anonymity factor.
- The anonymity frees students up to explore aspects of themselves they may not in real life. It can really help them grow as individuals in a safe environment.

The following comment from a student demonstrates how immersed they were in the role-play activity. They found switching roles difficult as they had to play a role that they were not comfortable with. This shows how real the learning in the virtual world is for them. The students were undertaking de Bono's (1985) Six Thinking Hats role-play exercise where they had to take on the personality of the coloured hat they were wearing and discuss a given topic with that personality.

- Wearing the green hat was easy as I am a creative person, but then I tried the black hat and even though I could think of things to say, it was hard being so cautious about something I believe so passionately in.

Following are general comments from students in relation to their learning experiences in a virtual world. These comments demonstrate how engaging the students found the virtual world and how very real their experiences were in the virtual environment.

- Every day I am more and more intrigued and excited and bewildered by the wonder of Second Life and its possibilities.
- At first I could only see problems with using it as a tool in a classroom; however, as I have learnt more I can see a huge benefit for students especially the quieter ones or even ones with a learning difficulty who may be able to be engaged through this type of learning. As we aim to engage all students, this is very important.
- Second Life gives students an opportunity to use so many different skills and to communicate in a way that they may otherwise be unable to. I will be very disappointed if I am unable to continue to use Second Life or something similar with my future students as I think this is the way education needs to go.

- Virtual worlds are an outstanding educational tool. They are exciting and empowering. They enable students to take control of their own learning, thus creating deeper learning experiences.
- Using the virtual world opened my eyes to a new learning tool. It has provided inspiration and opened possibilities that I previously did not know existed.
- I had my first visit to Second Life on Wednesday and it was a blast. I can see the students engaged in this environment and developing understanding in life skills and applying these to real life.
- As a distance student you feel alone but on Second Life you feel as though you a part of a group with the same challenges.
- Virtual worlds are incredibly stimulating educational environments. They are constructivist in essence, which means that every learning experience is meaningful and enjoyable. Virtual worlds have limitless educational possibilities and I am very excited to be at the forefront of this innovative new method of education. I am looking forward to being able to implement the use of virtual worlds into my own classroom.

Diener (2010) expresses the virtual world of Second Life as having a 'tangible sense of presence, co-location and self'. This is supported by the final student comments.

- I had a defining experience last week when we sat down in that open air lecture space and I sat on one side and the rest of you sat on the other side. Suddenly I felt lonely and without thinking got up and moved to where you were all sitting. And then I thought, that felt so real!
- I find Second Life pretty immersive. I feel like I'm chatting to you all in a meeting room.
- In a strange way I think exploring a virtual world can actually make that world more real than say looking at pictures, or reading texts or even viewing a video.
- I think Second Life has been good for me – I feel like a 'real' university student, and I do feel like I'm in a 'real' tutorial group.

SUMMING UP STUDENT COMMENTS

Over four semesters of educating students in Second Life using the model outlined, student comments are similar. Student perceptions have all been around the same themes of anonymity, engagement and feelings of really being there – that it is like a real life experience for them. The negative comments revolved around the technology. Some students were not able to participate because of technical reasons, such as bandwidth, wireless slow networks, inefficient graphics cards, or not having a headset. Technological difficulties are becoming less common as computers and virtual worlds improve to cater for bandwidth and computer capabilities worldwide.

FUTURE USE OF THE MODEL

The future use of virtual worlds appears endless. So long as there is access to the technology, students can immerse themselves synchronously or asynchronously in their learning as demonstrated in Table 1. This means that they can study anywhere and, on occasion, anytime.

As is often the case with technology, there is a lot of hype surrounding innovative, non-standard online tools. Media coverage can be both positive and negative. Even though Second Life is the tool of choice described here, it is just one virtual world of many to choose from. Second Life is undergoing dramatic changes at the moment. In June 2010, Linden Lab announced they were laying off 30% of their staff (Rao, 2010), in September they announced *Teen* Second Life was being decommissioned (Cummings, 2010b), which is a virtual world for the 13- to 18-year-olds, and finally, in October, Linden Lab announced that they were removing the 50% discount they provide to educational institutions and not-for-profit organisations from 2011 (Nelson, 2010).

Table 1. Synchronous and asynchronous uses of virtual world.

Synchronous Use of the Virtual World	Asynchronous Use of the Virtual World
• Guest lecturers • Virtual tours and excursions • Role play exercises • Building and scripting lessons • Collaborative projectes • Round table discussions & tutorials • Simulations in context • Using Second Life tools in groups • Group explorations	• Web quests • Receive note cards of activities to undertake tasks by self • Viewing "how to" machinima • Work on collaborative tasks by self • Individual exploration

As an educator, one could become 'stressed' by these changes. However, there are exciting developments happening with the introduction of *Teen* Second Life participants to the main grid (i.e., Second Life), the Second Life Marketplace that provides an incentive to create and sell digital objects, the integration of meshes for building more realistic objects, and finally a browser-based virtual world, so the true integration with the Internet can occur. Educators are currently developing many learning scenarios for their students due to the variety of content that Second Life offers.

All these things have caused educators to rethink their virtual world of choice. Many are moving over to Open Source virtual worlds where these problems do not currently occur. They will, of course, encounter other problems that may or may not serve them. It does not matter where educators take their students, the experiences outlined in this model can be gained in most virtual worlds, particularly with some imagination from the educator.

Educators may rethink their departure from Second Life and other virtual worlds due to developments that are emerging with the technology. The technology now exists for a person to wear specially created gloves (Hardesty, 2010), enabling interaction through physical gestures in the virtual world environment using hands and body movements (Beasley, 2010). The possibilities this brings are enormous. Imagine demonstrating an operation in a workshop. The students will be able to carry out tasks as they would in the physical world without risk to person or environment. Almost anything that requires precision and simulation and is in context, can now be achieved in real time and with accuracy. Using technology that combines X-Box's *Kinect* and Second Life, gestures made in real life can be viewed and experienced in Second Life (Phan, 2011). *Kinect* is controller-free software which responds to the user's movement (Microsoft, 2010).

Finally, ours and several other Australian institutions are about to create another dimension to what is offered to education students. Pre-service teachers will have the opportunity to observe and interact in a virtual world classroom where assessment, machinima (machine-based cinema), programming of bots and teaching in real classrooms will be provided with authentic learning and teaching experiences. The existing classroom on Australis4Learning will be transformed into a VirtualPREX a sophisticated, virtual, professional experience for pre-service teachers. VirtualPREX is a term coined for this innovation, which is also referred to as professional experience (PREX), practicum or workplace learning. Pre-service teachers will be provided with a full range of audiovisual interactivity of 3D simulations, enabling them to partake in realistic, diverse, versatile and dynamic activities that emulate real-life situations (Ferry et al, 2006; Gregory & Masters, 2010a; Gregory & Masters, 2010b).

A set of structured, collaborative role-plays will be developed to provide scenarios of common and challenging situations faced by teachers in a real classroom, for example class management that pre-service teachers may need to address during their real classroom professional experience. Pre-service teachers will be able to visit the virtual world classroom and adopt the role of teacher to practice their classroom skills with other students (synchronously) via role-play activities that require them to make decisions about the lesson, classroom management and responses to other students.

To afford greater equity and flexibility of access, especially for off-campus students, bots could be used, which will look and behave like school students. Bots will be programmed to talk to the pre-service teacher by answering and undertaking general conversation, as well as responding in a variety of ways to a student practicing their teaching skills. Machinima, like assessable video recordings used in assessment tasks, involve pre-production preparation and capture, editing and tagging of footage for easy reference (N. Dreher & Dreher, 2009). Machinima of online practice sessions will be available for viewing and used as learning aids. These are exciting developments that will enhance the tutorial model outlined to enable even more variety to be incorporated into the sessions.

CONCLUSIONS

Virtual worlds immerse the learners where they often lose track of time. Virtual worlds provide a space for interaction and engagement in an environment that emulates the context and is suited to collaboration and simulation.

This innovative tutorial model was devised in 2007 to cater to the diverse range of students that are being taught. As the years have progressed, the model has not changed a great deal. Different locations have been visited, new experts have been invited along to provide lectures, basic building and scripting has been taught, role-play activities have been conducted and Web quests have been undertaken, but the model remains basically the same. It is simple in its nature and execution and that makes it a very good model to use by experienced, but particularly new, educators in virtual worlds.

The success of the model is depicted in the manner in which students respond to their learning. They voluntarily spend a whole semester learning the virtues of virtual words when it is only a very small component of their overall assessable tasks. Each subject required different learning outcomes and were evaluated in a variety of formats, depending on the subject and how the student wished to present their assessment. Some were written in a report format and others opted to give demonstrations in Second Life. Many students return, even though they are no longer enrolled in the subject, course or university, and are always welcomed. Returning students value the learning they receive in the virtual world. The model is engaging for the students, and the roundtable discussions at the beginning of each session encourage the students to think about possibilities for their future teaching. The group comes together to learn from each other, which they would not normally do as they are studying different subjects at a distance.

Over the years, students enrolled at this regional Australian university have been able to attend sessions conducted in Second Life from their own home from expert educators worldwide. Many of the students showed scepticism about using a virtual world but were curious enough to try it. They state that they can see the potential of its use with their own students. So, this innovative tutorial model enables educators to use the environment without requiring skills for building or scripting. The model is very simple but effective and can be used at most public spaces in Second Life without the need to set up the institution's own space. This model would be impossible to implement in a physical learning situation due to time and financial constraints. As many of the students study from a distance, virtual world brings them together where it becomes increasingly difficult to distinguish between the physical world and the virtual world. The goal is to be there, and to engage there.

REFERENCES

Beasley, W. (2010, September). The most advanced 3D gesture recognition software platform. *Softkinetic*. Available at http://www.softkinetic.net/press-release.php?id=121&sid=122&pressid=197

Bodner, G. M. (1986). Constructivism: A theory of knowledge. *Journal of Chemical Education*, *63*, 873–878.

De Bono, E. (1985). *Six thinking hats*. London: Penguin Books.

Calonge, C. (2007). A view from Second Life's trenches: Are you a pioneer or a settler? In: R. S. Smith (Ed.), *NMC summer conference*. June 6–9, Indianapolis (pp. 111–119). Austin, TX: New Media Consortium.

Collins, C. (2008, November). *AVWW 2008 program: Australasian virtual worlds workshop*. Swinburne University of Technology, Hawthorn Campus and Second Life. Available at http://slenz.wordpress.com/2008/11/12/the-slenz-update-no-24-november-12-2008/

Constance, J. (2007, April). Second Life: Educational precedents and examples-Second Life feasibility study. In: K. M. Kraus (Ed.), *Second Life feasibility study* [wiki]. College Park, MD: University of Maryland. Available at http://manfromporlock.wetpaint.com/page/Second+Life%3A+Educational+Precedents+and+Examples

Cranton, P. (1992). *Working with adult learners.* Canada: Wall & Emerson.

Cummings, T. (2010a, March). *Education and the Second Life ecosystem.* Presented at the Virtual World Best Practices in Education (VWBPE) 2010, VWBPE North Second Life. Available at http://www.vwbpe.org/

Cummings, T. (2010b, September 28). Second life blogs: Features: Welcoming teen grid organizations to the main grid. Available at http://blogs.secondlife.com/community/features/blog/2010/09/28/welcoming-teen-grid-organizations-to-the-main-grid

Dabbagh, N., & Bannan-Ritland, B. (Eds.), (2005). *Online learning: Concepts, strategies and application.* (pp. 68–107). Upper Saddle River, NJ: Pearson.

Diener, S. (2010, October). Education discounts in second life: Loss or gain? *Hypergrid Business.* Available at http://www.hypergridbusiness.com/2010/10/education-discounts-in-second-life-loss-or-gain/

Dreher, N., & Dreher, H. (2009). Using machinima documentary in virtual environments to reinvigorate students' learning in system development. In: *Conference ICL2009* (pp. 1–11). Presented at the ICL2009, Villach, Austria.

Ferry, B., Cambourne, B., Jonassen, D., Turbill, J. B., Hedberg, J., Kervin, L., & Puglisi, S. (2006). Online classroom simulation: Using a virtual classroom to support preservice teacher thinking. In: A. Herrington & J. Herrington (Eds), *Virtual technologies: Concepts, methodologies, tools, and applications* (pp. 988–1007). Hershey, PA: Information Science Reference.

Finger, M., & Asun, J. M. (2001). *Adult education at the crossroads: Learning our way out.* New York: Zed Books.

de Freitas, S. (2008). *Emerging technologies for learning.* Vol. 3. Coventry, England: Becta.

Green, J. (1998). Andragogy: Teaching adults. *Encyclopaedia of Educational Technology.* Available at http://coe.sdsu.edu/eet/Articles/andragogy/index.htm

Gregory. S., Lee, M.J.W., Ellis, A., Gregory, B., Wood, D., Hillier, M., Campbell, M., Grenfell, J., Pace, S., Farley, H., Thomas, A., Cram, A., Sinnappan, S., Smith, K., Hay, L., Kennedy-Clark, S., Warren, I., Grant, S., Craven, D., Dreher, H., Matthews, C., Murdoch, D., McKeown, L. (2010). Australian higher education institutions transforming the future of teaching and learning through virtual worlds. In: C.H. Steel, M.J. Keppell, P. Gerbic & S. Housego (Eds.), *Curriculum, technology & transformation for an unknown future. Proceedings ascilite Sydney 2010* (pp. 399–415). Available at http://ascilite.org.au/conferences/sydney10/procs/Gregory-full.pdf

Gregory, S., & Masters, Y. (2010a). Six hats in Second Life: Enhancing preservice teacher learning in a virtual world. In: *iCTLT 2010.* Presented at the International Conference on Teaching and Learning with Technology 2010 (iCTLT), Singapore.

Gregory, S., & Masters, Y. (2010b). Virtual classrooms and playgrounds – Why would anyone use them? In: *Proceedings of the 4th annual postgraduate research conference* (pp. 120–129). Presented at the Bridging the Gap between Ideas and Doing Research, Faculty of The Professions: University of New England, Armidale, NSW, Australia.

Gregory, S., Reiners, T., & Tynan, B. (2010). Alternative realities: Immersive learning for and with students. In: H. Song (Ed.), *Distance learning technology, current instruction, and the future of education: Applications of today, practices of tomorrow* (pp. 245–271). Houston: IGI Global, Texas Southern University.

Gregory, S., & Smith, H. (2009). Virtual worlds: Can virtual worlds promote a higher level of collaboration, engagement and deeper thinking for students than traditional Web 2.0 tools? In *Proceedings of the 3rd Annual Postgraduate Research Conference* (pp. 85–92). Presented at the Bridging the Gap between Ideas and Doing Research, Faculty of The Professions: University of New England, Armidale, NSW, Australia.

Hardesty, L. (2010, May 20). Gesture-based computing on the cheap. *MIT News*. Available at http://web.mit.edu/newsoffice/2010/gesture-computing-0520.html

Hew, K. F., & Cheung, W. S. (2010). Use of three-dimensional (3-D) immersive virtual worlds in K-12 and higher education settings: A review of the research. *British Journal of Educational Technology*, *41*(1), 33–55.

Hollins, P., & Robbins, S. (2008). The educational affordances of Multi User Virtual Environments (MUVE). In: *Researching Learning in Virtual Environments International Conference* (pp. 172–180). Presented at the ReLIVE 08, The Open University, Milton Keynes, UK. Available at http://www.open.ac.uk/relive08/

Jennings, N., & Collins, C. (2007). Virtual or virtually U: Educational institutions in Second Life. *International Journal of Social Sciences*, *2*(3), 180–186.

Johnson, L., Levine, A. & Smith, R. (2008). *The Horizon report: 2008 Australia–New Zealand edition*. Austin, TX: New Media Consortium. Available at http://www.nmc.org/pdf/2008-Horizon-Report-ANZ.pdf

Kearsley, G. (2009a). Explorations in learning & instruction: The theory into practice database; andragogy (M. Knowles). Available at http://tip.psychology.org/knowles.html

Kearsley, G. (2009b). Explorations in learning & instruction: The theory into practice database; transformative learning (J. Mezirow). Available at http://tip.psychology.org/bruner.html

Kearsley, G. (2009c). Explorations in learning & instruction: The theory into practice database; constructivist theory (J. Bruner). Available at http://tip.psychology.org/bruner.html

Keesey, C. (2007). *YouTube-Ohio University Second Life Campus*. Available at http://www.youtube.com/watch?v=aFuNFRie8wA

Knowles, M. S. (1984). *Andragogy in action: Applying modern principles of adult learning*. San Francisco: Jossey-Bass.

Kovela, S. (2008). Virtual worlds and education 2.0: the "Second Life" perspective. Available at http://www.kingston.au.uk/~ku07009/Uni2/Kovela.pdf

Lee, M. J. W. (2009). How can 3D virtual worlds be used to support collaborative learning? An analysis of cases from the literature. *Journal of e-Learning and Knowledge Society*, *51*(1), 149–158.

Lee, M. J. W. (2010). 3D immersive virtual worlds in higher education: Emerging academic staff and student perspectives on learning and teaching in new online spaces. Unpublished manuscript.

Lester, J. (2008). Conversation with John Lester aka Pathfinder Linden in relation to educational institutions using Second Life. Available at http://www.glsconference.org/2006/pop/lindenp.htm

Linden Research. (2008). Second Life: Economic statistics. Available at http://secondlife.com/whatis/economy_stats.php

McLoughlin, C. & Lee, M.J.W. (2008). Mapping the digital terrain: New media and social software as catalysts for pedagogical change. In: R. Atkinson & C. McBeath

(Eds.), *Hello! Where are you in the landscape of educational technology? Proceedings of the 25th ASCILITE Conference* (pp. 641–652). Melbourne, Australia, November 30–December 3.

Microsoft. (2010). Kinect | Australia-Xbox.com. Available at http://www.xbox.com/en-au/kinect.

Minocha, S., & Reeves, A. (2010). Design of learning spaces in 3D virtual worlds: An empirical investigation of Second Life. *Learning, Media and Technology*, *35*(2), 111–137.

Nelson, R. (2010, October). Second Life blogs: Land and sea: Two important updates on 2011 land pricing. Available at http://blogs.secondlife.com/community/land/blog/2010/10/04/two-important-updates-on-2011-land-pricing

Phan, T. (2011, January). Using Kinect and OpenNI to embody an avatar in Second Life: Gesture & emotion transference. *ICT-Institute for Creative Technologies*. Available at http://ict.usc.edu/projects/gesture_emotion_transference_using_microsoft_kinect_and_second_life_avatars/

Rao, L. (2010, June). Linden Lab lays off 30 percent of staff. *Tech Crunch*. Available at http://techcrunch.com/2010/06/09/linden-labs-lays-off-30-percent-of-staff/

Reiners, T. (2010). University of Hamburg in 3D: Lesson learned. In: S. Wong (Ed.), *18th International Conference on Computers in Education*. Presented at the Asia-Pacific Society for Computers in Education, Putrajaya, Malaysia.

Robbins, S. (2007). Immersion and engagement in a virtual classroom: Using Second Life for higher education. Available at http://connect.educause.edu/library/abstract/ImmersionandEngageme/39328

Siemens, G. (2004, December). Connectivism: A learning theory for the digital age. *Elearnspace*. Available at http://www.elearnspace.org/Articles/connectivism.htm

Siemens, G. (2008). *Connectivisim: Networked learning*. Available at http://www.connectivism.ca/

Slone, D. J. (2009). A methodology for measuring usability evaluation skills using the constructivist theory and the Second Life virtual world. *Journal of Usability Studies*, *4*(4), 178–188.

Smith, M. K. (2002) Malcolm Knowles, informal adult education, self-direction and andragogy. *The encyclopedia of informal education*. Available at www.infed.org/thinkers/et-knowl.htm

Stamford, C. (2010a). Gartner says 80 percent of active Internet users will have a "Second Life" in the virtual world by the end of 2011. *Gartner Newsroom*. Available at http://www.gartner.com/it/page.jsp?id=503861

Stamford, C. (2010b, October). Gartner's 2010 hype cycle special report evaluates maturity of 1,800 technologies. *Gartner Newsroom*. Available at http://www.gartner.com/it/page.jsp?id=1447613

The New Media Consortium. (2007). *The Horizon report, 2007 edition*. Austin, Texas.

Warburton, S. (2009). Second Life in higher education: Assessing the potential for and the barriers to deploying virtual worlds in learning and teaching. *British Journal of Educational Technology*, *40*(3), 414–426.

LESSON PLAN: VIRTUAL WORLD WEB QUEST IN SECOND LIFE

This lesson plan is appropriate for pre-service and postgraduate higher education student, although it works well with any discipline, including school students.

Overview

Imagine being able to teach a class of students and not be there. The following task is designed for the educator to provide to students in advance of the due date so they can undertake in their own time. The lesson enables students to practice basic techniques in Second Life synchronously (with peers) or asynchronously (if they are not able to connect at the same time as their peers). Students will need to have prior knowledge of how to use Second Life, including how to create landmarks (like bookmarks and also referred to as SLURL), teleport to the location, take screenshots and create note cards (similar to a word-processed document). They will also need to know how to e-mail screenshots and transfer landmarks and note cards to the educator. Students can learn the skills required by reading and practising the technique through the 'how to' guides and/or viewing the videos (machinima) on http://www.virtualclassrooms.info.

This lesson demonstrates a way in which students can learn a variety of techniques whilst being immersed in the task at hand, without the educator. They will be able to search for places to visit in Second Life (also known as 'in-world'), take screenshots, teleport from location to location, search through their inventory and share items with others as they undertake the activities.

Purpose

The purpose of this activity is to introduce students to some basic skills in using Second Life. These skills will enable students to learn searching, bookmarking and sharing techniques in Second Life. They will also learn how to work collaboratively as the requirement is to work in teams, although this is not essential. If students are unable to log on at the same time, they can undertake the task by themselves. Students will also practice finding items in their inventory and sharing these items using a variety of techniques.

Objectives

In Second Life, students will be able to:

- Use search techniques within the virtual world and on the Internet to find locations;
- Teleport to these locations;
- Take screenshots (These can be e-mailed directly to the educator or downloaded to the computer to be e-mailed at a later time. They can also be shared in-world.);
- Create a landmark (SLURL) so that they can return in the future;
- Search and find items in their inventory and share with others;
- Work synchronously or asynchronously on the task;
- Develop team-building skills.

Activities

1. Log on to Second Life.
2. In teams of two to four people you are to find and visit at least three of the following locations (approximately 20 minutes for each location) in Second Life. If unable to log on at the same time as someone else, undertake the following tasks by yourself:

   - British Science Festival – Here you find interactive map of virtual world–based scientific research and educational activities, enabling a 3D journey into UK-based science.
   - Mad Pea Hunt – What did you find in the peas?
   - University of Western Australia – Artworks submitted monthly for a contest and is a place for teaching, research, art and architecture.
   - Virtual Mine – The virtual mine is an educational 3D environment and game that teaches about mountain top removal, coal-fired power production, alternative energies, and the amazing music and culture in the Appalachian mountains.
   - Skoolaborate – Transform learning experiences by using Internet-based technologies to deliver learning experiences around global understanding, tolerance and inclusion.
   - Virtual Ability – It is a space for people with disabilities and chronic illnesses to safely learn about virtual worlds.
   - Jokaydia – Virtual world community of practice – find bikes and ride around the island. Find out what you can do there.

- University of Auckland – Virtual Medical Centre – It is a hemorrhage unit.
- University of Adelaide – Transforming Assessment – It showcases examples of e-assessment in a virtual world.
- Virtual State Fair – There are games, rides, exhibits and learning tools. What activities did you do?

3. Create landmarks of all places visited.
4. Take screenshots of all locations visited;
5. Write a note card. Include on the note card all landmarks (SLURL) visited and a description of what was found and how the space could be used (i.e. just looking at things, using objects interactively, go on a ride etc.).
6. Transfer screenshots, landmarks and note card to the educator's avatar. Alternatively, screenshots can be emailed directly to the educator or downloaded to e-mail at a later time.

Resources Required

1. Computer (including sufficient RAM and video card to run software)
2. Second Life software
3. Internet connection (minimum of broadband)
4. Knowledge of basic techniques in Second Life – http://www.virtualclassrooms.info – for 'how to' information

SECOND LIFE URLS (LANDMARKS) – SLURLS (ANSWERS – IF REQUIRED)

- British Science Festival – http://slurl.com/secondlife/Birmingham%20Island/184/189/22/
- Mad Pea Hunt – http://slurl.com/secondlife/MadPea%202/73/96/34
- University of Western Australia – http://slurl.com/secondlife/UWA/45/133/249
- Virtual Mine – http://slurl.com/secondlife://Virtual%20Mine/128/128/0
- Skoolaborate – http://slurl.com/secondlife/Skoolaborate%202/128/112/30
- Virtual Ability – http://maps.secondlife.com/secondlife/Virtual%20Ability/132/129/23/

- Jokaydia – http://slurl.com/secondlife/jokaydia/168/85/24
- University of Auckland – http://slurl.com/secondlife/Long%20White%20Cloud/47/61/28
- University of Adelaide – http://slurl.com/secondlife/transforming%20assessment/254/254/23/
- Virtual State Fair – http://maps.secondlife.com/secondlife/Morrill/206/65/24/

ABOUT THE AUTHORS

Youngkyun Baek is professor of educational technology at Boise State University, USA. He had been teaching since 1991 at Korea National University of Education. Previously, he worked at Korea Educational Development Institute. His research interests are on instructional games, simulation, and mobile devices in education. He has presented several papers at SITE, NECC, AERA, and OECD Expert Meeting on gaming and simulations. Recently, he published two books on educational games and wrote several book chapters. Now he is designing a social network game on global warming and doing a research on intrinsic motivational factors in instructional games.

Simon Bignell is lecturer in psychology at University of Derby, UK. His research interests include autism, ADHD, and technology-enhanced learning. He has led several funded projects within Second Life and has served as reviewer for many scientific journals. He has been nominated for the UK's Times Higher Education "Most Innovative Teacher of the Year" Award and is committed to pushing the boundaries of innovation in learning at University.

Samantha J. Blevins is doctoral student in instructional design and technology as well as a graduate assistant for the Faculty Development Institute and Online Course Systems at Virginia Tech. She received her bachelor's degree from Radford University and her master's degree from Virginia Tech. In addition, Samantha also has previous teaching experience at the middle, high, and community college level. Her areas of research include distance learning, faculty training, and the use of virtual worlds within the classroom.

Irena Bojanova is a program director at the University of Maryland University College. She has managed academic programs at UMUC, Johns Hopkins University, and PIsoft Ltd. She also cofounded a software firm, currently employing hundreds of developers, and led the start-up of a successful educational company in Sofia, Bulgaria. Her current research interests are in educational innovations, knowledge management, virtual environments, and cloud computing. Dr. Bojanova has received awards for excellence in teaching, research, and program management. She received a Ph.D. degree in computer science/mathematics from the Bulgarian Academy of Sciences.

Aimee M. Brenner is currently pursuing her Ph.D. in instructional design and technology at Virginia Tech and is a graduate assistant for the Faculty Development Institute (FDI), which provides professional development workshops in learning technologies for faculty, staff and graduate students. She holds a B.A. in English from James Madison University, an M.A. in English Education from Virginia Tech, and an M.S. in Educational Leadership from Radford University. In addition, Aimee has taught middle school Communications and Language Arts, as well as education courses at Roanoke College and Radford University. Her research interests include studying how to improve K-12 student learning by effectively integrating emerging, learning technologies instruction into teacher education programs.

Melissa L. Burgess holds an education doctorate in reading with concentrations in instructional technologies and digital literacies. She is currently the director of the Texas Virtual Learning Center (TVLC) at Region VI Education Service Center. Although varied, her specific research interests are within the areas of emerging technologies applied to teaching and learning, multiuser virtual environments, e-Learning, and instructional design in distance education. Her research is heavily reliant upon theoretical frameworks/models including the Community of Inquiry (CoI), Bloom's Revised Taxonomy, and Optimal Experience. As the notion of virtual environments of all modalities undergoes the transformation from concept to instructional integration, these frameworks/models will increasingly become central to research within virtual environments. As the desired distance education delivery platform is heavily dependent upon access and sustainability, her research in these areas has resulted in numerous publications, presentations, book chapters, and invitations to keynote speaking engagements all around the world. Additionally, Dr. Burgess leads innovative partnerships linking K-12 classrooms to both higher educational institutions and the professional community.

Candido Cabo received the degree of Ingeniero Superior de Telecomunicacion from the Universidad Politecnica de Madrid in 1982, and a Ph.D. in biomedical engineering from Duke University in 1992. In 2000, he joined New York City College of Technology of the City University of New York (CUNY) where he is presently the chair of the Department of Computer Systems Technology. Since 2005, he has been a member of the doctoral faculty at the CUNY Graduate Center. His research interests include computer science and engineering education and the use of computational models to understand and solve problems in biology.

Dona Cady has degrees in history, English, and archeology, respectively, from University of the Pacific, University of Notre Dame and Somerville College, Oxford University, England. Dona is Associate Dean of Humanities and Asian Studies at Middlesex Community College and has taught with face to face, online, and learning community course loads that include a variety of humanity courses. Her online courses have won best practice awards in Massachusetts, and she has authored several articles as well as keynote presented at international conferences concerning her research on virtual worlds, with her current East-West Center and Carnegie Foundation research focusing on virtual worlds and Confucian role ethics – the Reality of Transcending the Virtual.

Donguk Cheong is adjunct professor teaching graduate students who are in-service teachers at Korea National University of Education. He was a visiting scholar at the University of Virginia's Curry School of Education for the coresearch on the ETIPS project. Previously, he worked at KeirNet as a researcher in South Korea. He managed several projects on developing e-Learning contents funded by Ministry of Education. His research interests include games and simulation, virtual worlds, and semantic web applications for education as well as teacher education and the future of learning. Recently, he has been doing a study on the educational use of Second Life.

Sue Gregory, a long-term adult educator and a lecturer in ICT Education, research fellow (DEHub), and NSW SiMERR-ICT representative at the University of New England, Armidale, NSW, Australia. She is the unit coordinator and lecturer in several ICT Education units, chairperson, DEHub Australia and New Zealand Virtual Worlds Working Group. Sue is researching adult learning in a virtual world and examines student experiences of engagement, collaboration, and immersion from their learning in a virtual world. The research explores adult learning theories and is a collection of student reactions to their learning with the emerging field of a virtual world. For four years, students have been given the opportunity to explore the educational potential of the virtual world of Second Life as a teaching and learning tool. Over 300 students have taken up the opportunity to explore value of teaching and learning in a virtual world with Sue (aka Jass Easterman) since 2007.

J. M. Grenier is an Instructor teaching Business and Communications at Middlesex Community College. Much of his work has focused on student engagement techniques, including the use of micro-lecture, multimedia, and virtual worlds. A former broadcaster, he has presented in both academic and corporate environments. He is presently the lead designer in creating learning spaces for MCC within the virtual world of Second Life. Outside of the classroom, he keeps a busy schedule as a media consultant and workshop leader.

Béatrice S. Hasler is research fellow in the Advanced Virtuality Lab of the Interdisciplinary Center Herzliya, Israel. She received her doctorate in psychology from the University of Zurich, Switzerland. She works at the intersection of computer science, media psychology, and communications. Her main research interests are in the design and evaluation of new technologies to support virtual team collaboration, with a focus on nonverbal communication, leadership, and conflict resolution in mediated cross-cultural encounters. She co-initiated a global lecture series (The ShanghAI Lectures) together with the Artificial Intelligence Lab of the University of Zurich. The ShanghAI Lectures serve as a platform for her large-scale international field studies on cross-cultural collaboration in virtual worlds. Her research is funded by the European Union and the Swiss National Science Foundation.

Randy Hinrichs is CEO of 2b3d, an award winning Internet media company, focused on emerging technologies. Randy holds former positions in Microsoft Research, Sun Microsystems, and Unisys. He pioneered work in web based multimedia, intranet technology, and immersive learning He holds patents in Internet network-based video conferencing, large-scale information collection in health care, and mining information based on relationships. Randy also serves on the faculty at the University of Washington's iSchool. As an avatar, Ran transforms business and learning inside a virtual world.

Phil Ice holds an education doctorate in curriculum and instruction with minor concentrations in Instructional Technology and Science Education. He is currently the VP of research and development at American Public University System (APUS) and holds the same title with Sage Road Analytics, LLC. His research is focused on the impact of new and emerging technologies on cognition in online learning environments. His work in this area has brought him international recognition in the form of three Effective Practice of the Year Awards (2007, 2009, and 2010) from the Sloan Consortium, which also recognized his leadership of an APUS team with the Gomory Award for Data Driven Quality Improvement in 2009. His other industry accomplishments include membership in Adobe's Education Leaders Group and Higher Education Advisory Board, as well as receiving the Adobe Higher Education Leaders Impact Award for 2010 and AliveTek, Inc. Innovation in Distance Learning Administration Award, 2011. Phil's vision for the future of technology in higher education is also demonstrated by his inclusion on the advisory council for the 2011 NMC/ELI Horizon Report. His work has covered the use of technology-mediated feedback, which has been adopted at over 50 institutions of higher education in five countries, multilevel institutional assessment techniques, and application of semantic analysis for mapping institutional learning assets. He has conducted more than 100 peer-reviewed and invited presentations and workshops as well as authored more than 20 articles, book chapters, and white papers related to the integration of emerging technologies in e-Learning.

Owen Kelly has worked as a community artist; a cultural consultant; an Apple Macintosh trainer; a freelance programmer; and a web designer. He currently lectures in online media at Arcada, a university of applied sciences in Helsinki, Finland; while completing his doctoral research at Aalto University. He is the author of *Community, Art and the State* (1984), and *Digital Creativity* (1996). He coauthored *Another Standard: Culture & Democracy* (1986), and *The Creative Bits* (1994); and has contributed to several more books. His latest published work is a chapter entitled "Sexton Blake and the Virtual Culture of Rosario: A Biji" in the book *Mashup Cultures*, edited by Stefan Sonvilla-Weiss, and published by Springer WienNewYork (2010).

Hoe Kyeung Kim is associate professor in the TESOL program of Department of Teacher Education at Cleveland State University. Her research interests include teacher education, educational technology, second language acquisition, culture and identity, and sociocultural theory.

Reneta D. Lansiquot is assistant professor of English at New York City College of Technology, where she earned a Bachelor of Technology Degree in computer systems technology. She earned her Ph.D. in educational communication and technology from New York University after completing her Master of Science Degree in Integrated Digital Media. Her educational approach emphasizes the importance of facilitating interdisciplinary studies and technology-based learning. Her mixed-methodology research focuses on interactive iconography, computer-mediated communication, problem-solving strategies, and virtual worlds. An avid gamer who enjoys exploring real and virtual worlds, she can be found in Second Life as her avatar, "Reneta Writer."

Matthew Olson is the Dean of Humanities and Social Sciences and was the former director of the Middlesex Interactive online learning program at Middlesex Community College in Bedford and Lowell, MA. He also serves as the senior e-Learning consultant for the online training firm of Instructional Solutions. He holds a doctorate degree in education from the University of Massachusetts Lowell, and his research interests focus on the relationship between online technologies and student learning. He has nineteen years of experience in community college education and online learning. In addition to his online learning expertise, Matthew has actively participated in a variety of consortia for distance education. He has vast experience in technological professional development for faculty, and has presented on the topic of online teaching and learning in a variety of local, national, and international venues.

Les Pang is a program director at the University of Maryland University College and teaches courses on cyber security, information technology, and homeland security. He is a former professor at the National Defense University, Washington, DC. He taught military and civilian leaders data management, enterprise applications, multimedia, simulation, Internet, and software technologies. He received a Ph.D. in engineering from the University of Utah and a MBA from the University of Maryland College Park. He is the 2004 recipient of the Stanley J. Drazek Teaching Excellence Award at the University of Maryland University College.

Vanessa Parson is lecturer in psychology at Sunderland University, UK. Her research interests are varied, but are primarily focused in the pedagogical uses of technology and attentional processing. In 2007 she was part of the group from Aston University short-listed for the "Times Higher Award for the Outstanding ICT Initiative of the Year."

Lesley Scopes aka Light Sequent in virtual worlds holds a BSc Honours degree in Applied Psychology and Computing from Bournemouth University and a Masters (MSc) in Computer based learning and training from the University of Southampton, has qualified teacher status (PGCE) from the University of Greenwich and currently works as a virtual worlds teaching and learning consultant. Based in UK, the developer of the model of Cybergogy of Learning Archetypes and Learning Domains, Lesley has been living and working in virtual worlds for over 5 years and has been instrumental in the implementation and development of teaching practices and learning environments on the Second Life® platform. The drive to bring robust methodology to 3D virtual environments for teaching and learning has led to projects involving various universities seeking to bring a blended learning strategy using virtual worlds. Lesley is currently supporting a number of developments including the integration of pedagogical practices in blended approaches in social centric virtual environments including the integration of language teaching to students of architecture as part of a European Commission project.

Peter Shea has a bachelor's degree in English literature from Fordham University as well as a master's in English education and a graduate certificate in instructional design from the University of South Florida. Currently, he is the Pedagogical/Instructional Designer for the Title III Strategies for Success program at Middlesex Community College in Massachusetts.

Jennifer L. V. Sparrow is the director of Emerging Technologies and New Ventures at Virginia Tech. She works with a great team of students and professional staff in the InnovationSpace, a New Media Center. She has a passion for working with faculty to explore new technologies to increase active and engaged learning. Her areas of research include emerging technologies, collaborative learning, and fostering collaboration with Web 2.0 technologies. Jennifer received her bachelor's degree from Smith College, her master's degree from Florida Gulf Coast University, and doctorate from the University of Central Florida. She currently serves on the EDUCAUSE Learning Initiative Advisory Board and the EDUCAUSE Evolving Technologies Committee.

Jenny S. Wakefield works as a web developer and instructional designer at the University of Texas at Dallas in the Office of Undergraduate Studies and the Office of Student Success and Assessment. As a doctoral student in the Educational Computing program at the University of North Texas department of Learning Technologies she focuses her research on instructional design, peer-led team learning, social networks learning, and virtual worlds. She has been the editor for several handbooks, magazines, and newsletters. She has also reviewed book chapters and also conference proposals for international organizations. Further, she has created and maintained websites for institutions, companies, organizations, and individuals and produced graphic design for several institutions. She holds a master of science in computer education and cognitive Systems, teaching and learning with technology from The University of North Texas.

Charles Wankel, associate professor of management at St. John's University, New York, earned his doctorate from New York University. Charles is on the Rotterdam School of Management Dissertation

Committee and is Honorary Vice Rector of the Poznan University of Business. He has authored and edited about 30 books including the best-selling *Management*, 3rd ed. (Prentice-Hall, 1986), ten volumes in the IAP series Research in Management Education and Development, the *Handbook of 21st Century Management* (SAGE, 2008), and the *Encyclopedia of Business in Today's World* (SAGE, 2009), which received the American Library Association's Outstanding Business Reference Source Award. He is the leading founder and director of scholarly virtual communities for management professors, currently directing eight with thousands of participants in more than seventy nations. He has been a visiting professor in Lithuania at the Kaunas University of Technology (Fulbright Fellowship) and the University of Vilnius (United Nations Development Program and Soros Open Society Foundation funding).

Scott J. Warren works as assistant professor of learning technologies at the University of North Texas. His current research examines the use of emerging online technologies such as immersive digital learning environments, educational games and simulations, and open source course management tools in complex systems in K-20 settings. Prior to working in higher education as a professor, researcher, and designer, he taught both social studies and English in public schools for nearly a decade. He has also worked on the Quest Atlantis National Science Foundation project, creating the Anytown world to support writing, reading, and problem solving. His current work with The Door, Broken Window, and The 2015 Project alternate reality courses is partly funded with grants from the University of North Texas. Further, he works with Created Realities on the development and research of the online literacy game Chalk House. He completed his Ph.D. in instructional systems technology at Indiana University-Bloomington.

John Woollard is lecturer in information technology education at the University of Southampton, UK. His research interests include e-learning, virtual world learning, and the teaching of computing concepts. John has written several books about learning theory and pedagogy, he supervises doctorate students and on a day-to-day basis is involved with pre-service ICT teachers and their training.

SUBJECT INDEX